THE EU AS A GLOBAL DIGITAL ACTOR

This is the first book length treatment of the advancement of EU global data flows and digital trade through the framework of European institutionalisation. Drawing on case studies of EU-US, EU-Japan and EU-China relations, it charts the theoretical and empirical approaches at play. It illustrates how the EU has pioneered high standards in data flows and how it engages in significant digital trade reforms committed to those standards. The book marks a major shift in how institutionalisation and the EU should be viewed as it relates to two of the more extraordinary areas of global governance: trade and data flows. This significant book will be of interest to EU lawyers, as well as those researching in the field of IT and data law.

Volume 111 in the Series Modern Studies in European Law

Modern Studies in European Law

Recent titles in this series:

Fundamental Rights and Mutual Recognition in the Area of Freedom, Security and Justice: A Role for Proportionality?
Ermioni Xanthopoulou

Law and Judicial Dialogue on the Return of Irregular Migrants from the European Union
Edited by Madalina Moraru, Galina Cornelisse and Philippe De Bruycker

Framing Convergence with the Global Legal Order: The EU and the World
Edited by Elaine Fahey

EU Citizenship at the Edges of Freedom of Movement
Katarina Hyltén-Cavallius

The Internal Market 2.0
Edited by Sacha Garben and Inge Govaere

New Directions in European Private Law
Edited by Mateja Durovic and Takis Tridimas

Standing to Enforce European Union Law before National Courts
Hilde Ellingsen

The Relative Authority of Judicial and Extra-Judicial Review: The EU Courts, the Boards of Appeal and the Ombudsman
Michal Krajewski

Responsive Human Rights: Vulnerability and the ECtHR
Corina Heri

The Architecture of Fundamental Rights in the European Union
Šejla Imamovic

The EU and its Member States' Joint Participation in International Agreements
Edited by Nicolas Levrat, Yuliya Kaspiarovich, Christine Kaddous and Ramses A Wessel

The UN Convention on the Rights of Persons with Disabilities and the European Union: The Impact on Law and Governance
Carmine Conte

EU Criminal Law, Second Edition
Valsamis Mitsilegas

The EU as a Global Digital Actor: Institutionalising Global Data Protection, Trade, and Cybersecurity
Elaine Fahey

For the complete list of titles in this series
see www.bloomsbury.com/uk/series/modern-studies-in-european-law/

The EU as a Global Digital Actor

Institutionalising Global Data Protection, Trade, and Cybersecurity

Elaine Fahey

•HART•
OXFORD • LONDON • NEW YORK • NEW DELHI • SYDNEY

HART PUBLISHING

Bloomsbury Publishing Plc

Kemp House, Chawley Park, Cumnor Hill, Oxford, OX2 9PH, UK

1385 Broadway, New York, NY 10018, USA

29 Earlsfort Terrace, Dublin 2, Ireland

First published in Great Britain 2022

A catalogue record for this book is available from the British Library.

A catalogue record for this book is available from the Library of Congress.

ISBN: HB: 978-1-50995-704-0
ePDF: 978-1-50995-706-4
ePub: 978-1-50995-705-7

Typeset by Compuscript Ltd, Shannon

'Rabbits, white rabbits'

In memory of my mother

ACKNOWLEDGEMENTS

The book project arises from the EUTIP Horizon 2020 funded research network, activities, symposia and events taking place in 2020 and 2021, as well as to the author's Erasmus+ Jean Monnet Chair in Law and Transatlantic Relations (funded 2019–2022). This project has been undertaken principally during fellowships at the European University Institute (EUI), Florence, iCourts Copenhagen and Keio University, Tokyo and throughout Covid-19, including involving an emergency 'evacuation' of the book project, cutting short a sabbatical from the EUI when academic activities were suspended and the retrieval of crates of papers and months several months later by shipment.

Various parts of the book were given as talks given at University of Nottingham Commercial Law group, Birmingham Law School Annual European Law Lecture, Durham European Law Institute (DELI) lectures, iCourts Copenhagen research seminar, International Studies Association (ISA) Spring 2021 (virtual) panels, Queen Mary-Northumbria Jean Monnet Chair conference, ULB Brussels, Keio Law School and City, University of London Cybersecurity Research Centre. I am extremely grateful to Ivanka Karaivanova for immense research assistance and project support assistance provided. Thanks also to Veronika Schleina.

I am grateful to the following, who have very kindly read drafts of chapters and/or given significant comments: Susan Aaronson, Nina Boeger, David Collins, Ben Farrand, Giulio Kowalski, Giuseppe Martinico, Lijun Zhao, Jed Odermatt, Eva Pander Maat, Mikael Madsen, Isabella Mancini, Yuliya Miadzvetskaya, Marc Mimler, Svetlana Yakovleva, Alex Joel, Maria Tzanou.

I am grateful to Hart Publishing for their patience and support with me. All errors or omissions are mine only. I endeavour to state the law as of 31 December 2021.

Elaine Fahey
January 2022

CONTENTS

ABBREVIATIONS AND ACRONYMS

AA	Association Agreement
AFSJ	Area of Freedom, Security and Justice
AI	Artificial Intelligence
APEC	Asia-Pacific Economic Cooperation
ARF	Asian Regional Forum
ASEAN	Association of Southeast Asian Nations
BIT	Bilateral Investment Treaty
BRI	Belt and Road Initiative
BRICS	Brazil, Russia, India, China, and South Africa
CAI	Comprehensive Agreement on Investment
CBC	Customs and Border Control
CBPR	Cross-Border Privacy Rules
CCPA	California Consumer Privacy Act
CETA	Comprehensive Economic and Trade Agreement
CFSP	Common Foreign and Security Policy
CJEU	Court of Justice of the European Union
CPTPP	Comprehensive and Progressive Agreement for Trans-Pacific Partnership
CSIRT	Computer Security Incidents Response Teams
DEA	Digital Economy Agreement
DEPA	Digital Economy Partnership Agreement
DGA	Date Governance Act
DMA	Digital Markets Act
DPA	Data Protection Authority
DPC	Data Protection Commission

DSA	Digital Services Act
DSB	Dispute Settlement Body
EC3	European Cybercrime Centre
EDPB	European Data Protection Board
EDPS	European Data Protection Supervisor
ENISA	EU Agency for Network and Information Security
EPA	Economic Partnership Agreement
EUCSS	EU Cybersecurity Strategy
FDI	Foreign Direct Investment
FTA	Free Trade Agreement
FTC	Federal Trade Commission
GATS	General Agreement on Trade in Services
GATT	General Agreement on Tariffs and Trade
GDP	Gross Domestic Product
GDPR	General Data Protection Regulation
GIs	Geographical Indications
ICANN	Internet Corporation for Assigned Names and Numbers
ICCPR	International Covenant on Civil and Political Rights
IGF	Internet Governance Forum
IMF	International Monetary Fund
INTCEN	EU Intelligence and Situation Centre
IoT	Internet of Things
ITU	International Telecommunication Union
JII	Joint Interpretative Instrument
JSEPA	Japan-Singapore Economic Agreement for a New Age Partnership
JSI	Joint Statement Initiative
KIIOs	Key Information Infrastructure Operators
NTA	New Transatlantic Agenda
OECD	Organisation for Economic Co-operation and Development

OEWG	Open-Ended Working Group
OSCE	Organisation for Security and Co-operation in Europe
PIPL	Personal Information Protection Law
PNR	Passenger Name Records
PPC	Personal Information Protection Commission
PTA	Preferential Trade Agreement
RCEP	Regional Comprehensive Economic Partnership
RTA	Regional Trade Agreement
SCC	Standard Contractual Clauses
SOEs	State-Owned Enterprises
SPA	Strategic Partnership Agreement
TABC	Trans-Atlantic Business Council
TABD	Trans-Atlantic Business Dialogue
TCA	Trade and Cooperation Agreement
TFTP	Terrorist Financing Tracking Program
TPP	Trans-Pacific Partnership
TTC	Trade and Technology Council
TTIP	Transatlantic Trade and Investment Partnership
UDHR	Universal Declaration of Human Rights
UNESCO	United Nations Educational, Scientific and Cultural Organisation
UNGA	United Nations General Assembly
USMCA	United States-Mexico-Canada Agreement
WSIS	World Summit on the Information Society
WTO	World Trade Organisation

TABLE OF CASES

China

Court of Justice of the European Union

European Court of Human Rights

European Commission

Ireland

Japan

United States

World Trade Organisation

TABLE OF INSTRUMENTS

International Agreements

TABLE OF LEGISLATION

China

European Union

United States

Japan

Introduction: The Framework of Data Institutionalisation

I. Overview

This book explores the waning and rising of EU institutionalisation in data. It argues that data embeds security into trade and trade into security and changes the face of institutionalisation, creating the need for cooperation, needs for trust, governance and rigour. This book exposes how the EU is ultimately an institutionalist, acting through and by institutions as a means of developing, advancing and changing the architecture of a field. It does this increasingly in the field of data. Institutionalisation is defined here as the process by which an organisation becomes increasingly subject to rules, procedures and stable practices.[1] It is thus arguably the most under-defined, under explored and misunderstood term deployed as to EU law and policy because of assumptions as to its existence or operation. Data operates as a key means to understand the breadth of the EU's approach to data law and governance. The EU's approach to AI policy development is to establish a European Artificial Intelligence Board or its approach to cyber law-making is to establish a European Cybercrime Centre (EC3) as a desk of Europol. Its approach to a new generation of trade agreements is to establish a broad architecture of bodies within trade agreements, from eg Joint Committees, specialised committees, civil society and Domestic Advisory Group entities. Institutionalisation is in the metaphorical DNA of the EU as an organisation as much as its modus operandi.

This volume is the first major legal book on institutionalisation, focusing on 'data' holistically, which one of the most cutting-edge areas of national, regional and international regulation. Institutionalisation is the *solution* to most of the world's problems but the concept is rarely scientifically developed. This book takes the EU's efforts at institutionalisation as its subject and the data transfer and governance regimes under EU law, from data privacy, data transfers to cyber law and policy, as its object. Data is the 'lifeblood' of economies across the world

[1] See further E Fahey, 'Introduction: Institutionalisation beyond the Nation State: New Paradigms? Transatlantic Relations: Data, Privacy and Trade Law' in E Fahey (ed), *Institutionalisation beyond the Nation State* (Springer, 2018); JE Alvarez, *The Impact of International Organizations on International Law* (Brill Nijhoff, 2016); F Terpan, 'Soft Law in the European Union – The Changing Nature of EU Law' (2014) 21 *European Law Journal* 68.

but is also the source of much concern about the future of individuals and their rights. Data is increasingly captured by new regimes globally yet its study is highly siloed. Few data privacy scholars focus on digital trade; few trade lawyers focus on cybersecurity and so forth. The study of institutionalisation has the capacity to synthesise these many cross-cutting themes.

In a world where its appears that there is too much data to regulate[2] and where Europe is not the hub for tech innovation, tech GDP or innovation creation, the EU is still the world's leading legislator, regulator and rule-making organisation in data governance. The EU is one of the most influential global actors in data and is constantly innovating in data transfer regimes, having some of the largest safe flow regimes in the world. Country after country replicates or builds on the General Data Protection Regulation (GDPR).[3] EU policy creep in data rises exponentially given the nature of data, which is evolving, malleable and cross-cutting. The EU is increasingly attempting to regulate all aspects of data, all of the value chain, all procedures, all geopolitics, through a so-called alphabet soup of regulation, from the DMA, DSA, AI, DGA, PNR to the GDPR – letters to be articulated throughout this book. Yet it has frequently regulated the previously unregulated and pushes the boundaries of extra-territoriality. This is to a certain degree because, for instance, there is no universal formula for data issues in a trade agreement, which may include many cross-cutting issues from cybersecurity, intellectual property, transparency to frictionless movement of tech workers. There is also still no global privacy, cybersecurity treaty. The EU has had 'first-mover' advantage in many, but not all, domains of data regulation – principally in data privacy. Trade negotiators might understand the importance of data governance questions but mainly operate without reliable data about the global digital economy. They also continue to overlook the losers of the digital transformation, underappreciate the right to regulate and misjudge the extent to which global digital corporations transcend territorial jurisdictional boundaries.[4] In contrast to other major international trade agreements, the EU's model agreements increasingly require its negotiating partners to sign up to the EU's conception of personal data protection and privacy as a fundamental right. An explicit carve-out ensures that the anti-localisation provisions cannot be directed against personal data protection and privacy safeguards.[5] Such carve-outs even extend to dialogues on regulatory issues in digital trade. Ostensibly, the carve-outs maximise the 'Brussels Effect' of voluntary adoption of its high privacy standards at transnational level in addition to requiring adequacy with the

[2] D Acemoglu et al, 'Too Much Data: Prices and Inefficiencies in Data Markets' (2019) National Bureau of Economic Research, Working Paper No 26296.

[3] eg Thailand, China, California: see A Bradford, *Brussels Effect: How the European Union Rules the World* (Oxford University Press, 2020).

[4] T Streinz, 'Digital Megaregulation Uncontested? TPP's Model for the Global Digital Economy' in B Kingsbury et al (eds), *Megaregulation Contested* (Oxford University Press, 2019) 317.

[5] European Commission, 'Horizontal provisions for cross-border data flows and for personal data protection (in EU trade and investment agreements)' (May 2018) Tradoc No 156884, template art B.1, https://trade.ec.europa.eu/doclib/docs/2018/may/tradoc_156884.pdf accessed 22 February 2022.

EU's GDPR in return for the facilitation of personal data exported out of the EU.[6] Yet there are risks in presupposing European dominance, which can easily appear as the 'law of everything', over-expansive, over-embracing and over-regulating of data.[7] There are also risks to understanding the EU as a monolithic entity: in reality its Court and legislator and even its European Council have all pulled in different directions on data matters.[8] Big Tech actively escape and circumvent EU data regulation but adopt it voluntarily in a variety of ways.[9] The EU's many new data regime proposals cover cybersecurity, digital tax and digital trade, and span both internal and external dimensions. All are equally significant components of the regulatory construct of data governance but reach in many different ways to a variety of subjects and objects.

This book argues that to capture a realistic and accurate picture of EU data institutionalisation practices, a more holistic focus on data is needed, including cross-cutting areas of data governance, transfer, digital trade, cyber regulation, law enforcement and the Internet of Things. In turn, a holistic focus on data helps us to understand institutionalisation, each subject feeding into the other. Topics never previously included in the study of international trade agreements are now part and parcel of FTA texts and strategic partnership agreements alike. They are the subject of more institutionalised regimes than ever.

This book aims to consider data institutionalisation holistically, as a composite area of contemporary regulation, by using cross-cutting studies of competence spanning internal and external dimensions but largely focusing on the external dimensions. It analyses *both* personal and non-personal data, looking at the heterogenous concept of data in the digital economy. It largely presents a descriptive rather than normative account of the need to frame legal, legislative and regulatory developments in this fashion.

This introduction contains the following sections: (II) the normalisation of institutionalisation; (III) defining institutionalisation; (IV) EU-centric

[6] Streinz (n 4) 317; Bradford (n 3).

[7] N Purtova, 'The Law of Everything. Broad Concept of Personal Data and Future of EU Data Protection Law' (2018) 10 *Law, Innovation and Technology* 40; Regulation (EU) 2016/679 of the European Parliament and of the Council of 27 April 2016 on the protection of natural persons with regard to the processing of personal data and on the free movement of such data, and repealing Directive 95/46/EC (GDPR) [2016] OJ L119/1; Regulation (EU) 2018/1807 of the European Parliament and of the Council of 14 November 2018 on a framework for the free flow of non-personal data in the European Union [2018] OJ L 303/59; Regulation (EU) 2019/881 of the European Parliament and of the Council of 17 April 2019 on ENISA (the European Union Agency for Cybersecurity) and on information and communications technology cybersecurity certification and repealing Regulation (EU) No 526/2013 (Cybersecurity Act) [2019] OJ L151/15; Directive (EU) 2019/1024 of the European Parliament and of the Council of 20 June 2019 on open data and the re-use of public sector information [2019] OJ L172/56.

[8] J Polakiewicz, 'The Emperor's New Clothes – Data Privacy and Cybersecurity from a European Perspective' in E Fahey and I Mancini (eds), *Understanding The EU As A Good Global Actor: Whose Metrics?* (Edward Elgar, forthcoming).

[9] Bradford (n 3).

institutionalisation; (V) comparative institutionalisation; (VI) institutionalisation beyond judicialisation; (VII) informal organisations and informal law-making; (VIII) institutionalising data: the data forum problem; and (IX) an outline of the chapters of the book.

II. Why Institutionalisation? The Normalisation of Institutionalisation

Institution building is a historic foundation stone of EU integration and the EU polity.[10] The creation of institutions to solve transnational problems is also one of the most consistent features of law-making, at national level, regional level and beyond the state. It is a key feature of some of the engagement with the most complex elements of globalisation. For example, it is at the heart of increased regulation of cross-border data flows, contemporary deeper trade agreements, and strengthened responses to cross-border migration flows. Such bodies increasingly raise, inter alia, legitimacy and accountability issues as to the powers they possess to engage in quasi-legislation, legislative substitution and forms of de facto and de jure regulation, with different forms of function, legitimation and accountability. This project explores how institutionalisation is fundamentally at the heart of these challenges. Although not well understood across disciplines, the process of the creation of institutions may be understand as institutionalisation.[11] Institutionalisation remains largely understood in highly *political* but not legal terms. The place of law, autonomy and legal norms within this matrix remains understudied. How does legal design contribute to understandings of processes of institutionalisation? What legal constructs relating to autonomy evolve institutionalisation? The EU continues to evolve innovations in institutionalisation. How are they understood outside of the EU? What legal norms have the capacity to open up processes of institutionalisation and expose their content, context and anatomy? Institutionalisation practices, studied in design, empirics or as transnational regimes, can shed light on increasingly salient interactions of bodies, actors or associations across legal orders. Political scientists pay insufficient attention to shifts in innovations through legal autonomy, to legal constructs and rule-making powers and competences. Unlike international courts and law-making beyond the state as a process, the transnational dimension to institutionalisation is understudied. In particular, as data protection and data transfer globally becomes more sensitised to concerns of standards, enforcement and compliance, institutional structures have evolved considerably. As the most unsolved puzzle of

[10] See A Vauchez, *Brokering Europe: Eurolawyers and the Making of a Transnational Polity* (Cambridge University Press, 2015).
[11] Fahey, *Institutionalisation beyond the Nation State* (n 1).

globalisation, migration has had a difficult policy journey to becoming strengthened by institutions and institutional structures. As trade agreements increasingly deepen in scale, outlook, objectives and reach, their core formative elements have also similarly advanced. This book asks in the chapters that follow, what is a most fruitful way to study the institutionalised dimension of new challenges? Is it 'top down' or 'bottom up'? How does independence operate here? What is oversight in institutionalisation beyond the state? What type of regulation or governance is it? Does it institutionalise actors who are non-institutions? How flexible or formal is it? What is the appropriate subject and object in the most complex areas of global governance? Institutionalisation provides a means to meaningfully frame and synthesise such questions and problematisations.

The EU's efforts on institutionalisation are argued here to be usefully studied through data, given that EU rules, actors and standards on data are considered internationally to be some of the highest global standards – or at worst to set complex bars for international cooperation and international debates on data flows.[12] Yet the EU's high privacy standards and shifts towards data localisation directly and indirectly are allegedly protectionist. This allegation is argued in this book to be overstated and best narrated through institutionalisation. The EU's institutionalisation practices are arguably hampered by other factors. For instance, adequacy decisions increasingly place indirectly complex constraints on trade negotiations. There are some who suggest that the EU has reached adequacy decisions unduly easily, for example that in relation to Japan.[13] It has also played an outsized role in the Brexit negotiations, as one area where the UK has actively sought to engage with the EU and show its demonstrable credentials to have such safe data flows. It has placed institutional strengthening, institutional innovations and actors as central entities therein, directly or indirectly. The EU has some longstanding efforts at collaboration in data flows with the US in both civil and criminal fields (Passenger Name Record, Umbrella Agreement, Privacy Shield (at least until recently), TFTP). EU-Japan is one of the world's largest safe flow of data regimes, and regulatory cooperation between the two in digital trade is cutting-edge. EU-China approaches to data regulation are as yet embryonic but characterised by China's voluntary adoption of EU law privacy rules and standards derived from the GDPR, in the absence of any formalised EU-China adequacy agreement on safe data flows or any treaty-based or formalised agreement. Yet there are some significant developments in Chinese data law and EU-China relations as well as global governance to suggest that the comparative study of these is of much value. This book thus examines the methodology of institutionalisation, focusing

[12] See EPIC (US civil liberties body) on the need for a US Data Protection Agency: https://epic.org/dpa/ accessed 31 December 2021; S Zuboff, *The Age of Surveillance Capitalism: The Fight for a Human Future at the New Frontier of Power* (Profile Books, 2019).

[13] G Greenleaf, 'Japan: EU Adequacy Discounted' (2018) 155 *Privacy Laws & Business International Report* 8.

on the case study of EU third-country data flows, cyber security and regulatory cooperation in trade. The case studies are examined from regional, international and transnational perspectives, in law, political science, international relations, political economy and sociology. The case studies also relate to third countries where significant data issues are arising in law enforcement issues, bilaterally or otherwise.

Three third-party country partners or negotiation partners of the EU have been selected as case studies for degrees of 'institutionalisation', from that 'furthest away' from institutionalisation (in Chapter 6 on EU-China relations), to those rather closer (Chapter 5 on EU-Japan relations and Chapter 4 on the EU-US). The latter two are longstanding key EU external relations partners, where significant developments, in particular since the 1990s, have seen a push to transatlantic cooperation and a pivot to Asia.[14] The three case studies relate to some of the largest scale trade agreements or negotiations or data flow agreements that the EU has, with two of the three countries being longstanding trade partners with highly developed economies of scale, and with China as a 'latecomer' to this metric but nonetheless today the largest trading actor globally. The three case studies relate to partners in very different states of negotiation in their EU relationship with regard to data flows and digital trade, from negotiations that have continued for over two decades, to most recent post-Treaty of Lisbon and post-GDPR negotiations with the EU, thus providing a variety of situations for the case studies.

III. On Origins and Terminology: Defining Institutionalisation

Institutions are foundational to most social sciences scholarship.[15] Over the past two decades, developments in Science and Technology Studies have contributed to our understanding of the socio-technical aspects of information infrastructures.[16] Such scholarship defines infrastructure as a stable sociotechnical substrate on which other systems and tools are built and that underpins, enables or constrains a wide variety of society intervention. Regulatory capacity over data governance in a digitised society is increasingly normalised.[17] Normalisation here becomes an issue. For many, 'institutionalisation' might seem to be an overly obvious term to use – barely worthy of definition – and possibly even a banal one. Its

[14] U Krotz et al, *Europe's Cold War Relations: The EC Towards a Global Role* (Bloomsbury, 2019). See F Bindi and I Angelescu (eds), *The Foreign Policy of the European Union: Assessing Europe's Role in the World*, 2nd edn (Brookings Institution Press, 2012) chs 1, 13, 17–21 in particular, and 33 also.

[15] eg DC North, *Institutions, Institutional Change, and Economic Performance* (Cambridge University Press, 1990).

[16] H Shen, *Alibaba: Infrastructuring Global China* (Routledge, 2022) 2.

[17] eg MG Jacobides and I Lianos, 'Regulating Platforms and Ecosystems: An Introduction' (2021) 30(5) *Industrial and Corporate Change* 1131.

official dictionary definition can be said to be highly variable as to its meaning.[18] It could be said that, for legal scholars, its 'blandness' is its worst offence, as an 'isation' of a word.[19] For example, the rapid development of digital technologies has been alleged to make possible a 'platform-isation' of infrastructures and an infra-structuralisation of platforms.[20] It is arguably a normalised discourse of social sciences and law without any explicit acknowledgement of it. It simply features greatly in many subjects, below the radar. However, this author argues that in the context of the EU, institutionalisation 'matters'. The adoption of stablished practices, ideals and processes make the EU more organised, bureaucratically sophisticated and effective, all through the medium of institutionalisation. It may also contribute to EU accountability and transparency requirements.

Institutionalisation is mostly about 'process'[21] and is not usually the subject of a definition, certainly not as far as EU law is concerned.[22] It usually involves probing incomplete situations or involves predictions as to what will prevail. For lawyers, the prediction of the future of EU law is not an easy task.[23] EU literature explicitly discussing the term largely emanates from discrete political science studies in the 1990s. Institutionalisation of the EU constitutes the joint processes of formalisation and stabilisation of procedures, institutional coordination, with the ability of individual actors to influence institutional development. It has dimensions moving in different directions, possibly inwards and outwards, or across actors and fields. EU institutionalisation was largely theorised, in the early days, as being 'bottom-up'.[24] Nowadays, the development of a policy field in the EU in external relations is also understood as a form of institutionalisation but without much emphasis on

[18] ie from (1) the *establishment* of ('something, typically a practice or activity') a convention or norm in an organisation or culture: the institutionalised *practice* of collaborative research on a grand scale ('as adjective, institutionalised') institutionalised religion; (2) to *place or keep (someone) in a residential institution*: he was institutionalised in a school for the destitute; and (3) ('as adjective, institutionalised') (of a person), *apathetic and dependent* after a long period in an institution: became less institutionalised, more able to function as an individual; See 'Institutionalisation': *Oxford English Dictionary*, 3rd edn (Oxford University Press, 2016) (British English spelling employed throughout).

[19] *cf* J Resnik, 'Globalization(s), Privatization(s), Constitutionalization, and Statization: Icons and Experiences of Sovereignty in the 21st Century' (2013) 11 *I-CON* 162, 163; see S Hofmann, 'Elastic Relations: Looking to Both Sides of the Atlantic in the 2020 US Presidential Election Year' (2021) 59(1) *Journal of Common Market Studies* 150, on 'institutional elasticity' without referencing any actual institutions. See Fahey, *Institutionalisation beyond the Nation State* (n 1).

[20] JC Plantin et al, 'Infrastructure Studies Meet Platform Studies in the Age of Google and Facebook' (2018) 20(1) *New Media & Society* 293; H Shen, *Alibaba: Infrastructuring Global China* (Routledge, 2022).

[21] D Soltys, 'Challenges to the Institutionalisation of Environmental NGOS in Kazakhstan's Corporate Policy Arena' (2014) 44 *Journal of Contemporary Asia* 342, 362; see also Fahey, *Institutionalisation beyond the Nation State* (n 1), as to transatlantic developments, policies and actions.

[22] Eg H Heclo, 'Thinking Institutionally' in SA Binder et al, *The Oxford Handbook of Political Institutions* (Oxford University Press, 2008) 732.

[23] See generally E Fahey, 'Future-Mapping the Directions of European Union (EU) Law: How Do We Predict the Future of EU Law?' (2020) 7(2) *Journal of International and Comparative Law* 265.

[24] M Smith, *Europe's Foreign and Security Policy: The Institutionalisation of Cooperation* (Cambridge University Press, 2004).

its legal provisions.[25] It is thus argued here to be a core characteristic of the EU's evolution as an international organisation.[26]

Institutionalisation at international level can be argued to take place as an antidote to concerns about the delegation of authority beyond the nation state. Institutionalisation shows the value of institutions and the faith held in the creation of public bodies, authorities and actors. It can allay concerns about transfers of authority and create sites for the creation of legitimacy, however imperfect. There are many vivid examples of the deepening and widening of institutionalisation studied in political science, eg the rising delegation by Member States of authority to international organisations, the growth of international organisations or the increase of majority-voting in international organisations.[27] Conceptually mapping and engaging with institutionalisation is thus of much value.

IV. Is Institutionalisation EU-Centric?

In the EU context, the EU's capacity to generate new configurations of institutions – for its own actors to evolve as agencies or quasi-agencies into autonomous agencies and to generate new international institutions – is a core feature of EU law and policy. It is also a core feature of its policies as to the global legal order. The EU espouses the view that international institutions reflect the EU's interests rather than shape them. It has taken many decades after the work of Robert Keohane to show how institutional effects are most visible not when regimes are first established, but at subsequent points where constellations of power and interests emerge.[28] The EU has thus advocated a longer-term vision of society, aligning with a particularly liberal non-realist view of institutions, that international institutions matter. However, it remains to be seen precisely how long-term the lifespan is of international organisations. *Externally*, the EU has a recent history of promoting new multilateral institutions, from the International Criminal Court to a Multilateral Investment Court, and reforming those it founded, eg the Word Trade Organisatino (WTO).[29] *Internally*, the EU struggles with partial institutionalisation as a solution to many complex policy fields, eg migration and the eurozone.[30]

[25] See A Moravcsik and C Emmons, 'A Liberal Intergovernmentalist Approach to EU External Action' in S Gstohl and S Schunz (eds), *The External Action of the European Union – Concepts, Approaches, Theories* (Macmillan, 2021).

[26] Ie differing from a variety of global practices of multilateral or treaty exit in recent times: eg African Union from the ICC, UK from the Council of Europe and European Union, US from WTO or UN.

[27] M Zürn, 'Opening up Europe: Next Steps in Politicisation Research' (2016) 39 *West European Politics* 16, 82; M Zürn, 'The Politicization of World Politics and its Effects: Eight Propositions' (2014) 6 *European Political Science Review* 47.

[28] *cf* the classic R Keohane, 'Ironies of Sovereignty: The European Union and the United States' (2002) 42 *Journal of Common Market Studies* 743.

[29] Fahey, *Institutionalisation beyond the Nation State* (n 1) 5.

[30] J Caporaso, 'Europe's Triple Crisis and the Uneven Role of Institutions: the Euro, Refugees and Brexit' (2018) 56 *Journal of Common Market Studies* 1345.

In the most crisis-ridden domains of the EU, partial-institutionalisation is often at the root of major challenges. Institutionalisation is also the default means by which the EU develops regulatory policy, as an entity grounded in the rule of law and rules-based law and governance. As noted above, the EU's approach to AI policy development has been to establish a European Artificial Intelligence Board, and its approach to cyber law-making was to establish a European Cybercrime Centre (EC3) as a desk of Europol. Its approach to a new generation of trade agreements has been to establish a broad architecture of bodies within trade agreements: joint committees, specialised committees, civil society and domestic advisory group entities. However, significant legitimacy concerns surround EU regulatory cooperation in all major trade agreements since the signing of the Lisbon Treaty.[31] The earliest migration solutions appear to fall short of full institutionalisation.[32] Yet institutionalisation has broadly positive – even laudable – public interest goals when pursued by the EU. Earlier EU scholarship contended that greater institutional adaptation and change had led to heightened formalisation and stabilisation the more institutionalised policy space became.[33] The more stable the governance arrangements were and the more institutionalised the policy area is, the more refined the established governance structures and procedures.

EU regimes evolve where the substantive rules underpinning them are as important as the institutional actors or configurations of actors themselves. The nature of the EU as an innovator but also an entity willing to expose itself to institutionalisation has meant that more, deeper, wider, institutionalisation practices reach into all fields and areas at the EU level, from areas of long-established competence, to cutting-edge regulatory issues, to sensitive complex areas, eg data to defence.[34] Indeed, the organisation responsible for regulating the Internet, the Internet Corporation for Assigned Names and Numbers (ICANN), noted in its comments on the EU's GDPR that the EU's development of a lead supervisory authority, a one-stop-shop mechanism under the GDPR, was a substantial development globally for organisations carrying out cross-border processing.[35]

However, in certain contexts the limits of EU institutionalisation may also possibly be said to have been reached – or perhaps the high-water mark thereof has been breached. As is outlined in Chapter 4, recent high-profile decisions

[31] W Weiß, 'Delegation to Treaty Bodies in EU Agreements: Constitutional Constraints and Proposals for Strengthening the European Parliament' (2018) 14(3) *European Constitutional Law Review* 532.

[32] A Rippoll Servant and F Trauner (eds), *Routledge Handbook of Justice and Home Affairs* (Routledge, 2017).

[33] A Stone Sweet et al, *The Institutionalization of Europe* (Oxford University Press, 2001).

[34] Fahey, *Institutionalisation beyond the State* (n 1); N Chrysoloras, 'EU Set to Allow US Participation in Joint Defence Projects' (*Bloomberg*, 4 November 2019), www.bloomberg.com/news/articles/2019-11-04/eu-set-to-allow-u-s-participation-in-joint-defense-projects accessed 23 February 2022.

[35] ICANN, 'ICANN Org Comments on the Two-Year Review Exercise of the GDPR' (April 2020), https://ec.europa.eu/info/law/better-regulation/have-your-say/initiatives/12322-Report-on-the-application-of-the-General-Data-Protection-Regulation/F514217 accessed 23 February 2022.

such as *Schrems II*, invalidating one of the world's largest data flow regimes (ie the EU-US Privacy Shield) that rested on a complex partial institutionalisation at transnational level, have been struck down in favour of significant privatisation and private actors. How should we understand the limits and flexibilities of institutionalisation in the EU context? Is the EU's push *towards* data localisation in trade agreements also generating more refined and localised understandings of EU institutionalisation?[36] How broadly should we define and understand institutionalisation? How do we understand the delicate balance between data as the lifeblood of modern economies and the increasing range of concerns in Europe about transferring data abroad? Is the balance founded in institutional design and de-institutionalising data? To the naked eye, the Court of Justice of the European Union (CJEU) increasingly appears to be blocking the institutionalisation negotiated by EU institutions. From the EU-US Privacy Shield to the EU-Canada Passenger Name Records Agreement – negotiated with one of the most sophisticated fundamental rights regimes in the world, Canada, who is also the EU's partner in a trade agreement and Strategic Partnership Agreement adjudged to be the gold standard of trade agreement – the CJEU has not been shy of finding faults in the structures negotiated with regard to international data transfer.[37] In other contexts, the CJEU has upheld limited institutionalisation structures of justice outside of the EU legal order, such as in the EU-Canada Economic and Trade agreement, in Opinion 1/17.[38]

How can the EU hope to build strong international and transnational institutionalisation when its own internal institutions suffer from continuous strain and pressure?[39] Upholding democracy remains a major issue, with the rise of social media giants seeking to develop their own autonomous transnational system, free from national, regional or international law constraints.[40] Arguably, the EU's

[36] A Chander and UP Lê, 'Breaking the Web: Data Localization vs. the Global Internet' (2014) UC Davis Legal Studies Research Paper No 378, https://ssrn.com/abstract=2407858 accessed 23 February 2022.

[37] Eg, Opinion 1/15 of the Court (Full Court) of 26 July 2017, EU:C:2016:656; Case C-311/18, *Facebook Ireland v Schrems*, EU:C:2020:559.

[38] However, we might say that this took place only on highly circumscribed terms, ie where EU law is not being applied and where a Joint Interpretative Instrument was agreed with Canada to delimit and limit the operation of CETA tribunals/appellate tribunals: Opinion 1/17 of the Court (Full Court) 30 April 2019, EU:C:2019:341; S Mayr, 'CETA, TTIP, TiSA, and Their Relationship with EU Law' in S Griller et al (eds), *Mega-Regional Trade Agreements: CETA, TTIP, and TiSA: New Orientations for EU External Economic Relations* (Oxford University Press, 2017); C Riffel, 'The CETA Opinion of the European Court of Justice and its Implications – Not that Selfish After All' (2019) 22 *Journal of International Economic Law* 503; M Fanou, 'The CETA ICS and the Autonomy of the EU Legal Order in Opinion 1/17 – A Compass for the Future' (2020) 22 *Cambridge Yearbook of European Legal Studies* 106.

[39] RD Kelemen, 'The European Union's Authoritarian Equilibrium' (2020) 27 *Journal of European Public Policy* 481.

[40] K Klonick et al, 'The Facebook Oversight Board' in City Law School Working Paper 2020/2 'The Law of Facebook'; E Benvenisti, 'Upholding Democracy Amid the Challenges of New Technology: What Role for the Law of Global Governance?' (2018) 29 *European Journal of International Law* 9.

longstanding tendency towards rules-based frameworks and developing consistent institutionalisation strategies insulates it from critiques. Data is arguably a litmus test of emerging practice here.

V. Whose Institutionalisation? Comparative Approaches to Institutionalisation

It may be said that the EU recently reached a point of multilateralism as one of the few remaining advocates of multilateralism and international institutions in an era of 'exit'.[41] There is an increasingly significant literature 'outside-in' on regional organisations where the EU plays an outsized role. Here, the place of the EU on institution building is widely studied, given the fact that the EU integration process was a relatively novel phenomenon in international politics, particularly with regard to the influence of the CJEU on generating other regional copies or the influence of the European Parliament on regional parliaments around the world.[42] It is said that the influence of the EU is more far-reaching than merely being a model and pattern for a new wave of regional organisations, eg Andean Community, Mercosur, ASEAN.[43] Institutionalisation makes an identifiable difference to regional organisations in other parts of the world, and others seek to catch up with the EU's level of institutionalisation.[44] However, there is also a widening gap between the rhetoric of multilateralism on the part of the EU and its more dominant practice of bilateralism, particularly in trade. Even adherents of the EU and those who passionately support it as an international organisation criticise its over-extensive diplomatic and regional ambitions, which appear immensely stretched relative to its useful engagements.[45] The nature of the EU as an innovator, and also an entity willing to expose itself to new levels of internal and external institutionalisation, reaches into all fields and areas at the EU level. On occasion, this has taken place outside of the treaties – for example, the creation of the Unified

[41] E Lazarou, 'The Future of Multilateralism: Crisis or Opportunity?' (2017) European Parliamentary Research Service Paper PE 603.922, www.europarl.europa.eu/RegData/etudes/BRIE/2017/603922/EPRS_BRI(2017)603922_EN.pdf accessed 23 February 2022.

[42] T Lenz, *Interorganizational Diffusion in International Relations: Regional Institutions and the Role of the European Union* (Oxford University Press, 2021) 22; see also C Dri, 'Limits of the Institutional Mimesis of the European Union: The Case of the Mercosur Parliament' (2010) 1(1) *Latin American Policy* 52; J Navarro, 'The Creation and Transformation of Regional Parliamentary Assemblies: Lessons from the Pan-African Parliament' (2010) 16(2) *Journal of Legislative Studies* 195; B Theodoro Luciano, 'A Clash between Creature and Creator? Contemporary Relations between the Pan-African Parliament and the European Parliament' (2020) 58 *Journal of Common Market Studies* 1182.

[43] Lenz (n 42) 33.

[44] ibid 9.

[45] A Gardner, *Stars with Stripes: The Essential Partnership Between the United States and the European Union* (Palgrave, 2020); *cf* R Bellamy et al (eds), *European Boundaries in Question?* (Routledge, 2018).

Patent Court. On other occasions, the EU has pushed for new institutionalisation at the margins of multilateralism through bilateralism, eg reform of the WTO's dispute settlement regime. The CJEU has settled for pragmatic fudges in certain instances, by splitting trade and investment or discreetly encouraging multilateralism along with a rising rigour for the autonomy of EU law after Opinion 2/15 and Opinion 1/17. Yet the EU's major efforts at multilateralism or institutionalisation beyond the state, eg the Multilateral Investment Court or the Unified Patent Court, look increasingly fragile, albeit for various different reasons.

As shown in Chapter 6, the Belt and Road Initiative (BRI) of China is understood to constitute a law-light, institution-light, treaty-light 'top-down' non-institutionalised form of globalisation, which differs from EU's globalisation through institutionalisation in 'bottom-up' structures at the core of the EU's deep and comprehensive post-Lisbon trade agreements.[46] China has used processes extrinsic to traditional frameworks for investments, and has disregarded social, environmental and labour laws.[47] These developments take place against the significant backdrop of China adopting a Civil Code in 2020, in force in 2021, the first for Communist China after half a century of codification efforts.[48] Does the BRI approach amount to an exception to globalisation? Does its legality have significance for the study of global governance? The EU's planned Global Gateway, discussed in Chapter 6, emerges as a counterbalance to this. Yet it largely proposes to adopt an investment-oriented view of infrastructure. Will it bring the EU and Asia closer together or push them further apart? Does it constitute an esoteric method for the EU to engage with globalisation? A gap between EU and Chinese approaches to globalisation creates an important series of question on institutionalisation. How do we understand the future of institutionalisation in globalisation? Does institutionalisation in this vein contribute to our understanding of EU-Asia relations generally, broader than EU-China relations? How bottom-up is institutionalisation in recent times? And what will it be like in future? Is it Europe-centric? Looking across the other side of the Atlantic to a 'closer' region, how can Europe and the US come closer to each other in methods of globalisation? What

[46] J Chaisse and J Kirkwood, 'Chinese Puzzle: Anatomy of the (Invisible) Belt and Road Investment Treaty' (2020) 23 *Journal of International Economic Law* 245; B Kingsbury, 'Infrastructure and InfraReg: on Rousing the International Law "Wizards of Is"' (2019) 8(2) *Cambridge International Law Journal* 171; M Wu, 'Digital Trade-Related Provisions in Regional Trade Agreements: Existing Models and Lessons for the Multilateral Trade System' (2017) RTA Exchange International Centre for Trade and Sustainable Development and Inter-American Development Bank; although see M Li, 'The Belt and Road Initiative: Geo-Economics and Indo-Pacific Security Competition' (2020) 96 *International Affairs* 169, on the role of Chinese officials.

[47] S Rolland and D Trubek, *Emerging Powers in the International Economic Order* (Cambridge University Press, 2019) 196.

[48] H Jiang, 'The Making of a Civil Code: Promises and Perils of a New Civil Law' (2021) 95 *Tulane Law Review* 777; H Wang, 'The Belt and Road Initiative Agreements: Characteristics, Rationale and Challenges' (2021) 20 *World Trade Review* 282.

place does Asia have in this matrix? How significant is the EU-Japan data flow agreement? Does EU institutionalisation work better at different stages of international agreement? How do we assess these claims in the current period and going forward? Is it Europe-centric? How revealing are case studies of sectoral differences?

This book thus examines comparative approaches to data institutionalisation through the EU's relationships with the US (Chapter 4), Japan (Chapter 5) and China (Chapter 6). It considers leading trade and EU external relations partners since the 1990s in particular – a major turning point for data and digital trade regulation, which has since blossomed. It examines how the EU engages with countries that have different approaches to law and institutions, explores the fundamental differences between Japan and China as to data issues: one a long standing partner and the other at arm's length, with a far smaller joint history of legal and institutional interaction. The EU's impact on third-country legal orders through esoteric adequacy processes such as data flows is understudied. Just how much change does it foist upon or demand from another order? Are findings transparent? The executive-led practice is generated by the Commission from somewhat opaque ideals. What are its effects? As will be noted above, the EU increasingly generates institutionalisation through its trade agreements, particularly in regulatory cooperation/digital trade. It may also be said that the adoption of EU rules, practices and ideas is partly managed through hard law but also partly through soft law processes, such as the power of EU markets. How does comparative law deal with the EU, and its capacity to generate rule transfer and indirect dissemination of rules and standards, given its status as a non-state and complex regional supranational entity? Is it a blind-spot of comparative law? The EU presents a unique case study for comparative law, with strong institutionalisation at the heart of its approach. Institutionalisation has been simultaneously opposed by many US lawyers, US laws and US views on market intervention, top-down intervention and the role of the private sector. Equally, EU institutionalisation practices contrast sharply with Asian approaches to law and rights. EU data infrastructures agreed with such entities generate questions as to blind spots of comparative law and comparative studies of the development of data regimes. Does comparative law embrace international economic law developments as to data and trade agreements? Are advances in comparative approaches being seen? Does the EU generate comparative shifts in institutionalisation in its partners' domains? Such questions are perhaps outside the scope of this work but are also predictably important future questions, eg in relation to a US privacy agency, which is increasingly under discussion. Chapter 6 outlines how developments in EU-China relations arguably eclipse these EU-US structures and developments and show deeper elements of institutionalisation of EU norms, values and rules, albeit embryonically.

As will be explored in this book, more generally the EU approach to digital trade in a global context is often thought to lie in the 'middle-ground', usually between polarised US and Chinese approaches.[49] As to data flows, US agreements frequently have unfettered cross-border data flows but have restrictive approaches to net neutrality and content moderation. Chinese approaches, bearning in mind its Great Firewall, have given economies of scale to data companies thanks to a huge population. Increasingly, China has adopted aspects of the EU's GDPR, but uses the BRI approach to support Chinese firms. It gives much power to an independent national data regulator, though its independence may be questioned. The EU has, in contrast, binding provisions on cross-border data flows, as in the EU-Japan Economic Partnership Agreement (EPA). It requires countries that want to exchange personal data to become 'adequate' in their protection of that data. Similarly, on the definition of digital trade, in WTO negotiations China has promoted a narrow view of digital trade, focusing on trade in goods online, while the US and others have subscribed to a more extensive approach. The US approach tends to focus more on the 'digital' nature of digital trade, while the Chinese approach prefers to address the issue from the traditional 'trade' perspective. The EU has arguably shifted to a midway point.[50] Still, despite its middle-ground stance, the EU will be shown to have an outsized role in its effects on regulation, its extra-territoriality, the force of its laws and the reach of its high standards. The difference arguably lies in the place of institutionalisation within the EU: the EU innovates, regulates and externalises through and by institutions.

This leads to broader questions relating to the place of law and checks and balances in institutionalisation and in major case studies of institutionalisation. Is their adjudication normatively significant for study?

VI. Arguing that Institutionalisation Goes Beyond Judicialisation

The latest debates about the methods and methodology of EU law are largely data-driven or advocate deeper law-in-context approaches or historical studies.[51]

[49] P Leblond, 'Digital Trade at the WTO – The CPTPP and CUSMA Pose Challenges to Canadian Data Regulation' (2019) CIGI Papers No 227, www.cigionline.org/sites/default/files/documents/no.227.pdf accessed 23 February 2022; S Aaronson, 'What Are We Talking about When We Talk about Digital Protectionism?' (2019) 18 *World Trade Review* 541.

[50] See further AD Mitchell, 'Towards Compatibility: The Future of Electronic Commerce within the Global Trading System' (2001) 4 *Journal of International Economic Law* 685; H Gao, 'Digital or Trade? The Contrasting Approaches of China and US to Digital Trade' (2017) 21 *Journal of International Economic Law* 297.

[51] Eg A Dyevre et al, 'The Future of European Legal Scholarship: Empirical Jurisprudence' (2019) 26 *Maastricht Journal of European and Comparative Law* 348; U Sadl and M Madsen, 'A "Selfie" from Luxembourg: The Court of Justice and the Fabrication of the Pre-Accession Case-Law Dossiers' (2016) 22 *Columbia Journal of European Law* 327; W Alschner et al, 'The Data-Driven Future of International Economic Law' (2017) 20 *Journal of International Economic Law* 217. See R van Gestel and H-W Micklitz, 'Why Methods Matter in European Legal Scholarship' (2014) 20 *European Law Journal* 292, 313–16; M Egan, 'Toward a New History in European Law: New Wine in Old Bottles?' (2013) 28 *American University International Law Review* 1223.

Certain schools now suggest, for example, that in future EU law must become more empirical in order to realise its scientific benefits and to develop the discipline.[52] Many of these advocates, however, are often heavily 'court-centric' and propose a highly court-centric understanding of EU integration as a modus operandi of EU law, or place the Court as the ultimate subject and object of the data analysis. Such an approach is by no means inevitable.[53] One of the first places in the world to teach EU law was Harvard Law School in the 1960s, where Koen Lenaerts (now President of the CJEU) taught the content of the EEC treaties.[54] To impugn such a 'court-centric' approach is not to denigrate it but rather to emphasise that organisational practice, law-making practice and Court judgments are different. Yet to suggest that a resolutely 'non-court-centric' look at the EU may be an option to consider is perhaps a 'minority' methodology. However, such non-court-centric views need to be taken into account in any realistic survey of contemporary and future EU law as part of the study of actors embedded in a specific socio-political context, eg as regards the relationship between courts and other institutions, or between courts and civil society more broadly.

The legalisation of society has contributed to this development and the growing sophistication of judicial review, although these developments are routinely imperilled. Legal scholarship and other fields of scholarship now invest considerably authority in the judicialisation of policy fields. Judicialisation relates to the central role played by courts in political systems, in particular with regard to the EU.[55] Judicialisation can be defined as the 'reliance on courts and judicial means for addressing core moral predicaments, public policy questions, and political controversies'.[56] Judicialisation is national, regional, international and supranational.[57]

[52] Dyevre et al (n 51); Sadl and Madsen (n 51); U Sadl and I Panagis, 'The Force of EU Case Law: An Empirical Study of Precedential Constraint' (May 31, 2016) iCourts Working Paper Series No 68, https://ssrn.com/abstract=2787119 accessed 23 February 2022; A Dyevre and M Ovádek, 'Experimental Legal Methods in the Classroom' (2020) 16 *Utrecht Law Review* 1.

[53] E Fahey, 'Future-Mapping the Directions of European Union (EU) Law: How Do We Predict the Future of EU Law?' (2020) 7(2) *Journal of International and Comparative Law* 265.

[54] Lecture of Koen Lenaerts, Brussels, 2013, author's notes.

[55] eg N Mussche and D Lens, 'The ECJ's Construction of an EU Mobility Regime-Judicialization and the Posting of Third-Country Nationals' (2019) 57 *Journal of Common Market Studies* 1247.

[56] See in the context of the EU-US Privacy Shield: E Fahey and F Terpan, 'Torn between Institutionalisation and Judicialisation: the Demise of the EU-US Privacy Shield' (2021) 28 *Indiana Journal of Global Legal Studies* 205. See further R Hirschl, 'The Judicialization of Politics' in GA Caldeira et al (eds), *The Oxford Handbook of Law and Politics* (Oxford University Press, 2018) 253.

[57] R Sieder et al (eds), *The Judicialization of Politics in Latin America* (Palgrave, 2016); B Dressel (ed), *The Judicialization of Politics in Asia* (Routledge, 2012); A-M Slaughter, 'Judicial Globalization' (2000) 40 *Virginia Journal of International Law* 1103; GI Hernández, 'The Judicialization of International Law: Reflections on the Empirical Turn' (2014) 25 *European Journal of International Law* 919; KJ Alter, *The New Terrain of International Law: Courts, Politics, Rights* (Princeton University Press, 2014).

In the EU, the role of the judiciary has been acknowledged first by lawyers seeing European integration as 'integration through law',[58] then by political scientists focusing on judicial politics in the EU,[59] and the CJEU as a 'political power'[60] or an activist court.[61] The CJEU is an unusually powerful court in international relations, for example, with powers, inter alia, of ex ante Opinion review pursuant to Article 218 TFEU, that are viewed as non-justiciable political questions in some legal orders. Beyond the EU, there is a broad scholarship on 'juristocracy' and the rise of judicial authority beyond the state in the light of the proliferation of international courts,[62] largely concerned with the upsurge in the number of courts and its significance.[63]

The more involvement and impact the courts and tribunals have, the more the judicialisation. The proliferation of international courts and tribunals is the most common focus of the study of institutions and the phenomenon of institutionalisation. Globally, the authority in transnational judicialisation has led to vast swathes of scholarship, research, actions on the legitimacy of the proliferation of courts and tribunals at international level.[64] The judicialisation beyond the state of all stages of law-making is an increasingly studied phenomenon. Its capacity to resolve the delegation of authority remains to be seen. Yet undue focus on judicialisation appears blinkered as to law-making or processes of decision-making. Indeed, in legal scholarship the role of courts as checks and balances overwhelmingly nudges analysis towards the output of law-making and procedural processes and legal scholarship interest in the design of institutions is less studied. This book considers the following: Is institutionalisation in the EU context judicialised? What advantages and disadvantages are there to relative consideration of judicialisation? The nature of the EU as a global digital actor arguably does not begin with the narrative of the courts, as is usual, but rather elsewhere. It is not landmark judgments that set the pace of development: it is rather institutionalisation itself that does.

[58] E Stein, 'Lawyers, Judges and the Making of a Transnational Constitution' (1981) 75 *American Journal of International Law* 1; M Cappelletti et al, *Integration through Law: Europe and the American Federal Experience*, vol 1 (De Gruyter, 1986).

[59] A Stone Sweet, *Governing with Judges: Constitutional Politics in Europe* (Oxford University Press, 2000); S Saurugger and F Terpan, *The Court of Justice of the European Union and the Politics of Law* (Red Globe Press, 2016).

[60] A-M Burley and W Mattli, 'Europe Before the Court: a Political Theory of Legal Integration' (1993) 47 *International Organization* 41.

[61] R Dehousse, *The European Court of Justice: the Politics of Judicial Integration* (Springer, 1998); RA Kagan, 'Globalization and Legal Change: the "Americanization" of European Law?' (2007) 1 *Regulation and Governance* 99; SK Schmidt, *The European Court of Justice and the Policy Process* (Oxford University Press, 2018); RD Kelemen, *Eurolegalism: the Transformation of Law and Regulation in the European Union* (Harvard University Press, 2011).

[62] R Hirschl, *Towards Juristocracy* (Harvard University Press, 2004 & 2007); KJ Alter et al, *International Court Authority* (Oxford University Press, 2018).

[63] See D Lustig and JH Weiler, 'Judicial Review in the Contemporary World – Retrospective and Prospective' (2018) 16 *I-CON* 1.

[64] Hirschl, *Towards Juristocracy* (n 62); Alter et al (n 62).

VII. Informal Organisations and Informal Law-Making: What Role for Institutionalisation?

The EU's institutionalisation practices are all the more exceptional when set in a broader context. Informal organisations are said to be proliferating in international law and policy.[65] In contemporary law and political science, informality of law-making and organisational practice continues to emerge as a key research agenda for understanding law and global governance. Informal international organisations are thus increasingly studied as entities that are less formal and more flexible than international organisations, and have emerged since the 1970s. It is now asserted that 30–40 per cent of all international organisations are informal organisations, thus constituting a substantial body of evidence.[66] It is important to highlight the EU's efforts to increasingly engage with more entities and actors, including private actors, as a driver *beyond* informal organisations.[67] International soft law literature reminds us of the desire of entities to regulate and generate 'mission creep' using soft law.[68]

Informality is thus a particularly powerful concept to consider in processes of institutionalisation because it becomes a *driver* thereof.[69] This book argues that the growing morass of informal law-making by EU institutions places more faith in institutional actors to develop institutional design and autonomy; this may be viewed as evidence of institutionalisation, thereby contributing to an understanding of this emerging research agenda and the esoteric nature of the EU. Formalisation through legal change is not ultimately well understood. It has been suggested that informal organisations have been driven by a desire to exclude developing countries from formal organisations at intra-state and inter-state level.[70] This is not necessarily the case with in relation to data, where organisations such as ICANN have been emancipated from the nation state and subjected to increasingly public regulation. There are many examples of informal organisations in trade, banking, antitrust (GATT, IMF, Basel Committee); the International Competition Network (ICN) was created informally outside of trade negotiations.[71] At a time of huge increase in state economies at the national level in the post-Covid world, there is

[65] See C Roger, *The Origins of Informality: Why the Legal Foundations of Global Governance are Shifting, and Why It Matters* (Oxford University Press, 2020) Ch 2.

[66] ibid; Roger understands the EU as state-like, using its competition powers as an example of its far-reaching competence.

[67] ibid, 1.

[68] A-M Slaughter, 'Agencies on the Loose: Holding Government Networks Accountable' in GA Bermann et al (eds), *Transatlantic Regulatory Cooperation* (Oxford University Press, 2000).

[69] O Stefan, 'The Future of EU Soft Law: A Research and Policy Agenda for the Aftermath of Covid-19' (2020) 7(2) *Journal of International and Comparative Law* 329; E Korkea-Aho, 'EU Soft Law in Domestic Legal Systems: Flexibility and Diversity Guaranteed?' (2009) 16(3) *Maastricht Journal of European and Comparative* Law 27.

[70] Roger (n 65).

[71] ibid. Roger gives the example of how the US forced the EU to create the ICN as an informal organisation: see ibid, Ch 7.

capacity to change the parameters of formal and informal, state versus private and so on. However, EU-specific literature on the state of EU soft law shows that the use of soft-law has exploded, from 15 per cent of all EU law-making some time ago to being a key tool of EU action in times of crisis (eurozone, health, migration etc).[72] Moreover, EU external relations law proliferates with examples of informal law-making from the EU institutions themselves.[73] From areas of stronger to weaker competence, informal law-making has increasingly more significant effects and increasing judicial – and other – accountability. Even in trade negotiations with key partners in areas of key EU exclusive external competences there is no shortage of examples. For example, one notable instance is the EU-US lobster deal and the EU-US Joint Statement in 2018, leading a long time later to a Commission Regulation – after the Joint Statement had seemed to become a binding instrument of sorts and created significant inter-institutional disputes as to the exclusion of the European Parliament.[74] In fact, within the EU, institutional key actors have been circumvented through the routine development of ad hoc informal processes – such as the exclusion of the European Parliament from recent trade negotiations with the US. The European Commission emerges as a clear actor generating new forms of law-making but it is not the only actor carrying out these practices. There are many incentives for institutional actors to use informal law-making, given the time and complexity of formal law-making, particularly in trade. Indeed, even the CJEU has arguably adopted an increasingly more benevolent and pragmatic view of informal law-making.[75] The Court of Justice in Opinion 1/17, inter alia, on the Joint Interpretative Instrument (JII) gives significant force to the legalisation, institutionalisation and entrenchment of informal law-making as a means to bolster legitimacy concerns about EU external relations.[76] The very fervent actions of the EU institutions, eg the Council and Commission, at the time of the signing of CETA placed great emphasis on the binding nature of the JII. As outlined in Chapter 4 below, there are significant developments in EU-US relations on data transfer law that are grounded in a series of letters obscurely linked to Commission

[72] E Fahey, 'Hyper-legalisation and Delegalisation in the AFSJ: on Contradictions in the External Management of EU Migration' in S Carrera et al (eds), *Constitutionalising the External Dimensions of EU Migration Policies in Times of Crisis: Legality, Rule of Law and Fundamental Rights Reconsidered* (Edward Elgar, 2019).

[73] Informal non-binding law-making here relates to law-making departing from Art 218 TFEU *stricto sensu*, where the latter relates to binding instruments. Informal law-making is not formless and there are many examples of it, eg MoU or administrative arrangements established in writing. Binding instruments are international agreements including exchange of letters of decisions of bodies established by international agreements.

[74] See also 'Joint statement of the 11th Union for the Mediterranean (UfM) Trade Ministers Conference (10th November 2020)' (2020) Tradoc 159033, https://trade.ec.europa.eu/doclib/docs/2020/november/tradoc_159033.pdf accessed 23 February 2022.

[75] The Court of Justice has had to consider the question of the effects of a MoU in the Swiss MoU decision and gave a highly practical answer: see Case C-660/13, *Council of the European Union v European Commission*, EU:C:2016:61.

[76] For example, in paras 220 and 221 of the CETA opinion, where much of the legal legitimacy under review therein apparently hinges upon such instruments; see Opinion 1/17 (n 38) paras 220–21.

decisions and which have far-reaching implications for the operation of a data transfer regime governing a billion citizens. Some suggest that the use of binding international law agreements – for example in EU-US evidence negotiations – is fanciful.[77] Thus, it is important to consider the place of institutionalisation in understanding these developments, because it assists in comprehending the roll-out of institutional design and the increasing autonomy of actors in law-making. In particular, informality of designs of law-making institutionalisation and its architecture are significant. Chapter 4 shows how EU-US hybrid governance in data transfers is increasingly legalised and evolving informally; similarly, Chapter 6 on EU-China relations, shows slow legalisation.

VIII. Institutionalising Data: The Data 'Forum' Problem

This book argues that the future of data as an entity entails engaging with the complexity of trust in standards. All over the world, many now grapple with the fact that trade agreements alone cannot solve the complexity of digital trade and data flows. This requires an acknowledgement of the practical nature of flows and the shortcomings of trade agreements which take a surprisingly limited view of data and its contours, links to privacy, localisation and security. Information has joined oil, tanks and money as the key currency of international affairs.[78] From a political science perspective, institutions do not solve distributional issues in which some win and some lose.[79] Yet from a legal perspective the curious and complex place of digital trade and data institutionalisation where it emerges represents perhaps a taxonomy challenge but also a victory for individual rights and the rule of law. The EU's GDPR is forecast to provoke even more legal disputes, possibly with the US and third countries, and may have profound consequences for social media companies' business models, amongst others. Yet political science is castigated by Farrell and Newman, for example, for its inability to fathom the new *politics* of information. This book contends that Big Data arguably has infrastructural effects and leads to the transformation of institutional infrastructures that existing regulatory frameworks tend to miss. It is thus a ripe area for the study of institutionalisation, given the challenges of capturing it coherently. The digitisation of trade as a reality is not reflected in the regulation of the world trading system, where WTO rules barely touch upon the matter, and only tangentially.[80] Existing

[77] T Christakis and F Terpan, 'EU-US Negotiations on Law Enforcement Access to Data: Divergences, Challenges and EU Law Procedures and Options' (2021) 11(2) *International Data Privacy Law* 81, discussed further in Ch 4.

[78] H Farrell and AL Newman, *Of Privacy and Power: The Transatlantic Struggle over Freedom and Security* (Princeton University Press, 2019) 173; *cf* A Fisher and T Streinz, 'Confronting Data Inequality' (2021) IILJ Working Paper 2021/1 and S Viljoen, 'Democratic Data: A Relational Theory for Data Governance' (2020) 131 *Yale Law Journal* 370.

[79] Farrell and Newman (n 78) 170.

[80] M Janow and P Mavroidis, 'Digital Trade, E-Commerce, the WTO and Regional Frameworks' (2019) 18(S1) *World Trade Review* 1.

WTO rules are also said to be limited in their ability to address the range of opportunities and challenges presented by digital trade.[81] Yet ironically, while every twentieth century trade agreement is in want of a chapter on electronic commerce, one of the politically and technically sensitive or challenging issues is the place of privacy therein. Data continuously suffers from the nexus problem – it is easily proximate but also paradoxically far from other issues.[82] Data has an increasingly voluminous yet also complex place in contemporary trade agreements. In the most large-scale formulation of trade agreements, such as the megaregionals CPTPP and USMCA, data may be understood to have been overlooked, at least with regard to its precise relationship with privacy. Data regulation has emerged as an extraordinary challenge of the twenty-first century, where the market is no longer invisible and the competitive struggle amongst surveillance capitalists produces the compulsion towards totality; see eg Mark Zuckerberg's notorious boast 'that Facebook would know every book, film and song a person had consumed' etc.[83] Data has become captured by surveillance capitalism whereby new economic imperatives emerge, whose mechanisms and effects cannot be grasped and which do not fit within existing models and assumptions.[84] Here, price, payment, free access and user integration constitute wholly new models of engagement. Yet this totality has not been matched by holistic views of the place of data, warranting a broader framework which captures the nature of EU practice with global effects – here through the place of institutionalisation.

IX. Outline of the Chapters in this Book

Chapter 1 outlines the conceptual framework that underpins the EU's role as a global digital actor. The EU now has data transfer regimes and flows with third countries, which count as some of the largest in the world and which feature significant institutional dimensions. The chapter examines questions of extra-territoriality that lie at the heart of these regimes, and their relationship to the global reach of EU data law. The chapter considers the global alternatives to the GDPR. It examines the development of the EU as a data localisation actor, championing high European

[81] M Burri, 'Should There Be New Multilateral Rules for Digital Trade?' (2013) E15 Expert Group on Trade and Innovation; M Burri, 'The International Economic Law Framework for Digital Trade' (2015) 135 *Zeitschrift für Schwezerisches Recht* 10; M Burri, 'Designing Future-Oriented Multilateral Rules for Digital Trade' in P Sauve and M Roy (eds), *Research Handbook on Trade in Services* (Edward Elgar, 2016).

[82] As Murray and Black remind us, discrete aspects of data regulation do not need to operate in isolation from existing regulatory regimes and much unnecessary energy can be spent on devising new regimes: J Black and A Murray, 'Regulating AI and Machine Learning: Setting the Regulatory Agenda' (2019) 10 *European Journal of Law and Technology*.

[83] Zuboff (n 12).

[84] ibid.

standards in the wake of the decision in *Schrems II* and including cloud computing regulatory plans. The chapter reflects upon EU digital sovereignty and its overall meaning. The EU as a global data actor is exemplified in the reach of the Brussels Effect, where digital frameworks on privacy and hate speech are adopted globally. From the DMA, DSA to AI civil liability, the EU has sought to write a new civil code for the Internet and digital society through its institutionalisation. It emerges as a constitution for the technical, trying to operationalise constitutional values through atypical institutional design and the rising autonomy of actors. The dense institutional design and autonomy of individual actors furthered by the GDPR continues to be a core hallmark of EU regulatory capture of data.

Chapter 2 then examines the development of the EU as a digital trade actor against the backdrop of a highly fragmented international framework on digital trade, lacking consensus and definition, with inadequate and tardy WTO developments. The chapter considers holistically the challenges of unity on digital trade, data flows and how they impinge on EU unity and actorness and its capacity to generate institutionalisation. The EU has, however, produced very significant developments in international economic law in the area of digital trade through championing best practice and high standards as to privacy, although often resting between US and Chinese developments thereon as a 'middle ground' actor. The EU appears increasingly to shift beyond a 'middle-ground actor' position in digital trade, aiming for higher standards of data privacy yet also advocating an ambitious digital trade agenda. However, its efforts appear increasingly stymied by data localisation allegations. The chapter examines the objectives of several key recent EU negotiations. Alongside digital trade, the chapter considers the place of data flows in negotiations, specifically as to adequacy decisions, and developments in practice after *Schrems II* and their capacity to generate further localisation. Here, the EU has sought to adopt an expansive approach to institutionalisation, eg with the US. Ultimately, it remains a challenge to see whether the EU's institutionalised vision of data can succeed in future negotiating forums, integrating high standards of privacy frameworks.

Chapter 3 moves on to examine how the EU's cyber law-making seems to have been long dominated by weak efforts at institutionalisation and few actors. This could change radically, given the unfolding internal market directions of cyber law-making. The reality of cyber law is dominated by a need to use Common Foreign and Security Policy (CFSP) sanctions; the overall matrix of law-making appears increasingly skewed in different directions, destined for partial institutionalisation. The EU's own complexity as an international organisation increasingly is also apparent, as developments on the Budapest Convention demonstrate. The history of EU cyber law-making is of the evolution of weak actors and a diversity of competences, from the single market to the CFSP. EU cyber action is significant to an understanding of EU integration practices, appearing until recently to be weakly institutionalised. The EU has had a limited range of institutionalisation activities as to cybersecurity in its trade agreements, largely dependent on soft law frameworks and voluntary cooperation, yet this is rapidly changing.

Chapter 4 reflects upon the development of transatlantic relations through dialogues and the development of many transatlantic data flow regimes (PNR, TFTP, Privacy Shield, Umbrella Agreement), focusing on the institutionalisation of data flows, in particular in the Privacy Shield. The chapter highlights how developments in EU-China relations arguably eclipse these EU-US structures and developments. The chapter considers EU-US developments as a weakly institutionalised mechanism with an Ombudsman and atypical transatlantic governance. The chapter examines the judicial review of EU-US data transfers in recent case law, which resulted in strong judicialisation of the Privacy Shield. The chapter further analyses developments in EU-US cyber law-making, and its tendencies towards internationalisation. The chapter explores how EU and US regulators may be finding significant convergence on the need to weaken Big Tech. Transatlantic convergence on regulatory standards from competition law to privacy and speech law suggests a commonality of regulatory capture, but is embedded within weak institutionalisation. The EU-US Joint Agenda for Global Change includes a Transatlantic Trade and Technology Council, putatively developing a loose institutionalisation of key global challenges currently not well covered or dealt with by, for example, the WTO; this seems like a useful forum to generate transatlantic convergence. Much remains to be seen as to the future of soft or weak institutionalisation and its sustainability in the face of the many other challenges arising globally, generated both internally and beyond the EU.

Chapter 5 then considers EU-Japan relations as a key study of the emerging place of data and digital trade with an Asian partner. The EU-Japan EPA and the EU-Japan Adequacy Decision cumulatively form one of the largest free trade areas in the world and one of the largest safe flow regimes of data. Significant convergence between the EU and Japanese legal orders seems apparent in recent case law: Japanese law has adopted aspects of the right to be forgotten, and is seemingly moving closer to European law. The digital trade/electronic commerce provisions of the EU-Japan EPA are particularly notable for their international best practice standards, their commitments to multilateralism, internationalisation and high standards of privacy protections. EU-Japanese cybersecurity cooperation is also embedded in multilateralism and commitments to international law; it has intensified in recent times and is the subject of institutionalised cooperation within the EU-Japan EPA. Chapter 5 reflects upon the institutionalisation of the relationship, particularly in regulatory cooperation and through convergence of standards which has generated deeper intersections between the two legal orders. Although the relationship is couched in weak institutionalisation, the EU enables and commits a key partner to significant convergence in data flows and digital trade.

Finally, Chapter 6 considers the relationship between the EU and China in data-related issues. Negotiations on investment have been ongoing between the EU and China for some time and do not cover data or digital trade. Many EU Member States have signed up the law-light institution-light BRI regime, in the absence of an EU agreement. There is a growing consensus that China has sought to utilise many EU GDPR concepts and principles in its recent cybersecurity law, but it does not institutionalise them internally in its domestic procedures, enforcement or compliance regimes, instead substantively committing 'away' from EU law. The Chinese legal order and its body politic appears open to forms of European institutionalisation. Limited convergence with EU law on some level does not equate to EU values and appears to indicate considerable distance between the parties. EU-China relations are nonetheless a significant study of law-light institution-light regimes. The chapter examines the absence of an overarching legal framework, the EU Member States' engagement with the BRI and the place of data localisation in the future. EU-China relations are technically the 'furthest' away and the least institutionalised of EU international relations, yet emerging infrastructures and the growing legalisation of the Chinese legal order indicate that convergence may well be in sight. It emerges thus as a clear study of reverse convergence rather than institutionalisation for now. EU-China relations are depicted as a source of manifold contradictions but predicated on reverse convergence.

1

EU as a Global Digital Actor

I. Overview: The EU The Internationalist: Becoming a Global Data Actor

In any discussion of the EU as a global actor it is important to remember that the EU appears as a distinctively consistent 'internationalist' in a world recently shifting towards populism and localism. Data institutionalisation can arguably now be understood to be a central part of this global agenda, as driving convergence in data protection laws and practices with global reach and effects of a once proclaimed law-free space, explicitly.[1] The success of the EU as a global data actor is argued here to have largely been constructed through the institutionalisation of data.

Moving towards international standards may inevitably involve deference to technocratic processes, as those of the EU amply demonstrate (it is arguably a specialisation of the EU).[2] However, many of those framing the discourse on global data flow increasingly single out EU data protection law as an impediment to digital trade.[3] Proponents of global data flows label the EU approach to personal data protection as 'overly restrictive', 'onerous', and 'protectionist'. Yet this presupposes a very specific view of the relationship between data and trade.[4] The 'economisation of human rights' other than privacy leads to human rights being instrumentalised for economic ends such as market access and creates tensions of this nature. The GDPR has been said to 'create[s] barriers to cross-border data transfers to such an extent that they are effectively data localization requirements'.[5] The hypothetical consequences for the EU, by frightening estimations, could lead

[1] European Commission, 'Communication from the Commission to the European Parliament and the Council: Exchanging and Protecting Personal Data in a Globalised World' COM(2017) 07 final; E Fahey, 'The Global Dimension of the EU's AFSJ: On Internal Transparency and External Practice' (2014) Jean Monnet Working Paper Series 2014/4. See also JP Barlow, 'A Declaration of the Independence of Cyberspace' (1996), www.eff.org/cyberspace-independence accessed 23 February 2022.

[2] A Chander, *The Electronic Silk Road: How the Web Binds the World Together in Commerce* (Yale University Press, 2013) 189.

[3] S Yakovleva and K Irion, 'Pitching Trade against Privacy: Reconciling EU Governance of Personal Data Flows with External Trade' (2020) 10(3) *International Data Privacy Law* 201.

[4] ibid; MF Ferracane et al, 'ECIPE Digital Trade Restrictiveness Survey Index' (ECIPE, 2018), https://ecipe.org/wp-content/uploads/2018/05/DTRI_FINAL.pdf accessed 23 February 2022.

[5] M Sharma, 'Approaching Data Localization' (*Medium*, 10 June 2019), https://medium.com/@madhavsharma/approaching-data-localization-cc90282cb975 accessed 23 February 2022.

to a 3.9 per cent loss in the EU's GDP, or up to $193 billion in absolute numbers.[6] It is probably also fair to say that the global debate on privacy has had an upward trajectory, towards the European discourses. The world's social media giants now argue for an EU GDPR and co-locate themselves strategically between Europe and the US and subject themselves to significant regulation. However, it seems fair to say that such views as to data localisation are important to bear in mind in a world of geo-blocking and internet divisions based on borders. More practically, there are many assertions of the unsuitability of the legal instruments used to protect privacy and grapple with surveillance and commercial concerns.[7] The place of setting and context is a broader one also. From a geopolitical perspective, many key questions arise, for instance, within the context of the recent so-called US China Silicon Curtain or tech war.[8] It raises the question of who was caught in the middle? The G7 countries no longer form a majority of the world's GDP and a significant split amongst G20 countries exists as to their relationship with China; the power balance of the global economy has never been more complex. The EU was also caught in the midst of one of the most complex tech wars ever, relating to the place of 5G, the future of many ICT industries and the place of digitisation in trade, arguably exacerbating the lack of agreement on digital trade.

The GDPR is highly significant because it establishes a coherent and consistent data protection framework by offering a uniform set of substantive rules that are enforced by a network structure of national data protection authorities, who cooperation with each other under the coordination of the European Data Protection Board (EDPB).[9] The resulting architecture is a complex system of bodies at EU and national level who are charged with responsibility for the enforcement of the rules in the GDPR. The sophistication and complexity of this regime is exacerbated by many of the world's social media networks having their European headquarters in

[6] Yakovleva and Irion (n 3).

[7] eg M Kaminski, 'Why Trade Is Not the Place for the EU to Negotiate Privacy' (*Internet Policy Review*, 23 January 2015), https://policyreview.info/articles/news/why-trade-not-place-eu-negotiate-privacy/354 accessed 23 February 2022.

[8] See also M Lewis, 'Criminalizing China' (2020) 111 *Journal of Criminal Law and Criminology* 145, on the China Initiative of the US Department of Justice launched in 2018 to counter national security threats emanating from China.

[9] Regulation (EU) 2016/679 of the European Parliament and of the Council of 27 April 2016 on the protection of natural persons with regard to the processing of personal data and on the free movement of such data, and repealing Directive 95/46/EC (GDPR) [2016] OJ L119/1, is a significant attempt on the part of EU law to modernise its approach to data protection and to engage in regulatory coherence in the aftermath of landmark CJEU decisions. The new Regulation is perceived to mark a significant extension of the extra territorial application of EU law with respect to EU and non-EU established companies pursuant to Art 3 thereof and thereby refining the landmark developments begun by the CJEU in Case-131/12, *Google Spain SL and Google Inc v Agencia Española de Protección de Datos (AEPD) and Mario Costeja González*, EU:C:2014:317. National authorities had not been satisfied with the pre-existing regime precisely because it had resulted in 'ad hoc transnational enforcement'. The GDPR is thus understood to have generated a process of 'Europeanisation' whereby there is a significant shift from decentralised application of data protection law to centralised enforcement.

Ireland, one of the smallest member states of the EU, with a data protection commission with de facto and de jure capacity to regulate all of Europe – and, by extension of law, many global social medial and tech companies. The scale of the resources and capacity to do is a matter for elsewhere. However, the institutional design of this system and its autonomy has already shown teething problems – as well as evolution and growth: the EDPB adopted its first Article 65 decision in November 2020 with respect to a dispute between the Irish Data Protection Commission and many other DPAs on a draft decision of the DPC concerning Twitter International Company breaching certain GDPR provisions. The respective places of enforcement, oversight, consistency and accountability are to the fore here. In its Grand Chamber decisions, the CJEU has developed significant case law to permit exceptions to the place of Ireland as lead supervisory authority.[10] The effects of such case law remain to be seen. The CJEU has re-emphasised the one-stop-shop in *Facebook Ireland Limited and Others v Gegevensbeschermingsautoriteit*[11] but is aware of the unevenness of resources and alive to risk of institutional forum shopping against that background.[12] However, it is clear that the dense institutional design and autonomy of individual actors furthered by the GDPR continues to be a core metric of its operation and a hallmark of EU regulatory capture of data and global reach.

Chapter 1 contains the following sections: (II) EU global reach over the web; (III) global reach through large-scale data flow regimes; (IV) global alternatives to the GDPR; (V) the EU as a soft data localisation actor; (VI) the EU the emerging digital sovereign; (VII) global capture of Big Tech in data spaces and the DMA/DSA; (VIII) the EU's emerging architectural infrastructure on AI; and (IX) Conclusions.

II. EU Global Reach Over the Web: An Architecture of Scale

Country after country around the world replicates the EU's GDPR.[13] Some struggle with its force and bureaucracy but ultimately comply.[14] However, many of the

[10] See Case C-645/19, *Facebook Ireland Ltd and Others v Gegevensbeschermingsautoriteit*, EU:C:2021:483.

[11] ibid.

[12] L Woods, 'Who Has Jurisdiction over Facebook Ireland? The CJEU Rules on the GDPR "One Stop Shop"' (*EU Law Analysis*, 16 June 2021), http://eulawanalysis.blogspot.com/2021/06/who-has-jurisdiction-over-facebook.html accessed 24 February 2022.

[13] eg Thailand, China, California. See A Bradford, *The Brussels Effect: How the European Union Rules the World* (Oxford University Press, 2020).

[14] F Lusa Bordin, 'Is the EU Engaging in Impermissible Indirect Regulation of UN Action? Controversies over the GDPR' (*EJIL: Talk!*, 11 December 2020) www.ejiltalk.org/is-the-eu-engaging-in-impermissible-indirect-regulation-of-un-action-controversies-over-the-general-data-protection-regulation/ accessed 24 February 2022.

most extraordinary developments of our times on jurisdictional issues, eg transatlantic 'showdowns' over the US CLOUD Act or liability for intermediaries, show international law-making mediated by major multinational cooperation.[15] Evidence indicates that, for example, Facebook was concerned about a possible change in the liability for intermediaries under the Digital Single Market back in 2015.[16] The E-Commerce Directive governing social media platforms does not hold companies such as Facebook liable for illegal content posted by their users.[17] However, companies must take down illegal content once it has been flagged as such. In 2016, Facebook lobbied that additional liability would be a barrier to Facebook and the new business models on the platform. These efforts were ultimately initially successful, as the E-Commerce Directive was not re-opened and Facebook became a repeat player in lobbying on EU law.[18] Significant regulatory shifts do not look likely under the EU's draft Digital Services Act (DSA), discussed below in further detail.[19] Instead, the 20-year-old legal infrastructure of the E-Commerce Directive remains mostly in place. The Digital Services Act (DSA) is proposed as a regulation rather than a directive, and does not repeal the E-Commerce Directive but builds on it, including the internal market principle found in Article 3 of the E-Commerce Directive. It provides for several types of online intermediary provider and a very broad range of exemptions. It allows intermediaries to continue to benefit from comprehensive liability exemptions so, as a result, will not be held liable for user content. The DSA provides for new due

[15] J Daskal 'Microsoft Ireland, the CLOUD Act, and International Law Making 2.0' (2018) 17 *Stanford Law Review Online*, 9.

[16] L Kayali, 'Inside Facebook's Fight against European Regulation' (*Politico*, 23 January 2019), www.politico.eu/article/inside-story-facebook-fight-against-european-regulation/ accessed 31 December 2021. Facebook Inc has now changed its name to 'Meta'.

[17] ibid.

[18] Regulation (EU) 2019/1150 of the European Parliament and of the Council of 20 June 2019 on promoting fairness and transparency for business users of online intermediation services [2019] OJ L186/57.

[19] European Commission, 'Proposal for a Regulation of the European Parliament and of the Council on a Single Market For Digital Services (Digital Services Act) and amending Directive 2000/31/EC' COM (2020) 825 final; Cf. European Commission, 'Proposal for a Regulation of the European Parliament and Council on contestable and fair markets in the digital sector (Digital Markets Act)' COM (2020) 842 final; European Commission, 'Press remarks by President von der Leyen on the Commission's new strategy: Shaping Europe's Digital Future' (19 February 2020), https://ec.europa.eu/commission/presscorner/detail/en/speech_20_294 accessed 24 February 2022; *cf* C Schmon and K Gullo, 'European Commission's Proposed Digital Services Act Got Several Things Right, But Improvements Are Necessary to Put Users in Control' (*Electronic Frontier Foundation*, 15 December 2020), www.eff.org/deeplinks/2020/12/european-commissions-proposed-regulations-require-platforms-let-users-appeal accessed 24 February 2022; A de Streel et al, 'Digital Markets Act: Making Economic Regulation of Platforms Fit for the Digital Age' (2020) CERRE Report, https://cerre.eu/wp-content/uploads/2020/11/CERRE_DMA_Making-economic-regulation-of-platforms-fit-for-the-digital-age_Full-report_December2020.pdf accessed 24 February 2022; M Schaake, 'EU Needs to Think Bigger than Big Tech' (*Tech Monitor*, 27 November 2020), https://techmonitor.ai/interviews/marietje-schaake-eu-think-bigger-than-big-tech accessed 24 February 2022.

diligence obligations for flagging illegal content for all providers of intermediary services, and establishes special type and size-oriented obligations for online platforms, including the very large ones.[20] The largest platforms can be fined up to six per cent of their annual revenue for violating rules about hate speech and the sale of illegal goods. At the time of writing, significant developments were ongoing as to eg improving the criteria for the designation of gatekeepers but clearly reach here is of much significance.

The case law of the CJEU also displays an increasingly reluctant approach to shielding online intermediaries with the immunities of the E-Commerce Directive, though arguably framed more 'glamorously'. Recent case law[21] offers a striking insight into the place of Facebook in the intricate regulatory jigsaw of EU law, in litigation instigated by an Austrian parliamentarian who had asked Facebook to delete a comment that was ultimately found by Austrian courts to be defamatory against her reputation. She had demanded that Facebook delete the post but in a geographically segmented way, including not just the specific post but also identical or equivalent posts. The novelty of the case is that one week previously the Court of Justice (Grand Chamber) had limited the reach of the infamous 'right to be forgotten' developed by the CJEU in 2014 in Case-131/12 *Google Spain*, allowing individuals to request search engines to remove links containing personal information from web results appearing under searches for their names.[22] In Case C-507/17 the CJEU in *Google v CNIL* were confronted with a notice served on Google by the French National Data Protection Authority for links to web pages to be removed from the list of results displayed following a search conducted to apply for removal of all the search engine's domain name extensions.[23] The CNIL regarded Google's geo-blocking proposal as insufficient. The CJEU held that a search engine operator could not, under current EU law, be required to de-reference on all versions of its search engine.[24] Rather, the internet was a global network without borders.[25] Many suggested that *Google v CNIL* would de jure predict the result in *Eva Glawischnig-Piesczek*, and that the latter case could conceivably trigger a global assault on freedom of speech.[26] However, this is arguably not the case. The Austrian Supreme Court in *Eva Glawischnig-Piesczek* asked the CJEU to determine whether the wording of Article 15(1) of

[20] M Eifert et al, 'Taming the Giants: The DMA/DSA Package' (2021) 58 *Common Market Law Review* 987.

[21] Case C-18/18, *Eva Glawischnig-Piesczek v Facebook Ireland Limited*, EU:C:2019:821.

[22] *Google Spain* (n 9).

[23] Case C-507/17, *Google LLC v Commission nationale de l'informatique et des libertés (CNIL)*, EU:C:2019:772.

[24] ibid para 72.

[25] ibid para 56.

[26] J Daskal and K Klonick 'When a Politician Is Called a "Lousy Traitor", Should Facebook Censor It?' (*New York Times*, 27 June 2019), www.nytimes.com/2019/06/27/opinion/facebook-censorship-speech-law.html accessed 24 February 2022.

Directive 2000/31 covered removal not just of illegal or defamatory information but also other information: (1) worldwide; (2) in EU Member States; (3) of the relevant worldwide user; or (4) of the user in the circumstances. Although willing to consider the extraterritorial effects of EU law, Advocate General Szpunar in his Opinion said that the proceedings did not come within the scope of EU law. He held that Directive 2000/31 had to be interpreted as meaning that it did not preclude a host provider from being ordered to remove information characterised as illegal. In contrast, the CJEU in its decision found that although Facebook was not liable for the disparaging comments that had been posted, it had an obligation to remove comments after they were found to be defamatory. It held that, in view of the global nature of e-commerce, the Directive did not preclude injunctive measures with worldwide effect. The Court found that the lower court had jurisdiction to require the host provider to block access to the information stored. It also held, somewhat cryptically, that global injunctions would be limited 'by the relevant international law', possibly making reference here to issues of comity.[27]

Case C-18/18 exposes a considerable gap between the Court's decision and the Opinion of the Advocate General in the case, who was also the Advocate General in the recent *Google v CNIL* decision. This could be indicative of significant disputes internally in the Court. Arguably, however, the most significant difference between the two cases relates to the role of the latter case as concerning a public figure and political speech. For some, the case gives the green light for global orders against the thrust of the E-Commerce Directive and assumes a level of technological sophistication and specificity that does not exist. What must Facebook (the overarching owner of which has been renamed as Meta, but the Facebook platform name remains unchanged) do? Take down a particular post globally and look for other additional posts?[28] Others argue that it represents an important shift in the burden of proving legal exceptions to 'Big Tech'.[29] Or is there a shift in power inside the Court room?[30] Such cases expose interesting power dynamics, in which EU law continuously intervenes against Big Tech in the realm of data but arguably only goes so far – just far enough for EU institutions to fairly assert that they have considerable ongoing authority over it through the institutionalisation of the web. Facebook has ultimately shown itself to be a Europeanist, as it ostensibly now

[27] *Eva Glawischnig-Piesczek* (n 21) para 53. See A Keane Woods, 'Litigating Data Sovereignty' (2018) 128 *Yale Law Journal* 328.

[28] J Daskal, 'A European Court Decision May Usher in Global Censorship' (*State*, 3 October 2019), https://slate.com/technology/2019/10/european-court-justice-glawischnig-piesczek-facebook-censorship.html accessed 24 February 2022.

[29] D Desierto, 'Human Rights Regulation in the Tech Sector? The European Court of Justice's Facebook Decision and California's AB5 Gig Economy Bill' (*EJIL:Talk!*, 8 October 2019), www.ejiltalk.org/human-rights-regulation-in-the-tech-sector-the-european-court-of-justices-facebook-decision-and-californias-ab5-gig-economy-bill/ accessed 24 February 2022.

[30] Daskal, 'A European Court Decision May Usher in Global Censorship' (n 28).

adheres to significant amounts of EU law, eg the GDPR and voluntary EU codes on hate speech.[31] On the face of it, this is no surprise: 250 million users in Europe contribute 25 per cent of Facebook's global revenue. However, although Facebook stated that it would apply the GDPR in spirit across the globe, in practice matters were different. The company made internal logistical changes to ensure that the GDPR would not circumscribe the majority of its operations, 'quietly' moving 1.5 billion user files from Ireland to the US in April 2018 so that they would hence be governed by US privacy law. Similarly, Google swiftly moved millions of UK Google users to US 'control' post-Brexit in 2020, to reduce the impact of the GDPR and eliminate the possibility of any of those users filing claims in the Irish courts.[32] However, Facebook purportedly remains a 'strong' advocate of EU law, at least as regards certain aspects of data law, even to the point of increasingly advocating for the GDPR to be the global standard, in the absence of any truly global equivalent. It has helped, along with Apple, Microsoft and Google, to create a position where concern for privacy has the same canonical status as freedom of speech does in the US. Privacy has been 'nudged' and is now being touted as Europe's 'First Amendment'.[33] It has also fostered debates and developments on a US Federal Privacy law, pre-empting developments in Californian law.[34] Facebook continues to object to intense efforts on the part of EU regulators to subject it to EU law and to demonstrate EU law's authority over a vast range of evolving regulatory domains. This is both a direct and indirect call for institutionalisation of immense significance.

III. EU Global Reach Through Large-Scale Data Flow Regimes: On Adequacy

Global reach is how pop music, fashion, sport and art achieve critical mass and acclaim. EU law is no different. The GDPR is particularly relevant to the future of global digital trade because it leaves countries that want to access a market of 400 million consumers with no alternative. Such countries must update their

[31] Bradford (n 13); GDPR.

[32] D Ingram, 'Exclusive: Facebook to Put 1.5 Billion Users out of Reach of New EU Privacy Law' (*Reuters*, 19 April 2018), www.reuters.com/article/us-facebook-privacy-eu-exclusive-idUSKBN-1HQ00P accessed 24 February 2022; 'Google Moves UK User Data to US to Avert Brexit Risks' (*Financial Times*, 20 February 2020), www.ft.com/content/135e5b66-53fb-11ea-90ad-25e377c0ee1f accessed 24 February 2022. Africa, Asia, Australia and Latin American are governed by terms of service issued by the company's international headquarters in Ireland: see S Zuboff, *The Age of Surveillance Capitalism: The Fight for a Human Future at the New Frontier of Power* (Profile Books, 2019) Ch 17.

[33] B Petkova, 'Privacy as Europe's First Amendment' (2019) 25 *European Law Journal* 140.

[34] eg C Kerry et al, 'Bridging the Gaps: A Path Forward to Federal Privacy Legislation' (2020), www.brookings.edu/wp-content/uploads/2020/06/Bridging-the-gaps_a-path-forward-to-federal-privacy-legislation.pdf accessed 24 February 2022.

domestic laws to comply with the EU regime or enter into specific individual regimes with the EU.[35] The EU now has data transfer regimes and flows with third countries which count as some of the largest on the globe – eg the EU-US Privacy Shield, 2016, covering over a billion citizens; the EU-Japan Data Adequacy Decision, 2018, relating to the world's largest safe data flow area between the EU and Japan.[36] These regimes evolved through somewhat different legal processes but ultimately hinge upon a process of negotiating convergence. The European Commission has the power to determine, on the basis of Article 45 of the GDPR, whether a country outside the EU offers an adequate level of data protection. In doing so, it examines wider factors such as the country's judicial system, the rule of law and its national security policies. The overall system for data protection must be deemed 'essentially equivalent' to the EU's before a positive decision will be made. The decision is periodically reviewed by the European Commission and it can be revoked at any time. While the European Commission has never revoked an adequacy decision following a review, the CJEU has. It is a complex practice but also an interesting one, where the EU's institutionalisation practices have dominated and where it has had a significant impact on third country partners, sometimes beyond the scope of what was anticipated.

The concept of an 'adequate' level of protection has been significantly developed by the CJEU in Case C-263/14, *Schrems v Data Protection Commissioner*, relating to arrangements with the US, where 'partial' adequacy decisions exist involving self-certification practices, similar to the arrangements in place with Canada. These adequacy decisions do not cover data exchanges in the law enforcement sector, which are governed by the 'Police Directive' (Article 36 of Directive (EU) 2016/680). The notion of adequacy has been put under considerable strain during the Covid-19 crisis, where many key EU partners with adequacy decisions have adopted measures that impinge on privacy or that strengthen surveillance.[37] Adequacy has now also been subjected to extraordinary pressures by the CJEU decision in *Schrems II*, discussed in particular in Chapter 4 below. There, the Court has added layers of complexity to the possibility of truly free flows of data and has presented significant challenges to business and data protection authorities. The capacity of the CJEU to 'insert' itself into the adequacy procedure and upset and overturn adequacy decisions made by the European Commission – reached after immense negotiations – leaves international partners at the mercy of extremely stringent European values. Adequacy in the time of Covid-19 posed many additional challenges, as the activities, freedom and essential health data of all citizens

[35] P Sauvé and M Soprana, 'The Evolution of the EU Digital Trade Policy' in M Hahn and G Van der Loo (eds), *Law and Practice of the Common Commercial Policy* (Brill Nijhoff, 2020) 298–99.

[36] See S Stefano, 'The EU as a Global Standard Setting Actor: The Case of Data Transfers to Third Countries' in E Carpanelli and N Lazzerini (eds), *Use and Misuse of New Technologies* (Springer, 2019).

[37] C Docksey, 'The Coronavirus Crisis and EU Adequacy Decisions for Data Transfers' (*European Law Blog*, 3 April 2020), https://europeanlawblog.eu/2020/04/03/the-coronavirus-crisis-and-eu-adequacy-decisions-for-data-transfers/ accessed 24 February 2022.

globally have become an everyday part of life in ways that could not have previously been imagined. The time limitations on adequacy decisions, and the fact that they are capable of being withdrawn, are also of much concern because of their possible impact on partners. Whether EU data protection standards are relevant to data-gathering activities carried out in third countries to combat Covid-19 remains to be seen, not least in those countries who are considered to be handling the crisis most effectively. It is clear that there is an equivocality at root here which is difficult to capture – forcing the world to accept high standards and possibly divorcing Europe from lesser global standards of protection.

The EU's data adequacy system is ultimately highly politicised and institutionalised, as the CJEU has inserted itself into the adequacy process, institutionalising global data flows like no other process, in its extraordinary interventions in its landmark decisions in *Schrems I* and *II* relating to the EU-US Privacy Shield and previous Safe Harbour Agreement.[38] This means that data flow agreements are politicised but also heavily legalised and have autonomously generated a significant jurisprudence and analytical outline. These processes self-evidently present themselves as forms of institutionalisation and have failed because of weak institutionalisation (eg in *Schrems II* where the Ombudsman was found by the CJEU to be insufficiently robust and independent in the EU-US regime). The EU's approach to data flows was originally unilateral and 'treaty-light' in its locus and is now inserted into provisions of its trade agreements in much detail, eg the EU-UK Trade and Cooperation Agreement (TCA), which has significantly evolved its institutional design. These global data flows are subject to layers of bureaucratisation and convergence requirements, which generate significant forms of institutional interaction.

Some contend that the European Commission 'cloaks efforts to promote the spread of EU law in the language of encouraging third countries and international organisations to adopt strong data protection standards'.[39] However, this promotes a rather skewed vision of a process that is an evolution of convergence. The institutional configurations of this transfer of data matter considerably. The EU's data regimes vary in scale and complexity and very much in terms of institutional design. A turn to institutions and deeper forms of institutional oversight, accountability and legitimation is regarded as 'European' or 'EU-centric' and differs substantially from US and Asian models of looser accountability and oversight.[40] The EU-US Privacy Shield came into force in 2017, as a legal instrument intended to replace the US Safe Harbour Agreement, the voluntary self-certification system with public enforcement by the US FTC, which requires US companies to treat data

[38] Case C-362/14, *Maximillian Schrems v Data Protection Commissioner*, EU:C:2015:650 (*Schrems I*) and Case C-311/18, *Facebook Ireland v Schrems*, EU:C:2020:559 (*Schrems II*).

[39] C Kuner, 'The Internet and the Global Reach of EU Law' in M Cremona and J Scott (eds), *EU Law Beyond EU Borders: The Extraterritorial Reach of EU Law* (Oxford University Press, 2019) 112, 137.

[40] P Schwartz, 'The EU-U.S. Privacy Collision: A Turn to Institutions and Procedures' (2013) 126 *Harvard Law Review* 1966.

on EU citizens as if the data were physically in Europe.[41] As further developed in Chapter 4, it specifically addresses the concerns about data collection and privacy that arose in the case of *Schrems I*.[42] In 2018, the European Parliament threatened to vote for suspension of the Privacy Shield unless considerable changes were made, to comply with EU data protection rules on clarity on data control, remedies and oversight. It remains the subject of much scrutiny and litigation.[43] The CJEU ultimately struck down the Privacy Shield in *Schrems II*, drawing attention to its weakly institutionalised oversight *and* US surveillance laws.[44] The development of a Trans-Atlantic Privacy Framework Agreement comprises a court and robust independent scrutiny mechanisms. Will the mechanisms developed after the decision be understood as institutionalisation of EU-US relations?

Other regimes are important too: the US regime is not in fact the only large-scale regime of significance. In 2018, the EU and Japan agreed to recognise each other's data protection systems as 'equivalent', to allow data to flow safely between the EU and Japan.[45] The EU maintains that its mutual adequacy arrangement will create the world's largest area of safe transfers of data based on a high level of protection for personal data and also complement the EU-Japan Economic Partnership Agreement (EPA), though not a leading innovation in trade terms.[46] It is thus another significant global endeavour, ostensibly creating global reach. The instruments surveyed now constitute some of the broadest and increasingly important global legal instruments adopted, with enormous regulatory reach across the Atlantic and global territory, literally and metaphorically, and show the scale of the EU's intent. Substantial critique has been levied against the EU-Japan data adequacy agreement for its lack of both institutionalisation and transparency.[47] Countries 'closest' to the EU in terms of agreements reached often have partial adequacy decisions (eg EU-US). The EU-Japan agreement is heralded as one of the most far-reaching of all time in terms of 'area' *qua* adequacy decision. What forms of checks and balances are appropriate and sufficient of this space?

[41] Commission Implementing Decision (EU) 2016/1250 of 12 July 2016 pursuant to Directive 95/46/EC of the European Parliament and of the Council on the adequacy of the protection provided by the EU-US Privacy Shield (notified under Document C (2016) 4176) [2016] OJ L207/1.

[42] *Schrems I* (n 38).

[43] 'Civil Liberties MEPs Want EU-US Privacy Shield Suspended by September' (*Euractiv*, June 2018), www.euractiv.com/section/data-protection/news/civil-liberties-meps-want-eu-us-privacy-shield-suspended-by-september/ accessed 24 February 2022.

[44] *Schrems II* (n 38).

[45] Agreement between the European Union and Japan for an Economic Partnership (EU-Japan EPA) [2018] OJ L330/3; EU-Japan Adequacy Decision: Commission Implementing Decision (EU) 2019/419 of 23 January 2019 pursuant to Regulation (EU) 2016/679 of the European Parliament and of the Council on the adequate protection of personal data by Japan under the Act on the Protection of Personal Information (EU-Japan Adequacy Decision) [2019] OJ L 76/1.

[46] H Suzuki, 'The New Politics of Trade: EU-Japan' (2017) 39 *Journal of European Integration* 875.

[47] M Bartl and K Irion, 'The Japan EU Economic Partnership Agreement: Flows of Personal Data to the Land of the Rising Sun' (2017) Amsterdam Centre for Information Law Institute Working Paper, www.ivir.nl/publicaties/download/Transfer-of-personal-data-to-the-land-of-the-rising-sun-FINAL.pdf accessed 24 February 2022.

How can the concerns of civil society be abated? What evidence is there of 'learning' in institutional design? What role is given to civil society in the development of initiatives to abate concerns? And what about regimes that appear to fail to enforce any theoretical rights?

The EU-Japan adequacy decision was also said to complement the EU-Japan EPA.[48] However, it has been criticised for the ease with which Japan received the decision relative to its capacity to satisfy a stricter view of equivalence, and so the politicisation of the process has come to the fore. While the EU is typically described as a global actor in trade, the EU-Japan trade negotiations and the parallel data adequacy negotiations provide a setting to study how the EU actorness in data has developed alongside its actorness in trade.

China is an extraordinary potential partner for the EU. It has adopted EU law GDPR principles and relevant case law into its recent cybersecurity law, yet it severely restricts the regulation of data and appears to constitute a form of reverse Brussels Effect. An adequacy decision with China seems increasingly unlikely and improbable. It is only recently, after years of dialogue, that China is beginning to engage with the EU in trade in a legalistic sense. China has notably for years only engaged with individual Member States on law enforcement. This sits against a broader backdrop of many EU Member States engaging with China's Belt and Road Initiative (BRI) whilst the EU was taking part in rounds of negotiations with China on an investment agreement; this is considered further in Chapter 6.

Nonetheless, the reviews of all EU adequacy decisions planned in 2022, of all 14 to date, including high-profile decisions with the UK and Korea in 2021, make this likely to become an extraordinary period of reflection on the future of convergence with EU values and the institutional design structures of the adequacy process itself.

IV. Global Alternatives to the GDPR Lack Institutionalisation

As human rights go, privacy is relatively new; Samuel Warren and Louis Brandeis were the first to advance the notion that privacy is a right deserving of legal protection.[49] Privacy is distinctive among the core civil and political rights, because it was enshrined in international law before it was comprehensively guaranteed by any domestic constitutional system.[50] Prior to the adoption of the Universal

[48] Suzuki (n 46).

[49] S Warren and L Brandeis, 'The Right to Privacy' (1980) 4 *Harvard Law Review* 193.

[50] S Schulhofer, 'An International Right to Privacy? Be Careful What You Wish For' (2016) 14 *International Journal of Constitutional Law* 238; V Krishnamurthy, 'A Tale of Two Privacy Laws: The GDPR and the International Right to Privacy' (2020) 114 *American Journal of International Law Unbound* 26; D Cole and F Fabbrini, 'Bridging the Transatlantic Divide? The United States, the European Union, and the Protection of Privacy across Borders' (2016) 14 *International Journal of Constitutional Law* 220.

Declaration of Human Rights (UDHR) in 1948, a tiny number of domestic legal systems had only protected certain aspects of what we now consider the right to privacy.[51] The *travaux préparatoires* of the UDHR, the ICCPR, and the European Convention on Human Rights indicate that the right to privacy was included as an afterthought. Some illumination of the meaning of the right to privacy enshrined in Article 17 of the ICCPR may be found in General Comment 16, which the UN Human Rights Committee adopted in 1988 and which recognises that the right to privacy 'is required to be guaranteed against all [arbitrary or unlawful] interferences and attacks whether they emanate from State authorities or from natural or legal persons'.

As Krishnamurthy states,

> the GDPR certainly provides the strongest privacy protections of any law in the world today for those matters within its material scope. No comparable law endows individuals [...] with such strong rights over data relating to them, and no other law imposes such strong conditions on the collection and use of personal data by private- and public-sector entities [...]. This is doubtless why privacy campaigners around the world have held up the GDPR as a model that their own jurisdictions should emulate.[52]

However, it is 'neither sufficient on its own to comprehensively protect the right to privacy, nor a necessary means for states to meet their obligations under Article 17 of the ICCPR'.[53] Arguably, other international standards such as the Asia-Pacific Economic Cooperation (APEC) Cross Border Privacy Rules (CBPR) could become geographically more significant in the advent of broader membership, particularly from larger jurisdictions, such as the UK post-Brexit, if it joins the Comprehensive and Progressive Agreement for Trans-Pacific Partnership (CPTPP) successfully. The 'first-mover' advantage of the EU in data regulation is arguably frequently over-stated as to its reach – data privacy comprises only one specific facet or contour thereof. Digital trade is frequently omitted from this analytical rubric yet is the site of significant developments as the EU attempts to evolve its global actorness into trade agreements.

In *The Brussels Effect: How the European Union Rules the World*, Bradford describes how EU regulations impact standards around the world through the process of unilateral regulatory globalisation.[54] There is a significant challenge in formulating EU global action in law and its effects. Many authors diverge on its precise delineation as a subject field and also as a methodological question. The EU is not a unified or homogenous global actor. The precise movement of EU rules beyond borders is also highly contested as an idea across disciplines. Arguably one of the clearest accounts is as to the digital economy in relation to the acceptance by leading social media tech giants in the US of EU law principles, from hate speech to the GDPR.[55]

[51] Krishnamurthy (n 50).
[52] ibid 28.
[53] ibid 29.
[54] Bradford (n 13) Ch 5.
[55] ibid Ch 5.

When dealing with transborder data flows, the EU is faced with different systems of personal data protection, which has resulted in both fragmentation and competition in standard setting. As trade and the global economy rely ever more on data, countries from North America to Asia are becoming aware of the importance of data flows in trade and potential challenges for data protection, which explains the increase of regulation on cross-border data flows in recent years.[56] Legal frameworks at the international and regional level have existed since the 1980s, under the auspices of the UN,[57] the OECD,[58] the APEC Privacy Framework, the Council of Europe Convention 108.[59] One week before the GDPR came into force in 2018, the modernisation of data protection Convention 108 was completed by the Council of Europe.[60] Most arguments as to the force of Convention 108+ assume a controversial understanding of the reach of the jurisprudence of the Council of Europe and European Court of Human Rights, which seems difficult to maintain.[61] Convention 108+ lacks a sanctions regime and significantly lacks extraterritoriality in the sense of the GDPR – thus lacking 'bite'.[62] The CBPR system was first established in 2011 by the APEC as a 'regional economic forum' of 21 Asia-Pacific member economies.[63] The APEC Privacy Framework is a set of principles and implementation guidelines that were created in order to establish effective privacy protections that avoid barriers to information flows, and ensure

[56] C Kuner, *Transborder Data Flows and Data Privacy Law* (Oxford University Press, 2013) 10.

[57] General Assembly of the United Nations, 'Guidelines for the Regulation of Computerized Personal Data Files' UN Doc.E/CN.4/1990/72 of 14 December 1990.

[58] OECD Council Recommendation, 'Guidelines on the Protection of Privacy and Transborder Flows of Personal Data' (OECD, 1980).

[59] Convention for the Protection of Individuals with Regard to Automatic Processing of Personal Data (1981) CETS 108 28 January 1981.

[60] G Greenleaf, '"Modernised" Data Protection Convention 108 and the GDPR' (2018) 154 *Privacy Laws and Business International Report* 22; C Sullivan, 'EU GDPR or APEC CBPR? A Comparative Analysis of the Approach of the EU and APEC to Cross Border Data Transfers and Protection of Personal Data in the IoT Era' (2019) 35(4) *Computer Law & Security Review* 380; G Greenleaf, 'Renewing Convention 108: The CoE's "GDPR Lite" Initiatives' (2016) 142 *Privacy Laws & Business International Report* 14; LA Bygrave, 'The "Strasbourg Effect" on Data Protection in Light of the "Brussels Effect": Logic, Mechanics and Prospects' (2021) 40 *Computer Law & Security Review* 1; G Greenleaf, 'A World Data Privacy Treaty? "Globalisation" and "Modernisation" of Council of Europe Convention 108' in N Witzleb et al (eds), *Emerging Challenges in Privacy Law: Comparative Perspectives* (Cambridge University Press, 2014) 92.

[61] eg Bygrave (n 60) 3: '… the Strasbourg Effect on data protection did not begin with the adoption of C108 +. Ever since the 1970s, the CoE has been enormously influential in shaping regulatory discourse in the field, primarily within Europe but also beyond'. See ibid 10. There is currently little appetite in major economies outside the EU to accede.

[62] G Greenleaf, 'Modernised Data Protection Convention 108 and the GDPR' (2018) 154 *Privacy Laws and Business International Report* 22–23.

[63] Like the EU GDPR, the CBPR also governs the transfer of personal information across the borders of participating nations. To date, eight nations have joined the CBPR system: the US, Canada, Mexico, Japan, Singapore, Taiwan, Australia and the Republic of Korea; G Greenleaf, *Asian Data Privacy Laws: Trade and Human Rights Perspectives* (Oxford University Press, 2014); G Greenleaf, 'The Right to Privacy in Asian Constitutions' (2020) University of New South Wales Law Research Series No 53.

continued trade and economic growth in all 27 countries of the APEC region. The APEC Privacy Framework set in motion the process of creating the APEC CBPR system. However, unlike the GRPR – which is a binding regulation that applies to all EU countries – the CBPR is a voluntary, principles-based framework that only extends to APEC members that have formally joined.

The CPTPP includes commitments to privacy in its Chapter 14 (on e-commerce), but *without* specifying the APEC CBPR. TPP endorsed the 'Silicon Valley Consensus' mainly as to data governance, preventing its parties from restricting transnational data flows and from requiring the use of domestic computing facilities.[64] However, it let the mere existence of a legal framework for the protection of personal information suffice.[65] Yet, CPTPP is arguably a good example of how trade negotiators might understand the importance of data governance questions. Regulators and trade negotiators have in the main long operated without reliable data about the global digital economy and continue to overlook the losers of the digital transformation, underappreciate the right to regulate and misjudge the extent to which global digital corporations transcend territorial jurisdictional boundaries.[66] CPTPP is also notable because it interested countries with privacy authorities which were members of the Asia-Pacific privacy authorities' forum and institutionalised intersections. With respect to the e-commerce chapter, the CPTPP text remains the same as that found in the earlier versions of TPP, particularly with regard to the key provision, Article 14.8 on personal information protection, which imposes positive obligations on each party to maintain or adopt a legal framework that provides for the protection of the personal information of the users of electronic commerce. It includes references to broader international frameworks, possibly the APEC CBPR system.[67] This raises the question of the meaning of 'globalness'.

In 2017, 44 trade agreements were shown to have established specific provisions on personal information protection.[68] By 2021, data suggested truly significant global convergence on personal data protection laws: over 98 per cent of

[64] T Streinz, 'Digital Megaregulation Uncontested? TPP's Model for the Global Digital Economy' in B Kingsbury et al (eds), *Megaregulation Contested* (Oxford University Press, 2019).

[65] See Comprehensive and Progressive Agreement for Trans-Pacific Partnership (CPTPP) Art 14.8 (personal information protection), Art 14.11 (cross border transfer of information by electronic means) and Art 14.13 (location of computing facilities).

[66] See eg Streinz (n 64) 313; M Burri, 'Data Flows and Global Trade Law' in M Burri (ed), *Big Data and Global Trade Law* (Cambridge University Press, 2021); G Greenleaf, 'Looming Free Trade Agreements Pose Threats to Privacy' (2018) 152 *Privacy Laws & Business International Report* 23; E Oh, 'Digital Trade Regulation in the Asia-Pacific: Where Does It Stand? Comparing the RCEP E-commerce Chapter with the CPTPP and the JSI' (2021) 48 *Legal Issues of Economic Integration* 403.

[67] Notably the UK intends to pursue accession to the CPTPP as part of its trade negotiations programme.

[68] J-A Monteiro and R Teh, 'Provisions on Electronic Commerce in Regional Trade Agreements' (2017) WTO Working Paper ERSD-2017-11, 51.

nations have a personal data protection law and 64 per cent have a comprehensive approach.[69] The overall picture is still one of extraordinary legal fragmentation,[70] reflecting divergent approaches, preferences and priorities, split between the EU's high standards and the self-regulatory approaches of the US and Asia.[71] In addition to national legislation, less than ten years ago there were around 10 binding bilateral agreements and instruments to govern transborder data flows in place,[72] as well as a series of private sector instruments, such as contractual clauses and non-binding codes of practice.[73] Elsig and Klotz have analysed 91 digital trade-related provisions in 347 trade agreements signed 2000–2019, and find that almost half (48 per cent) of such provisions were first introduced in trade agreements to which the US is a member.[74] These developments demonstrate why there is no global standard on privacy and nothing coming close to rivalling the GDPR; but still, it is only one facet of the overall 'jigsaw'.

Calls for a global regulatory framework have not dissipated even in the US, as discussed in Chapter 4. In the face of rising expectations of digital protection, there are increasingly calls for 'global data laws'[75] and 'international privacy standards'.[76]

[69] See the Digital Trade and Data Governance Hub: https://datagovhub.letsnod.com/ accessed 24 February 2022.

[70] Kuner, *Transborder Data Flows and Data Privacy Law* (n 56) 26.

[71] RH Weber, 'Transborder Data Transfers: Concepts, Regulatory Approaches and New Legislative Initiatives' (2013) 3 *International Data Privacy Law* 117.

[72] ibid. See Binding Corporate Rules: Article 29 Working Party, 'Working Document setting up a framework for Binding Corporate Rules' (WP 154, 24 June 2008); Standard Contractual Clauses: Commission Decision 2010/87/EU of 5 February 2010 on standard contractual clauses for the transfer of personal data to processors established in third countries under Directive 95/46/EC of the European Parliament and of the Council [2010] OJ L39/5; Commission Decision 2004/915/EC of 27 December 2004 amending Decision (EC) 2001/497 as regards the introduction of an alternative set of standard contractual clauses for the transfer of personal data to third countries [2004] OJ L385/74; Safe Harbor Privacy Principles issued by the US Department of Commerce on 21 July 2000, and recognized as 'adequate' under European Commission Decision 2000/520/EC of 26 July 2000 [2000] OJ L215/7; Agreement between the European Union and Australia on the processing and transfer of European Union-sourced passenger name record (PNR) data by air carriers to the Australian Customs Service [2008] OJ L213/49; Agreement between the United States of America and the European Union on the use and transfer of passenger name records to the United States Department of Homeland Security [2012] OJ L215/5; Agreement between the European Union and the United States of America on the processing and transfer of Financial Messaging Data from the European Union to the United States for purposes of the Terrorist Finance Tracking Program [2010] OJ L8/11; Reports by the High Level Contact Group (HLCG) on information sharing and privacy and personal data protection (23 November 2009); Infocomm Development Authority of Singapore (IDA) and the National Trust Council of Singapore (NTC) Voluntary Model Data Protection Code for the Private Sector; Madrid Resolution 'International Standards on the Protection of Personal Data and Privacy' (non-binding); Treasury Board of Canada, 'Taking Privacy into Account before Making Contracting Decisions' (2006).

[73] Kuner, *Transborder Data Flows and Data Privacy Law* (n 56) 21.

[74] M Elsig and S Klotz, 'Initiator Conditions and the Diffusion of Digital Trade-related Provisions in PTAs' (2021) *International Interactions*.

[75] See eg Satya Nadella, Microsoft CEO, in D Hurst, 'Japan Calls for Global Consensus on Data Governance' (*The Diplomat*, 2 February 2019), https://thediplomat.com/2019/02/japan-calls-for-global-consensus-on-data-governance/ accessed 24 February 2022.

[76] P Fleischer, Global Privacy Counsel, 'Call for Global Privacy Standards' (*Public Policy*, 14 September 2007), https://publicpolicy.googleblog.com/2007/09/call-for-global-privacy-standards.html accessed

Nonetheless, the EU has the advantage of being the 'first mover', and also the first mover with the highest standards and some of the deepest institutionalisation to date, as well as ambitious extra-territorial reach to follow through on its internationalist ambitions in generating a global standard.[77]

V. Is the EU a 'Soft Data Localisation' Actor?

Data transfers are one of the most significant and complex areas that the EU attempts to regulate. The EU has invested much political and legal capital in transnational cooperation and cross-border data regulation projects.[78] It has also, however, invested soft power resources into them too.[79] Information control is central to the survival of authoritarian regimes but is also a device with many economic and social benefits and challenges. One useful area for 'narrower' reflection, where the EU appears to increasingly push for institutionalisation, is cloud computing. The origins of cloud computing are disputed but it is understood to date back to around 2010, when it had complex vague contours.[80] Far from being vague, cloud computing has dictated how companies, business and consumers alike store, utilise and assess data. This revolution has led to security issues, with an increasing number of countries asserting the need for a national cloud.[81] The circularity in the processes of evolution here are remarkable. Data localisation requirements may ultimately prevent access to global cloud computing services.[82] While governments assume that global services will simply erect local data server farms, this may mean that local companies are denied access to the many companies that might help them scale up, or to go global.[83] In the European Commission's Data Strategy of 2020, the European Commission has proposed to invest and developed a cloud infrastructure to store and process data in Europe and to support European

24 February 2022; C de Terwangne, 'Is a Global Data Protection Regulatory Model Possible?' in S Gutwirth et al (eds), *Reinventing Data Protection?* (Springer, 2009).

[77] P de Hert and M Czerniawski, 'Expanding the European Data Protection Scope Beyond Territory: Article 3 of the General Data Protection Regulation in Its Wider Scope' (2016) 6 *International Data Privacy Law* 3; PM Schwartz, 'Global Data Privacy: The EU Way' (2019) 94 *New York University Law Journal* 771; Yakovleva and Irion (n 3); Krishnamurthy (n 50).

[78] eg Amendments to the Council of Europe Budapest Convention, discussed in Ch 3 below.

[79] eg the Phaedra project: www.phaedra-project.eu/the-phaedra-project/ accessed 31 December 2021.

[80] A Regalado, 'Who Coined "Cloud Computing"' (*MIT Technology Review*, 31 October 2011), www.technologyreview.com/2011/10/31/257406/who-coined-cloud-computing/ accessed 24 February 2022.

[81] eg 2018 BSA Global Cloud Computing Scorecard: https://cloudscorecard.bsa.org/2018/ accessed 31 December 2021.

[82] A Chander, 'Googling Freedom' (2011) 99 *California Law Review* 1, 20.

[83] See A Chander and U Lê, 'Breaking the Web: Data Localization vs. the Global Internet' (2014) UC Davis Legal Studies Research Paper No 378, https://ssrn.com/abstract=2407858 accessed 24 February 2022.

cloud providers in a significant attempt to bolster the institutionalisation of data through localisation.[84] Prior to this, the European Commission proposed to create an enabling and trust-building policy framework for cloud services in Europe. The European Cloud Initiative of 2016 presented a strategy for public investments to build European Open Science Cloud and European Data Infrastructure, building upon the 2012 European Cloud Strategy.[85] These are significant institutionalisation investments on the part of the EU in grounding cloud computing on EU soil. This increasing territorialisation of data is, of course, not uncontroversial.

Cross-border data flows are hallmarks of twenty-first century globalisation and perceived as 'glue' holding the global economy together.[86] One estimate shows that cross-border data flows added $2.8 trillion to world GDP in 2014.[87] Their valuation process is computationally complex.[88] It is not only the sheer amount of data and global dependence on data that has exponentially increased; there are more actors – specifically governments – seeking to assert control over global data flows. From China to Europe and beyond, there are many important examples arising as to control of data flows. A new generation of regulation of internet controls seeks to keep information from going out of a country rather than stopping it from

[84] See European Commission, 'Shaping Europe's Digital Future: Cloud Computing' (Policy), https://ec.europa.eu/digital-single-market/en/cloud accessed 24 February 2022.

[85] See European Commission, 'Communication from the Commission to the European Parliament, the Council, the European Economic and Social Committee and the Committee of the Regions: European Cloud Initiative – Building a competitive data and knowledge economy in Europe' COM (2016) 178 final; European Commission, 'Communication from the Commission to the European Parliament, the Council, the European Economic and Social Committee and the Committee of the Regions: Unleashing the Potential of Cloud Computing in Europe' COM (2012) 529 final.

[86] WG Voss, 'Cross-Border Data Flows, the GDPR, and Data Governance' (2020) 29 *Washington International Law Journal* 485.

[87] US Department of Commerce, 'Measuring the Value of Cross-Border Data Flows' (2016) 2, www.ntia.doc.gov/files/ntia/publications/measuring_cross_border_data_flows.pdf accessed 24 February 2022; McKinsey Global Institute, 'DigitalGlobalization: The New Era of Global Flows' (2016), www.mckinsey.com/business-functions/digital-mckinsey/our-insights/digital-globalization-the-new-era-of-global-flows accessed 24 February 2022; McKinsey Global Institute, 'By 2025, Internet of Things Applications Could Have US$11 Trillion Impact' (2015), www.mckinsey.com/mgi/overview/in-the-news/by-2025-internet-of-things-applications-could-have-11-trillion-impact accessed 24 February 2022; Voss, 'Cross-Border Data Flows, the GDPR, and Data Governance' (n 86).

[88] A Gardner, *Stars with Stripes: The Essential Partnership between the European Union and the United States* (Palgrave, 2020) 164 and 225. See OECD Digital Economy Papers, 'Measuring the Economic Value of Data and Cross-border Data Flows' (*OECD*, 26 August 2020), www.oecd-ilibrary.org/docserver/6345995e-en.pdf?expires=1605107203&id=id&accname=guest&checksum=7631AE9F2929B79DAB35E25BC1124DEE accessed 24 February 2022. Cross-border data flows include in one US government taxonomy the following interesting outline: 1) Purely non-commercial data traffic, including government and military communications; 2) Transaction data flows between buyers and sellers at a market price, including direct purchases between buyers and sellers, such as in online banking or advertising, and services transactions that involve digital platforms acting as intermediaries between buyers and sellers; 3) Commercial data and services exchanged between or within businesses or other related parties, including supply chain, personnel, or design information; 4) Digital data and services delivered to and from end-users, including free email, search engine results, maps and directions, and information via social media: see US Department of Commerce, 'Measuring the Value of Cross-Border Data Flows' (n 87) 3.

entering the sovereign state space. It is arguably a clear example of the global institutionalisation of data flows. Some contend that this is not a new phenomenon and is in fact widespread, as a form of informational sovereignty.[89] Arguments for and against extending such boundaries to the Internet are arguably reflected in the debate from the late 1990s and early 2000s between David Post and Jack Goldsmith with regard to closed electronic networks.[90] As Kuner eloquently puts it, the transfer of national borders to the online space reflects society's ambivalence about globalisation: on the one hand, we are all accustomed to the global availability of goods and services, but on the other hand, we are unsettled by the breakdown of barriers that threatens national and regional identities which makes us suspicious and uneasy about barriers to data flows.[91]

One important way of viewing these developments is to consider them through the lexicon and prism of the phenomenon of data localisation. Data localisation is a growing phenomenon where globally more attempts are made to impose structures, architecture, actors, controls, reviews and access controls on data. Data localisation is a complex trend to regulate because it is about *reducing* access to data and digital technologies. It seems to address cybersecurity concerns of data vulnerability by requiring data to be kept in a single jurisdiction, making it easier to target and possibly preventing data back-ups in globally distributed data centres.[92] However, data localisation also raises the costs of access to, and use of, data, thereby reducing gains from digital trade.[93] Of course, data localisation laws affect businesses and ordinary individuals in countries in various ways: data localisation is a cost that possibly falls disproportionately on digital exporters, who are required to meet the data localisation requirements. This is challenging for small and medium-sized enterprises.[94] Most literature is heavily centred on the economic, and law and economics, understandings of the costs and implications of regulation of data. For instance, there is a concern that where the data relates to the provision of services, data flow restrictions can also undermine the value of WTO members' GATS services commitments.[95] As a result, it is sometimes stated that countries pushing for data localisation are 'hotbeds' of cyber crimes.[96] Governments across the world also increasingly cite foreign surveillance as an

[89] C Kuner, 'Data Nationalism and Its Discontents' (2015) *Emory Law Journal Online* 2089.

[90] Kuner, *Transborder Data Flows and Data Privacy Law* (n 56) 28–31; JL Goldsmith, 'Against Cyberanarchy' (1996) 65 *University of Chicago Law Review* 1199; DR Johnson and D Post, 'Law and Borders: The Rise of Law in Cyberspace' (1996) 48 *Stanford Law Review* 1367; D Post, 'Against "Against Cyberanarchy"' (2002) 17 *Berkeley Technology Law Review* 1365, 2092.

[91] Kuner, 'Data Nationalism and Its Discontents' (n 89).

[92] J Meltzer, 'Governing Digital Trade' (2019) 18 *World Trade Review* 23, 25.

[93] ibid.

[94] ibid 25.

[95] ibid, giving the example of where WTO members have scheduled a GATS commitment, they must also allow the data flow to deliver the service. Yet localisation measures can reduce access to, or raise the cost of transferring, such data.

[96] A Chander and UP Lê, 'Data Nationalism' (2015) 64 *Emory Law Journal* 677.

argument for preventing data from leaving their borders, allegedly into foreign hands.[97] Consequently, governments are increasingly said to localise data within their jurisdiction.[98] Data localisation can be understood as measures that encumber the transfer of data across jurisdictional borders.[99] It includes rules preventing information from being sent outside the country, rules requiring prior consent of the data subject before information is transmitted across national borders, rules requiring copies of information to be stored domestically, and even a tax on the export of data. Quite *how* the phenomenon plays out is another matter. Some contend that since much data sharing seems to be carried out between different intelligence services around the world, in the end data nationalism may only facilitate access by local intelligence services.[100] Others contend that data localisation measures are in fact likely to undermine security, privacy, economic development, and innovation where adopted.[101] Requiring local data storage arguably weakens, rather than strengthens, fundamental rights if it facilitates the access of intelligence services to data locally, who then share that data with other countries.[102] For instance, French intelligence services conducting widespread Internet surveillance in France and sharing the data collected with the US inevitably makes it unclear what the privacy benefits are of French data localisation.[103]

As countries increasingly apply their national law to cross-border activities on the Internet, will it become increasingly necessary to 'tag' or otherwise mark data to indicate the country whose law is processing it? This is where the EU has a different 'story' to tell. The landmark decision of the CJEU in *Schrems II* is said to mark a key shift towards data localisation in Europe and less openness, evinced through technology surveillance.[104] In either case, market pressures will contribute to the current increase of data localisation measures, as much as the rise of firewalls, yet redress issues will remain.[105] For instance, a number of US Internet

[97] ibid 680.

[98] M Burri, 'The Governance of Data and Data Flows in Trade Agreements: The Pitfalls of Legal Adaptation' (2017) 51(56) *University of California Davis Law Review* 65, 70; Chander and Lê, 'Data Nationalism' (n 96).

[99] Chander and Lê, 'Data Nationalism' (n 96).

[100] Kuner, 'Data Nationalism and Its Discontents' (n 89).

[101] Chander and Lê, 'Data Nationalism' (n 96) 682, reviewing measures in Australia, Brazil, Canada, China, France, Germany, India, Indonesia, Kazakhstan, Malaysia, Nigeria, Russia, South Korea, Sweden, Taiwan, Thailand, and Vietnam, as well as the EU and a handful of other countries ('an astonishing array of countries …').

[102] C Kuner, 'Requiring Local Storage of Internet Data Will Not Protect Privacy' (*OUP Blog*, 6 December 2013) https://blog.oup.com/2013/12/data-security-privacy-storage-law/ accessed 24 February 2022; Kuner, *Transborder Data Flows and Data Privacy Law* (n 56).

[103] ibid.

[104] *Schrems II* (n 38); European Council, 'Special meeting of the European Council (1 and 2 October 2020) – Conclusions' EUCO 13/20 (2020): '… to be digitally sovereign, the EU must build a truly digital single market. Define its own rules, to make autonomous technological choices. At international level, the EU will leverage its tools and regulatory powers to help shape global rules and standards …'.

[105] C Kuner, 'Data Nationalism and Its Discontents' (n 89), 2094; K Propp and P Swire, 'After *Schrems II*: A Proposal to Meet the Individual Redress Challenge' (*Lawfare Blog*, 13 August 2020), www.lawfareblog.com/after-schrems-ii-proposal-meet-individual-redress-challenge accessed 22 February 2022.

companies have set up local data processing centres as a way to deal with strict European standards, which means that market pressures dictate location. They also indirectly then enhance the EU's own institutionalisation of data notably, as to capacity, reach, authority and regulatory capabilities. It might be contended that similar issues exist as to so many other regimes, particularly strict and/or authoritarian regimes, to the effect that those jurisdictions also seek to institutionalise data. Such a claim is not denied; on the contrary, institutionalisation of data unquestionably constitutes a growing phenomenon.

These issues matter because barriers to data flows impinge upon trade and the capacity of a data-innovative economy to succeed. In recent years, many PTAs have started to include provisions on data localisation, either banning or limiting requirements on the location or use of data. An important difference with the data flows provisions is that almost all data location provisions found in trade agreements are of a binding nature.[106] Yet whether data localisation is actually harmful to the institutional structures of trade is a much larger intellectual question. Arguably, most analysis is heavily economically-oriented and wedded to modelling of barriers to trade that take little cognisance of rights and obligations. Is it correct to argue that those criticising the harmful effects of data localisation adopt a weak framework of fundamental rights protections? Can an open and free internet be achieved in the absence of a global pact on the subject matter? What about its intersection in all contemporary trade agreements? It can be argued that data localisation threatens Big Data by limiting data aggregation by country, increasing costs and adding complexity to the collection and maintenance of data. Data localisation requirements can reduce the size of potential data sets, eroding the informational value that can be gained by cross-jurisdictional studies.[107] It is likely to have quite a pernicious effect on cloud computing, innovation and data agility. In addition to digital services taxes, the Digital Markets Act (DMA) and the DSA, combined with data localisation measures, could cumulatively amount to a litany of measures to develop a de facto and de jure European firewall.[108] As a result, it is consistently argued that EU digital protectionism is stifling and hampers trade and diplomatic ties.[109]

The EU rejects, in principle, the assumption of an obligation to allow cross-border data flows.[110] Instead, it argues for a form of data localisation, outlawing

[106] M Burri and R Polanco, 'Digital Trade Provisions in Preferential Trade Agreements: Introducing a New Dataset' (2020) 23 *Journal of International Economic Law* 187, 214.

[107] Chander and Lê, 'Data Nationalism' (n 96) 729.

[108] European Commission, 'Proposal for a Regulation of the European Parliament and of the Council on a Single Market for Digital Services (Digital Services Act) and amending Directive 2000/31/EC' COM (2020) 825 final.

[109] C Barshefsky, 'EU Digital Protectionism Risks Damaging Ties with the US' (*Financial Times*, 2 August 2020), www.ft.com/content/9edea4f5-5f34-4e17-89cd-f9b9ba698103 accessed 24 February 2022 (former USTR).

[110] See K Propp, 'Data Flows across the Channel: The Emerging UK-EU Digital Trade Relationship' (*Atlantic Council*, 3 June 2020), www.atlanticcouncil.org/blogs/new-atlanticist/data-flows-across-the-channel-the-emerging-uk-eu-digital-trade-relationship/ accessed 24 February 2022.

rules that require a company to locate its computing facilities or network in the territory of the other party or that require data to be stored or processed there. The EU also advocates giving each party an absolute right to maintain any data privacy safeguards it deems appropriate, with no objective trade disciplines of the nature proposed by others in trade negotiations, such as the UK. The EU thus faces manifold criticisms of the *Schrems II* ruling, for the emphasis that it places upon data localisation directly or indirectly and the manner in which it appears to champion digital sovereignty.[111] Some suggest that the *Schrems II* decision is unworkable for the EU if it wishes to be a global actor.[112] While *Schrems II* is discussed in greater detail in Chapter 4, it is difficult to disagree with the thrust of how Chander depicts its legacy:

> The end result of [...] *Schrems* II is to reduce the available channels for transferring personal information from the [EU] to the [US]: two of the principal mechanisms for transferring personal data to the United States have either been repudiated outright or made unstable. The CJEU struck down the EU-US Privacy Shield, an agreement that more than 5,300 companies (both European and American) use to transfer data across the Atlantic. And while the CJEU upheld the validity of Standard Contractual Clauses (SCCs) for transferring data outside the EU, it conditioned that transfer on a determination by the transferring parties that the transfer would not risk unwarranted surveillance by the US government. While the putative defendant in the case was Facebook, it was the U.S. government that was on trial.[113]

The CJEU suggested using supplementary measures to protect data under the SCCs but did not explain what these measures could be, and in effect SCCs became mini-adequacy decisions.[114] 'Soft' data localisation is thus the likely result there.[115] However, keeping the information in the EU does not insulate the data from the surveillance of the EU Member States' own intelligence services and there has been a wealth of recent case law to this effect, putting contours on their actions and scope. There is a further argument to the effect that even the EU itself does not really know what EU data localisation looks like or means in the post-*Schrems II* world. Ultimately, the Internet itself appears to be likely to be further

[111] *Schrems II* (n 38); A Chander, 'Is Data Localization a Solution for Schrems II?' (2020) 23 *Journal of International Economic Law* 771.

[112] Propp and Swire, 'After Schrems II: A Proposal to Meet the Individual Redress Challenge' (n 105); C Kuner, 'The Schrems II Judgment of the Court of Justice and the Future of Data Transfer Regulation' (*European Law Blog*, 17 July 2020), https://europeanlawblog.eu/2020/07/17/the-schrems-ii-judgment-of-the-court-of-justice-and-the-future-of-data-transfer-regulation/ accessed 24 February 2022; M Rotenberg, '*Schrems II*, from Snowden to China: Toward a New Alignment on Transatlantic Data Protection' (2020) 26 *European Law Journal* 141.

[113] Chander, 'Is Data Localization a Solution for Schrems II?' (n 111) 774.

[114] Kuner, 'The Schrems II judgment of the Court of Justice and the future of data transfer regulation' (n 112).

[115] Case C-623/17, *Privacy International*, EU:C:2020:790; Joined Cases C-511/18, C-512/18 and C-520/18, *La Quadrature du Net and Others*, EU:C:2020:791. See Chander, 'Is Data Localization a Solution for Schrems II?' (n 111).

split or divided between regulatory regimes, beyond that which the EU GDPR has initiated, from the Great Firewall of China to the West of Europe, a gigantic span of regulation.[116] The 'larger view' of data localisation is that it entrenches the protectionism allegations that the EU faces post-Brexit, as the European Council Conclusions of October 2020 unambiguously state: to be digitally sovereign, the EU must develop its own generic idea of the digital sphere that it inhabits.[117] This must entail that it defines its own rules to make autonomous technological choices. At the international level, the EU will leverage its tools and regulatory powers to help shape global rules and standards. Moreover, it is worth making the point that trade agreements follow a complex logic for these debates, ie that these issues play out in many forums beyond data flow agreements. For example, in one of the EU's most advanced FTAs on digital trade, the EU-Japan EPA, the requesting of source code is prohibited, while the location of computing facilities is not covered. Some key elements of this digital trade chapter relate to soft law obligations.[118]

Notably, the EU introduced a significant Regulation in 2018, when it sought to ban data localisation restrictions in order to ensure the free flow of data.[119] Regulation 2018/1807 on a framework for the free flow of non-personal data in the European Union was adopted as part of the Single Market for data storage and processing services, such as cloud computing. The Regulation was adopted with the intention of ensuring that the freedom to choose a data service provider anywhere in Europe would lead to more innovative data-driven services and more competitive prices for businesses, consumers and public administrations. Although on its face the Regulation intended to permit data to flow freely, allowing companies and public administrations to store and process non-personal data wherever they choose in the EU, important constraints on data within the territory of Europe are imposed. The Regulation removes any restrictions imposed by Member States' public authorities on the geographical location for storing or processing non-personal data, unless such restrictions are justified on grounds of public security. The Regulation defines non-personal data to include the rapidly expanding Internet of Things, artificial intelligence and machine learning. Whether it will have a more significant impact on the understanding of localisation remains to be seen. The EU's complex position on data localisation is developed further in Chapter 2 on digital trade.

Data localisation links also to the place of digital sovereignty.

[116] eg: EU users of US websites found themselves blacklisted from many US sites post-GDPR introduction or have to accept a site's user values when accessing a site: 'European readers still blocked from some US news sites' (*BBC News*, 26 June 2018), www.bbc.co.uk/news/technology-44614885 accessed 24 February 2022.

[117] European Council, 'Special Meeting of the European Council (1 and 2 October 2020) – Conclusions' (n 104).

[118] See S Hamanaka, 'The future impact of Trans-Pacific Partnership's rule-making achievements: The case study of e-commerce' (2019) 42 *World Economy* 552.

[119] Regulation (EU) 2018/1807 of the European Parliament and of the Council of 14 November 2018 on a framework for the free flow of non-personal data in the European Union [2018] OJ L 303/59.

VI. The EU, the Emerging Digital Sovereign

The EU has increasingly begun to advocate a message of tech sovereignty as its future. The evolution of this concept is far from clear-cut. It appears to have a long pedigree, though its association with the era of the Trump presidency and increasingly challenging global engagement seems beyond doubt. For the optimistic, it is a natural evolution of the so-called Brussels Effect.[120] Initially, EU digital sovereignty was cast in the era of the Trump administration, generating a Sino-US tech war, with little development of multilateralism or any meaningful WTO agenda on digital trade, and the increased dominance of China in tech wars.[121] It advocated developing the capability for the EU to make its own choices on its own values and own rules, predicated on an emerging regime of institutionalisation of compliance, enforcement and governance.[122] It also aligned with the development of a new generation of the regulation of internet controls to keep information from going out of a country rather than stopping it from entering the sovereign state space *qua* informational sovereignty. Still, it appears as a new EU lexicon in recent times.[123] The European Council in late 2020 advocated technological sovereignty as follows:

> The Covid-19 pandemic has further underlined the need to accelerate the digital transition in Europe. Seizing the opportunities of this transition is crucial to strengthening our economic base, ensuring our technological sovereignty, reinforcing our global competitiveness, facilitating the green transition, creating jobs and improving the lives of citizens. Building a truly digital Single Market will provide a home-based framework allowing European companies to grow and scale up.[124]

The definitional breadth of digital sovereignty in this is vast, and is increasingly understood in EU official documents and by EU Member State actors[125] and institutions[126] to warrant a holistic formulation of regulatory capture of the digital

[120] T Christakis, '"European Digital Sovereignty": Successfully Navigating Between the "Brussels Effect" and Europe's Quest for Strategic Autonomy' (2020) Multidisciplinary Institute on Artificial Intelligence/Grenoble Alpes Data Institute, https://ssrn.com/abstract=3748098 accessed 24 February 2022.

[121] Although it has older origins: V Reding, 'Digital Sovereignty: Europe at a Crossroads' (*EIB Institute*, 2016), https://institute.eib.org/wp-content/uploads/2016/01/Digital-Sovereignty-Europe-at-a-Crossroads.pdf accessed 24 February 2022. See P Grüll, '"Geopolitical" Europe Aims to Extend its Digital Sovereignty from China' (*Euractive*, 9 September 2020), www.euractiv.com/section/digital/news/geopolitical-europe-aims-to-extend-its-digital-sovereignty-versus-china/ accessed 24 February 2022.

[122] European Commission, 'Press remarks by President von der Leyen on the Commission's new strategy: Shaping Europe's Digital Future' (19 February 2020).

[123] Kuner, 'Data Nationalism and Its Discontents' (n 89).

[124] European Council, 'Special meeting of the European Council (1 and 2 October 2020) – Conclusions' (n 104).

[125] eg Opinion of the Economic, Social and Environmental Council (France), 'Towards a European Digital Sovereignty Policy' (*ESEC*, 13 March 2019), www.lecese.fr/sites/default/files/travaux_multilingue/2019_07_souverainete_europeenne_numerique_GB_reduit.pdf accessed 24 February 2022.

[126] European Parliament, 'Digital Sovereignty for Europe' (2020) EPRS Ideas Paper Briefing, www.europarl.europa.eu/RegData/etudes/BRIE/2020/651992/EPRS_BRI(2020)651992_EN.pdf accessed 24 February 2022. See European Parliament resolution on security threats connected with the rising Chinese technological presence in the EU and possible action on the EU level to reduce them

in an unprecedented way, albeit mostly referring to Europe's ability to act independently in the digital world.[127] There are those who criticise European digital sovereignty as a circular oxymoron, confusing human-centered autonomy – each individual citizen is personally sovereign over their data, interactions with AI, etc – with a more Westphalian understanding of sovereignty: each state has an undisputed power monopoly within its border.[128] It is also criticised for the conflicting EU bureaucracies involved in its implementation, where competition policy, one of the EU's most powerful competences and areas of strength, still pales in contrast to the gigantic regulatory tasks involved in non-competition areas. We might say that all digital matters in theory may ostensibly appear to be incapable of being adequately institutionalised despite their need for it. A seemingly conflictual agenda of regulating digital platforms, net neutrality and an EU ecosystem of values appears to constitute the 'surface' meaning thereof.[129] Ultimately, however, a significant amount of institutionalisation of digital sovereignty appears at its heart, which renders it such a rich Europeanised construct.

For many, the defensiveness at the heart of the EU digital sovereignty agenda is striking. Some understand its rhetoric to be predominantly based in the need for robust cyber sanctions and to flight information wars with Russia and China in the future.[130] It can be seen as a means to support EU tech champions. Mostly, it is understood as a defensive reaction to an increasingly hostile environment of the US-China tech wars, at least during the Trump administration, and an era of a lack of multilateralism.[131] Sovereignty is an increasingly dated and provocative subject, castigated for its lack of relevance in contemporary sovereignty in

(2019), 2019/2575(RSP) – 12/03/2019, https://oeil.secure.europarl.europa.eu/oeil/popups/summary.do?id=1577382&t=d&l=en accessed 24 February 2022.

[127] European Parliament, 'Digital Sovereignty for Europe' (n 126); *cf* European Commission, 'Europe: The Keys to Sovereignty' (News) (11 September 2020), https://ec.europa.eu/commission/commissioners/2019-2024/breton/announcements/europe-keys-sovereignty_en accessed 24 February 2022; FG Burwell and K Propp, 'The European Union and the Search for Digital Sovereignty: Building "Fortress Europe" or Preparing for a New World?' (*Atlantic Council*, June 2020), www.atlanticcouncil.org/wp-content/uploads/2020/06/The-European-Union-and-the-Search-for-Digital-Sovereignty-Building-Fortress-Europe-or-Preparing-for-a-New-World.pdf accessed 24 February 2022.

[128] See T Barker, 'Europe Can't Win the Tech War It Just Started' (*Foreign Policy*, 16 January 2020), https://foreignpolicy.com/2020/01/16/europe-technology-sovereignty-von-der-leyen/ accessed 24 February 2022.

[129] K Komaitis, 'Europe's Pursuit of Digital Sovereignty Could Affect the Future of the Internet' (*TechEU*, 7 September 2020), https://tech.eu/features/32780/europe-digital-sovereignty/ accessed 24 February 2022.

[130] V Manancourt and M Heikkilä, 'EU Eyes Tighter Grip on Data in "Tech Sovereignty" Push' (*Politico*, 29 October 2020), www.politico.eu/article/in-small-steps-europe-looks-to-tighten-grip-on-data/ accessed 24 February 2022.

[131] C Hobbs (ed), *Europe's Digital Sovereignty: From Rulemaker to Superpower in the Age of US-China Rivalry* (Essay Collection, European Council of Foreign Affairs 2020), https://ecfr.eu/wp-content/uploads/europe_digital_sovereignty_rulemaker_superpower_age_us_china_rivalry.pdf accessed 24 February 2022.

an age of globalisation and long the subject of many contentious applications to the EU.[132] Digital sovereignty is no less controversial for the EU and is innately a concept about conflict and contestation. EU digital sovereignty above all is conceived as a language of strife, might and fight – through institutions.[133] This is arguably as close as the EU gets to a shared construction of digital sovereignty with the US and China in particular. At heart, digital sovereignty links closely to ideas of digital protectionism, but in itself this is quite a fluid concept and the 'free' nature of 'free flows' is not a straightforward idea.[134] Putting down demarcations of territory in the digital leads to convoluted forms of globalisation, as Chander reminds us eloquently in the electronic Silk Road.[135] As Floridi states, '[t]he fight for digital sovereignty is an epochal struggle not only of all against all, but also of anyone allied with anyone, with variable alliances changing according to interests and opportunities'.[136] It is a clash where tech companies may try to trick or bypass states and their legislation, fight each other or become embroiled in the questions of home soil and transnationalism, disputes that Facebook, Google, Microsoft and Twitter have all been party to.[137] It cannot be forgotten that the EU has adopted sanctions against 35 countries and four thematic sanctions regimes regarding chemical weapons and terrorism and most recently cyber sanctions and human rights and has, along with the US, one of the world's largest sanction regimes.[138] It begs the question about the definition of sovereignty emerging. However, the 'holisticness' of digital sovereignty as a concept is arguably highly complex to evaluate. For instance, the robustness of some of the most institutionalised areas of EU policy, eg competition law, are increasingly under development

[132] eg D Herzog, *RIP Sovereignty* (Yale University Press, 2020); R Keohane, 'Ironies of Sovereignty: The European Union and the United States' (2002) 42 *Journal of Common Market Studies* 743; see SD Krasner, *Sovereignty. Organised Hypocrisy* (Princeton University Press, 1999); S Sassen, *Losing Control? Sovereignty in the Age of Globalization* (Columbia University Press, 1996); J Cohen, *Globalization and Sovereignty Rethinking Legality, Legitimacy, and Constitutionalism* (Cambridge University Press, 2012); N Walker, 'Late Sovereignty in the European Union' in N Walker (ed), *Sovereignty in Transition* (Hart Publishing, 2003).

[133] J Borrell, 'Europe Must Learn Quickly to Speak the Language of Power' (*EJIL:Talk!*, 25 October 2020), www.ejiltalk.org/europe-must-learn-quickly-to-speak-the-language-of-power-part-i/ accessed 24 February 2022.

[134] S Aaronson, 'What Are We Talking about When We Talk about Digital Protectionism?' (2019) 18(4) *World Trade Review* 541.

[135] A Chander, *The Electronic Silk Road: How the Web Binds the World Together in Commerce* (Yale University Press 2013), Ch 8 in particular.

[136] L Floridi, 'The Fight for Digital Sovereignty: What It Is, and Why It Matters, Especially for the EU' (2020) 33 *Philosophy and Technology* 369.

[137] 'Apple and Facebook Trade Accusations over Data Privacy' (*Financial Times*, 20 November 2020), www.ft.com/content/54c54efb-7c80-4468-bf8f-c646e2bbe07f accessed 24 February 2022.

[138] C Portela, 'The Spread of Horizontal Sanctions' (*CEPS*, 7 March 2019), www.ceps.eu/the-spread-of-horizontal-sanctions/ accessed 24 February 2022; European Parliamentary Research Service, 'EU Sanctions: A Key Foreign and Security Policy Instrument' (2018) PE 621.870; C Eckes, 'The Law and Practice of EU Sanctions' in S Blockmans and P Koutrakos (eds), *Research Handbook on EU Common Foreign and Security Policy* (Edward Elgar, 2019); EU Sanctions Map (2019): https://www.sanctionsmap.eu accessed 24 February 2022; as to Russian sanctions see https://www.consilium.europa.eu/en/policies/sanctions/restrictive-measures-against-russia-over-ukraine/.

with respect to the regulation of Big Tech, eg the DMA or new competition tools for digital markets. Equally, the institutionalisation of data flows and data governance through far-reaching new EU instruments is at the core of the proposed Data Governance Act.[139] To a degree, the EU here appears to give itself carte blanche with regard to at least one the three most problematic concepts of global governance – sovereignty, territory and jurisdiction – by evolving such a defensive and offensive conceptual tool as digital sovereignty, and giving its own efforts at extraterritoriality, for example, more legitimacy and 'respectability'.[140]

Digital sovereignty self-evidently thus gives identity and unity to EU data regulation. Arguably, however, it is a hallmark of a new era of trade and data regulation on account of its defensiveness and even its protectionism. It even appears outmoded and uncharacteristic to some extent as a development of the EU as a global actor. Digital sovereignty also has a complex relationship with strategic autonomy.[141] The infrastructure dimension of digital sovereignty thus appears

[139] The DGA is intended to create a standardised framework of trusted tools and techniques to encourage data reuse by setting 'secure and privacy-compliant conditions' for sharing data: European Commission, 'Proposal for a Regulation of the European Parliament and of the Council on European data governance' (Data Governance Act) COM (2020) 767 final. Concerns have been expressed as to the EU Data Governance Act, on localisation and its capacity to manage the distinction between personal and non-personal data: see EDPB-EDPS, 'Joint Opinion 03/2021 on the Proposal for a regulation of the European Parliament and of the Council on European data governance (Data Governance Act)' (2021), https://edpb.europa.eu/system/files/2021-03/edpb-edps_joint_opinion_dga_en.pdf accessed 24 February 2022. See also EDPB, 'Recommendations 01/2020 on measures that supplement transfer tools to ensure compliance with the EU level of protection of personal data' (2020), https://edpb.europa.eu/sites/edpb/files/consultation/edpb_recommendations_202001_supplementarymeasurestransferstools_en.pdf accessed 24 February 2022. On the understandings of market power relative to architectural power through its institutional design see C Doctorow and C Schmon, 'The EU's Digital Markets Act: There is a Lot to Like, but Room for Improvement' (*Electronic Frontier Foundation*, 15 December 2020), www.eff.org/deeplinks/2020/12/eus-digital-markets-act-there-lot-room-improvement accessed 24 February 2022.

[140] See E Fahey, *Introduction to Law and Global Governance* (Edward Elgar, 2018) 91. See H Buxbaum 'Territory, Territoriality and the Resolution of Jurisdictional Conflict' (2009) 57(2) *American Journal of Comparative Law* 631.

[141] See eg European Parliament, 'Legislative resolution of 17 April 2019 on the proposal for a regulation of the European Parliament and of the Council establishing the Digital Europe programme for the period 2021–2027 (COM(2018)0434 – C8-0256/2018 – 2018/0227(COD))' (2019) P8_TA(2019)0403; European External Action Service, 'Why European strategic autonomy matters' (3 December 2020), https://eeas.europa.eu/headquarters/headquarters-homepage/89865/why-european-strategic-autonomy-matters_en accessed 24 February 2022; European Council, 'Digital sovereignty is central to European strategic autonomy – Speech by President Charles Michel at "Masters of Digital 2021" online event' (3 February 2021), www.consilium.europa.eu/en/press/press-releases/2021/02/03/speech-by-president-charles-michel-at-the-digitaleurope-masters-of-digital-online-event/ accessed 24 February 2022; B Lippert et al (eds), 'European Strategic Autonomy: Actors, Issues, Conflicts of Interests' (2019) SWP Research Paper 2019/RP 04; G Grevi, 'Strategic Autonomy for European Choices: The Key to Europe's Shaping Power' (2019) European Policy Centre Discussion Paper; S Anghel et al, 'On the Path to "Strategic Autonomy": The EU in an Evolving Geopolitical Environment' (2020) European Parliamentary Research Service, PE 652.096; '10 Point-Manifesto Towards European Digital Strategic Autonomy' (*Eurosmart*, 2019), https://www.eurosmart.com/towards-european-digital-strategic-autonomy-digital-sovereignty/ accessed 24 February 2022; P Tamma, 'Europe wants "strategic autonomy" – it just has to decide what that means' (*Politico*, 15 October 2020), www.politico.eu/article/europe-trade-wants-strategic-autonomy-decide-what-means/ accessed 24 February 2022.

all the more ambiguous post-*Schrems II*. Data localisation generated through the 'negative' institutionalisation of the CJEU is not easy to regulate, to govern or to implement. It ultimately appears predicated on certain barriers and obstacles and the hindering of the free flow of data, somehow in the public interest, through complex hybrid public regulation of private actors who are increasingly public and increasingly transnational.[142]

VII. Global Capture of Big Tech? European Data Spaces and the DMA/DSA

A European Strategy for Data was published in February 2020, designed to develop a Single Market in Data by 2025 and a Common European Data Space. It focused on tackling, inter alia, fragmentation between Member States in nine areas, ranging from industrial manufacturing to health, financial, energy, and agricultural data,[143] and was accompanied by a significant White Paper on Artificial Intelligence.[144] This construction of regulatory spaces takes institutionalisation of data to a new level for the EU. It seeks to design a space relative to economic power on the basis of a single market therein, enabling the EU to obtain by 2030 a share of the data economy. However, it is notably predicated on voluntary cooperation by market participants, entailing a requirement to join the data space, and to assess and certify compliance. This 'law-light' 'institution-light' formulation was rolled out with a sharply contrasting vision of the reach of EU law. On 29 January 2020, the European Commission's Work Programme 2020 was published. Under the second priority – 'A Europe fit for the digital age' – the Commission proposed a new DSA and a new DMA in 2020 in order to reinforce the single market for digital services and help provide smaller businesses with the legal clarity and level playing field they need.[145] It develops complex means to understand gatekeepers on a company level. Arguably, as regulatory interventions (ongoing through the legislative process at the time of writing), they are mostly characterised by their restraint. The EU has sought through two key Acts – the DSA and the DMA – and to a degree through a third, the Digital Governance Act, to build on the political successes of the GDPR and the political capital it has unleashed against Big Tech but also by departing from the GDPR philosophy. The Acts constitute an architecture

[142] Burwell and Propp (n 127).
[143] European Commission, 'Communication from the Commission to the European Parliament, the Council, the European Economic and Social Committee and the Committee of the Regions "A European Strategy for Data"' COM (2020) 66 final.
[144] European Commission, 'White Paper "On Artificial Intelligence – A European Approach to Excellence and Trust"' COM (2020) 65 final.
[145] European Commission, 'Commission Work Programme: A Union That Strives for More' COM (2020) 37 final.

of horizontal regulation applying to all processes involving personal information, whether they occur online or offline or by private, public or commercial actors.[146] They are controversial pieces of legislation for many reasons, principally because of their relationship to competition law and their effects on innovation through a regulatory infrastructure with unprecedented reach.

The EU's introduction of the DMA has seen it attempt to radically evolve the regulation of Big Tech. It has drawn the EU into much controversy over the reach of conventional competition law powers and regulatory powers to capture ex ante actions.[147] Some commentators point out that for Article 114 TFEU to be a valid legal basis for the DMA, it necessitated important adaptations to ensure harmonisation of national laws and respect for the principle of proportionality and for companies' fundamental rights, and to reduce the Commission's margin for discretion.[148] Others warn that the DMA would probably have a chilling effect on research, development and innovation. The framework that is proposed by the EU is of much significance for its ambit. It attempts in Article 3 to define gatekeepers as entities with a significant impact on the EU internal market that operate one or more important gateways to customers and enjoy an entrenched and durable position in their operations. The term is intended to apply to a particular dominant actor where economic significance, scope or size provide grounds for concern about control over the economy. The DMA also sets certain quantitative criteria that establish a presumption for gatekeeper status. It has ultimately started to ignite in shifts in regulation globally through its selection of subjects and objects. It proposes to set narrowly defined objective criteria by which a large online platform can qualify as a so-called gatekeeper, with the aim of tackling large systemic online platforms and institutionalising them as subjects and objects of EU law in a manner that has not previously been achievable. The draft DMA is based upon the premise that competition law principles would not limit administrative action but this raises questions as to the robustness of its institutional design.[149] It is stated that it is unusual for the Commission to build a regulatory regime based on autonomous legal concepts wholly from scratch. Can gatekeepers be constrained as providers of core platform services in this legislation? There is little opposition from within the EU and among its law-makers to the possibility of a European infrastructure that can engage with the scale of regulating Big Tech.

[146] H Lee-Makiyama, 'On New Regulation of Europe's Digital Markets' (*Wilson Center*, 5 April 2021), www.wilsoncenter.org/article/new-regulation-europes-digital-markets accessed 24 February 2022.

[147] European Commission, 'Proposal for Digital Markets Act' (n 19).

[148] See A Lamadrid de Pablo and N Bayón Fernández, 'Why The Proposed DMA Might be Illegal under Article 114 TFEU, and How To Fix It' (2021), https://antitrustlair.files.wordpress.com/2021/04/why-the-proposed-dma-might-be-illegal-under-article-114-tfeu-and-how-to-fix-it-3.pdf accessed 24 February 2022.

[149] See P Ibáñez Colomo, 'The Draft Digital Markets Act: A Legal and Institutional Analysis' (2021) SSRN Paper, https://papers.ssrn.com/sol3/papers.cfm?abstract_id=3790276 accessed 24 February 2022.

For instance, the European Parliament appears to agree with the Commission that the proposal needs to include ex ante rules on systemic operators with a gate-keeper role pursuant to the internal market, with the potential to open up markets to new entrants.[150] The DMA has faced many accusations as to the EU's capacity to limit innovation here or whether the Act is a 'game changer' in addressing digital market distortions, including anti-market practices.[151] Nonetheless, from a regulatory perspective, the EU's actions in the digital space are undoubtedly primarily defensive, as is evident from the framing of digital sovereignty. Given the lack of success of competition law or antitrust in engaging with tech platforms, new formulations of engagement form the core of the DMA.

The DSA provides for a so-called horizontal framework for transparency, accountability and regulatory oversight of the EU online space, not to replace but to complement the E-Commerce Directive and other legislation, eg Platform to Business regulation. It has four specifically key sets of rules on intermediary services, hosting services, online platform services and very large online platform services. It is said to be a horizontal instrument because it puts in place a framework of layered responsibilities targeted at different types of intermediary services. All online intermediaries offering their services in the EU would have to comply with the new rules, including those established outside of the EU. However, the obligations are said to be asymmetric because they would create a range of harmonised EU-wide symmetric obligations. The extent to which such terminology is over-stated or even facetious remains to be seen. On its face, it places a range of obligations on the providers of intermediary services and on online platforms and hosting service providers. The DSA is similarly poised to legislate in a far-reaching way on various issues relating to technology platforms, including competition, data sharing and content moderation. What is striking about the proposed institutionalisation of the DSA is its engagement with 33,000 stakeholders and the multiplicity of actors therein.[152]

The DSA was proposed by the Commission in the form of a regulation on a single market on digital services on the basis of Article 114 TFEU to prevent

[150] See European Parliament, 'Digital Markets Act' (2021) European Parliamentary Research Service PE 662.641, www.europarl.europa.eu/RegData/etudes/BRIE/2021/662641/EPRS_BRI(2021)662641_EN.pdf accessed 24 February 2022 and European Commission, European Commission, Communication from the Commission to The European Parliament, The Council, The European Economic and Social Committee and The Committee of The Regions, 'Shaping Europe's digital future' COM (2020) 67 final. The European Parliament here cites the Commission statement: 'Among the key actions envisaged in the communication was a digital services act package to "further explore … ex ante rules to ensure that markets characterised by large platforms with significant network effects acting as gate-keepers, remain fair and contestable for innovators, businesses, and new market entrants"'.

[151] On the eve of the first EU-US Summit in 2021, the Biden administration even argued that the DMA was anti-American: J Espinoza and J Politi, 'US Warns EU against Anti-American Tech Policy' *Financial Times* (15 June 2021), www.ft.com/content/2036d7e9-daa2-445d-8f88-6fcee745a259 accessed 24 February 2022.

[152] Commission Staff Working Document, 'Impact Assessment: Accompanying the document Proposal for a Regulation of the European Parliament and of the Council on a Single Market For Digital Services (Digital Services Act) and amending Directive 2000/31/EC' SWD(2020) 348 final, 1.

divergences from hampering the free provision of cross-border digital services and to guarantee the uniform protection of rights and uniform obligations for business and consumers across the internal market.[153] The DSA has a complex relationship with the DMA and is said to both bolster it and synergise with it. Its key legal link appears striking, with its legal base being rooted in Article 114 TFEU. It is important to state that the EU has a longstanding history of the broadest use of Article 114 TFEU and an extensive CJEU jurisprudence exists on the parameters of its use, which is largely benevolent. There was a significant cross-institutional alignment of the EU institutions to regulate online marketplaces, eg Amazon, eBay and Alibaba, seeking more requirements for e-commerce platforms. Whatever the outcomes of these law-making negotiations, the depth of the regulatory capture is far-reaching and explicit. The EU is repeatedly criticised for its negative regulatory vision of 'reining in' Big Tech rather than creating a positive one to foster innovation.[154] Herein lies the dilemma: the EU has immense capacity to generate institutionalisation, but whether that is what will actually be generated here remains to be seen, particularly because of the autonomy of actors emerging and the likely stabilisation of the projects. It is hard to better the words of Schaake: '[the] EU is somewhat coasting on its reputation for introducing measures such as GDPR. Instead, it needs to embrace a positive vision and plans to grow the European tech market … in addition to regulatory measures'.[155]

It is asserted that the DSA will turn online platforms into judge, jury and executioner when it comes to removing online content, in line with other copyright law developments. It is also said to give vast powers to the European Commission and national governments to suppress opposing voices, particularly arising from suggestions that platforms be ordered to make legality assessments of content in the absence of public scrutiny within 24 hours if the content can, for example, harm public policy.[156] The DSA aims to introduce more transparency and accountability with regard to social media platforms and online speech. The DSA is not per se about content but rather the processes to ensure that digital services work to support decisions made in democracies. The institutional and procedural innovations of the DSA are manifold. It sets up mechanisms for users to complain or to seek redress if their posts or profiles are removed. The DSA also requires general risk assessments, whereby tech companies will need to ask themselves whether their platforms will invite threats to democracy and how they can mitigate those risks. The DSA

[153] European Commission, 'Proposal for a Regulation of the European Parliament and of the Council on a Single Market for Digital Services (Digital Services Act) and amending Directive 2000/31/EC' COM (2020) 825 final.

[154] Schaake (n 19).

[155] ibid.

[156] European Parliament Committee on the Internal Market and Consumer Protection, 'Draft Report with recommendations to the Commission on Digital Services Act: Improving the functioning of the Single Market' (2020) 2020/2018(INL); See also J Penfrat, 'DSA should promote open and fair digital environment, not undermine the rule of law' (*EDRi*, 2020), https://edri.org/our-work/dsa-must-promote-open-and-fair-digital-environment-not-undermine-the-rule-of-law/ accessed 24 February 2022.

is a main centrepiece of EU law-making, with much focus on disinformation.[157] It is significant that the DSA is accompanied by a DMA designed to address the concentration of power in digital markets, rooted in the internal market legal base of Article 114 TFEU.[158] Notably, other forms of EU disinformation efforts have been undertaken through soft law, through self-regulatory Codes of Practice on Disinformation in force since October 2018 yet with limited success in the face of rising tides of disinformation becoming regularised in social media. It was allegedly 'strengthened' as a co-regulatory instrument along with the DSA in 2021, yet much remains to be seen as to the capacity of the EU concretely to evolve its content.[159]

The DSA and DMA follow atypical EU regulatory models of infrastructure, actors, agencies and regulatory structures, based upon robust intuitional design because they are single-market related. Their capacity to have external relations powers de facto or de jure remains to be seen. Nonetheless, the institutionalisation of data appears significantly 'ratcheted up' by these two core planks of the EU's digital strategy. The use here of the internal market is significant in bolstering the breadth of the Acts. Yet it also constrains them and shows an uneasy use of the intersection of internal market and competition law.

VIII. The EU's Emerging Architectural Infrastructure of AI: Global Lead on Regulatory Capture

The EU has introduced the first all-encompassing AI regulation in the world, immediately welcomed by the US and a host of civil society organisations.[160] The EU has

[157] B Martins dos Santos and D Morar, 'Four lessons for U.S. legislators from the EU Digital Services Act' (*Brookings*, 6 January 2021), www.brookings.edu/blog/techtank/2021/01/06/four-lessons-for-u-s-legislators-from-the-eu-digital-services-act/ accessed 24 February 2022; C de Froment, 'Digital Services Act: New Forms of Work' (*Institut Montaigne*, 15 September 2020), www.institutmontaigne.org/en/blog/digital-services-act-new-forms-work accessed 24 February 2022; C Schmon and K Gullo, 'European Commission's Proposed Digital Services Act Got Several Things Right, but Improvements Are Necessary to Put Users in Control' (*Electronic Frontier Foundation*, 15 December 2020), www.eff.org/deeplinks/2020/12/european-commissions-proposed-regulations-require-platforms-let-users-appeal accessed 24 February 2022; G Babinet et al, 'Digital Services Act: Moderating Content and Protecting Minors' (*Institut Montaigne*, 18 September 2020), www.institutmontaigne.org/en/blog/digital-services-act-moderating-content-and-protecting-minors accessed 24 February 2022.

[158] European Parliament, 'Digital Markets Act' (n 150); European Parliament, 'Digital Services Act' (2021) European Parliamentary Research Service PE 689.357, www.europarl.europa.eu/RegData/etudes/BRIE/2021/689357/EPRS_BRI(2021)689357_EN.pdf accessed 24 February 2022.

[159] Code of Practice on Disinformation: https://digital-strategy.ec.europa.eu/en/policies/code-practice-disinformation accessed 24 February 2022. The Code of Practice was signed by the online platforms Facebook, Google and Twitter, Mozilla, as well as by advertisers and parts of the advertising industry in October 2018, all of whom then later presented their roadmaps to implementation. Microsoft and Tiktok became signatories in 2019 and 2020.

[160] See European Commission, 'Communication: 'Shaping Europe's digital future' (n 150). See 'A Union that strives for more: My agenda for Europe – By candidate for President of the European Commission Ursula von der Leyen; Political Guidelines for the Next European Commission 2019–2024', 13, https://ec.europa.eu/info/sites/default/files/political-guidelines-next-commission_en_0.pdf accessed 24 February 2022.

sought to frame AI using OECD terminology and definitions thereof as widely accepted as possible to encompass human-produced systems and to understand AI in similar terms to product safety, ie as a human product. The EU is attempting here to shift discussions beyond mere ethics to form binding rules – all-pervasive to society in all areas. The first legally binding law on AI would be no small global achievement. For the EU, institutionalising AI in this way amounts to an issue of power: regulating power to corporations over countries and people. The legislative process as to the EU's AI regulation can be described as a 'finding process', to ascertain the core thereof. During the law-making process of the GDPR, a significant amount of US lobbying sought to water down the proposals. Interestingly, the US has welcomed the EU's AI proposals, marking a significant shift from its reaction to the EU's GDPR legislation. The EU is understood in this law making process to be following its values by putting structures, design and autonomous actors in place to support them. Under the EU's proposal, most AI systems will not be high risk (see draft titles IV and IX). One of the features of the legislation is the transparency obligations (pursuant to Article 52) to notify humans that they are interacting with an AI system. The EU has sought here to move from the ethics-probing challenges of many parties, including within the Commission and also in the Member States, to legal proposal, where a transition from talk and ethics to law is perceived as a gigantic leap. The EU's law fundamentally challenges the infamous Barlow discourse on the law-free nature of the Internet – which has now been consigned to history in the EU – and does so in Washington DC. The EU's efforts show that AI regulation is similarly neither law-free nor democracy-free. EU legislation subverts the claim that the Internet could be free from regulatory capture, 'Barlow-esque'.[161] The EU's process of law-making has also been fundamental in procuring a design of this nature, as participation is key for the EU in law-making, including extensive stakeholder engagement, considerable involvement of civil society and the far-reaching bottom-up development of proposals. In this regard, the AI regulation is far from merely a technical debate. Thus from the DMA, DSA to AI civil liability, the EU has sought to write a new *code civil* for the Internet and digital society through its institutionalisation. It emerges as a constitution for the technical which is trying to operationalise constitutional values – previously the preserve of specialists and ethicists. Institutionalisation here is an important value encapsulating the actions taking place. It thus challenges the complexity, opacity, unpredictability and autonomy of data, and addresses directly the many reasons to not regulate in the usual way, but rather to retain AI within the preserve of ethics – thus engaging directly with safety risks, fundamental rights risks, enforcement, legal certainty, mistrust and fragmentation. The definition and scope of the regulation is provided for in Article 6. It is defined as neutrally as possible, and provides in Annexe i a catalogue list of techniques and approaches that can be amended/proposed. It differentiates four risk groups in a pyramid: those permitted with no restrictions; those permitted with information obligations; those that are high risk

[161] Barlow (n 1).

eg recruitment, medical devices permitted subject to compliance with AI requirements and ex ante Conformity assessment; unacceptable risk eg social scoring which is prohibited. In so doing, it has adopted many principles of the internal market, eg as to product conformity assessments, and applied them to AI. It has thus sought to widen the reach of its most successful internal policy field, itself highly institutionalised.

IX. Conclusions

The EU has essentially developed an approach to data protection because it is widely understood to have had extra-territorial reach and effects, both de facto and de jure. The resulting architecture is a complex system of bodies at EU and national level who are charged with responsibility for the enforcement of the rules in the GDPR. The dense institutional design and autonomy of individual actors furthered by the GDPR continue to be core hallmarks of EU regulatory capture of data. The EU now has data transfer regimes and flows with third countries, which count as some of the largest in the world, featuring significant institutional dimensions. As has been outlined above, the EU's data adequacy system is ultimately both highly politicised and institutionalised: the Court of Justice has inserted itself into the adequacy process, institutionalising global data flows like no other process, in its extraordinary interventions in its landmark decisions in *Schrems I* and *II* relating to the EU-US Privacy Shield and previous Safe Harbour Agreement. The EU's data regimes vary in scale and complexity and most of all in institutional design. A turn to institutions and deeper forms of institutional oversight, accountability and legitimations is definitively 'European' and differs substantially from US and Asian models of looser accountability and oversight. The EU has the advantage of being the first mover, and also the first mover with the highest standards and some of the deepest institutionalisation to date, as well as ambitious extra-territorial reach to follow through on its internationalist ambitions in generating a global standard.

EU digital sovereignty has emerged as a strange lexicon, as a language of strife. As has been argued here and elsewhere, from the DMA, DSA to AI civil liability, the EU has evidently sought to write a new *code* for the Internet and digital society through its institutionalisation. This constitution for the technical emerges which tries to operationalise constitutional values through atypical institutional design and the rising autonomy of actors. The depth of the design, eg its agencification, and the success of the breadth of its regulatory capture, given its many subjects and objects, remains to be seen.[162]

[162] See G De Gregorio and O Pollicino, 'The European Constitutional Road to Address Platform Power' (*Verfassungsblog*, 31 August 2021) https://verfassungsblog.de/power-dsa-dma-03/ accessed 24 February 2022; see The Digital Constitutionalist Project: https://digi-con.org/ accessed 24 February 2022.

2

The EU as a Digital Trade Actor

I. Overview: Digital Trade – A Fragmented and De-institutionalised Landscape?

Across many disciplines and subject fields, digital trade and the digital economy are widely agreed to be key elements in the successful development of the future economy.[1] Companies and governments are encouraged to use the potential of data and to mobilise their resources appropriately so as to make the data-drive economy real. Digital trade is already one of the main driving forces behind sustained economic growth, because it helps countries to improve productivity, a key indicator for technological advancement and the chief source of future economic welfare.[2] However, the perils of reliance on data and Big Data with respect to the protection of privacy are also repeatedly highlighted.[3] While data and digital information may have joined 'oil, tanks and money' as the key currency of international affairs,[4] from a legal perspective the curious and complex place of data represents a challenge. However, the newly emerged framework of digital trade governance, despite increasing numbers of digital trade provisions in digital trade chapters, is increasingly fragmented, patchy and complex.[5] While there may be some regulatory convergence on certain objectives and principles, significant

[1] World Bank 'World Development Report 2021: Data For Better Lives', www.worldbank.org/en/publication/wdr2021 accessed 24 February 2022. In the transatlantic context, see generally D Hamilton and J Quinlan, US Chamber of Commerce, *The Transatlantic Economy 2021* (2021), www.amchameu.eu/sites/default/files/publications/files/transatlanticeconomy2021_fullreporthr.pdf accessed 24 February 2022.

[2] MF Ferracane et al, 'ECIPE Digital Trade Restrictiveness Survey Index' (ECIPE, 2018), https://ecipe.org/wp-content/uploads/2018/05/DTRI_FINAL.pdf accessed 24 February 2022.

[3] M Burri, 'The Governance of Data and Data Flows in Trade Agreements: The Pitfalls of Legal Adaptation' (2017) 51(56) *University of California Davis Law Review* 65, 67; Council of Europe, 'Guidelines on the Protection of Individuals with Regard to the Processing of Personal Data in a World of Big Data' (23 January 2017) T-PD(2017)01, https://rm.coe.int/16806ebe7a accessed 24 February 2022; Federal Trade Commission Staff Report, 'Internet of Things: Privacy and Security in a Connected World' (2015), www.ftc.gov/system/files/documents/reports/federal-trade-commission-staff-report-november-2013-workshop-entitled-internet-things-privacy/150127iotrpt.pdf accessed 24 February 2022.

[4] H Farrell and A Newman, *Of Privacy and Power: The Transatlantic Struggle over Freedom and Security* (Princeton University Press, 2019) 173.

[5] M Burri and R Polanco, 'Digital Trade Provisions in Preferential Trade Agreements: Introducing a New Dataset' (2020) 23 *Journal of International Economic Law* 187, 220.

differences remain with regard to the treatment of cross-border data flows, data localisation and personal data protection. Also, despite the growing importance of digital trade, little is known about its scale. New studies of digital trade restrictiveness globally are only recently beginning to emerge.[6] Reliable and internationally comparable statistics on digital trade that are coherent with national accounting frameworks are limited.[7] Any reasonable enquiry into the relationship between data and digital trade arguably needs also to be partly descriptive in order to attempt to map the field. With the exception of the framework developed jointly by the Organisation for Economic Co-operation and Development (OECD), World Trade Organisation (WTO) and International Monetary Fund (IMF), there have been few attempts to systematically define digital trade.[8] Perhaps unsurprisingly, there have also been few attempts to systematically map the content of digital trade, at least until recently.[9]

There is no global or legally agreed definition for either data or digital trade in an international trade agreement.[10] Data comprises a broad church of concepts and forms, from cybersecurity, intellectual property and transparency to frictionless

[6] There are several new databases on digital trade policy measures as provided by the Global Trade Alert, the OECD Digital Services Trade Restrictiveness Index and ECIPE's Digital Trade Estimates project and the Global Data Governance Mapping Project at the Digital Trade and Data Governance Hub. See respectively, Digital Trade Alert Website: www.globaltradealert.org/digital_policy; OECD Digital Services Trade Restrictiveness Index: https://stats.oecd.org/Index.aspx?DataSetCode=STRI_DIGITAL; Digital Trade Estimates, https://ecipe.org/dte/ and Datahub Global Data Governance Mapping Project: https://datagovhub.elliott.gwu.edu/, all accessed 24 February 2022.

[7] Cambridge Econometrics for UK Department of International Trade and Department of Digital, Culture, Media & Sport, 'Understanding and Measuring Cross-border Digital Trade' (14 May 2020), https://assets.publishing.service.gov.uk/government/uploads/system/uploads/attachment_data/file/885174/Understanding-and-measuring-cross-border-digital-trade.pdf accessed 24 February 2022, who state that the OECD-WTO-IMF framework is a useful starting point for understanding and measuring the different components of digital trade. The OECD-WTO-IMF framework defines digital trade as trade that is 'digitally ordered' (synonymous to e-commerce) and/or 'digitally delivered' (services transactions that are delivered remotely through computer networks).

[8] OECD-WTO-IMF framework from the United Nations Conference on Trade and Development paper 'Information Economy Report 2017: Digitalization, Trade and Development' considers that there are broadly three levels of digital economy: (1) core digital IT/ICT sector: the ICT-producing sector comprising of both IT infrastructure and IT services; (2) narrow scope (digital economy): adds to the core definition with digital services (eg outsourced call centre services) and the platform economy (eg Facebook and Google); and (3) broad scope (digitalised economy): includes the use of various digital technologies for performing activities such as e-business, e-commerce, automation and artificial intelligence. The biggest challenges to measuring digital trade are said to relate to: transactions involving intermediaries; (free) cross-border data flows that involve no monetary transactions; imports of e-services (such as digital downloads, or streaming services) by households; de minimis trade; options to measure emergent innovations in the digital domain eg cloud computing, or crypto-assets). See United Nations Conference on Trade and Development, 'Information Economy Report 2017: Digitalization, Trade and Development' (2017), https://unctad.org/system/files/official-document/ier2017_en.pdf accessed 24 February 2022. See also J Lopez-Gonzalez and MA Jouanjean, 'Digital Trade: Developing a Framework for Analysis' (2017) OECD Trade Policy Papers No 205.

[9] See ibid. See also United States Trade Representative, 'Key Barriers to Digital Trade' (2017), https://ustr.gov/about-us/policy-offices/press-office/fact-sheets/2017/march/key-barriers-digital-trade accessed 27 February 2022.

[10] *cf* Datahub Global Data Governance Mapping Project (n 6).

movement of tech workers. Many activities, such as sharing information, regulation, laws and programs on data protection, domestic regimes for the protection of personal data, technical assistance in the form of exchange of information and experts, research and training activities, joint programmes, dialogues, consultations on data protection, etc, constitute activities involving cooperation relating to data.[11] It is a truism that every twenty-first century trade agreement wants a holistic and robust chapter on electronic commerce or digital trade – but rarely obtains it.[12] WTO law stands at an embarrassing juncture and is sorely in need of modernisation. Digital taxation remains outside of trade agreements but is a key peripheral area, affecting the scope and ambition of trade agreements in some instances. Free Trade Agreements (FTAs) are understood to have generated considerable rule fragmentation in the area of data and digital trade because of the overarching outdated state of WTO provisions on digital trade.[13] The era of the Internet and of the wholesale digitisation of Covid-19 society has given rise to an explosion of 'data localisation' measures, which involve data about a nation's citizens or residents being collected, processed, and/or stored in that country. Data localisation is a particularly significant flashpoint in the rule-making, explored further in this chapter. Thus, states around the world have taken to trade agreements to 'fill in the gaps' of the outdated WTO framework, discussed further below.[14] As a result, however, the framework that now regulates contemporary digital trade is understood to be extremely fragmented, from a legal point of view.[15] Ultimately, it is far removed from being an 'institutionalised' landscape in any shape or form.

It is also worth stating that no WTO member classified as a developing country by the United Nations or as a low-income country by the World Bank has agreed a Regional Trade Agreement (RTA) that contains an e-commerce chapter.[16] No WTO member in sub-Saharan Africa has ever agreed an RTA that contains an e-commerce chapter. Until very recently, even developed economies did not seek to include a chapter on e-commerce or digital trade.[17] However, the most developed global economies tend to have been most active in negotiating

[11] M Burri, 'Should There Be New Multilateral Rules for Digital Trade?' (2013) E15 Expert Group on Trade and Innovation 15–16.

[12] R Wolfe, 'Learning about Digital Trade: Privacy and E-Commerce in CETA and TPP' (2019) 18(S1) *World Trade Review* 63, 63–64.

[13] Burri, 'The Governance of Data and Data Flows in Trade Agreements: The Pitfalls of Legal Adaptation' (n 3) 127.

[14] Burri and Polanco (n 5); H Gao, 'The Regulation of Digital Trade in the TPP: Trade Rules for the Digital Age' in J Chaisse et al (eds), *Paradigm Shift in International Economic Law Rule-Making* (Springer, 2017) 345.

[15] Burri and Polanco (n 5) 220.

[16] M Wu, 'Digital Trade-Related Provisions in Regional Trade Agreements: Existing Models and Lessons for the Multilateral Trade System' (2017) RTA Exchange International Centre for Trade and Sustainable Development and Inter-American Development Bank. See E Fahey, 'Digital Trade and Data Equivalency: Research Briefing for the Welsh Parliament' (Welsh Parliament, 2020).

[17] Wu (n 16) 8.

agreements with e-commerce provisions.[18] Certain country agreements have been uniquely consistent across their respective provisions relating to data, eg South Korea e-commerce chapters as to consumer protection, paperless trading and data protection. But mostly this inequity and practice of inconsistency prevails. Certain countries and regions are notable for their commitment to significantly *changing* their approaches over the year.[19] EU trade agreements have historically merged trade in services with establishment and electronic commerce, rather than giving e-commerce a standalone chapter.[20] In more contemporary post-Lisbon trade agreements with developed global economies, such as the EU-Canada Comprehensive Economic and Trade Agreement (CETA), initial practice saw a standalone e-commerce chapter. The EU subsequently negotiated the EU-Japan Economic Partnership Agreement (EPA), which has an e-commerce chapter covering trade in services, investment liberalisation *and* e-commerce. More recent negotiations with Australia, Mexico and the UK have seen the EU adopt US terminology on digital trade and tend to provide for a separate chapter on digital trade aligned with services to a degree but still standing more apart than in earlier agreements, discussed further below, with provisions for very high levels of protection for data.[21] These developments underscore the unsettled state of digital trade globally. Yet this is where the EU has stepped in, at ultilateral level, to make a significant contribution; this the focus of this chapter.

Digital trade sits within a complex broader matrix. Until recently there were no reliable measurements of data flows, and any assessment of their contribution to value-creation lacked solid methodological grounds.[22] Rather, wholesale extrapolations from estimations of data flows and their value to the effect of domestic privacy regulation have resulted in a skewed picture. Internet traffic suffers from double counting because Internet protocol traffic is not linear and can be routed through several countries.[23] There is no agreed definition of digital trade or, more broadly, of digital economy. As a result, the methodology to be applied to data flows may be said to be doubly flawed. It is said that framing the protection of personal data as a barrier to trade focuses only on the cost side of things, ignoring the individual and societal benefits of stronger data protection. Ultimately, this approach generates a polarised landscape that ignores the possibility of a win-win between the protection of privacy and personal data, on the one hand, and of cross-border data flows, on the other. Digital trade is increasingly fragmented and

[18] J-A Monteiro and R Teh, 'Provisions on Electronic Commerce in Regional Trade Agreements' (2017) WTO Working Paper ERSD-2017-11, 10.

[19] ibid 11.

[20] Fahey (n 16).

[21] Advanced economies closely connected to the EU, such as the EEA, have historically not necessarily sought a broad e-commerce chapter either: Wu (n 16) 8.

[22] See Datahub Global Data Governance Mapping Project (n 6); Burri, 'The Governance of Data and Data Flows in Trade Agreements: The Pitfalls of Legal Adaptation' (n 3).

[23] S Yakovleva and K Irion, 'Pitching Trade Against Privacy: Reconciling EU Governance of Personal Data Flows with External Trade' (2020) 10(3) *International Data Privacy Law* 201.

dependent on data flows and the broader regulatory capture of data. This chapter argues that the EU is a complex emerging actor in digital trade, leading with exceptionally high standards and a highly bureaucratised design for its regulation. The EU is generally agreed to be cautious and to have repurposed itself with modest innovations, but it largely constitutes an outlier because of its focus on rights. The EU faces many challenges in upholding this position but by subscribing to internationalisation and multilateralism it seeks to make significant inroads in global governance. Regulatory cooperation is shown in this chapter (and further in Chapter 5) to be a tool that the EU uses to develop deeper partnerships with developed economies. The 'Brussels Effect' alone does not explain the success of the EU, nor explain the EU's complexity. This chapter shows how a commitment to multilateralism in institutional design and institutional practice is important in contemporary digital trade.

Chapter 2 contains the following sections: (II) the EU's shift beyond a mid-way position on digital trade; (III) the WTO as a forum for digital trade; (IV) data localisation in trade agreements; (V) FTAs and data privacy; (VI) the EU's horizontal strategy on data internationalisation and the institutionalisation of data privacy; (VII) EU digital trade regulatory cooperation; and (VIII) Conclusions.

II. The EU Moving Beyond the 'Mid-Way' Position on Digital Trade

There is no one accepted or objective definition of 'digital trade' or 'electronic commerce'; international economic law is understood to be mired in archaic understandings of these terms because of uncertainty as to its goods or services characterisation.[24] Digital trade usually relates to provisions on data and consumer protection, provisions on cross-border data flows and data localisation provisions, temporary prohibition of custom duties levied on electronic transmissions, provisions on regulatory cooperation and definitions of e-commerce and digital products. Whilst this debate as to what is old or new terminology goes on, other regions of the world have moved on from digital trade terminology altogether, towards modular discussions of regional cooperation on digital economy issues, viewed in the broadest of terms.[25] Digital trade is still conventionally understood to have evolved in two genres – narrow and broad – with the EU traditionally falling between the two extremes of the US's more digital-focused understanding of trade, and the Chinese approach, focused on the 'trade' aspect.[26] Thus, historically,

[24] AD Mitchell, 'Towards Compatibility: The Future of Electronic Commerce within the Global Trading System' (2001) 4 *Journal of International Economic Law* 685.

[25] Thereby differing from the WTO's single undertaking approach that comprehensive FTAs have replaced.

[26] Mitchell (n 24); H Gao, 'Digital or Trade? The Contrasting Approaches of China and US to Digital Trade' (2017) 21 *Journal of International Economic Law* 297.

China has promoted a narrow view of digital trade, focusing on trade in goods online, while the US and others have subscribed to a more inclusive approach.

Structurally, e-commerce was elevated from a small number of articles in other chapters into a standalone chapter in trade agreements. The EU is thought to stand out amongst WTO members for having made the greatest changes in its approach to e-commerce in Preferential Trade Agreements (PTAs) over the years, although for very different economic and geopolitical factors than others such as the US and China.[27] It is regarded as a latecomer to many key issues in digital trade and most of its earlier efforts lack real 'normative' value and are not regarded as game-changers. These factors have seen the EU carve out cultural and audio-visual services from its Common Commercial Policy whilst reconciling the differing policy perspective of DG Trade and DG Justice towards digital governance over a relatively short period of time. The EU is said to subsequently pursue a much more activist free trade agenda as to digital content and cross-border data flows in PTAs, while China has adopted a more restrictive stance towards information and communication technologies.[28] E-commerce disciplines expanded from passive non-interference obligations into more positive requirements that specify what the government needs to do for e-commerce businesses. This new model of e-commerce obligations started out in the 2004 FTAs signed by the US with Australia, Chile, and Singapore, respectively, and culminated in the Trans-Pacific Partnership (TPP) that was concluded in 2016. While the Trump administration withdrew from the TPP, its e-commerce chapter was heavily influenced by the US and has been incorporated into the new Comprehensive and Progressive Agreement for Trans-Pacific Partnership (CPTPP) that the remaining 11 TPP members signed in March 2018.[29] The TPP is not the first FTA to have an e-commerce chapter, and as discussed below, many FTAs signed by Australia and Singapore have substantial e-commerce chapters, which paved the way to the TPP negotiations.[30] The 'digital trade' provisions in the US-Mexico-Canada Agreement (USMCA) largely follow TPP's model, promoting the so-called Silicon Valley consensus of this era. However, the USMCA deviates from TPP in its framing.

[27] P Sauvé and M Soprana, 'The Evolution of the EU Digital Trade Policy' in M Hahn and G Van der Loo (eds), *Law and Practice of the Common Commercial Policy* (Brill Nijhoff, 2020) 287; Wu (n 16); H Horn et al, 'Beyond the WTO? An Anatomy of EU and US Preferential Trade Agreements' (2010) 33 *The World Economy* 1565; Ferracane et al (n 2).

[28] Sauvé and Soprana (n 27) 288.

[29] The chapter on e-commerce in CPTPP was not changed from that in TPP. However, several side letters have been added, which seem to have an implication to the bindingness of the rules. Most notably, Vietnam and the partners signed side letters on cybersecurity. It was agreed that the partners shall refrain from having recourse to dispute settlement with respect to measures adopted or maintained pursuant to the Cybersecurity Law of Vietnam or related legislation, which are alleged to be in violation of Vietnam's obligation under Art 14.11 (Cross-Border Transfer of Information by Electronic Means) and Art 14.13 (Location of Computing Facilities), for a period of five years. See S Hamanaka, 'The Future Impact of Trans-Pacific Partnership's Rule-Making Achievements: The Case Study of E-Commerce' (2019) 42 *World Economy* 552.

[30] Hamanaka (n 29).

While TPP used 'electronic commerce' as an umbrella term, in line with WTO terminology, USMCA has shifted towards 'digital trade', which avoids some of the confusion caused by the colloquial use of the term 'e-commerce' to mean online shopping.[31] The USMCA thus has a chapter (Chapter 19) on digital trade rather than e commerce, unlike the CPTPP (Chapter 14), the successor to TPP. It is reasonable to expect that similar provisions will be reflected in future US FTAs. While the EU's approach to data institutionalisation has been progressive and holistic, post-Lisbon the EU has merged e-commerce with trade in services and only recently moved to separate digital trade. It has thus moved closer to the US negotiation position and lexicon but also notably merged digital trade and services in some key recent trade agreements, eg the UK-EU TCA.

Historically, many preferential trade agreements signed by the EU also contain provisions addressing issues relating to electronic commerce that are treated in other parts of the agreement. Most frequently, such provisions can be found under a different section within the trade agreement chapters dedicated to trade in services, investment and electronic commerce.[32] In particular, examples relate to provisions governing access to and use of the Internet, which are typically found in PTA sections addressing electronic communication networks and services. Provisions as to digital trade and data processing have been found in sections on financial services or intellectual property other than electronic commerce. Privacy provisions or provisions as to personal data protection are typically scattered across parts of EU agreements, although with considerable variance. A question arises as to the dominance of 'Silicon Valley logic' or the so-called 'Washington Consensus' in digital trade going forward, as to pro-market liberalisation in a likely future era of Big Tech regulation. It seems clear that a certain trade policy continuity from the Obama to the Trump administration took effect through the survival of CPTPP and thus beyond ideological divisions on the nature of the future digital economy.[33] While the Obama administration maintained close contacts with Silicon Valley companies, efforts by the Trump administration to build connections to the tech sector quickly withered and the sector has toed a complex line on America First. Nevertheless, US Internet corporations remain 'first' in the world, rivalled only by their Chinese counterparts. Furthermore, US tech companies' delivery of online services abroad creates a trade surplus that counterbalances the US trade deficit generated by trade in goods – one of the key fixations of former US President Trump and some of his advisors. The collapse of the TTIP negotiations and the incarnation of TPP in CPTPP without the US, yet adopting key US principles and norms, are thus of significance in understanding the place of the EU here. This is particularly the case in relation to data standards, where US law seems

[31] T Streinz, 'Digital Megaregulation Uncontested? TPP's Model for the Global Digital Economy' in B Kingsbury et al (eds), *Megaregulation Contested* (Oxford University Press, 2019) 317.

[32] Sauvé and Soprana (n 27) 294.

[33] Streinz (n 31).

to be shifting closer to EU law, largely spurred by US tech companies with world headquarters or substantial markets in the EU, as is explored in Chapter 4 and in the light of RCEP developments, discussed in Chapter 6.

While data has continued to occupy a complex place in all major global trade agreements in recent times, large trade agreements, such as the megaregionals CPTPP and USMCA, data's precise relationship to privacy has been somewhat overlooked. For example, USMCA contains a chapter (Chapter 19) on digital trade, rather than e-commerce like the CPTPP (Chapter 14) and so distinct differences between the two major agreements exist as to international privacy regimes cited, data localisation, interactive computer services etc.[34] They have an unclear relationship with the human right to access information or control information and privacy.[35] They reflect the broader trend that transnational consumer protection and cybersecurity are weak. More substantively, one might say that USMCA deviates significantly from TPP in its framing, as TPP had used electronic commerce as an umbrella term, in line with WTO terminology. As noted above, the USMCA shifted towards the term digital trade, which avoids the confusion caused by colloquial use of e-commerce for online shopping.[36] Similarly, the EU has notably shifted towards the US terminology. However, the economic as opposed to rights-based construction of privacy as between APEC and the General Data Protection Regulation (GDPR) constitutes a significant challenge for the future in the search for global standards or the workability of data localisation in an era of privacy.

The place of the EU as a first-mover internationally on best practice in data protection and data flows on account of the high standards of the GDPR will be unavoidably significant for many countries. The EU's Digital Strategies published in 2018 and 2020 indicated unambiguously the institutional, regulatory and international contours of the EU as a global digital player.[37] A European Strategy for Data was published in February 2020. The Strategy, which was accompanied by a significant White Paper on Artificial Intelligence,[38] was designed to develop a Single Market in data by 2025 and a Common European Data Space, focusing upon tackling, inter alia, fragmentation between Member States in nine areas, ranging

[34] See Streinz (n 31); P Leblond, 'Digital Trade at the WTO – The CPTPP and CUSMA Pose Challenges to Canadian Data Regulation' (2019) CIGI Papers No 227, https://www.cigionline.org/sites/default/files/documents/no.227.pdf accessed 27 February 2022.

[35] Burri and Polanco (n 5).

[36] Contrast USMCA ch 19 with TPP ch 14. See Streinz (n 31) 315.

[37] European Commission, 'Communication from the Commission: European Commission Digital Strategy; A digitally transformed, user-focused and data-driven administration by 2022' C (2018) 7118 final; European Commission, Communication from the Commission to The European Parliament, The Council, The European Economic and Social Committee and The Committee of The Regions, 'Shaping Europe's digital future' COM (2020) 67 final.

[38] European Commission, White Paper 'On Artificial Intelligence – A European Approach to Excellence and Trust' COM (2020) 65 final.

from industrial manufacturing to health, financial, energy, and agricultural data.[39] Indeed, its approach to regulating such a cutting-edge area as AI is to embed EU policies heavily in international and multilateral frameworks, from the OECD, G20, Council of Europe and UNESCO to the International Telecommunications Union and the WTO with respect to policies of third countries that limit data flows and create undue restrictions on bilateral trade negotiations, whilst establishing a High Level Expert Working Group on AI. Overall, the EU advocates a message of tech sovereignty as its future, promoting the capability the EU must have to make its own choices on its own values and own rules, predicated on an emerging regime of institutionalisation of compliance, enforcement and governance.[40] It is a highly ambitious set of objectives. However, time will tell whether its implementation is plausible, given the many delays in the roll-out of data matters; the lack of complete implementation of prior policies, eg Digital Single Market, indicate that ambition can have severe limitations in data matters.

III. The WTO as a Forum for the Future of Digital Trade?

As considered above, e-commerce is said to be no longer a marginal chapter in FTAs.[41] However, there is no settled definition of electronic commerce or e-commerce. At its broadest, electronic commerce involves conducting business using most modern communication instruments: telephone, fax, television, electronic payment and money transfer systems, Electronic Data Interchange, and the Internet. Yet these developments were not reflected at the WTO until recently, as its role appeared to be ever-diminishing amongst the innovations taking place at bilateral and region level. The WTO recognises that commercial transactions can be broken into three stages: the advertising and searching stage; the ordering and payment stage; and the delivery stage. It is commonly assumed that the digital trade provisions in PTAs build upon the rules of the WTO. Although one study showed that 108 PTAs had e-commerce chapters, only 48 agreements had a reference to the applicability of WTO rules to e-commerce, and these were mainly found in agreements where the EU is a party.[42] The *US–Gambling WTO Appellate*

[39] European Commission, Communication from the Commission to The European Parliament, The Council, The European Economic and Social Committee and The Committee of The Regions, 'A European Strategy for Data' COM (2020) 66 final.

[40] European Commission, Press remarks by President von der Leyen on the Commission's new strategy: Shaping Europe's Digital Future (19 February 2020).

[41] P Mavroidis, 'Trade Regulation, and Digital Trade' (2017) Columbia School of International and Public Affairs Working Paper; Gao (n 26); Hamanaka (n 29). It is often said that one of the major contributions of TPP was its inclusion of e-commerce although as a term it appears surpassed by digital trade as an agenda: see Gao (n 26).

[42] Burri and Polanco (n 5) 197.

Body case saw the General Agreement on Trade in Services (GATS) commitments apply to electronically supplied services but it also clarified key notions of services regulation, such as the application of the likeness test and the scope of the 'public morals/public order' defence under the general exceptions of GATS Article XIV.[43] However, much WTO law – in particular GATS provisions – was designed to allow WTO members to tailor their commitments. Others relate to outdated, pre-internet classifications of goods, services and sectors, upon which these commitments were based and which have become increasingly disconnected from modern trade practices.[44]

In early 2016, e-commerce gained 'renewed interest' among WTO members: seven proposals were tabled by major WTO members such as the US, the EU, Japan and Brazil. The US proposal appeared to be encouraged by its success in the Trade in Services Agreement – although that has subsequently disappeared – and TPP negotiations. Electronic commerce has wound its way into both a WTO Ministerial Decision and a Joint Ministerial Statement, but also became the subject of a joint initiative by the WTO, the World Economic Forum, and the Electronic World Trade Platform (eWTP), the first of its kind in the WTO. With these signs, e-commerce was set to become one of the first 'Doha' issues to bear fruit in the form of the Joint Statement Initiative (JSI) on e-commerce.[45] Currently, however, negotiations on a plurilateral agreement on e-commerce, which began in 2019 and cover a range of rules on digital trade, have stalled. The negotiations have been structured around six focus groups, 'enabling digital trade/e-commerce', 'openness and digital trade/e-commerce', trust, cross-cutting issues and telecommunications. Notably the EU is actively attempting to promote its model articles; thus, as a forum it has much potential but arguably less promise. There has been some concern from civil society about the manner in which this JSI is perceived to be more representative of the views of Big Tech. The EU space for policy innovation eg as to AI, high privacy protection, spam and disinformation, 'ratchets' upwards. The complex position of the EU here becomes more interesting for its rights-based focus, as examined below, and for its capacity to engage with areas that are a key focus of China, such as sovereignty and security, though these terms may have radically different meanings for different parties.

Due to the widely diverging views of WTO members, efforts to revamp the rules in the WTO have historically largely failed in this area. Given the lack of progress in the WTO, the US, as the champion of digital trade, had turned to various bilateral, plurilateral, and regional initiatives to push for the internationalisation of digital trade rules that are based on the regulatory philosophy and

[43] *United States – Measures Affecting the Cross-Border Supply of Gambling and Betting Services* App no WT/DS285/26 (WTO).

[44] M Burri, 'The Regulation of Data Flows Through Trade Agreements' (2017) 48 *Georgetown Journal of International Law* 407, 413.

[45] See WTO, 'Joint Statement on E-commerce News Archives', www.wto.org/english/news_e/archive_e/jsec_arc_e.htm accessed 27 February 2022.

approach in the US to tackle trade barriers facing the US companies. Meanwhile, although initially reluctant to engage, China has also become more willing to negotiate e-commerce rules in its recent FTAs, eg RCEP, discussed in detail in Chapter 6. A 1998 WTO moratorium on import duties on e-commerce transmissions was due to lapse in 2020, with concerns from developing countries about lost government revenue where trade becomes less goods-intensive and more digital. On 10 December 2019, WTO members adopted a decision on the Work Programme on Electronic Commerce.[46] In that decision they agreed to reinvigorate the Work Programme and to renew the practice of not imposing customs duties on electronic transmissions until Ministerial Conference 12 (MC12) in Geneva in 2021. These developments have doubtless been exacerbated by Covid-19, which has put increasing pressure on states and organisations for revenue, as the EU Digital Services Tax indicates, and has hampered much multilateral progress across the board with regard to law-making and regulation, discussed below. However, from an EU perspective, the place of the transatlantic relationship in leading change on a Transatlantic Trade and Technology Council (EU-US TTC), as proposed by the EU in late 2020 and already in place by Autumn 2021, could provide an important foundation on which multilateral developments can be built – discussed further in Chapter 4.[47] Much also depends on the future of the WTO and its dispute settlement system, the traditional forum for the navigation of disputes. The WTO has not yet explored the boundaries of barriers to trade in relation to the Internet in a robustly institutionalised format.

IV. Data Localisation in Trade Agreements

Digital protectionism has been defined by some to include laws and regulations that block the flow of data across borders or impede the provision of services such as cloud computing.[48] There are limits to digital trade and there are also many broad philosophical debates about what the contours of digital protectionism might be. The EU has been accused of digital protectionism in many contexts, despite its broader organisational goals of promoting free and fair trade and protecting consumer rights. It thus remains a somewhat complex idea to frame realistically. As noted above in Chapter 1, data-related provisions are a relatively new phenomenon in trade agreements. Before the year 2000, only 19 measures had been imposed globally. However, by 2008, that number had more than doubled, and it has doubled again since then.[49] These measures are primarily found in

[46] WTO, 'Work Programme On Electronic Commerce: General Council Decision, Adopted on 10 December 2019' (2019) WT/L/1079.
[47] See the discussion below in Ch 4.
[48] Eg United States Trade Representative (n 9).
[49] Ferracane et al (n 2).

dedicated e-commerce chapters. Where they appear in agreements, they outline rules either referring to the cross-border flow of data or banning or limiting data such localisation requirements. Provisions on the cross-border flow of data can, however, also be found in chapters dealing with discrete services sectors, where data flows are key or indeed inherent to the very definition of those services, eg telecommunications and the financial services sector. As Burri and Polanco state, data localisation now constitutes in the vast majority of trade agreements a *hard law* or binding measure as opposed to the soft law locus of data-related measures in earlier agreements: almost all localisation measures are binding now.[50] Recent surveys of digital trade restrictiveness show that the majority of contemporary data localisation measures impose conditional flow regimes, ie there are certain conditions that have to be fulfilled before the data can be transferred abroad.[51] In addition, many belong to the most restrictive category of bans on transfer and local processing requirements, eg requiring a company to use a local server for the main processing of the data and, in the case of a ban on transfer, not even a copy of the data can leave the implementing jurisdiction.[52] Finally, a smaller cohort contains local storage requirements, which means that a copy of certain data has to remain within the country, although the data itself can be processed abroad.[53] It is important to note that recent OECD data on digital trade-related restrictions indicates a solid rise in restrictions since 2014.[54] However, the Covid-19 pandemic has witnessed a significant lessening of restrictions, eg digital signatures law globally. Internet restrictions on data flows also continue to rise.[55]

The first agreement to include data localisation provisions was the 2015 Japan-Mongolia FTA, and Asia continues to be a key focus for digital trade matters. The Japan-Mongolia FTA provides that neither party 'shall require a service supplier of the other party, an investor of the other party, or an investment of an investor of the other party in the area of the former party, to use or locate computing facilities in that area as a condition for conducting its business'. The 2016 TPP included provisions on the location of computing facilities, in Article 14.13, kept without change in the CPTPP.[56] The TPP explicitly sought to restrict the use of data localisation measures. Measures restricting digital flows or localisation requirements under Article 14.13 of the TPP were permitted only if they did not amount to an arbitrary or unjustifiable discrimination or a disguised restriction on trade and did not impose restrictions on transfers of information greater than required to achieve the objective. The ban on localisation measures was softened as regards

[50] Burri and Polanco (n 5) 212, 214.
[51] Ferracane et al (n 2) 56.
[52] ibid.
[53] ibid.
[54] See OECD Digital Services Trade Restrictiveness Index (n 6).
[55] Ferracane et al (n 2).
[56] See Trans-Pacific Partnership Agreement (TPP), Art 14.14 and Comprehensive and Progressive Agreement for Trans-Pacific Partnership (CPTTP) (2016), Art 14.13. See also Japan-Mongolia Economic Partnership Agreement (7 June 2016), Art 5.36.

financial services and institutions, which has some merit.[57] As Burri states, the provisions of the TPP were ultimately interesting but did not simply entail a clarification of existing bans on discrimination or set higher standards.[58] Rather, they shaped the regulatory space domestically and could actually lower certain standards. In fact, Burri contends that a commitment to lower standards on privacy and data protection was palpable, with respect for Article 14.82.1 requiring every party to the TPP to adopt or maintain a legal framework that provides for the protection of the personal information of users of electronic commerce.[59] In fact, TPP parties were invited to promote compatibility between their data protection regimes by essentially treating lower standards as equivalent.[60] After TPP/CPTPP, a hard rule on data localisation, largely following the same wording, was included in the 2016 Chile-Uruguay FTA, Article 8.11 and the 2016 updated ASAFT, Article 14.15. A variation on this is to be found in the USMCA, stipulating that no party shall require a covered person to use or locate computing facilities in that party's territory as a condition for conducting business in that territory without considering any further exception, except in the USMCA, which includes a special rule for financial services.[61] Ultimately, we are at a crucial crossroads in relation to the actial meaning of data localisation. For the EU, as outlined above, recent trade agreements have increasingly provided for free flows of data and set out provisions prohibiting 'bad' data localisation.

V. FTAs and Data Privacy: Why the EU's Institutionalisation of Data Privacy Matters

The EU is a very late comer to the place of privacy within trade agremeents, and for long was not considered to be innovative or cutting-edge in its approaches. The EU has, broadly speaking, at least three forms of trade agreement in this domain: (i) preferential trade agreements (PTAs) that are part of a broader framework agreement, encompassing Deep and Comprehensive FTAs, including Association Agreements (AA), eg the EU-Georgia AA 2014, the EU-Moldova AA 2014, the EU-Ukraine AA 2014, and the EU-Serbia 2013 Stabilisation and Association Agreement; (ii) standalone preferential trade agreements (such as the EU-Canada CETA 2016), EPAs, eg the EU-Cariforum EPA 2008, the EU-Japan EPA 2017, and (iii) more recent or next-generation FTAs, such as EU-South Korea FTA 2010, the EU-Colombia and Peru

[57] TPP, Art 14.2.4.

[58] Burri, 'The Governance of Data and Data Flows in Trade Agreements: The Pitfalls of Legal Adaptation' (n 3) 115.

[59] ibid.

[60] TPP, Art 14.8.5.

[61] Agreement between the United States of America, the United Mexican States, and Canada (in force 1 July 2020) (USMCA), Art 19.12.

FTA 2012, the EU-Singapore FTA 2018, and the EU-Vietnam FTA 2019. Digital technology for commercial purposes is nonetheless a relatively recent phenomenon dating back to the 1990s, as is evidenced from the scant provisions in the legal texts on electronic transmissions of the WTO from 1994.[62] Some studies indicate that just 30 per cent of all 274 PTAs notified to the WTO by 2017 featured e-commerce provisions.[63] Currently, approximately 80 or more FTAs include provisions on privacy.[64] Yet even in the most large-scale formulation of trade agreements, such as the CPTPP and USMCA, data is understood to be mostly overlooked in the sense that it is difficult to find evidence of a robust and precise relationship between trade and privacy.[65] Most of the earlier agreements dealing with privacy issues largely consisted of non-binding declarations of mere programmatic form, such as the 2000 Jordan-US FTA, which contained a joint statement on electronic commerce where parties could deem it necessary to ensure the effective protection of privacy in the processing of personal data on global information networks.[66] The US-Jordan FTA was the very first FTA to have an e-commerce chapter, though it does not contain any hard obligations. It even recommended the OECD Privacy Guidelines as the appropriate basis for policy developments, although even the OECD points out that this framework has been surpassed by digitisation, interconnected networks and the nature and volume of data flows.[67] However, the shortcomings of trade agreements here need to be acknowledged: they are not holistic tools, are not regulatory forums, they create limited institutions and mostly have weak global centrifugal points underpinning them. They self-evidently mean that further regulation and multilateralism is required.

There have been many schools thought on digital trade, evidencing its evolving contours, from studies on e-commerce allowing for an understanding of how to identify and classify provisions relating to digital trade based on the content and scope of application, to all disciplines and obligations impacting digital trade beyond e-commerce. As will be outlined here, a significant shift eventually took place in EU agreements, where the EU has sought to elevate the place of privacy protection in electronic communications requiring transfers of data, following the broader trends of trade agreements – generally affirmatively protecting individuals' rights.[68] This has been done, for example, by increasingly referencing the

[62] Sauvé and Soprana (n 27) 286.

[63] See WTO Database on Preferential Trade Arrangements: http://ptadb.wto.org/?lang=1 accessed 27 February 2022.

[64] Monteiro and Teh (n 18).

[65] Burri, 'The Governance of Data and Data Flows in Trade Agreements: The Pitfalls of Legal Adaptation' (n 3). See Monteiro and Teh (n 18).

[66] Burri and Polanco (n 5).

[67] Jordan-US Joint Statement on Electronic Commerce (7 June 2000) Art II; The OECD Privacy Framework: Supplementary explanatory memorandum to the revised recommendation of the council concerning guidelines governing the protection of privacy and transborder flows of personal data (2013); OECD Guidelines on the Protection of Privacy and Transborder Flows of Personal Data (1980).

[68] Association Agreement between the European Union and the European Atomic Energy Community and their Member States, of the one part, and the Republic of Moldova, of the other part [2014] OJ L260/4, Art 13.1 and Art 99(d).

processing and dissemination of data, introducing administrative measures, or adopting non-disciplinary practices.[69]

The EU has adopted a range of perspectives as to international standards and data protection:[70] eg EU-Central America, EU-Columbia, or EU-Peru, all providing that e-commerce shall be consistent with international standards of data protection; or EU-Ukraine, which provides that e-commerce must be fully compatible with the highest international standards of data protection. EU agreements include qualifications to these standards, for example giving the parties the right to define and regulate their own levels of protection of personal data in pursuit of public policy objectives and not to be required to disclose confidential or sensitive information or data.[71] The EU has subsequently pioneered special chapters on the protection of personal data including discrete principles.[72] I argue here that the EU ultimately pioneered these developments through the institutionalisation of data.

As developed further below and above, other trade agreements reference or place the criteria or guidelines from relevant international organisations or bodies into their agreements, eg APEC Cross-Border Privacy Rules system Privacy Framework or OECD Recommendations of the Council concerning guidelines governing the protection of privacy and transborder flows of data (2013).[73] These references could in theory be significant for the locating of internationalisation as the centre of gravity in a world of conflicting regimes and conceptual framing. USMCA explicitly recognises the APEC as a valid mechanism to facilitate cross-border information transfers while protecting personal information. Distinct differences exist between major agreements with respect to the international privacy regimes cited, data localisation, interactive computer services and so on which some label to be a 'missed

[69] Burri, 'The Governance of Data and Data Flows in Trade Agreements: The Pitfalls of Legal Adaptation' (n 3).

[70] Free Trade Agreement Between the European Union and the Republic of Singapore [2019] OJ L 294/2 Art 8.57.4; Comprehensive and enhanced Partnership Agreement between the European Union and the European Atomic Energy Community and their Member States, of the one part, and the Republic of Armenia, of the other part [2018] OJ L23/4 Art 197.2; Economic Partnership Agreement between the CARIFORUM States, of the one part, and the European Community and its Member States, of the other part [2008] OJ L289/3 Art 119.2; Agreement establishing an association between the European Community and its Member States, of the one part, and the Republic of Chile, of the other part [2002] OJ 359/3, Art 202; Monteiro and Teh (n 18) 52.

[71] Agreement between the European Union and Japan for an Economic Partnership (EU-Japan EPA) [2018] OJ L 330/3, Art 18.1.2.h and Art 18.16.7.

[72] Such as purpose limitation, data quality, proportionality, transparency, security, right to access, rectification and opposition, restrictions on onwards transfers, protection of sensitive data, enforcement mechanisms, coherence with international commitments and cooperation between the parties to ensure an adequate level of protection of personal data. See Interim Agreement with a view to an Economic Partnership Agreement between the European Community and its Member States, of the one part, and the Central Africa Party, of the other part [2008] OJ L57/2 ch 6, Arts 61–65; Economic Partnership Agreement between the CARIFORUM States, of the one part, and the European Community and its Member States, of the other part, ch 6, Arts 197–201.

[73] USMCA, Art 19.8.2.

opportunity'.[74] The Australia-Singapore Digital Economy Agreement (DEA) is noted to be a world first – an agreement calling for 'interoperability' of data protection regimes, making data protection more effective and coherent internationally.[75] These developments do not change the fact that the EU's regimes are philosophically significantly at odds with economic understandings of privacy, and that interoperability may not be as intellectually robust as its flexible terminology might suggest.[76]

Data-related provisions in trade agreements are a relatively new phenomenon, found primarily in dedicated e-commerce chapters of PTAs as to cross-border flows of data or banning or limiting data localisation rules. Provisions on cross-border data flows are also found in chapters on service sectors, where data flows are inherent to the definition of the service, eg telecommunications and financial services.[77] Non-binding provisions on data flows have appeared since 2000, eg in Jordan-US FTA. In the 2006 Taiwan-Nicaragua FTA the parties affirmed the importance of working to maintain cross-border flows of information as an essential element of promoting a dynamic environment for electronic commerce.[78] An intermediate type of provision, positioned between hard and soft commitments, is found in the 2007 South Korea-US FTA, where the parties – after recognising the importance of the free flow of information in facilitating trade and acknowledging the importance of protecting personal information – declare that they shall endeavour to refrain from imposing or maintaining unnecessary barriers to electronic information flows across borders.[79] The first agreement with a *binding* provision on cross-border information flows was the 2014 Mexico-Panama FTA, allowing the parties to transmit electronic information from and to their respective territories when required in accordance with the applicable legislation on the protection of personal data and taking into account international practices. The 2016 TPP text appears to have greatly influenced all subsequent agreements, with data flow provisions, stipulating that each party 'shall allow the cross-border transfer of information by electronic means, including personal information when it was for the conduct of the business of a covered person'. It would not prevent a party from 'adopting or maintaining measures to achieve a legitimate public policy objective' provided that the measure was not applied in a manner which

[74] See Leblond (n 34); E Fahey and I Mancini, 'The EU as an Intentional or Accidental Convergence Actor? Learning from the EU-Japan Data Adequacy Negotiations' (2020) 26(2) *International Trade Law and Regulation* 99.

[75] Article 18.7: 'each Party shall encourage the development of mechanisms to promote compatibility between these different regimes. These mechanisms may include the recognition of regulatory outcomes, whether accorded autonomously or by mutual arrangement or broader international frameworks'.

[76] S Aaronson 'Could Trade Agreements Help Address the Wicked Problem of Cross Border Disinformation' (2021) SSRN Paper, 19, https://papers.ssrn.com/sol3/papers.cfm?abstract_id=3820213 accessed 27 February 2022.

[77] Burri and Polanco (n 5) 211.

[78] *cf* Canada-Peru FTA (2009); Peru-Korea FTA (2011); Central America-Mexico FTA (2013); Columbia-Costa Rica FTA (2013); Canada-Honduras FTA (2014); Canada-Korea FTA (2015); Japan-Mongolia EPA (2016).

[79] South Korea-US FTA (2007) Art 15.8. See Burri, 'The Governance of Data and Data Flows in Trade Agreements: The Pitfalls of Legal Adaptation' (n 3).

could constitute a means of arbitrary or unjustifiable discrimination or a disguised restriction on trade and does not impose restrictions on transfers of information greater than are required to achieve the objective. This provision and the entire e-commerce chapter of the TPP was transposed without change into the 2018 CPTPP. Thereafter, hard rules on data flows have been incorporated into a large range of agreements, maintaining exactly the same wording.[80] It is considered path-breaking that certain countries have sought to consider in future negotiations commitments relating to cross-border flows of information, such as in the 2018 EU-Japan EPA Article 8.81 or in the EU-Mexico Global Agreement under negotiation. This naturally leads to a consideration of the place of the EU.[81]

VI. The EU Horizontal Strategy for Data: The Impact of the Model Clauses

While overall it may be said that the EU's approach to data institutionalisation has been progressive, it is certainly only a recent phenomenon. Similarly, post-Lisbon, the EU has merged electronic commerce with trade in services and has only recently moved to dedicated digital trade chapters, thus moving closer to the US position. The EU has developed a horizontal strategy on cross-border flows of personal data in external trade policy.[82] This strategy was developed in the wake of the introduction of the EU's far-reaching GDPR and the significant post-Lisbon trade agreements negotiated with many leading developed economies.[83] The European Parliament had argued vociferously for internal consistency of external trade policy.[84] Thereafter, the European Commission developed highly significant so-called model 'horizontal' provisions on cross-border data flows and personal data protection in EU trade and investment agreements.[85] The provisions are of value in so far as they purport to incorporate the complex position of the EU into model texts, placing extremely high standards and individual rights at the core thereof, whilst also committing to free data

[80] Chile-Uruguay FTA (2016) Art 8.10; Argentina-Chile FTA (2017) Art 11.6; Singapore-Sri-Lanka FTA (2018) Art 9.9; Peru-Australia FTA (2018) Art 13.11; USMCA (2018); Brazil-Chile FTA (2018); Australia-Indonesia FTA (2019) Art 13.11; Japan-US FTA (2019) Art 11.

[81] See EU-Mexico Agreement in Principle (under negotiation), Art XX, https://trade.ec.europa.eu/doclib/press/index.cfm?id=1833 accessed 27 February 2022.

[82] European Commission, 'Horizontal provisions for cross-border data flows and for personal data protection (in EU trade and investment agreements)' (2018) Tradoc 156884, https://trade.ec.europa.eu/doclib/docs/2018/may/tradoc_156884.pdf accessed 27 February 2022.

[83] The European Commission has set out the mechanisms for international transfers of personal data and clarified the criteria to be taken into account in the adequacy mechanism when selecting third countries, in particular in Asia and Latin America: European Commission, 'Communication from the Commission to the European Parliament and the Council: Exchanging and Protecting Personal Data in a Globalised World' COM(2017) 07 final.

[84] See European Parliament, 'Resolution Towards a Digital Trade Strategy' (2017) (2017/2065(INI)), www.europarl.europa.eu/doceo/document/A-8-2017-0384_EN.html accessed 27 February 2022.

[85] European Commission, 'Horizontal provisions for cross-border data flows and for personal data protection' (n 82). Article A on cross-border data flows reads:

flows and condemning 'bad' data localisation. The clauses have three main elements: so-called Articles A, B and X. Article A provides for a declaratory commitment on cross-border data flows and prohibits restrictions in four data and IT localisation requirements. Article B sets out counterbalancing provisions for national measures as to personal data. Article X on regulatory cooperation with respect to digital trade then provides a carve-out for cross-border data flows and the protection of personal data from the dialogue on regulatory issues. The Commission thereafter submitted these provisions to trade negotiations with Australia, Chile, Indonesia, Mexico, New Zealand, Tunisia and the UK – mostly successfully – and has sought to replace the EU-Japan EPA rendezvous clause, to a degree also in the EU-Mexico modernised FTA.[86] It has also sought to bring its complex position to WTO negotiations on electronic commerce in the Joint Statement Initiative (JSI), discussed above.[87] This particular forum is an important one, at least superficially, because of the EU's unlikely prospect of success in gaining global consensus.[88] Yet the WTO negotiations

> '1. The Parties are committed to ensuring cross-border data flows to facilitate trade in the digital economy. To that end, cross-border data flows shall not be restricted between the Parties by:
>
> (i) requiring the use of computing facilities or network elements in the Party's territory for processing, including by imposing the use of computing facilities or network elements that are certified or approved in the territory of a Party;
> (ii) requiring the localisation of data in the Party's territory for storage or processing;
> (iii) prohibiting storage or processing in the territory of the other Party;
> (iv) making the cross-border transfer of data contingent upon use of computing facilities or network elements in the Parties' territory or upon localisation requirements in the Parties' territory.
>
> 2. The Parties shall keep the implementation of this provision under review and assess its functioning in 3 years following the entry into force of this Agreement. A Party may at any time propose to the other Party to review the list of restrictions listed in the preceding paragraph. Such request shall be accorded sympathetic consideration.'

Article B on Protection of personal data and privacy states:

> '1. Each Party recognises that the protection of personal data and privacy is a fundamental right and that high standards in this regard contribute to trust in the digital economy and to the development of trade.
> 2. Each Party may adopt and maintain the safeguards it deems appropriate to ensure the protection of personal data and privacy, including through the adoption and application of rules for the cross-border transfer of personal data. Nothing in this agreement shall affect the protection of personal data and privacy afforded by the Parties' respective safeguards.
> 3. For the purposes of this agreement, "personal data" means any information relating to an identified or identifiable natural person.
> 4. For greater certainty, the Investment Court System does not apply to the provisions in Articles A and B.'

[86] JA Micallef, 'Digital Trade in EU FTAs: Are EU FTAs Allowing Cross Border Digital Trade to Reach Its Full Potential?' (2019) 53 *Journal of World Trade* 855, 867. See also M Burri, 'A WTO Agreement On Electronic Commerce: An Enquiry Into Its Legal Substance And Viability' (2021) Trade Law 4.0 Working Paper No 01/2021, 18; E Fahey, 'The EU as a Digital Trade Actor' in D Collins (ed) *Research Handbook on Digital Trade* (Edward Elgar, forthcoming) and Yakovleva and Irion (n 23) 214.

[87] Communication from the European Union, Joint Statement on Electronic Commerce, 'EU Proposal For WTO Disciplines and Commitments Relating to Electronic Commerce' INF/ECOM/22 (2019), https://trade.ec.europa.eu/doclib/docs/2019/may/tradoc_157880.pdf accessed 27 February 2022.

[88] A large coalition of civil society organisations is critical of the JSI and the proposals currently under discussion, particularly because of concerns that it would enshrine the current status quo, which favours the dominant internet companies.

provide a forum for the EU to seek further institutionalisation of its complex views and this is currently of some importance. This is because the horizontal strategy is understood to be highly ambitious and of much significance to the deeper trade era, as a counterbalance to provisions on labour standards, environmental protections and sustainable development in many trade agreements.[89] The EU confirms that parties safeguards to protect privacy need to be agreed and are not a pretext for abuse or unjustifiable data localisation. It marks an important shift in the EU's trade agreements and normative approach to the protection of data through its institutionalisation. The complex position held by the EU is not entirely without precedent in the era of FTAs: during the CETA negotiations, the EU voiced concerns about the impact on privacy of the disclosure obligations in the agreement.

Afterwards, it has been no less easy, eg the place of free flows of data and privacy were left undetermined and postponed as to the EU-Japan EPA, as noted above and as discussed in detail in Chapter 5, despite the EPA containing many notable provisions on privacy.[90] The horizontal strategy has been only partially accepted by the UK in the EU-UK TCA, where the UK has clearly made known its ambitions to join the CPTPP. In this regard, data flows and localisation bans also feature in the TCA, alongside the replication of the model clauses on the protection of data as a right. However, the word 'fundamental' has been removed from 'data as a fundamental right', and this has caused considerable discussion in analyses which followed. Still, the model clauses are understood to contain a narrower prohibition on restrictions of cross-border data flows than in the so-called US models implemented in the CPTPP, USMCA, US-Japan DTA and China's model implementation of the RCEP; they thus provide the EU with the broad autonomy to protect privacy and personal data.[91] Hence, rather than making provision for an open prohibition to restrict cross-border data flows, the EU model clauses provide for an exhaustive list of the types of restrictions that may be imposed on cross border data flows. Overall, the balance achieved by the model clauses is to assert the EU position more concretely and to be explicit as to the depth of protection.[92] Whether the EU's clauses will cause difficulty for future public policy or ultimately

[89] Yakovleva and Irion (n 23) 219–20.

[90] Eg EU-Japan EPA: Art 10.4.2 (subjecting data sharing regarding temporary entry of business persons to each party's privacy and data protection law); Art 20.5 (affirming that intellectual property related disclose of information was not required if except under either party's privacy laws); Art 21.4.e (subjecting provision of proposed regulations to applicable privacy law) or Art 32.1 of the Protocol on rules of origin and origin procedures (affirming that furnishing or access to information was not required if contrary to either party's personal data protection and privacy law).

[91] See S Yakovleva, 'EU's Policy on Cross-border Data Flows: Navigating the Thin Line between Liberalizing Digital Trade, Promoting Rules-based Multilateralism and Safeguarding Fundamental Rights and Values' in E Fahey and I Mancini (eds), *Understanding the EU as a Good Global Actor: Whose Metrics?* (Edward Elgar, forthcoming).

[92] Some argue that the EU's restrictions aim to protect fundamental rights in a manner which is formulated satisfactorily and meet minimum requirements for plausibility under WTO law: see Yakovleva (n 91). See also Mira Burri, 'A WTO Agreement On Electronic Commerce: An Enquiry Into Its Legal Substance And Viability' (2021) Trade Law 4.0 Working Paper No 01/202, 18.

undermine the EU's goals regarding the liberalisation of data flows remains to be seen.

As Yakovleva argues, when comparing the EU's exception from data flows with the narrower exception in US digital trade chapters, it is clear that the US national security exception grants the US and its trading partners much broader autonomy to restrict cross-border data flows than the proposed EU exception, when those restrictions are framed as national security interests.[93] Although the national security exception in US-led trade agreements gives a broad leeway to the US to restrict data flows, it limits the possibilities for restricting such flows on data protection grounds for *other* parties to those agreements. Given that the trading partners with which the EU maintains a free flow of personal data (eg the UK, Japan and Canada) are also parties to those trade agreements with the US, the routing of personal data from the EEA through those countries may allow the circumvention of the GDPR restrictions on data flows, which perceived as unduly onerous under the US-led trade agreements. As a result, Yakovleva argues that the EU is being surrounded by free data flow areas created by US-led trade agreements, which makes it harder in practice for the EU to maintain its stance on data protection. Such a position, however, assumes little from the US as it is likely to shift towards federal protection for privacy and regulation. Such developments, examined in Chapter 4, may not emerge quickly but appear increasingly like to occur as some stage and will change the parameters of many debates in this field, not least the accuracy of where to place the EU within the 'spaghetti-bowl' mixture of trade agreements internationally, intersecting in awkward and messy spaces.

VII. EU Digital Trade Regulatory Cooperation: Deepening the Nature of Institutionalisation

Forms of institutionalisation of digital trade in PTAs

Establishment of sub-committee/working group on e-commerce
Functions of sub-committee/working group
Coordination of information exchange
Possibility to establish a working group on e-commerce
Establishment of joint/sub-committee on paperless trading
Establishment of committee on trade in services, establishment and e-commerce
Possibility to conclude implementing arrangements

Source: J-A Monteiro and R Teh, 'Provisions on Electronic Commerce in Regional Trade Agreements' (2017) WTO Working Paper ERSD-2017-11.

[93] ibid.

Only a very limited number of trade agreements establish specific institutional arrangements for e-commerce and it is important to emphasise that existing provisions vary enormously across agreements. Thus, the idea of an institutional infrastructure within digital trade is still highly limited and the account here draws from the work of Monteiro and Teh to typologise this. Some such institutional arrangements establish sub-committees to review and monitor the implementation and operation of the chapter. Some supervise and assess implementation of the relevant chapter (eg EU-Korea), whilst others establish a dedicated joint committee.[94] Other forms of intuitional arrangements include working groups or the possibility of creating a working group in charge of certain tasks.[95] Others envisage working groups of experts. Post-Lisbon, EU trade agreements include a vast array of institutional arrangements for their implementation.[96] Historically, the most usual form of institutionalised cooperation envisioned by the EU in digital trade is regulatory cooperation overseen by joint committees. More recent chapters on digital trade, eg those in the EU-UK TCA or the EU-Australia agreements suggest that there has been a significant shift away from these structures to more lithe and sparse arrangements, which tend to be shorter, set out fewer cooperation provisions generally and contain few commitments to multilateralism, indicating a different vision for engagement.

From the OECD to the EU, regulatory cooperation has a variety of meanings and is a broad church of ideas, schemas and practices. For instance, the OECD definition of 'regulatory cooperation' is the range of institutional and procedural frameworks within which national governments, sub-national governments, and the wider public can work together to build more integrated systems for rule making and implementation, subject to the constraints of democratic values such as accountability, openness, and sovereignty.[97] Yet regulatory cooperation

[94] eg on paperless trading: see Japan-Singapore EPA, entered into force 30 November 2002, revised 2007. See Monteiro and Teh (n 18) 68, who find only 16 agreements.

[95] eg regulatory issues as to trade in services, establishment and e-commerce: Trade Agreement between the European Union and its Member States, of the one part, and Colombia and Peru, of the other part (EU-Colombia-Peru FTA) [2012] OJ L354/3.

[96] I Mancini, 'Fundamental Rights in the EU's External Trade Relations: From Promotion "Through" Trade Agreements to Protection "In" Trade Agreements' in E Kassoti and R Wessel (eds), *EU Trade Agreements and the Duty to Respect Human Rights Abroad* (CLEER, 2020).

[97] OECD, 'International Regulatory Co-operation – Adapting Rules to an Interconnected World' (2020), www.oecd.org/gov/regulatory-policy/irc.htm accessed 27 February 2022; B Hoekman, 'International Regulatory Cooperation and Trade Agreements' in E Brousseau et al (eds), *The Oxford Handbook of Institutions of International Economic Governance and Market Regulation* (Oxford University Press, 2019); J Wouters and A Andrione-Moylan, 'The Changing International Cooperation Network of the EU: The Inclusion of Informal (Regulatory) Bodies' in RA Wessel and J Odermatt (eds), *Research Handbook on the European Union and International Organizations* (Edward Elgar, 2019); J Nakagawa, 'Regulatory Co-operation and Regulatory Coherence through Mega-FTAs: Possibilities and Challenges' in J Chaisse and T Lin (eds), *International Economic Law and Governance: Essays in Honour of Mitsuo Matsushita* (Oxford University Press, 2016); AR Young, 'Liberalizing Trade, Not Exporting Rules: The Limits to Regulatory Co-ordination in the EU's "New Generation" Preferential Trade Agreements' (2015) 22 *Journal of European Public Policy* 1253; B Hoekman, 'Fostering Transatlantic Regulatory Cooperation and Gradual Multilateralization' (2015) 18 *Journal of International Economic Law* 609; R Quick, 'Regulatory Cooperation – A Subject of Bilateral Trade Negotiations or Even for the WTO' (2008) 42 *Journal of World Trade* 391; E Golberg, 'Regulatory Cooperation – A Reality Check'

ranges from relatively informal and unstructured, occasional or ad hoc – eg sharing best practices or simply sharing information – to the more formal, such as mutual recognition agreements and wholesale harmonisation of regulatory frameworks. International regulatory cooperation is more conventionally understood to involve shaping and complying with international agreements, utilising international evidence, collaborating with international counterparts – either bilaterally or through multilateral forums when designing and enforcing regulations.[98] Recognising existing regulations and standards that achieve the same policy objective at lower costs can, to some, be seen as regulatory cooperation.[99] In the transatlantic context, some define regulatory cooperation as the process of interaction between US and EU regulators, founded on the benefits that regulators can achieve through closer partnership and greater regulatory interoperability.[100] Thus, irrespective of the precise definition, there is a significant dimension of institutional action to generate convergence in rule-making. Regulatory cooperation has become of immense international significance because it prevents regulatory divergences and non-tariff barriers. It is to be found dealing with the most important impediments to trade in many leading contemporary international trade agreements, eg the CPTPP and latest deep EU FTAs with South Korea, Canada, the UK, Singapore and Japan. There is no shared idea of regulatory cooperation as to digital trade in regional trade agreements but a rising prevalence of data regulation and no shortage of examples of significant regulatory cooperation. Regulatory cooperation bodies within trade agreements do not formally constitute institutions or fit within standard taxonomies of institutions. But they do form part of the architecture of bodies found within trade agreements.

Provisions calling on parties to cooperate on regulatory issues relating to e-commerce through regular dialogue and exchanges of information are found amongst the most recent PTAs signed by the EU in the last decade. The issues most frequently listed in the vast majority of EU PTAs include: recognition of certificates of electronic signatures issued to the public and facilitation of cross-border certification services; the liability of intermediary service providers with

(2019) M-RCBG Associate Working Paper Series No 115, www.hks.harvard.edu/sites/default/files/centers/mrcbg/img/115_final.pdf accessed 27 February 2022.

[98] J Wiener and A Alemanno, 'The Future of International Regulatory Cooperation: TTIP as a Learning Process Toward a Global Policy Laboratory' (2015) 78 *Law and Contemporary Problems* 103; R Bull et al, 'New Approaches to International Regulatory Cooperation: The Challenge of TTIP, TPP, and Mega-Regional Trade Agreements' (2015) 78 *Law and Contemporary Problems* 1; W Mattli and N Woods, 'In Whose Benefit? Explaining Regulatory Change in Global Politics' in W Mattli and N Woods (eds), *The Politics of Global Regulation* (Princeton University Press, 2009).

[99] UK Department for Business, Energy & Industrial Strategy, 'International Regulatory Cooperation for a Global Britain: Government Response to an OECD Review' (2020), https://assets.publishing.service.gov.uk/government/uploads/system/uploads/attachment_data/file/913730/international-regulatory-cooperation-for-a-global-britain.pdf accessed 27 February 2022.

[100] US Chamber of Commerce, 'Regulatory Coherence & Cooperation in the Transatlantic Trade and Investment Partnership (TTIP)', www.uschamber.com/sites/default/files/regulatory_coherence_regulatory_cooperation_-chamber_ttip_paper_-_final_3-02.pdf accessed 27 February 2022.

respect to the transmission or storage of information; the protection of consumers in the ambit of e-commerce. Other issues to be found in EU FTAs signed in the early 2000s called for regulatory cooperation relating to paperless trading and the protection of personal data.[101] The EU has sought to include regulatory cooperation its post-Lisbon trade agreements with all major developed global economies. This is particularly so in the area of digital trade or e-commerce in all of its post-Lisbon trade agreements with all major developed global economies.[102] Many such articles of the regulatory cooperation chapters are heavily embedded in multilateralism. Article 16.4 of the CETA provides for international standards of data protection for both parties into the concepts of trust and confidence in e-commerce. Arguably, articles such as CETA Article 16.6, which thus embeds internationalisation into dialogue on e-commerce to include multilateral forums constitute more far-reaching commitments to multilateralism. To similar effect is Article 8.80 of the EU-Japan EPA, which provides that:

1. The Parties shall, where appropriate, cooperate and participate actively in multilateral fora to promote the development of electronic commerce.
2. The Parties agree to maintain a dialogue on regulatory matters relating to electronic commerce with a view to sharing information and experience … including on related laws, regulations and their implementation, and best practices with respective to electronic commerce. (…).

The span is important because it suggests a very broad relationship and many instruments to underpin that relationship. What is thus significant about regulatory cooperation provided for in Article 16.6 of CETA and Article 8.88 of the EU-Japan EPA is the extent to which internationalisation and multilateralism are embedded within the dialogue for engagement.[103] Still, regulatory cooperation becomes a key mechanism with which the EU and other leading international partners can develop economy studies and central features of the digital trade landscape. It is important to state that the dialogue that is taking place in these post-Lisbon trade agreements on digital trade or e-commerce generally has a broad reach and may be extremely ambitious. CETA enables dialogue to take place in a variety of forums and ways but in particular in multilateral forums, for example in CETA Article 16.6

[101] Eg Free Trade Agreement between the European Union and its Member States, of the one part, and the Republic of Korea, of the other part [2011] OJ L127/6, Art 7.49; EU-Columbia-Peru FTA, Art 163.

[102] Eg Comprehensive Economic and Trade Agreement (CETA) between Canada, of the one part, and the European Union and its Member States, of the other part [2017] OJ L11/23, Ch 16 or EU-Japan EPA, Ch 8.

[103] By contrast, in more recent EU trade agreements such as the Trade and Cooperation Agreement between the European Union and the European Atomic Energy Community, of the one part, and the United Kingdom of Great Britain and Northern Ireland, of the other part ST/5198/2021/INIT (EU-UK TCA) [2021] OJ L149/10, we see in the regulatory cooperation chapter there and in the entire chapter a significantly *lesser* interest in the internationalisation of regulatory cooperation and multilateralism. We also see this in more recent negotiations, for example between the EU and Australia, similarly outlining a slimmer component of the areas for regulatory cooperation engagement.

paragraph 3. This insertion of international cooperation within regulatory dialogues is a very new form of engagement with international partners; it is also replicated in the EU-Japan EPA, in Article 8.88.[104]

These commitments to multilateralism in the EU's efforts at regulatory cooperation are notable and distinctive. Yet they sit uncomfortably against the backdrop of a severe lack of activity at a multilateral level, in particular at the WTO. As noted above, only in 2016, did e-commerce garner 'renewed interest' among WTO Members, where seven proposals were tabled by major WTO Members such as the US, the EU, Japan and Brazil, now the subject at the WTO of a Joint Statement Initiative (JSI) on e-commerce.[105] The EU has been leading technical discussions in plenary and in small group and the co-convenors include Australia, Japan and Singapore. Notably, the EU is actively attempting there to promote its model horizontal articles to embed data flows and data privacy within digital privacy – including key provisions on regulatory cooperation. Many remain unconvinced that the WTO can realistically act as a locus for the scale of law-making ahead. Such law-making has a vast array of key objectives, because it needs to modernise digital trade *and* to engage with the global split between East and West on economic or individualised privacy etc; this constitutes a lengthy shopping list.[106] The EU thus in its relations with third countries champions regulatory cooperation predicated on international standards and seeks regulatory cooperation in the absence of a global consensus on standards. Frequently, the EU appears to agree with partners that multilateralism, international standards and global forums are the starting point.

Returning to the broader point then, bilateral regulatory cooperation is thus a very important means by which the EU can develop its institutionalisation of data regimes. The EU has formulated many significant innovations in the field of data in its trade agreements. All in all, regulatory cooperation is a very important way of engaging with third country partners in this new era of deeper trade agreements because it demonstrates that willingness to be a global leader but also to lead with other significant global matters.

These engagements lead to important multilateral developments and participation structures. In other words, institutionalisation *appears to lead to further institutionalisation*. The international dimension of this have taken their engagement to extremely positive heights, ie the EU and Japan in the context of the WTO have made important efforts to evolve the WTO institutional AB stalemate out of its current impasse. The international dimension of this institutionalisation is thus a key springboard for the *reach* of institutionalisation.

[104] There are significant nuances in how the EU engages with cybersecurity, discussed in Chapter 3.

[105] WTO, 'Joint statement on e-commerce news archives' (n 45). The negotiations have been structured around six focus groups. Negotiations on a plurilateral agreement on e-commerce, covering a range of rules on digital trade, have yet to come to a conclusion.

[106] See S Aaronson and P Leblond, 'Another Digital Divide: The Rise of Data Realms and its Implications for the WTO' (2018) 21 *Journal of International Economic Law* 245.

VIII. Conclusion

Digital trade may be used as a key case study of the EU's development, along with its partners, of institutional design and the rollout of high-level binding standards for the flow of data, an area previously neglected in international economic law. The EU advocates, mostly with developed third countries, for regulatory cooperation predicated on international standards. It seeks regulatory cooperation even in the absence of a global consensus on such standards. This has formed part of the EU's key push for trade in the post-Lisbon era, striving to write the global rule-book. The EU continues to implement and propagate its complex position on digital trade at a multilateralism level and has developed important practices on how to implement best practice through institutions. Digital trade involves many actors, bottom-up, and suffers from an identity crisis as to its facets and functions in the contemporary legal order. The global legal order appears increasingly fragmented, with multiple regimes in digital trade with respect to data flows – split between the EU and many other forms of regime. The high standards of the EU represent an important counterbalance to a variety of global actors who would promote economic standards over individual rights. The WTO, for various reasons, appears unlikely to constitute the forum for significant change for now. Most of the world seems to be coming closer to the EU's position but significant gaps still remain. How to maintain high standards of privacy yet also advocate a liberal stance remains a conundrum for the EU. The EU has largely a mixed position, mid-way between key actors such as the US and China, as a middle ground actor in digital, yet this metaphor appears rapidly surpassed by practice. In Chapter 4 the future of the EU-US relationship on data flows is explored. This seems to have an outsized impact on the future of data privacy in digital trade provisions. Ultimately, it remains a challenge to see whether the EU's institutionalised vision of data can succeed in future negotiating forums.

3

The EU as a Cyber Actor

The Evolving Architecture of EU Cyber Law: Beyond Weak Institutionalisation

I. Overview: The EU as an International Cyber Actor

It is increasingly argued by public international law specialists that cyberspace does not to constitute a new legal domain.[1] EU lawyers could also credibly make such a claim. Nevertheless, the EU is well represented in all international forums on cyber law-making and is explicitly committed to the promotion of international law.[2] This is unsurprising, as it is one of over 50 countries and regions that have adopted cybersecurity policies.[3] Indeed, some suggest that it is one of the EU's most significant policy fields in recent times – however new and increasingly externalised despite its initially internal focus – making it a highly prominent and active locus for external relations.[4] As a result, the EU also increasingly appears to nudge international cybersecurity developments.[5] The EU has been a core

[1] eg R Buchan, *Cyber-Espionage and International Law* (Hart Publishing, 2018).

[2] eg RA Wessel, 'Towards EU Cybersecurity Law: Regulating a New Policy Field' in N Tsagourias and R Buchan (eds), *Research Handbook on International Law and Cyberspace* (Edward Elgar, 2015); J Odermatt, 'The European Union as a Cybersecurity Actor' in S Blockmans and P Koutrakos (eds), *Research Handbook on the EU's Common Foreign and Security Policy* (Edward Elgar, 2018).

[3] A Kasper, 'EU Cybersecurity Governance – Stakeholders and Normative Intentions Towards Integration' in M Harwood et al (eds), *The Future of the European Union: Demisting the Debate* (Msida, 2020); Wessel (n 2); W Voss, 'The Concept of Accountability in the Context of the Evolving Role of ENISA in Data Protection, ePrivacy and Cybersecurity' in A Arcuri and F Coman-Kund (eds), *Technocracy and the Law: Accountability, Governance and Expertise* (Routledge, 2021).

[4] Wessel (n 2) 507.

[5] A Kasper and A Antonov, 'Towards Conceptualizing EU Cybersecurity Law' (2019) ZEI Discussion Paper C253, www.researchgate.net/profile/Center-For-European-Integration-Studies/publication/338038206_ZEI_Discussion_Paper_C_253_Towards_Conceptualizing_EU_Cybersecurity_Law/links/5dfb5630a6fdcc28372c19eb/ZEI-Discussion-Paper-C-253-Towards-Conceptualizing-EU-Cybersecurity-Law.pdf accessed 25 February 2022; A Bendiek, 'The EU as a Force for Peace in International Cyber Diplomacy' (2018) SWP Comment No 19/2018, www.ssoar.info/ssoar/handle/document/57428 accessed 25 February 2022; A Verhelst and J Wouters, 'Filling Global Governance Gaps in Cybersecurity: International and European Legal Perspectives' (2020) 15(2) *International Organization* 141; D Markopoulou et al, 'The New EU Cybersecurity Framework: The NIS Directive, ENISA's Role and the General Data Protection Regulation' (2019) 35(6) *Computer Law & Security Review* 105336; H Carrapico and B Farrand, 'Discursive Continuity and Change in the Time of Covid-19: the Case of EU Cybersecurity Policy' (2020) 42 *Journal of European Integration* 1111; T Renard,

proponent of the Council of Europe Budapest Convention forum for global law-making but is running into difficulties there on account of the autonomy of the EU legal order concept.[6] It also has an increasingly broad range of cyber partnerships linked explicitly to both trade and multilateralism. The EU Cybersecurity Strategy (CSS) expressly advocates that the EU create a coherent international cyberspace policy to promote EU values.[7] The EU is thus active in many international organisations where cyber matters are being developed.[8] As is outlined below, the roles of the UN and Council of Europe are of most significance in this area, yet the EU also struggles with its esoteric stance as an international organisation. The two key global cyberspace developments in recent times are framed as law-making exercises on state behaviour (the UN Group of Governmental Experts and the parallel UN Open Ended Working Group).[9] A key issue then emerges as to the external policy being presented by the EU and the restrictons that adhering to EU law's autonomy place on the EU's participation in international forums, which are shown here to be great.

Cyber diplomacy is considered by many to be an important means of evolution for the subject of cyber rule-making, given the complexity of public and private law in this domain. Diplomacy here is a multilevel and multiforum concept.[10] Yet diplomacy has a wide variety of meanings and reach. A good example of this is the Framework for a Joint EU Diplomatic Response to Malicious Cyber Activities (cyber diplomacy toolbox), which sets out measures, including restrictive measures, which can be used to prevent and respond to malicious cyber activities.[11]

'EU Cyber Partnerships: Assessing the EU Strategic Partnerships with Third Countries in The Cyber Domain' (2018) 19(3) *European Politics and Society* 321.

[6] J Polakiewicz, 'The Emperor's New Clothes – Data Privacy and Cybersecurity from a European Perspective' in E Fahey and I Mancini (eds), *Understanding The EU as a Good Global Actor: Whose Metrics?* (Edward Elgar, forthcoming).

[7] European Commission, 'Joint Communication to the European Parliament, the Council, the European Economic and Social Committee and the Committee of the Regions – Cybersecurity Strategy of the European Union: An Open, Safe and Secure Cyberspace' JOIN (2013) 01 final.

[8] eg Council of Europe Convention, Organisation for Economic Co-operation and Development (OECD), United Nations General Assembly (UNGA), Organisation for Security and Co-operation in Europe (OSCE), International Telecommunication Union (ITU), World Summit on the Information Society (WSIS) and the Internet Governance Forum (IGF).

[9] See H Aitken 'The Pandemic, UN Cyber Negotiations and International Law and Norms' (*EJIL Talk!*, 13 September 2021), www.ejiltalk.org/the-pandemic-un-cyber-negotiations-and-international-law-and-norms/ accessed 25 February 2022.

[10] eg in 2017, the Council underlined the need to address cybersecurity with a coherent approach at national, EU and global level: see Council of the European Union, 'Outcome of Proceedings – General Secretariat of the Council to Delegations' No 14435/17 (20 November 2017).

[11] On 28 June 2018, the European Council, in its Conclusions, called on institutions and Member States to implement the measures referred to in the Joint Communication on increasing resilience and bolstering capabilities to address hybrid threats, including the work on attribution of cyber-attacks and the practical use of the cyber diplomacy toolbox. On 18 October 2018, the European Council adopted conclusions calling for work on the capacity to respond to and deter cyber-attacks through EU restrictive measures to be taken forward. As a follow up, on 17 May 2019, the Council adopted the necessary legal acts establishing a framework for targeted restrictive measures to deter and respond to cyber-attacks with a significant effect which constitute an external threat to the Union or its Member

Here, the EU's usual soft law and soft power approach to legal tactics is 'hardened' when seen in a broader context. Significant non-state governance in the cyber domain has transformed national cyber law-making as much as global initiatives have, mired in the quest to constrain private actors and complex state entities. Cyberspace has also had a complex relationship with international law, as no global cyber law exists.[12] The emerging role of private entities in cyber law-making poses many challenges for enforcement, accountability and transparency.[13] Arguably, however, the real focus of EU cyber diplomacy is alongside and even within the EU's trade agreements with its many third-country partners. The EU is embedding cyber law-making more deeply within multilateralism and soft-law strategic partnership agreements. Even in such contexts, the picture that emerges is very dynamic but also highly fragmented. The EU is the world's second-most active user of restrictive measures after the US, with four thematic sanctions regimes: chemical weapons and terrorism and, more recently, cyber sanctions and human rights.[14] Sanctions regimes permit restrictive measures to be applied in response to cyber-attacks with a significant effect against third states or international organisations, pursuant to Article 21 TEU. This raises many human rights issues, particularly for the attribution of responsibility through the widening institutionalisation of cyber law-making.[15] There is now significant political pressure on the EU to act, as many states and business in the EU have been the target of cyber-attacks. The capacity of the EU to evolve a robust, credible and sustainable set of tools in cyberspace in an era of strategic autonomy and rising defensiveness to global threats had long been anticipated.[16] The EU has taken

States. See respectively, European Council, 'From General Secretariat of the Council to Delegations – Conclusions 28 June 2018' (2018) EUCO 9/18; European Council, 'From General Secretariat of the Council to Delegations – Conclusions 18 October 2018' (2018) EUCO 13/18; European Council, 'From General Secretariat of the Council to Delegations – Conclusions 18 October 2018' (2018) EUCO 13/18; European Council, Council Decision (CFSP) 2019/797 of 17 May 2019 concerning restrictive measures against cyber-attacks threatening the Union or its Member States [2019] OJ L 129I/13; Council Regulation (EU) 2019/796 of 17 May 2019 concerning restrictive measures against cyber-attacks threatening the Union or its Member States [2019] OJ L 129I/1.

[12] Buchan (n 1).

[13] E Fahey, 'Institutionalising EU Cyber Law: Can the EU Institutionalise its Many Subjects and Objects?' (2020) EIF Working Paper Series 01/2020.

[14] C Portela, 'The Spread of Horizontal Sanctions' (*CEPS*, 7 March 2019), www.ceps.eu/the-spread-of-horizontal-sanctions/ accessed 25 February 2022; European Parliamentary Research Service, 'EU Sanctions: A Key Foreign and Security Policy Instrument' (2018) PE 621.870; 'EU Sanctions Map' (2019), www.sanctionsmap.eu accessed 25 February 2022. In 2018, the European Council adopted conclusions calling for work on the capacity to respond to and deter cyber-attacks through EU restrictive measures to be taken forward.

[15] F Dumortier et al, 'EU Sanctions against Cyber-Attacks and Defense Rights: Wanna Cry?' (*European Law Blog*, 28 September 2020), https://europeanlawblog.eu/2020/09/28/eu-sanctions-against-cyber-attacks-imposed-and-defense-rights-wanna-cry/ accessed 25 February 2022. It is also worth noting the widening of the scope of judicial review of the CFSP by the CJEU, eg Case C-134/19 *P Bank Refah Kargaran v Council* EU:C:2020:793.

[16] E Moret and P Pawlak, 'The EU Cyber Diplomacy Toolbox: Towards a Cyber Sanctions Regime?' (2017) European Union Institute for Security Studies, 24 Brief Issue, www.iss.europa.eu/sites/default/files/EUISSFiles/Brief%2024%20Cyber%20sanctions.pdf accessed 25 February 2022; MG Porcedda, 'Patching the Patchwork: Appraising the EU Regulatory Framework on Cyber Security Breaches'

significant action, using new powers in this domain swiftly and replicating them in many other significant sanctions regimes, going beyond the powers of international law in several respects. Sanctions thus represent a hardening of the EU's legal tools in a domain where international diplomacy has been the initial currency of action, going beyond the economics of the internal market as a legal starting point for regulation. Its global dimensions or international characterisation is of much note. As Borell stated, while the EU 'prioritise[d] international cooperation and dialogue to tackle these malicious activities', believing in 'respect for international law and the continued work in the United Nations on norms of responsible state behaviour … [in] maintaining international security and stability in cyberspace] cybersanctions also became inevitable'.[17] Thus, in 2019, the Council established a framework pursuant to Article 21 TEU that allows the EU to impose targeted restrictive measures to deter and respond to cyber-attacks which constitute an external threat to the EU or its Member States, including cyber-attacks against third states or international organisations where restricted measures are considered necessary to achieve the objectives of the Common Foreign and Security Policy (CFSP).[18] In 2020, the EU imposed its first ever targeted restrictive measures against Chinese and Russian individuals and also legal entities, for their involvement in significant cyber-attacks and attempted cyber-attacks against the EU and its Member States. The EU used its new sanctions regime to impose travel bans and freeze the assets of six individuals, as well as carrying out assets freezes against three entities or bodies. These individuals and entities were said to have been involved in cyber-attacks against companies located in the EU, such as those known as WannaCry, NotPetya, Operation Cloud Hopper or the attempted cyber-attack against the Organisation for the Prohibition of Chemical Weapons. The reach of such actions was evidently immense. The EU has adopted a vast range of sanctions in early 2022 in response to the Ukraine crisis and digital cyber war waged by Russia, including a range of disinformation and cyber sanctions. This appears to form a concrete realisation of real strategic autonomy and EU technological sovereignty.[19] Sanctions were intended to represent a hardening of relevant legal 'fire power' and a distinct

(2018) 34 *Computer Law & Security Review* 1077; P Pawlak and T Biersteke (eds), 'Guardian of the Galaxy: EU Cyber Sanctions and Norms in Cyberspace' (2019) European Union Institute for Security Studies, Chaillot Paper 155, www.iss.europa.eu/sites/default/files/EUISSFiles/cp155.pdf accessed 25 February 2022.

[17] J Borrell, 'Cyber Sanctions: Time to Act' (*European External Action Service*, 30 July 2020), https://eeas.europa.eu/headquarters/headquarters-homepage/83627/cyber-sanctions-time-act_en accessed 25 February 2022; Council of the European Union, 'European Parliament calls for increased EU cybersecurity capacity' (Press Release, 17 May 2021), www.consilium.europa.eu/en/press/press-releases/2021/05/17/cyber-attacks-council-prolongs-framework-for-sanctions-for-another-year/ accessed 25 February 2022.

[18] Council Decision 2019/797; European Council, 'Conclusions 18 October 2018' (n 11).

[19] Council of the European Union, 'Malicious cyber-attacks: EU sanctions two individuals and one body over 2015 Bundestag hack' (Press Release, 22 October 2020), www.consilium.europa.eu/en/press/press-releases/2020/10/22/malicious-cyber-attacks-eu-sanctions-two-individuals-and-one-body-over-2015-bundestag-hack/ accessed 25 February 2022; Council Decision 2019/797; https://www.consilium.europa.eu/en/policies/sanctions/restrictive-measures-against-russia-over-ukraine/.

shift in legal tools, in a field where the European Court of Justice (CJEU) has heavily legalised and judicialised the contours of the CFSP.[20] Indeed, the EU appears to be mainstreaming cyber issues throughout its existing foreign and security policy as it becomes more difficult to separate internal and external threats.[21]

This chapter attempts to sketch the evolution of the EU as a cyber actor as a significant example of the EU institutionalisation that is taking place, often caught between complex global challenges and contested taxonomies. Cyber law-making demonstrates an evolution of autonomy of actors, yet the effectiveness and salience of the volume of law-making measures adopted in relation to the internal market remain to be seen. In the past, the EU has appeared afflicted, somewhat paradoxically, by both over-legalisation and under-legalisation of cyber law-making. The state of cyber policy in trade law-making is embryonic but is already taking shape in more recent trade agreements in a manner never thought possible, eg the EU-UK Trade and Cooperation Agreement (TCA).[22] The autonomy of EU law increasingly poses challenges for international law-making. Perversely, there have been both many and few cyber actors emerging in EU law: many 'bottom up' with limited powers, oversight or accountability, and few 'top down' with similarly minimal legal fire-power, negligible autonomy and a complex relationship with the internal market.

This chapter contains the following sections: (II) the evolution of EU cyber law-making as an international cyber actor; (III) international trade and cybersecurity; (IV) cybersecurity provisions in EU trade and cooperation agreements; (V) the EU Cybersecurity Act 2019; (VI) the institutional design of 5G regulation; (VII) EU-Council of Europe relations; (VIII) case studies; and (IX) conclusions.

II. The Evolution of EU Cyber Law-Making: Towards Regulatory Capture

Several decades ago, Barlow famously declared the Internet and cyberspace to be a law-free zone. Such a claim is certainly not now possible as a matter of EU law.[23] Cyber law-making is arguably composite and multi-level in its structure, and poses a challenge for state-centric international law, arguably less so for contemporary EU law. From cybercrime to cybersecurity, cyber defence to cyber governance, law-making is increasingly defined by private actors, both by stealth and by design. The EU has made considerable efforts with cyber law-making

[20] C Eckes, 'Common Foreign and Security Policy: The Consequences of the Court's Extended Jurisdiction' (2016) 22 *European Law Journal* 492.

[21] Wessel (n 2) 506.

[22] Trade and Cooperation Agreement between the European Union and the European Atomic Energy Community, of the one part, and the United Kingdom of Great Britain and Northern Ireland, of the other part ST/5198/2021/INIT (EU-UK TCA) [2021] OJ L149/10.

[23] JP Barlow, 'A Declaration of the Independence of Cyberspace' (1996), www.eff.org/cyberspace-independence accessed 25 February 2022.

over the course of two decades, culminating in a Cybersecurity Act and Cyber Agency in 2019, whose succinct titles belie their journeys.[24] Historically, the EU has approached cyber regulation with an unwieldly mix of powers, sanctions and 'agencification' and as a somewhat incoherent external actor.[25] Cyber law-making has arguably often exposed the EU as a weaker global actor, conflicted, beholden to private actors and vexed by its competences, but also highly innovative and transparent.[26] EU cyber action is useful in understanding EU integration practices because it exposes a partially institutionalised field, with incomplete and awkwardly non-intersecting competences, straddling incomplete Security and Digital Single Market policies, evolving sanctions and new agencies.[27] Cyber laws and policies fall, as a law-making exercise, only partly within EU security and more rather as to the internal market. Cyber law is particularly complex as a result, in its breadth and reach. Recently, major efforts have been made in the Area of Freedom, Security and Justice (AFSJ) to develop new autonomous systems, actors and practices to expand the securitisation of the EU, ranging from the evolution of existing AFSJ agencies to new systems in databases, eg as Europol (Regulation 2016/794),[28] Eurojust (Regulation 2018/1727),[29] a European Border and Coast Guard (Regulation (EU) 2016/1624),[30] eu-LISA (Regulation (EU) 2018/1726),[31] ETIAS-TCN (Regulation (EU) 2019/816).[32] Certain 'new entities', for example

[24] See for an overview of past efforts: E Fahey, 'The EU's Cybercrime and Cybersecurity Rule-Making: Mapping the Internal and External Dimensions of EU Security' (2014) 5 *European Journal of Risk Regulation* 46.

[25] eg H Carrapico and A Barrinha, 'The EU as a Coherent (Cyber)Security Actor?' (2017) 55 *Journal of Common Market Studies* 1254; H Carrapico and B Farrand, 'Blurring Public and Private: Cybersecurity in the Age of Regulatory Capitalism' in O Bures and H Carrapico (eds), *Security Privatization: How Non-Security-Related Businesses Shape Security Governance* (Springer, 2018).

[26] Fahey, 'Institutionalising EU Cyber Law: Can the EU Institutionalise Its Many Subjects and Objects?' (n 13) 3.

[27] ibid; E Fahey, 'Developing EU Cybercrime and Cybersecurity: On Legal Challenges of EU Institutionalisation of Cyber Law-Making' in T Hoerber et al (eds), *The Routledge Handbook of European Integrations* (Routledge, 2022) Ch 15.

[28] Regulation (EU) 2016/794 of the European Parliament and of the Council of 11 May 2016 on the European Union Agency for Law Enforcement Cooperation (Europol) and replacing and repealing Council Decisions 2009/371/JHA, 2009/934/JHA, 2009/935/JHA, 2009/936/JHA and 2009/968/JHA [2016] OJ L135/53.

[29] Regulation (EU) 2018/1727 of the European Parliament and of the Council of 14 November 2018 on the European Union Agency for Criminal Justice Cooperation (Eurojust), and replacing and repealing Council Decision 2002/187/JHA [2018] OJ L295/138.

[30] Regulation (EU) 2016/1624 of the European Parliament and of the Council of 14 September 2016 on the European Border and Coast Guard and amending Regulation (EU) 2016/399 of the European Parliament and of the Council and repealing Regulation (EC) No 863/2007 of the European Parliament and of the Council, Council Regulation (EC) No 2007/2004 and Council Decision 2005/267/EC [2016] OJ L251/1.

[31] Regulation (EU) 2018/1726 of the European Parliament and of the Council of 14 November 2018 on the European Union Agency for the Operational Management of Large-Scale IT Systems in the Area of Freedom, Security and Justice (eu-LISA), and amending Regulation (EC) No 1987/2006 and Council Decision 2007/533/JHA and repealing Regulation (EU) No 1077/2011 [2018] OJ L295/99,

[32] Regulation (EU) 2019/816 of the European Parliament and of the Council of 17 April 2019 establishing a centralised system for the identification of Member States holding conviction information

the European Border and Coast Guard, are part of a continuing trend towards the growth of autonomous actors in the AFSJ.[33] These developments are clearly replicated in cyber law-making. The future of the EU Agency for Network and Information Security (ENISA) as a cyber agency remains to be seen. A robust and appropriately empowered cyber agency will probably also constitute a significant intersection of internal and external activities and competences of the EU in cyber law-making.[34]

The definition of cyber law-making is challenging on a global level, not merely for EU law, with over 400 definitions of cybersecurity worldwide, and multiple conceptual disputes as to the appropriate framing of cybercrime and cybersecurity.[35] This chapter principally examines the international and external relations dimensions of cyber law-making. This includes, for example, a consideration of 5G regulation to trade to bilateral relations with third countries and participation in international organisations. Further, it is important to engage with the 'transversal' nature of cyber law-making. One consequence of the contemporary digital age and smart products and smart data may be an age of products which 'own the user' rather than the reverse. Regulation, governance and enforcement may capture products, services and transfers of data, thus spanning the internal and external of EU law.[36] While technologies across a wide range of sectors offer real benefits, the core cultural and legal shifts that they present strike another blow against ownership in the digital economy and impact on the role of the state.[37] EU law in this domain is far from proscriptive. However, data and its sale has become a core part of many contemporary businesses and their practices. There is now a broad commitment to the use of surveillance and surveillance technologies as a way of life that is at the heart of the EU's digital ambitions as a regulator both internally and externally. Technology companies have increasingly difficult relationships with states and governments whereby their practices, for example as to surveillance and its links to policing, or its holding of data and the State's interests in that data, form new modes of interaction which appear to cause more and more concern.[38] In this regard, the relationship between the Internet of

on third-country nationals and stateless persons (ECRIS-TCN) to supplement the European Criminal Records Information System and amending Regulation (EU) 2018/1726 [2019] OJ L135/1.

[33] V Mitsilegas, 'Autonomous Concepts Diversity Management and Mutual Trust in Europe's Area of Criminal Justice' (2020) 57 *Common Market Law Review* 45; E Fahey, 'The Rise and Fall of International Law in the Post-Lisbon AFSJ Legislation Cycles' (2021) 1 *Groningen Journal of European Law* 1.

[34] I am grateful to Ben Farrand for suggestions on this issue.

[35] See R Deibert, 'Toward a Human-Centric Approach to Cybersecurity' (2018) 32 *Ethics & International Affairs* 411.

[36] For example, the IoT covers a range of devices from smartphones and networked thermostats to self-driving cars and wearable technology. These are all products that combine embedded software, network connectivity, microscopic sensors and large-scale data analytics; they are effectively computers: see E Fahey, *Introduction to Law and Global Governance* (Edward Elgar, 2018) 120–21.

[37] See A Perzanowski and J Schultz, *The End of Ownership: Personal Property in the Digital Economy* (MIT Press, 2016) Ch 8.

[38] E Joh, 'The Undue Influence of Surveillance Technology Companies on Policing' (2017) 92 *New York University Law Review* 19; D Yadron et al, 'Inside the FBI's encryption battle with Apple'

Things (IoT) and EU law becomes more salient, particularly as to its cross-border element. Surveillance in the contemporary world also has a central place within this policing: it functions as a regulatory mechanism where policing is replacing law in the framework within which collectives act, or where Big Data is replacing law as the framework of reference, and is a common goal of many frameworks and actors.[39] This chapter thus aims for a deliberately expansive understanding of cyber law-making, to include and accommodate these issues. The EU as a cyber actor appears increasingly to institutionalise cyber matters – yet is also subject to an increasingly wide variety of subjects and objects through its sanctions policy. Major developments in EU cyber action, both internally and externally, increasingly focus on institutionalisation and also on the co-opting of private actors into governance. It is argued here that this is not consistent.[40] It is conceivable that the future of EU cyber law will be constituted by multilevel action and increasingly powerful agencies battling with digital platforms. But this is no different from many other areas of EU law. Indeed, inter-agency cooperation is ultimately seen as the most significant international goal for the development of cyber law, as a means of sharing expertise, deepening learning and coordinating efforts for engagement. Evidently, the outsized role of private actors constitutes a more thorny element of this evolution. As ever, the EU's signature mode of response is to seek to co-opt such actors, to encourage self-regulation with the pretext of developing a regulatory framework and a broader institutional design – even as to the Internet – as in the case of the EU Internet Referral Unit.[41]

III. International Trade and Cybersecurity: The EU Exportation of Institutionalisation?

Data flows present many challenges for the global economy and also for the stability of legal orders. Data flows can risk the security of data systems and networks.[42] They create unique privacy challenges. Data flows also create information

The Guardian (18 February 2016), www.theguardian.com/technology/2016/feb/17/inside-the-fbis-encryption-battle-with-apple accessed 25 February 2022; J Daskal, 'Privacy and Security across Borders' (2019) *Yale Law Journal Forum* 1029, www.yalelawjournal.org/pdf/Daskal_v3q35qwf.pdf accessed 25 February 2022.

[39] L Catá Backer, 'Global Panopticism: States, Corporations and the Governance Effects of Monitoring Regimes' (2008) 15(1) *Indiana Journal of Global Legal Studies* 101.

[40] Carrapico and Farrand, 'Blurring Public and Private: Cybersecurity in the Age of Regulatory Capitalism' (n 25); Carrapico and Barrinha (n 25).

[41] Set up in 2015 as part of the Europol Counter Terrorism Centre, with an objective to refer terrorist and extremist content to Online Service Providers and to provide support to Member States in the context of internet investigations. See the website of Europol, dedicated to EU IRU: www.europol.europa.eu/about-europol/eu-internet-referal-unit-eu-iru accessed 25 February 2022.

[42] E Laidlaw, 'Privacy and Cybersecurity in Digital Trade: The Challenge of Cross Border Data Flows' (2021) *Global Affairs Canada Paper*, 3, https://ssrn.com/abstract=3790936 accessed 25 February 2022.

challenges and can be used to spread misinformation.[43] While the global nature of the digital economy means that cross-border data flows are now intrinsic to commerce, and that all the aforementioned challenges are well known, there is still no global agreement on the relationship between cybersecurity and privacy.[44] However, cybersecurity has a range of meanings, definitions and applications and does not fall into a neat set of rules in any legal jurisdiction, least of all in the EU. It spans espionage, theft, privacy and data protection cross-border trade and investment in Information and Communications Technology.[45] Given the broad range of the potential meanings of 'cybersecurity', the possibility for it to contribute to the creation of trade barriers appears high. It is increasingly stated that trade and cybersecurity are ever more intertwined through the global use of the Internet, the use of data flows, e-commerce and the evolution of international trade, including the spread of AI, the Internet of Things (IoT) and cloud computing.[46] EU law has only recently begun to bring cybersecurity within the ambit of trade agreements with more detail, agency, operations and standards-based reflections. The EU has yet to be involved at WTO level in disputes relating to GATT national security exceptions, a body of jurisprudence which is limited and sparse and is mainly populated by disputes about Asia and BRICS countries.[47] Ultimately, cybersecurity has only become a key issue for trade very recently, and most trade rules were not conceived of with the digital age in mind. There is still much uncertainty about the interaction of cybersecurity and international trade, and the EU's efforts in this field are very interesting, given its ambitions internally and externally.[48] As more countries develop offensive and defensive cyber-attack capabilities, more

[43] ibid, citing U Ahmed, 'The Importance of Cross-Border Regulatory Cooperation in an Era of Digital Trade' (2019) 18 *World Trade Law Review* 99, 99.

[44] Laidlaw (n 42) 4; see D Ciuriak, 'Cybersecurity, National Security and Trade in the Digital Era' (2021) SSRN Paper, https://ssrn.com/abstract=3374886 accessed 25 February 2022; J Meltzer and C Kerry, 'Cybersecurity and Digital Trade: Getting it Right' (*Brookings*, 18 September 2019), www.brookings.edu/research/cybersecurity-and-digital-trade-getting-it-right/ accessed 25 February 2022; J Meltzer, 'The Internet, Cross-Border Data Flows and International Trade' (2013) Center for Technology Innovation at Brookings, Issues in Technology Innovation No 22, 1, www.brookings.edu/wp-content/uploads/2016/06/internet-data-and-trade-meltzer.pdf accessed 25 February 2022.

[45] J Lockett, 'What Cybersecurity Means for Global Trade' (*World Economic Forum*, 15 September 2015), www.weforum.org/agenda/2015/09/what-cybersecurity-means-for-global-trade/ accessed 25 February 2022.

[46] Meltzer and Kerry (n 44); Meltzer, 'The Internet, Cross-Border Data Flows and International Trade' (n 44).

[47] *Russia – Measures Concerning Traffic in Transit* [2019] WT/DS512 (WTO); *United Arab Emirates – Measures Relating to Trade in Goods and Services, and Trade-Related Aspects of Intellectual Property Rights* [2019] WT/DS526 (WTO) not yet reported; *Japan – Measures Related to the Exportation of Products and Technology to Korea: Request for Consultations by the Republic of Korea* [2020] DS590 (WTO). See WTO, 'Members adopt draft decision to improve tariff and import data, discuss trade concerns' (28 May 2019), www.wto.org/english/news_e/news19_e/mark_28may19_e.htm accessed 25 February 2022; WTO, 'Minutes of the Committee on Market Access, 9 October 2018' (2018) G/MA/M/68; D Ciuriak and M Ptashkina, 'Toward a Robust Architecture for the Regulation of Data and Digital Trade' (2020) CIGI Paper No 240.

[48] K Huang et al, 'Framework for Understanding Cybersecurity Impacts on International Trade' (2019) CISL Working Paper No 2019-23, https://ssrn.com/abstract=3555341 accessed 25 February 2022.

countries gravitate towards the logic that in cyberspace, the offence has the upper hand.[49] In recent years, more than 50 countries have started to publish their cybersecurity strategies, to define the security of the online environment.[50] The EU has been in the vanguard of the development of holistic policies for the entire bloc, with the evolution of the EU Cyber Security Act 2019 and the EU Agency for Cybersecurity ENISA to establish an EU-wide certification scheme. Still, cybersecurity is a highly complex regulatory phenomenon that is heavily dependent on incomplete international law, private power, soft law and practical cooperation, eg information sharing, standard setting (ISO), all of which makes it a somewhat uneasy bedfellow for a trade agreement.

Increasingly, data sovereignty is being emphasised by countries such as Russia and Vietnam as much as by the EU.[51] Data localisation policies which restrict the transfer of data across borders are also on the increase[52] and as a result have become increasingly salient for trade negotiations. Cybersecurity incidents and concerns present many challenges, not least that they potentially present significant barriers to trade and investment.[53] As noted in previous chapters, the EU straddles many of these concerns awkwardly, with its soft data localisation policies and the span of its vast emerging framework on digital regulation. Cybersecurity concerns are also a major source of growing commercial disputes where divergent cybersecurity policies have been evolved. Some commentators present cybersecurity concerns in international trade as more than a regulation compliance issue, and rather as a supply chain and geopolitical problem.[54] Vague definitions of cyber issues, eg critical infrastructures, are also perceived to be highly problematic. Trade agreements increasingly include references to cybersecurity, though the precise formulation varies dramatically, with some placing much emphasis on risk-based approaches to cybersecurity and others relying on consensus-based international standards and practices.[55] The EU's approach to cybersecurity is only embryonic in some of the key trade agreements and negotiations studied in this book. The EU's approach is also reasonably cautious with third countries and even with developed economies is purely voluntary. Yet even in trade agreements, the EU has placed cybersecurity cooperation within regulatory cooperation frameworks as well as in soft law strategic partnership agreement documents. Notably, one of the most ambitious recent agreements, though not the subject of fuller analysis in

[49] ibid, citing W Lynn, 'Defending a New Domain the Pentagon's Cyber Strategy' (2010) 89(5) *Foreign Affairs* 98.

[50] ibid, citing A Klimburg, *National Cyber Security Framework Manual. NATO CCD COE Publication* (NATO, 2013).

[51] Laidlaw (n 42).

[52] M Burri, 'How Should the WTO Respond to the Data-driven Economy' (*CIGI*, 4 May 2020), www.cigionline.org/articles/how-should-wto-respond-data-driven-economy accessed 25 February 2022.

[53] Huang et al (n 48) 3.

[54] ibid.

[55] US-Mexico-Canada Agreement (USMCA), Art 19.15.

this book, is the UK-EU agreement.[56] Cybersecurity can generate import-related trade barriers such as 'prohibition, authorisation or registration requirements' to restrict certain imports or require the importer to obtain authorisations etc. Other barriers relate to the requirement for information traceability concerning the origins of materials and parts, processing history and distribution and location of products after delivery.

The broader framing of cybersecurity also poses challenges, for example, the framing of the IoT and trade in goods and investment in manufacturing.[57] International trade and cybersecurity are increasingly intertwined because of the rise of the Internet and increased use of data flows by businesses and consumers; the end result is the transformation of contemporary trade.[58] Cybersecurity poses many challenges to the digital space, eg cybercrime, as well as the physical space, such as critical infrastructure (eg telecommunications, transport, and health care) and IoT, which relies on software to network services. The task of balancing security and trade is a highly complex one for the institutions involved and for decision-makers and adjudicators. Defining the threats and challenges is itself an incredibly murky area in an era of ever-expanding dual use technologies. Some argue that the large majority of cybersecurity measures do not fall within the limited set of exceptional circumstances provided for in WTO law or that their adjudication and interpretation will generate unfair balances of trade and security interests in an environment of political, technological and policy uncertainty.[59] Cybersecurity and trade thus have further and more broadly complex relationships with the regulation of cross-border data flows.[60]

IV. Cybersecurity Provisions in EU Trade and Cooperation Agreements

Cyber security provisions are increasingly found in EU international relations but mainly in EU strategic partnership agreements, ie soft law agreements, negotiated, signed and ratified alongside trade provisions with partners. They appear to occupy an interesting space in the EU's institutionalisation activities in a variety

[56] More contemporary trade agreements, such as USMCA and DEPA, have retained the national security example language of GATT Art XXI but have dropped the examples and not entered new ones.

[57] In this regard, some consider regulatory cooperation to constitute the key driver for international collaboration on cybersecurity and trade. The EU has largely adopted this stance generally: J Trachtman, 'Cybersecurity Versus Trade in Internet of Things Products' (2019) 16 *Manchester Journal of International Economic Law* 301.

[58] J Meltzer, 'Cybersecurity, Digital Trade, and Data Flows: Re-thinking a Role for International Trade Rules' (2020) Global Economy & Development WP 132.

[59] N Mishra, 'The Trade: (Cyber)Security Dilemma and Its Impact on Global Cybersecurity Governance' (2020) 54 *Journal of World Trade* 567.

[60] AD Mitchell and J Hepburn, 'Don't Fence Me In: Reforming Trade and Investment Law to Better Facilitate Cross-Border Data Transfer' (2016) *The Yale Journal of Law and Technology* 1.

of ways. The EU-Japan Strategic Partnership Agreement (SPA)'s provisions in Article 36 on cybersecurity provided, until recently, a good example of the EU's most robust and broad-ranging set of cybersecurity provisions for a key developed economy trade partner, and could operate as a template for multilevel cooperation. Multilateralism and international law form a key plank of this cooperation and there is a significant effort to learn to collaborate. The EU-Japan SPA thus provides:

1. The Parties shall enhance the exchange of views and information on their respective policies and activities on cyber issues, and shall encourage such exchange of views and information in international and regional fora.
2. The Parties shall enhance cooperation in order to promote and protect human rights and free flow of information to the maximum extent possible in cyberspace. For this purpose, and based on the understanding that international law applies in cyberspace, they shall cooperate, where appropriate, in establishing and developing international norms and promoting confidence building in cyberspace.
3. The Parties shall cooperate, where appropriate, to enhance the ability of third countries to strengthen their cybersecurity and to fight against cybercrime.
4. The Parties shall enhance cooperation in preventing and combating cybercrime, including the distribution of illegal content via the internet.

These provisions on cybersecurity mirror to a degree the provisions in the e-commerce chapters of the EU-Japan Economic Partnership Agreement (EPA) with respect to regulatory cooperation, where cybersecurity cooperation is also referenced. As is outlined further in Chapter 5, the provisions of the EU-Japan EPA in Article 8.80 on regulatory cooperation in digital trade explicitly mention cybersecurity, particularly in Article 8.80.2(b), and this signifies the EPA's place as a next generation agreement of data matters. Such dialogues are a notable and important form of engagement when seen against this backdrop of the SPA grounded in multilateralism. The soft law provisions of the SPA thus interact with and complement the EPA through dual-faceted institutionalisation, ie both bilateral and multilateral. The EU-Japan provisions are of note and may been seen as a high-water mark when contrasted with its predecessor, the EU-Canada SPA of 2016, which made provision for a shorter and lighter form of cyber-based cooperation. The text in the EU-Canada SPA is less predicated upon broader aspects of multilateralism and cyberspace and is instead focused mainly on cybercrime. Arguably, it is a less impressive engagement in the area of cyber cooperation, which probably reflects the significantly more prominent role played by Japan in relation to cyber issues in multilateral forums.[61] The EU-Canada SPA 2016 thus makes provision, in Article 22 on cybercrime, that:[62]

1. The Parties recognise that cybercrime is a global problem requiring global responses. To that end, the Parties shall strengthen cooperation to prevent and combat cybercrime through the exchange of information and practical knowledge,

[61] See Ch 5.

[62] Strategic Partnership Agreement between the European Union and its Member States, of the one part, and Canada, of the other part [2016] OJ L 329/45.

in compliance with their respective legal frameworks and laws. The Parties shall endeavour to work together, where appropriate, to provide assistance and support to other states in the development of effective laws, policies and practices to prevent and combat cybercrime wherever it occurs.

2. The Parties shall, as appropriate within their respective legal frameworks and laws, exchange information in fields including the education and training of cybercrime investigators, the conduct of cybercrime investigations and digital forensics.

The EU-Korea SPA, 2013, was one of the EU's earliest next generation agreements. Similar to the earlier EU-Canada SPA, it contained analogous provisions with respect to breadth, depth and scope, and was subsequently overtaken by considerable innovations in practice which reflect the rising place of cybersecurity as a global challenge for international relations.[63] Although not the focus of this book as a case study, the provisions of the EU-UK TCA mark a highly significant shift in EU trade agreements as to cybersecurity. There, cybersecurity occupies a highly central position unlike in its predecessors. Title II of the TCA makes highly significant provision for thematic cooperation, alongside health cooperation. In a trade agreement devoid of more recent provisions on regulatory cooperation and dialogues based upon multilateralism, the cybersecurity provisions of the TCA are notable for their exceptional commitments to cooperation and multilateralism and also for the breadth of the cooperation, couched in institutional cooperation, eg Article 707 enables participation in ENISA. The provisions are striking also for their detail and their extent, despite being, strictly speaking, essentially voluntary in nature.[64] The provisions also reflect well the 'global challenges' dimension of cybersecurity but ultimately are not well linked to the digital trade chapter of the TCA and despite their depth and breath, ultimately seem to be a missed opportunity.[65] What is noticeable here is a significant shift in the place of

[63] Framework Agreement between the European Union and its Member States, on the one part, and the Republic of Korea, on the other part (EU-Korea Framework Agreement) [2013] OJ L 20/2, Art 37 'Combating cybercrime': '1. The Parties will strengthen cooperation to prevent and combat high technology, cyber and electronic crimes and the distribution of terrorist content via the Internet through exchanging information and practical experiences in compliance with their national legislation within the limits of their responsibility. 2. The Parties will exchange information in the fields of the education and training of cybercrime investigators, the investigation of cybercrime, and digital forensic science.'

[64] The TCA makes extensive provision for participation in EU institutions and EU bodies as to cybersecurity and thus provides for significant forms of institutionalisation. See EU-UK TCA Part Four: Thematic cooperation, Title II: Cybersecurity.

[65] Article CYB.5: Cooperation with the EU Agency for Cybersecurity (ENISA) '1 With a view to promoting cooperation on cyber security while ensuring the autonomy of th Union decision-making process, the United Kingdom may participate at the invitation, which the United Kingdom may also request, of the Management Board of the EU Cybersecurity Agency (ENISA), in the following activities carried out by ENISA: (a) capacity building; (b) knowledge and information; and (c) awareness raising and education. 2. The conditions for the participation of the United Kingdom in ENISA's activities referred to in paragraph 1, including an appropriate financial contribution, shall be set out in working arrangements adopted by the Management Board of ENISA subject to prior approval by the Commission and agreed with the United Kingdom. 3. The exchange of information, experiences and best practices between ENISA and the United Kingdom shall be voluntary and, where appropriate, reciprocal.

cybersecurity in EU international relations and the form of trade agreements, as they widen and deepen.[66] Whether this trend can continue, in the face of limited international law treaties on cybersecurity, remains to be seen.

V. The EU Cybersecurity 'Act', 2019: The Beginnings of 'Strong' Internal and External Institutionalisation?

Internal EU cybercrime policy has historically been situated in an internal market rationale but perhaps mainly theoretically rather than practically.[67] However, a new Cybersecurity Act in 2019 has shifted EU cybersecurity substantially towards the internal market. Internal EU cybercrime and security policies additionally have a relevance to the operation of the internal market, to the safety of consumers and the functioning of business. However, cybersecurity also recently takes its legal position to some degree from CFSP measures. The key legal instrument of the EU's cyber law-making reforms in recent times is the Cybersecurity Act, adopted on the basis of Article 114 TFEU, the key legal basis for the approximation of the internal market. This complex intersection of economic and security policies is underestimated on a regulatory level in its impact on the depth of the institutional framework and architecture of cyber policies. Cybercrime is conventionally said to be differentiated from cybersecurity in a temporal sense: cybercrime relates to the past, whereas cybersecurity relates to the future.[68] The historical absence of a common EU framework on cybersecurity has been the subject of much debate. The EU's law-making in cybercrime and cybersecurity begins in policy terms most concretely with its Cybersecurity Strategy in 2013, which defined cybersecurity extremely broadly.[69] What is significant about the Strategy is its focus on security, and a lack of specificity about the definition of cybercrime to be used.[70] An overwhelming number of legal and policy documents relating to cybersecurity often

[66] See also EU-Korea Framework Agreement, Article 37 Combating cybercrime: '1. The Parties will strengthen cooperation to prevent and combat high technology, cyber and electronic crimes and the distribution of terrorist content via the Internet through exchanging information and practical experiences in compliance with their national legislation within the limits of their responsibility. 2. The Parties will exchange information in the fields of the education and training of cybercrime investigators, the investigation of cybercrime, and digital forensic science'.

[67] Fahey, 'The EU's Cybercrime and Cybersecurity Rule-Making: Mapping the Internal and External Dimensions of EU Security' (n 24).

[68] I Bernik, *Cybercrime and Cyber Warfare* (John Wiley and Sons, 2014) 143.

[69] European Commission, 'Joint Communication to the European Parliament, the Council, the European Economic and Social Committee and the Committee of the Regions – Cybersecurity Strategy of the European Union: An Open, Safe and Secure Cyberspace' JOIN (2013) 1 Final.

[70] Others point to the narrower definition of cybersecurity used by ENISA, distinguishing cybercrime, cyber espionage and cyber warfare: see Odermatt, 'The European Union as a Cybersecurity Actor' (n 2) 356; European Commission, 'Joint Communication – Cybersecurity Strategy of the European Union: An Open, Safe and Secure Cyberspace' (n 69).

begin with a conceptual discussion about what exactly is meant by the term.[71] There are several key questions as a result here with respect to the place of data protection matters, militarisation of EU policy and the place of cybercrime defined imprecisely and somewhat at variance with the Council of Europe Convention.[72]

Earlier EU cyber actors were also particularly weak. For instance, the EU Cybercrime Centre, the so-called 'EC3', was established in 2012 as a 'desk' within Europol.[73] Arguably, this emphasised how earlier EU policy was ideologically antipathetic to institutions. The 2019 Act evolves the powers of ENISA significantly and changes this mindset. ENISA is one of the EU's earliest efforts to institutionalise cyber law-making. At its inception, ENISA had a restricted mandate which involved it mainly engaging with national law enforcement bodies on security aspects of cybercrime.[74] The Act of 2019 has enlarged ENISA's mandate, giving it more powers and resources to support Member States, a permanent status and authority to establish cybersecurity certification. Ultimately, it is heavily reliant on many national and technical support actors. Thus bifurcated action challenges its capacity to generate strong and autonomous institutions. It is also important to say that there are other internal developments of note as to other actors. In the new European Commission of 2019, cybercrime and security traverse many general directorates beyond the internal market.[75] It is a very broad, institutionalised and balanced composition of teams on one level, but also seeks to separate content in ways that are not necessarily aligned with actual law-making. Post-Lisbon, there are also ostensibly several legal bases in the treaties *outside* of the internal market rationale that are not yet used to regulate cybercrime and security. Instead, aside

[71] Odermatt, 'The European Union as a Cybersecurity Actor' (n 2).

[72] eg NM Schmitt (ed), *Prepared by the International Group of Experts at the Invitation of the NATO Cooperative Cyber Defence Centre of Excellence: Talinn Manual on the International Law applicable to Cyber-Warfare* (Cambridge University Press, 2013); The European Data Protection Supervisor, 'Opinion of the European Data Protection Supervisor on the Cyber Security Strategy and Directive' (2013), https://secure.edps.europa.eu/EDPSWEB/edps/Consultation/OpinionsC accessed 25 February 2022.

[73] European Commission, 'Communication from the Commission to the Council and the European Parliament: Tackling Crime in our Digital Age: Establishing a European Cybercrime Centre' COM (2012) 140 final. Its purpose was institutional and strategic and has been established within an evolving EU agency, Europol, thereby forming an EU focal point in fighting cybercrime, fusing information and informing Member States of threats. EC3 notably had no explicit association with cybersecurity. Thus an EU actor for cybercrime monitoring was established arguably *prior* to the development of a cybercrime and cybersecurity strategy, which may be described as a complex form of institutionalisation. See Fahey, 'Institutionalising EU Cyber Law: Can the EU Institutionalise Its Many Subjects and Objects?' (n 13) 17.

[74] Fahey, 'Institutionalising EU Cyber Law: Can the EU Institutionalise Its Many Subjects and Objects?' (n 13) 15. This task built on ENISA's role as secretariat of the National Computer Security Incident Response Teams (CSIRTs) Network, established by Directive (EU) 2016/1148 of the European Parliament and of the Council of 6 July 2016 concerning measures for a high common level of security of network and information systems across the Union (2016) OJ L194/1.

[75] Fahey, 'Developing EU Cybercrime and Cybersecurity: On Legal Challenges of EU Institutionalisation of Cyber Law-Making' (n 27).

from the internal market, sanctions constitute the major alternative law-making tool,[76] as executive led law-making and are discussed next. It suffices to say that the external relations dimensions of these questions are highly significant and arguably awkwardly dominant despite the legal tools deployed.

VI. The Institutional Design of 5G Regulation: The Periphery of the Single Market and the Global

Data is an increasingly multifaceted concept that is bound up with trade and commercial matters as much as security and law enforcement issues, as the global issues relating to Huawei 5G indicate.[77] This means that it is essential to pay combined attention to trade and security, particularly law enforcement issues. Increased digitalisation of information, the rising power of private companies, delimiting access to that information, and the cross-border nature of investigations involving digital evidence have changed our understanding of access to data and jurisdictional limits on access.[78] The challenge of the security/trade nexus as to data regulatory capture cannot be overstated. The EU law applicable to 5G networks is at best sketchy and dominated by a lack of clarity about where national law ends and EU law could possibly begin. This is because it is also dominated by internal market considerations and its internal and external dimensions are difficult to unpack.[79] It is pivotal to many other EU data policies, from AI to trade, and so this remains something of a legal vacuum. Data policies are increasingly embedded in subjects such as security where significant national competences exist. In theory, EU Member States retain sole competence for matters of national security and the EU's role is merely complementary. In 2019 the European Commission issued a non-binding recommendation on the cybersecurity of 5G networks. On the one hand, however, it identified technical factors as risks to 5G network security, such

[76] For example, there are grounds in the treaties to legislate for procedural EU criminal law in Art 82 TFEU, allowing for the Parliament and Council to establish minimum rules to the extent necessary to facilitate mutual recognition of judgments and judicial decisions and police and judicial cooperation in criminal matters having a cross-border dimension. In Art 83 TFEU, there is competence for the EU to enact substantive criminal law. More specifically, Art 83(1) TFEU provides that the Parliament and Council may establish minimum rules concerning the definition of criminal law offences and sanctions in the area of particularly serious crime with a cross border dimension resulting from the impact of such offences or need to combat such offences jointly. This provision includes thereafter a list of crimes in which the EU has legislative competence which specifically includes terrorism. Article 83(2) TFEU also provides for harmonisation in the event to ensure the effective implementation of EU policy already subject to harmonisation measures.

[77] M Stevis-Gridneff, 'Without Naming Huawei, EU Warns Against 5G Firms From "Hostile" Powers' (*New York Times*, 9 October 2019), www.nytimes.com/2019/10/09/world/europe/eu-huawei-report.html accessed 25 February 2022.

[78] Daskal (n 38).

[79] M Varju, '5G Networks, (Cyber)security Harmonisation and the Internal Market: The Limits of Article 114 TFEU' (2020) 45 *European Law Review* 471.

as communication networks' technological vulnerability to cyber-attacks. On the other, the recommendation specifically warned that 5G technology suppliers may pose a security risk, especially those from third states.[80] It might also be said that recent case law creates significant challenges for the EU legislature, setting out important national security exemptions in a series of cases that appeared to stamp out surveillance generally. In this instance, the institutionalisation of data becomes a parallel track of regulatory development.[81]

The new fifth generation of telecommunications systems of 5G will be one of the most critical blocks of the digital economy and society. 5G will provide virtually ubiquitous ultra-high bandwidth and low latency connectivity and will serve a wide range of applications and sectors. It will be the eyes and ears of AI systems and is said to bring the cloud to a new dimension.[82] As the EU's cybersecurity agency, ENISA, has outlined, the threat landscape for 5G networks is immense. Yet the legal dimension of this remains highly ambiguous.[83] EU law matters relating to 5G is currently regulated by a complex web of provisions but ultimately depend on national strategies. A European 5G Observatory has been established with a view to deepening exchanges at the EU level. A European Parliament resolution of 1 June 2017 on internet connectivity for growth, competitiveness and cohesion welcomed the Commission's proposal to draw up a 5G action plan aimed at making the EU a world leader in the deployment of standardised 5G networks from 2020 to 2025 as part of a developed strategy for a 'European Gigabit Society'. A Ministerial Declaration on making 5G a success for Europe was signed in 2017 to establish a common baseline on future 5G standards. Parallel negotiations on a European Electronic Communications Code have progressed also to set the conditions to facilitate the deployment of future networks. All Member States have adopted a National Broadband Plan and a few Member Ctates are close to reaching the targets set out in the Digital Agenda for Europe. Several Member States have already published preliminary proposals to facilitate the rollout of 5G networks. In ongoing work, working groups could not identify any major actions relating to national security at national level. One of the most significant features of the EU's 5G vision is that it is intended to enhance Internet *architectures and structures* in existing and emerging areas, such as machine-to-machine communication and the IoT. It is thus atypical of EU regulatory capture in many other domains. Ultimately, as Varju states, this securitisation and politicisation of the EU's 5G policy means that it is unlikely that its implementation can rely solely on the well-tried tactic of adopting internal market harmonisation measures under Article 114 TFEU.[84]

[80] ibid 474.

[81] Case C-311/18 *Data Protection Commissioner v Facebook Ireland Limited, Maximillian Schrems* (*Schrems II*) EU:C:2020:559; Case C-623/17 *Privacy International* EU:C:2020:790; Joined Cases C-511/18, C-512/18 and C-520/18 *La Quadrature du Net and Others*, EU:C:2020:791.

[82] European Commission, 'Shaping Europe's Digital future: Towards 5G' (2020).

[83] ENISA, 'ENISA Threat Landscape for 5G Networks: Threat Assessment for the fifth generation of mobile telecommunications networks (5G)' (November 2019).

[84] Varju (n 79) 485.

Yet many other regulatory measures relating to 5G appear to be increasingly based on Article 114 TFEU, eg as part of the Shaping Europe's Future Initiative or a Directive on a Communications Code, showing the nature of the EU's use of this key legal 'fire-power'.[85] It is difficult within any of these initiatives to garner sensitivity to international relations issues beyond defensive bluster. The significant disputes with the Chinese corporation, Huawei, discussed further in Chapter 6 put these developments into perspective. In fact, here the place of the internal market has yet to achieve an institutional equilibrium and shows the complexity of the EU's position as to cyber law-making.

VII. EU-Council of Europe Relations: Fostering Stronger Institutionalised Spaces?

The Council of Europe Cybercrime Convention (the Budapest Convention) is considered the most significant multilateral arrangement that specifically addresses aspects of cyber-attacks and exploitation. It is a law-enforcement treaty focusing on many types of action against the integrity of cyber systems. The Budapest Convention forms the basis for all EU, EU-US and to some extent US law as a form of 'transnational gold standard'. It is over 20 years old and has one of the largest global memberships of states in the field.[86] In addition, many other states align their laws with the Convention.[87] The Budapest Convention can be criticised for its appearance of unduly reflecting law enforcement standards or for its complex broader relationship with the regulatory framework of the Council of Europe, particularly as to individual rights, eg privacy. Most EU Member States have signed and ratified the Convention.[88] The Budapest Convention adopts a broad perspective on cybercrime.[89] It is the most far-reaching multilateral agreement on cybercrime in existence, purporting to harmonise national legislation procedurally. There is a particular emphasis in contemporary Council of Europe

[85] Thanks to Ben Farrand for this suggestion. See European Commission, 'Communication from the Commission to The European Parliament, The Council, The European Economic and Social Committee and The Committee of The Regions: Shaping Europe's digital future' COM (2020) 67 final; Directive (EU) 2018/1972 of the European Parliament and of the Council of 11 December 2018 establishing the European Electronic Communications Code [2018] OJ L321/36.

[86] See Council of Europe, 'Parties/Observers to the Budapest Convention and Observer Organisations to the T-CY', www.coe.int/en/web/cybercrime/parties-observers accessed 25 February 2022.

[87] See also Fahey, 'The EU's Cybercrime and Cybersecurity Rule-Making: Mapping the Internal and External Dimensions of EU Security' (n 24).

[88] Council of Europe, 'Chart of signatures and ratifications of Treaty 185, Convention on Cybercrime' (10 December 2019), www.coe.int/en/web/conventions/full-list/-/conventions/treaty/185/signatures accessed 25 February 2022.

[89] It is criticised for its overbroad content, its lack of provision for cross-border enforcement and the obligations it imposes on Internet Service Providers, and also for the fact that it does not purport to regulate cybersecurity. The Convention distinguishes between various types of offences. In addition, criminal terms such as cyber terrorism or phishing cover acts that may fall within several different categories. The Convention does not contain as many definitional conceptions of cybercrime.

cybercrime policy on its effect on the dichotomy of hard and soft law and the relevance of jurisdiction, conceptual focuses that appear surprising.[90] For the Council of Europe, placing limits on the extra-territorial exercise of jurisdiction in relation to transnational cybercrimes has been essential; this contrasts with the position under US law.[91] Yet what should the Convention be aiming for? Is its focus in reality conventional rather than progressive? Such a focus appears troubling from the transnational 'gold-standard', as one centred exclusively around enforcement as opposed to rights-based law-making.

The Budapest Convention has only recently adopted significant reforms on transborder access to data and cloud evidence in the form of a protocol.[92] In June 2017, the parties agreed terms of reference for the preparation of the Protocol and negotiations commenced in September 2017.[93] The EU has had to consider the impact of such reforms on its other legislation, eg GDPR. In its negotiation directives, the EU raised the issue of e-evidence regimes and third countries, such as the US.[94] The Commission and other EU institutions had a key role in the development of the Protocol, strikingly similar to the privileged place of the CJEU at the negotiation on accession to the European Convention on Human Rights (ECHR).[95] In fact an EU-specific 'disconnection' clause caused much controversy when it appeared to suggest that only EU law would be applied between EU Member States; whether this might accord with the autonomy of EU law seems to be of much significance.[96] As Polakiewicz states, a rather successful outcome nonetheless arguably resulted

[90] Council of Europe, 'Recommendation and Explanatory Memorandum – The Protection of Individuals with Regard to Automatic Processing of Personal Data in the Context of Profiling' CM/Rec 13 (Council of Europe Publishing 2010).

[91] O Hathaway et al, 'The Law of Cyber-Attack' (2012) 100 *California Law Review* 817.

[92] Polakiewicz, 'The Emperor's New Clothes – Data Privacy and Cybersecurity from a European Perspective' (n 6); J Daskal and D Kennedy-Mayo, 'Budapest Convention: What Is It and How Is It Being Updated?' (*Cross Border Data Forum*, 2 July 2020), www.crossborderdataforum.org/budapest-convention-what-is-it-and-how-is-it-being-updated/ accessed 25 February 2022. See also Daskal (n 38); T Christakis and F Terpan, 'EU-US Negotiations on Law Enforcement Access to Data: Divergences, Challenges and EU Law Procedures and Options' (2021) *International Data Privacy Law* 1.

[93] Provisions on more efficient mutual legal assistance; provisions on direct cooperation with providers in other jurisdictions; framework and safeguards for existing practices of extending searches transborder; rule of law and data protection safeguards. The Parties to the Convention have been looking to reform access to electronic evidence by judicial and police authorities through a Second Additional Protocol which would address those challenges by ensuring greater international cooperation.

[94] Two recommendations to participate in the Second Additional protocol and to open negotiation with the US were adopted by the Commission in 2019: see European Commission, 'Recommendation for a Council Decision Authorising the Opening of Negotiations in View of an Agreement between the European Union and the United States of America on Cross-Border Access to Electronic Evidence for Judicial Cooperation in Criminal Matters' COM(2019) 70 final; European Commission, 'Recommendation for a Council Decision Authorising the Participation in Negotiations on a Second Additional Protocol to the Council of Europe Convention on Cybercrime (CETS No. 185)' COM(2019) 71 final.

[95] ibid.

[96] 'Legal Opinion on Budapest Cybercrime Convention: use of disconnection clause in Second Additional Protocol to the Council of Europe Convention on Cybercrime' (29 April 2019), www.coe.int/en/web/dlapil/-/use-of-a-disconnection-clause-in-the-second-additional-protocol-to-the-budapest-convention-on-cybercri-1 accessed 25 February 2022.

from this.[97] The Member States of the EU are bound by the GDPR and the Data Protection Law Enforcement Directive (Directive 2016/680).[98] The CJEU held in *La Quadrature du Net* that any processing of personal data by service providers, be it the mere disclosure or the transmission of personal data to state authorities for law enforcement purposes, falls within the scope of the GDPR and the e-Privacy Directive.[99] There was no margin for EU Member States to apply any standards other than EU law, eg international law. After lengthy and difficult negotiations, a compromise between the EU and the Council of Europe was reached, providing for flexibility to permit adaptation to different legal systems and to evolving technology, business models and interpretation by the courts, arguably giving significant precedence to Convention 108.[100] It is understood to have sufficient leeway to engage with the EU-US Umbrella Agreement and its evolution. The compromise reached formulates a freestanding set of data protection safeguards[101] and requirements for the onward transfer of data.[102]

A broader phenomenon of EU international relations law has still seen the autonomy of EU law operate as a barrier to deeper institutionalisation.[103] It has emerged as a complex statement of EU distinctiveness. It has origins in a vast array of case law covering an immense span of EU legal subjects over a number of years. The resulting uneasy relationship between EU and international law was the subject of, for example, inconclusive studies by the International Law Commission and also the Council of Europe's Committee of Legal Advisers on Public International Law.[104] The autonomy of EU law has seen the case law of the CJEU increasingly inhibit institutionalisation beyond the state (eg Opinion 2/13 ECHR accession). More recent case law such as Opinion 2/17 may indicate a step back from the most extreme version of this position.[105] The autonomy of EU law

[97] Polakiewicz, 'The Emperor's New Clothes – Data Privacy and Cybersecurity from a European Perspective' (n 6). However, after the Cybercrime Committee rushed through the last steps of the negotiations to finalise the new Additional Protocol, there is concern that as an international agreement of the EU, the Protocol will be superior to EU secondary laws and may undermine important safeguards in these instruments.

[98] Directive (EU) 2016/680 of the European Parliament and of the Council of 27 April 2016 on the protection of natural persons with regard to the processing of personal data by competent authorities for the purposes of the prevention, investigation, detection or prosecution of criminal offences or the execution of criminal penalties, and on the free movement of such data, and repealing Council Framework Decision 2008/977/JHA [2016] OJ L 119/89.

[99] *La Quadrature du Net and Others* (n 81) 162–63.

[100] See Council of Europe, 'Summary of comments on opinions by Council of Europe Committees and submissions by other stakeholders on the draft 2nd Additional Protocol to the Convention on Cybercrime' (May 2021), Note prepared by T-CY Secretariat, T-CY (2021)12 dated 28 May 2021, 3–4.

[101] ibid 12 as regards Art 14 – Protection of personal data.

[102] ibid 12 as to Art 14 (10) – Onward transfer to another State or international organisation.

[103] Polakiewicz, 'The Emperor's New Clothes – Data Privacy and Cybersecurity from a European Perspective' (n 6); M Cremona, 'The Opinion Procedure under Article 218(11) TFEU: Reflections in the Light of Opinion 1/17' (2020) *Europe and the World: A Law Review*, www.scienceopen.com/hosted-document?doi=10.14324/111.444.ewlj.2020.22 accessed 25 February 2022.

[104] Council of Europe, 'Report on the consequences of the so-called "disconnection clause" in international law in general and for Council of Europe conventions, containing such a clause, in particular' (8 October 2008).

[105] Cremona (n 103); Opinion 2/13 of the ECJ on EU Accession to the ECHR of 18 December 2014, EU:C:2014:2454.

increasingly still 'bites' and complicates how the EU engages with international law, international organisations and third countries, from the UK Brexit negotiations to the ongoing negotiations with the US with respect to e-evidence.[106] Autonomy, or a claim to a legal order autonomous from the national law of Member States, as well as from international law, has been even labelled the single most far-reaching, and probably most disputed, principle of the EU.[107] Famously, the principle of the autonomy of EU law was given force in Opinion 2/13, where the CJEU concluded that the draft agreement on the EU's accession to the ECHR was not in accordance with the Treaties and Protocol. Autonomy is regularly and explicitly mentioned in external relations case law when the CJEU has sought to preserve its exclusive jurisdiction to interpret and apply EU law, see eg *MOX Plant*,[108] *Achmea*,[109] *Wightman*[110] or *Komstroy*.[111] The extent to which it is a principle, rule or theory remains a finer point of EU law yet to be resolution. It has evolved into a significant range of CJEU case law as a blockade against further integration, further institutionalisation or deeper engagement with international organisations, as a shield and sword.[112] This principle increasingly has become also problematic for US negotiations with the EU on e-evidence issues and the Council of Europe. How the autonomy of EU law is understood outside of the EU legal order is increasingly a matter of concern in a wide variety of legal fields. Does it acutely affect the US if deeper forms of convergence are proposed or planned? Does it exacerbate existing differences?[113] Perhaps ironically given the challenges

[106] KS Ziegler and V Moreno-Lax, 'Autonomy of the EU Legal Order – A General Principle? On the Risks of Normative Functionalism and Selective Constitutionalisation' in K Ziegler et al (eds), *Research Handbook on General Principles in EU Law: Constructing Legal Orders in Europe* (Edward Elgar, forthcoming); Christakis and Terpan (n 92); Cremona (n 103).

[107] D Kukuvec, 'The Court of Justice of the European Union for Hedgehogs' (2021) *Jean Monnet Working Paper* 1/21, https://jeanmonnetprogram.org/wp-content/uploads/JMWP-01_Damjan-Kukovec.pdf accessed 25 February 2022.

[108] Case C-459/03 *Commission of the European Communities v Ireland (MOX Plant)* EU:C:2006:345.

[109] Case C-284/16 *Slowakische Republik v Achmea BV* EU:C:2018:158.

[110] Case C-621/18 *Andy Wightman and Others v Secretary of State for Exiting the European Union* EU:C:2018:999.

[111] Case C-741/19 *République de Moldavie v Komstroy LLC* EU:C:2021:655.

[112] Odermatt, 'The European Union as a Cybersecurity Actor' (n 2); Polakiewicz, 'The Emperor's New Clothes – Data Privacy and Cybersecurity from a European Perspective' (n 6).

[113] Case C-459/03 *Commission v Ireland* ECLI:EU:C:2006:345; Joined Cases C-402/05 P and C-415/05 P *Yassin Abdullah Kadi and Al Barakaat International Foundation v Council of the European Union and Commission of the European Communities* EU:C:2008:461; Opinion 1/09 of the Court (Full Court) (European Patent Court) EU:C:2011:123; Opinion 2/13 of the Court (Full Court) (Accession to ECHR) EU:C:2014:2454; Opinion 2/15 of the Court (Full Court) of 16 May 2017 EU:C:2017:376; Case C-284/16 *Slowakische Republik v Achmea BV* EU:C:2018:158; Opinion 1/17 of the Court (Full Court) 30 April 2019 EU:C:2019:341; Case C-621/18 *Andy Wightman and Others v Secretary of State for Exiting the European Union* EU:C:2018:999; *Micula v Romania*, Case No 17-cv-02332 (DDC 11 September 2019) US Court of Appeals (2nd Circ); *Micula v Romania*, Case No 17-cv-02332 (DDC 11 September 2019) US Court of Appeals (2nd Circ), Brief for Amicus Curiae the Commission of the European Union in Support of Defendant-Appellant, 4 February 2016; X Groussot and ML Öberg, 'The Web of Autonomy of the EU Legal Order: Achmea' in G Butler and R Wessel (eds), *EU External Relations Law: The Cases in Context* (Bloomsbury, forthcoming); C Binder and J Hofbauer, 'The Perception of the EU Legal Order in International Law: An In- and Outside View' (2017) 8 *European Yearbook of International*

of EU-ECHR accession, EU-Council of Europe cooperation is arguably the most collaborative and flexible engagement that the EU has in terms of its autonomy in the cyber domain. Cooperation between the Council of Europe and the EU has been – and could continue to be – strengthened through a more rational, rules-based approach. Amendments to the Budapest Convention demonstrate the challenges of the EU seeking to act as a global actor and a very important limitation of the 'global' in a forum where the EU can, in theory, have influence. In particular, it is suggested that the two systems should jointly agree on a series of basic principles on the treaty-making process, providing for horizontal application by the introduction of specific rules on, for example, voting and speaking rights of the EU, the sharing of reporting obligations between the EU and its Member States under Council of Europe monitoring mechanisms, and financial arrangements. The EU's participation and financial contribution to monitoring follow-up could always be considered on a case-by-case basis, taking into account the specificities of each mechanism.[114]

Next, three specific third countries are considered in relation to their cybersecurity links with the EU. Cybersecurity cooperation between the EU-US, the EU-Japan and the EU-China are considered, in a brief introduction to the three major third countries that form the following chapters.

VIII. Case Studies

A. EU-US Cybercrime and Cybersecurity Cooperation

The difference in cybersecurity approaches between the EU and US presents major regulatory challenges for many businesses operating in the EU and US, with the voluntary approach of the US contrasting with the compulsory approach provided for by the EU.[115] The US cybersecurity approach involves private actors at all stages

Economic Law 139; J Odermatt, 'When a Fence Becomes a Cage: The Principle of Autonomy in EU External Relations Law' (2016) EUI Working Paper MWP 2016/07; M Fanou, 'The CETA ICS and the Autonomy of the EU Legal Order in Opinion 1/17 – A Compass for the Future' (2020) 22 *Cambridge Yearbook of European Legal Studies* 1; P Eeckhout, 'Opinion 2/13 on EU Accession to the ECHR and Judicial Dialogue: Autonomy or Autarky' (2015) 38(4) *Fordham International Law Journal* 955; T Lock, 'Walking on a Tightrope: The Draft ECHR Accession Agreement and the Autonomy of the EU Legal Order' (2011) 48 *Common Market Law Review* 1025.

[114] J Polakiewicz, 'A Council of Europe Perspective on the European Union: Crucial and complex cooperation' (April 2021) *Europe and the World: a Law Review*, www.scienceopen.com/document?vid=fa37e975-2539-4343-93dc-f92efbf7ec95 accessed 25 February 2022.

[115] See European Union – External Action, 'Fact Sheet: EU-US cooperation on cyber security and cyberspace' (26 March 2014), http://eeas.europa.eu/archives/docs/statements/docs/2014/140326_01_en.pdf accessed 25 February 2022; European Parliament, 'Understanding the EU's approach to cyber diplomacy and cyber defence' (2020) EPRS Policy Brief, www.europarl.europa.eu/RegData/etudes/BRIE/2020/651937/EPRS_BRI(2020)651937_EN.pdf accessed 25 February 2022.

of rule-making and enforcement; the EU AFSJ is becoming increasingly similar.[116] The EU-US Working Group on Cybersecurity and Cybercrime was the first major transatlantic cooperation in security a decade after 9/11, as a different form of cooperation from the post-9/11 terrorism related cooperation. The origins of this cooperation date back to the Joint EC-US Task Force on Critical Infrastructure Protection a decade earlier, and at about the same time, the Budapest Convention was adopted, forming a central legal element of EU-US cooperation.[117] The degree of institutionalisation of cyber cooperation between the EU and US has increased significantly irrespective of the administrations, and follows other forms of transatlantic security institutionalisation in placing staff on the ground. For example, the EU Cybercrime Centre, 'EC3', within Europol has a full-time liaison officer from the FBI working in The Hague.[118] The State Department and the European External Action Service remain core partners in cyber diplomacy. Some assert that out of the dozens of instruments available to the EU and US to achieve their cybersecurity policy goals, many are common to both sides and, of those, approximately 20 are feasible tools for joint implementation.[119] The number of legal instruments that unifies the EU and US in reality relates only to one, the Budapest Cybercrime Convention. Nonetheless, it seems beyond dispute that transatlantic cooperation would be beneficially globally, given the stalemate at the UN in cyber matters.[120] Closer cooperation with the US, with its own equally significant interagency process, could ultimately improve awareness of threats.[121] As noted above, the

[116] H Carrapico and B Farrand, 'When Trust Fades, Facebook Is No Longer a Friend: Shifting Privatisation Dynamics in the Context of Cybersecurity as a Result of Disinformation, Populism and Political Uncertainty' (2021) 59 *Journal of Common Market Studies* 1160.

[117] It entered into force on 1 July 2004 and was drafted by the Council of Europe Member States and Canada, Japan, South Africa and the US. See E Fahey, *The Global Reach of EU Law* (Routledge 2017) 127.

[118] Europol, Operational Agreements, www.europol.europa.eu/partners-agreements/operational-agreements?page=1 accessed 25 February 2022.

[119] J Schuetze, 'The Future for EU-US Cybersecurity Cooperation' (*Directions*, 26 November 2020), https://directionsblog.eu/the-future-for-eu-us-cybersecurity-cooperation/ accessed 25 February 2022.

[120] F Delarue, *Cyber Operations and International Law* (Cambridge University Press, 2020); G Christou, 'Transatlantic Cooperation in Cybersecurity: Converging on Security as Resilience?' in G Christou, *Cybersecurity in the European Union* (Palgrave Macmillan, 2016). The practical need for more US-EU collaboration on cybersecurity policy is identified by policymakers and diplomats from the EU and the US in their official Cyber Dialogues 2018 and 2019 as well as by international cybersecurity policy scholars such as George Christou and Julia Schuetze. See respectively European Commission, 'Joint Communication to the European Parliament, the European Council and the Council: A new EU-US Agenda for Global Change' JOIN (2020) 22 final; Schuetze, 'The Future for EU-US Cybersecurity Cooperation' (n 119).

[121] Schuetze, 'The Future for EU-US Cybersecurity Cooperation' (n 119). Regular exchanges regarding the cyber threat landscape would enable the development of a shared understanding over malicious cyber activities and their effects, creating an opportunity for the EU and the US to coordinate responses. These could be driven by the EU Intelligence and Situation Centre (INTCEN), an intelligence body of the European External Action Service, to gather information, prepare analyses and political assessments about a single event, or across events. This role is pursued in close cooperation with the CSIRTs network chaired by the rotating EU Presidency, the EC3, ENISA or CERT-EU: S Herpig and J Schuetze, 'Transatlantic Cyber Forum – Cooperating on Borderless Cyber Security Challenges' in

parties to the Budapest Convention searched for solutions for some time on trans-border access to data and cloud evidence.[122] In its negotiation directives, the EU has raised the issue of consistency with respect to e-evidence regimes and third countries, in particular the US after the CLOUD Act and the autonomy of the EU legal order. The place of the US as an innovator with the EU remains to be seen and is discussed further in Chapter 4.

B. EU-Japan Cybersecurity Cooperation

EU cybersecurity cooperation with Japan has many soft law and hard law comparisons of note and has a vibrant multilevel dimension. As outlined above, and further considered in Chapter 5, the provisions of the EU-Japan EPA regulatory cooperation in digital trade explicitly mention cybersecurity, in Article 8.80.2(b); this signifies the EPA's place as a next generation agreement on data matters. EU-Japan cybersecurity cooperation is also an explicit part of the related SPA. This dual-faceted reference to cyber law-making in both hard and soft law is of much importance.[123] Japan has significantly internationalised its cybersecurity policy in recent years, putting multilateralism and internationalisation at the forefront thereof, as is evident from its first and second national security strategy on information security.[124] The central place of Europe, along with the US, as a key partner of Japan, which participates in about 10 key cyber dialogues, is evident from the Japan-EU Internet Security Forum and the Convention on Cybercrime initiated by the Council of Europe, as well as the bilateral Japan-UK Cyber Dialogue.[125]

In 2013, Japan issued its first Cybersecurity Strategy with the objective of becoming a 'world-leading' cyberspace power.[126] The Strategy was updated and revised, in particular in 2018.[127] Japan is signatory to the Budapest Convention and has

D Feldner (ed), *Redesigning Organizations* (Springer 2020); J Schuetze, 'EU-US Cybersecurity Policy Coming Together: Recommendations for Instruments to Accomplish Joint Strategic Goals' (2020) EU Cyber Direct Research Paper, https://eucyberdirect.eu/content_research/eu-us-cybersecurity-policy-coming-together-recommendations-for-instruments-to-accomplish-joint-strategic-goals/ accessed 25 February 2022.

[122] Polakiewicz, 'The Emperor's New Clothes – Data Privacy and Cybersecurity from a European Perspective' (n 6); Daskal and Kennedy-Mayo (n 92); Daskal (n 38); Christakis and Terpan (n 92).

[123] This dual-faceted trend increasingly emerges in trade agreements, where cybersecurity emerges in the agreement, ie *beyond* a soft law strategic partnership agreement (or other non-binding document to accompany the trade agreement). However, in the EU-UK TCA, the cybersecurity cooperation provisions are particularly detailed.

[124] Information Security Policy Council Japan, 'International Strategy on Cybersecurity Cooperation: J-Initiative for Cybersecurity' (2013), www.nisc.go.jp/eng/pdf/InternationalStrategyonCybersecurityCooperation_e.pdf accessed 25 February 2022.

[125] W Vosse, *Japan's Cyber Diplomacy* (2019), 6, https://eucyberdirect.eu/research/japans-cyber-diplomacy accessed 7 March 2022.

[126] ibid 3. See also Y Nitta, 'Japan's Approach Towards International Strategy on Cyber Security Cooperation' (2013) 2013 World Cyberspace Cooperation Summit IV (WCC4), https://cybersummit.info/sites/cybersummit.info/files/Japan_edited%20v2.pdf-FINAL.pdf accessed 25 February 2022.

[127] Japan's 2018 update of its Cybersecurity Strategy is available in Japanese only: www.nisc.go.jp/conference/cs/dai17/pdf/17shiryou02.pdf accessed 25 February 2022. See M Matsubara, 'How Japan's

emphasised the importance of multilateralism, for example, in its Cybersecurity Strategies of 2013 and 2015.[128] It is significant, in terms of Japan's cooperation with the EU and US in this domain, that Japan's cooperation is underpinned by international institutions. This commitment to multilateralism is also a key plank of the EU-Japan EPA regulatory cooperation in digital trade, which explicitly mentions cybersecurity and the capacity to work together in multilateral forums in Article 8.80.2(b). In 2014, an EU-Japan cyber dialogue was launched in recognition of the necessity for a safe, open and secure cyberspace, to promote cooperation on cyberspace through exchanges of experience and knowledge. The EU has also been active in forums such as the Asian Regional Forum and the Association of Southeast Asian Nations (ASEAN), where it has sought to support discussion on cybersecurity confidence building measures. The EU has sponsored events and workshops[129] to enable it to work effectively with Japan in such forums as the UN, ASEAN, the OECD and NATO in particular. It is said that whilst the Japanese emphasis on deterrence and militarisation implies a more enhanced strategic relationship with the US in the area of cyber defence, its broader strategic interests and vision for security in cyberspace also point to strategic cooperation with like-minded regional organisations such as the EU (and its Member States), in order to address what are perceived as common challenges (cybercrime, cyber espionage, securing the business environment) to ensure that their common normative vision for the Internet and the norms and laws of cyberspace constructed around it (UN Charter, international humanitarian law) are applied, enforced and adhered to globally.[130] It is reasonable to state that, from a legal perspective, such views are borne out well in the early years of the post-EPA/ SPA collaborations. With China perceived by Japan to be the main threat to its cybersecurity and broader security, the EU and Japan are understood to stand on shared intellectual ground.[131] In 2020 and later in 2021, the EU and Japan were engaged in cybersecurity drills.[132] This is an important backdrop against which to view the EPA and its implementation. EU-Japan collaboration on cybersecurity has been led by ENISA, eg capacity building with Japan in 2020.

The nature of the convergence taking place appears significant on one level but also strategically aligned and well placed for further development, a partnership

New Cybersecurity Strategy Will Bring the Country up to Par With the Rest of the World' (*Council on Foreign Relations*, 4 June 2018), www.cfr.org/blog/how-japans-new-cybersecurity-strategy-will-bring-country-par-rest-world accessed 25 February 2022.

[128] G Christou, 'The EU's Approach to Cybersecurity' (2017) University of Essex Discussion Paper: EU-Japan Security Cooperation: Challenges and Opportunities project.

[129] ibid 8–9.

[130] ibid 9.

[131] ibid.

[132] See Y Tajima, 'Japan to lead first cyber defense drill with ASEAN, US and Europe' (*Nikkei Asia*, 9 August 2020), https://asia.nikkei.com/Business/Technology/Japan-to-lead-first-cyber-defense-drill-with-ASEAN-US-and-Europe accessed 25 February 2022; European Commission, 'International cooperation: EU, Japan and the US in joint cybersecurity training' (15 March 2021), https://digital-strategy.ec.europa.eu/en/news/international-cooperation-eu-japan-and-us-joint-cybersecurity-training accessed 25 February 2022.

of interesting 'like-mindedness'. These developments matter because they show institutionalisation provisions on regulatory cooperation taking effect with multilateral consequences. This differs sharply from, for example, the EU-UK TCA, which disconnects digital trade and cybersecurity as binding provisions and places cybersecurity in less binding dialogue oriented thematic cooperation (ie not in Part II title III along with digital trade) although it does have many key cybersecurity cooperation provisions of note, as outlined above.[133]

C. EU-China Cybersecurity

As outlined further below, one the greatest challenges for understanding China and cyber law issues is that there is no agreed understanding of the meaning of the Chinese 'State', ie what China is in this context, despite its increasing significance in global technology.[134] Network connectivity has been critical in China's post-2008 restructuring, and the unprecedented role of the Internet in China's contemporary political economy.[135] China introduced a Cybersecurity Law (CSL) in 2019, with the aim to protect national security.[136] Article 1 of the CSL emphasises cyberspace sovereignty, national security, social and public interest to protect the lawful rights and interests of citizens. It imposes additional obligations on critical information infrastructure operators and other infrastructure that may endanger national security, pursuant to Article 31. As there is a data localisation requirement for operators of critical information infrastructure, such a provision can extend the scope of information access by the government. Strikingly, China has ostensibly sought to emulate the EU's GDPR in its Personal Information Protection Law in 2021, as outlined further in Chapter 6, but mainly incorporating several GDPR concepts into Chinese law merely de jure rather than de facto. Unlike to the EU approach to cybersecurity, which is defensive, centred on law and resilience, and focused on multi-stakeholder approaches, China's approach to cybersecurity is driven by the central objective of establishing cyber sovereignty within China. It ensures that the respect for national sovereignty becomes one of the guiding principles governing global cyberspace. The authoritarian dimensions to cyber sovereignty exercised are manifested, for example as to Chinese control of key Internet corporations such as Alibaba, where there is significant evidence of the state exercising disciplinary power over the company, with conflict between

[133] See n 22.
[134] M Wu, 'The "China, Inc." Challenge to Global Trade Governance' (2016) 57 *Harvard International Law Journal* 261; D Mac Síthigh and M Siems, 'The Chinese Social Credit System: A Model for Other Countries?' (2019) 82 *Modern Law Review* 1071; M Erie, and T Streinz, 'The Beijing Effect: China's "Digital Silk Road" as Transnational Data Governance' (2021) 54 *New York University Journal of International Law and Politics* 1. See further Ch 6.
[135] H Shen, *Alibaba: Infrastructuring Global China* (Routledge, 2022).
[136] EDPB, 'Government access to data in third countries (Final report)' (2021) EDPS/2019/02-13, https://edpb.europa.eu/system/files/2022-01/legalstudy_on_government_access_0.pdf accessed 25 February 2022, p 12.

Jack Ma and Chinese banking authorities over the lending activities of Alibaba's fintech group. As Shen states: '[…] the growing power and influence of Alibaba in both the Chinese global political economy has […] pushed the state to exercise regulatory power to keep this extremely powerful unit of internet capital in check […]'.[137] This comes directly from China's national security culture, with an emphasis on securing China's so-called cyber sovereign borders.[138] The EU-China Strategic 2020 Agenda for Cooperation notably agreed enhanced cooperation and mutual trust as core pillars of cooperation.[139] However, the diverse approaches of the EU and China in cyberspace are said to be too diametrically opposed for any concrete outcome to be achieved.[140] The EU has also largely focused on soft cyber power and this is understood to be too far apart from the Chinese approach to amount to a credible engagement. China and the EU apply different approaches towards global cyber governance, with China adopting a state-centric view.[141] EU-China collaboration in the field of cybersecurity is thus a complex yet also embryonic affair, because of and in spite of China's so-called great firewall.

IX. Conclusions

The EU's cyber law-making has historically been dominated by weak efforts at institutionalisation and few actors. This now seems to be changing significantly, given the unfolding internal market directions of cyber law-making and 'turn' to hard law. Externally, the EU has had a limited range of institutionalisation activities as to cybersecurity in its trade agreements, largely dependent on soft law frameworks and voluntary cooperation. However, this reflects broader trends and developments and the EU still projects immense soft power in this domain. Cooperation with other international third partners is still based on heavily institutionalised ideals, such as the evolution of the Council of Europe. The autonomy of EU law is increasingly problematic for the EU's law-making efforts. Still, while cyber diplomacy is pursued through soft and hard law powers, the EU's sanction regimes, some of the most active in the world, feature executive-led institutionalised regimes. The reality of cyber law is dominated by the need to use CFSP sanctions and to date most significant law-making has not been constrained by the autonomy of EU law issues. This securitised dimension of cyber law-making is of significance, perhaps constraining the evolution of the EU's global actorness.

[137] Shen (n 135).

[138] S Bersick et al, 'Cybersecurity and EU–China Relations' in EJ Kirchner et al (eds), *Security Relations between China and the European Union: From Convergence to Cooperation?* (Cambridge University Press, 2016) 169.

[139] European Commission and HR/VP contribution to the European Council, 'EU-China – A Strategic Outlook' (2019).

[140] ibid; *cf* Chinese Ministry of Foreign Affairs, 'China's Policy Paper on the EU: Deepen the China-EU Comprehensive Strategic Partnership for Mutual Benefit and Win-Win Cooperation' (2014).

[141] F Russo, 'Assessing the EU-China Relationship in Cyberspace' (*EIAS*, 2020), https://eias.org/op-ed/assessing-the-eu-china-relationship-in-cyberspace/ accessed 25 February 2022.

4

On the Transatlantic Divide: Beyond Weak Institutionalisation

I. Overview

Many landmarks in the history of EU-US relations date to the Transatlantic Declaration of 1990, expanded through the New Transatlantic Agenda in 1995.[1] Yet these arrangements are couched in soft law rather than being formally binding agreements, and have never sought to legalise or institutionalise transatlantic relations.[2] The defining characteristic of contemporary transatlantic relations is that there are constant complex shifts to and from institutional integration – and few judicial engagements with its contours. As further explored below, more novel or hybrid structures such as 'dialogues' have perhaps superficially characterised the main mode of transatlantic operations. The place of hard law or binding legal provisions has proved to be complex, as have questions of governance and sovereignty. Traditionally, political science accounts have contended that EU-US relations are law-light and institution-light.[3] Lawyers have struggled with this view of law and politics.[4] Some, such as the present author, have argued that there are many institutional and legal components of transatlantic relations not usually accounted for, evolving through various presidencies.[5] In terms of institutional design, some of the most notable novelties and developments in EU-US relations from a legal perspective took effect during the Obama administration. The advent of the Trump administration appeared to give effect to the most unprecedented shift in transatlantic relations since before World War II, but mostly in terms of institutions, structures and institutional design. The US even refused

[1] M Pollack, 'The New Transatlantic Agenda at Ten: Reflections in an Experiment in International Governance' (2005) 43 *Journal of Common Market Studies* 899, 900.

[2] Pollack, 'The New Transatlantic Agenda at Ten: Reflections in an Experiment in International Governance' (n 1) 902 and 916.

[3] ibid 916.

[4] E-U Petersmann, 'Transformative Transatlantic Free Trade Agreements without Rights and Remedies of Citizens?' (2015) 18 *Journal of International Economic Law* 579, 589; see M Pollack and G Shaffer, *When Cooperation Fails: The International Law and Politics of Genetically* (Oxford University Press, 2009).

[5] E Fahey, 'On The Use of Law in Transatlantic Relations: Legal Dialogues Between the EU and US' (2014) 20(3) *European Law Journal* 368, 370.

to diplomatically recognise the European Union at one point.[6] Prior to this, the Obama-era Transatlantic Trade and Investment Partnership (TTIP) negotiations had brought the EU and US closer, with much deeper forms of institutionalisation and cooperation, but these were ultimate 'iced' by the Trump administration.[7] For Europe, the effect of the Trump Presidency has been the dramatic movement of a former ally into a foe, with countless trade wars, diplomatic spats, active hostility and a general withdrawal from multilateral leadership by the EU and US acting together.[8] This looks likely to change with the Biden administration, as signalled by the Transatlantic Trade and Technology Council (EU-US TTC) proposed immediately by the European Commission, which has been swiftly implemented and is already taking effect.[9] Yet its law-light, institution-light characteristics are beyond dispute. While many longstanding disputes between the EU and US have been swiftly resolved, paused or halted at the outset of the Biden administration, ie Airbus-Boeing WTO disputes and the section 232 National Security Tariffs on Steel and Aluminum, a future agreed transatlantic form of cooperation on the WTO appears in some doubt.[10] Many of the incoming Biden administration – which was itself a seachange in transatlantic cooperation – were former members of the Obama administration, 'battle-scarred' by the TTIP negotiations; this fact alone made it quite unlikely that such levels of institutional cooperation would be

[6] 'US Downgraded E.U.'s Diplomatic Status (but Didn't Say Anything)' *New York Times* (8 January 2019), www.nytimes.com/2019/01/08/world/europe/eu-us-diplomatic-status.html accessed 25 February 2022.

[7] M Bartl and E Fahey 'A Postnational Marketplace: Negotiating the Transatlantic Trade and Investment Partnership (TTIP)' in E Fahey and D Curtin (eds), *A Transatlantic Community of Law: Legal Perspectives on the Relationship between the EU and US Legal Orders* (Cambridge University Press, 2014).

[8] Many key aspects of trade policy appear replicated from the Trump to the Biden adminsitration but with 'softer' contours.

[9] European Commission and High Representative of the Union for Foreign Affairs and Security Policy, 'Joint Communication to the European Parliament, the European Council and the Council: A new EU-US agenda for global change' JOIN (2020) 22 final; European Commission, 'EU-US Trade and Technology Council Inaugural Joint Statement' (Statement, 29 September 2021), https://ec.europa.eu/commission/presscorner/detail/en/statement_21_4951 accessed 25 February 2022; European Commission, 'EU-US launch Trade and Technology Council to lead values-based global digital transformation' (Press Release, 15 June 2021), https://ec.europa.eu/commission/presscorner/detail/en/IP_21_2990 accessed 25 February 2022; The White House, 'US-EU Trade and Technology Council Inaugural Joint Statement' (Briefing, 29 September 2021), www.whitehouse.gov/briefing-room/statements-releases/2021/09/29/u-s-eu-trade-and-technology-council-inaugural-joint-statement/ accessed 25 February 2022; G Van Der Loo et al, 'The EU-US Trade and Technology Council: Mapping the Challenges and Opportunities for Transatlantic Cooperation on Trade, Climate, and Digital' (2021) Egmont Paper 113; J Hillman and S Grundhoefer, 'Can the US-EU Trade and Technology Council Succeed?' (*Council on Foreign Affairs*, 29 October 2021), www.cfr.org/blog/can-us-eu-trade-and-technology-council-succeed accessed 25 February 2022; European Commission, 'Joint Communication to the European Parliament, the European Council and the Council: A new EU-US agenda for global change' JOIN (2020)22 final, https://ec.europa.eu/info/sites/info/files/joint-communication-eu-us-agenda_en.pdf accessed 25 February 2022.

[10] E Zalan, 'EU and US reach steel truce in effort to reset relations' (*EU Observer*, 18 May 2021), https://euobserver.com/world/151870?utm_source=euobs&utm_medium=email accessed 25 February 2022; E Fahey (eds), 'The Future of Transatlantic Trade' (2021) 52 *EU Law Live Special Issue*.

proposed by such an administration. Yet, irrespective of the administration, the transatlantic relationship forms a key longer-term case study of limited institutionalisation and patchy aspirations.

There have been many so-called transatlantic dialogues over the years.[11] The term 'dialogue' appears to emphasise its soft law or informal credentials as a safe space for exchange of views and cooperation. These dialogues cover a diverse range of subject matter and their focus appears to have incrementally moved towards considerable degrees of specialisation, a recent one being the Joint Competition Technology Dialogue.[12] Certain dialogues appear more permanent or high-profile, whereas others have been less than transparent and their business dominance or less than citizen-centric nature in the past has been heavily criticised.[13] Indeed, the Transatlantic Business Dialogue appears to have been rebranded as the Transatlantic Business Council, perhaps for that very reason, but still retaining dialogue at the core of its mission.[14] To the present day the place of

[11] M Pollack and G Shaffer (eds), *Transatlantic Governance in the Global Economy* (Rowman & Littlefield, 2001) 25–34, 298; E Fahey, 'On The Use of Law in Transatlantic Relations: Legal Dialogues Between the EU and US' (n 5).

[12] See Fahey, 'On the Use of Law in Transatlantic Relations: Legal Dialogues Between the EU and US' (n 5).

[13] eg The Transatlantic Business Dialogue, Transatlantic Labour Dialogue, Transatlantic Consumer Dialogue; Transatlantic Environment Dialogue, the Transatlantic Dialogue on Sustainable Development, Aviation and Climate Change, Policy Networks and Donors Dialogue, the Transatlantic Dialogue on Higher Education and the Transatlantic Dialogues on Humanitarian Action. See respectively, Transatlantic Business Dialogue Website: https://transatlanticbusiness.org/tabd/ accessed 25 February 2022; M Green Cowles, 'The Transatlantic Business Dialogue: Transforming the New Transatlantic Dialogue' in Pollack and Shaffer, *Transatlantic Governance in the Global Economy* (n 11) 213; J Knauss and D Trubek, 'The Transatlantic Labor Dialogue: Minimal Action in a Weak Structure' in Pollack and Shaffer, *Transatlantic Governance in the Global Economy* (n 11); see Transatlantic Consumer Dialogue Website: https://tacd.org/ accessed 25 February 2022; see also 'Transatlantic Environment Dialogue suspended' (*Euractive*, 23 November 2000), www.euractiv.com/section/climate-environment/news/transatlantic-environment-dialogue-suspended/ accessed 25 February 2022; F Bignami and S Charnovitz, 'Transnational Civil Society Dialogues' in Pollack and Shaffer, *Transatlantic Governance in the Global Economy* (n 11) 275–76; on the Transatlantic Sustainable Development Dialogue: 'Transatlantic dialogue on sustainable development' (*Euractive*, 26 February 2002), www.euractiv.com/section/sustainable-dev/news/transatlantic-dialogue-on-sustainable-development/ accessed 25 February 2022; The Transatlantic Policy Networks Dialogue Website, www.tpnonline.org accessed 25 February 2022; on the Transatlantic Climate Dialogue: F Simon, 'Europe ready to restart transatlantic climate dialogue after Trump "parenthesis"' (*Euractive*, 9 November 2020), www.euractiv.com/section/energy-environment/news/europe-ready-to-restart-transatlantic-climate-dialogue-after-trump-parenthesis accessed 25 February 2022; European University Association, 'Transatlantic Dialogue', www.eua.eu/component/tags/tag/74-transatlantic-dialogue.html accessed 25 February 2022; U Kriebernegg, *The Transatlantic Dialogue on Higher Education: An Analysis of Cultural Narratives* (Logos Verlag Berlin GmbH, 2011) and also M Green and L Purser 'The Faculty of the Future: A Transatlantic Dialogue' (2000), www.acenet.edu/Documents/transatlantic-dialogue.pdf accessed 25 February 2022; 'Transatlantic Dialogues on Humanitarian Action' (Global Public Policy Institute), www.disastergovernance.net/events/transatlantic_dialogues_on_humanitarian_action/ accessed 25 February 2022; European Parliament, 'EU-US Security and Defence Dialogue' (2021), www.europarl.europa.eu/cmsdata/227845/20210127-sede-d-us-meeting-expo-carrousel.pdf accessed 25 February 2022.

[14] 'The Trans-Atlantic Business Dialogue (TABD) is the executive council of the Trans-Atlantic Business Council. The TABD program is the highest forum within the TABC and brings together chief

transparency and consumer rights is complex and if anything, intensifying in its significance. Indeed, the Transatlantic Consumer Dialogue has become increasingly high-profile in the age of Big Tech, assessing the need for voluntary and transparent exchanges between regulators, the involvement of all stakeholders and the sharing of best practice, particularly as to privacy.[15] At the time of writing, there are ongoing talks looking, for example, into the possibilities for a future transatlantic dialogue in security and defence and an EU-US dialogue on China.[16] There are many NGOs and thinktanks also conducting parallel informal transatlantic dialogues, such as the Atlantic Council. It is still remarkably difficult to find information about all of the aforementioned more 'formal' entities and the publicly available materials, particularly websites, vary greatly.[17] Some increasingly appear more evident or active, with the era of digitisation a contributory factor, eg some now with active Twitter accounts, websites and platform activities.[18] It is particularly difficult then to assess overall their accessibility, participation or effectiveness as entities. In fact, several dialogues have historically been perceived to have given certain economic actors privileged access to policy makers at the expense of other sectors of 'transatlantic society'; whether this is a valid critique remains unclear.[19] Yet dialogues constitute a longer-term structured process of informal non-institutional law-making of note.[20] Dialogues are also the common lexicon of EU-US relations. For example, the EU in its initial proposal for a transatlantic TTC showed a dialogue to be a standard communication method, open, flexible and ongoing. The TTC is also predicated on multiple working groups that align with this formula of flexibility, ie Technology Standards Cooperation, Climate and Clean Tech, Secure Supply Chains, ICT Security and Competitiveness, Data Governance and Technology Platforms, Misuse of Technology Threatening Security & Human Rights, Export Controls Cooperation, Investment Screening Cooperation, Promoting SME Access to and Use of Digital Technologies and

executive officers and C-Suite executives from leading American and European companies operating in the US, Europe, and globally who advocate for a barrier-free transatlantic market that will contribute to growth, employment, innovation and sustainability in the global economy. "Dialogue" is part of TABD because it is a key aspect of how TABD operates – bringing together business and government at the highest levels to allow candid exchange of views and discussion on the opportunities to further integrate the world's largest trading bloc': see the website of the Trans-Atlantic Business Dialogue (TABD): https://transatlanticbusiness.org/tabd/ accessed 25 February 2022.

[15] Trans Atlantic Consumer Dialogue (TACD), 'Lack of transparency could thwart the strong consumer safeguards that must be the goal of EU-US cooperation dialogues' (*TACD*, 28 September 2021), https://tacd.org/eu-us-organisations-transparency-ttc-pr/ accessed 25 February 2022. It is a remarkable entity, with 75 members across countries, entirely independently funded.

[16] European Parliament, 'EU-US Security and Defence Dialogue' (n 13).

[17] Fahey, 'On the Use of Law in Transatlantic Relations: Legal Dialogues between the EU and US' (n 5).

[18] The Transatlantic Consumers Dialogue has been particularly prominent and active in relation to the future of the EU-US Privacy Shield; see Transatlantic Consumer Dialogue website: https://tacd.org accessed 25 February 2022.

[19] Cowles, 'The Transatlantic Business Dialogue: Transforming the New Transatlantic Dialogue' (n 13) 213.

[20] Fahey, 'On the Use of Law in Transatlantic Relations: Legal Dialogues Between the EU and US' (n 5); E Fahey, *Introduction to Law and Global Governance* (Edward Elgar, 2018) Ch 1.

Global Trade Challenges.[21] What is also notable about the TTC is the extent to which it is based upon a large number of working groups that reflect the EU's modus operandi in trade. For instance, it could be said to 'mimic' certain aspects of most contemporary EU trade agreements, for example the EU-UK Trade and Cooperation Agreement (TCA). However, the initial TTC meeting was plagued by allegations of a lack of transparency, giving excessive influence to the US, not aligning enough on the place of transparency for consumers and instead providing a platform for business groups to influence the EU.[22] It could also be said that the early reports of the TTC indicate engagement only from business and to a much lesser extent from civil society and Member States or sub-national units despite the use of online platforms and extensive social media engagement efforts. In this regard, transatlantic cooperation is frequently plagued by its multilevel nature and the composite place of public and private actors therein.

Many other *formal* law-making processes take place against this difficult backdrop or context.[23] One of the most significant sites of transatlantic 'law-making' – if one can use that term – has until recently been at the WTO. Most disputes between the EU and US have taken place before the WTO Dispute Settlement Body (DSB) in recent times, at least until its demise in late 2020.[24] There, the EU and US have historically been involved in most disputes and are opposing parties in some of the longest running litigation of all time.[25] The resolution of such WTO

[21] See the EU-US TTC website: https://futurium.ec.europa.eu/en/EU-US-TTC accessed 25 February 2022.

[22] TACD, 'Lack of transparency could thwart the strong consumer safeguards that must be the goal of EU-US cooperation dialogues' (n 13).

[23] Fahey, 'On the Use of Law in Transatlantic Relations: Legal Dialogues Between the EU and US' (n 5); D Jančić, 'Transatlantic Regulatory Interdependence, Law and Governance: The Evolving Roles of the EU and US Legislatures' (2015) 17 *Cambridge Yearbook of European Legal Studies* 334.

[24] Panel Report, *European Communities – Measures Affecting the Approval and Marketing of Biotech Products* (EC – Approval and Marketing of Biotech Products), WT/DS291/R, WT/DS292/R, WT/DS293/R (29 September 2006); Panel Report, *European Communities – Measures Concerning Meat and Meat Products* (EC– Hormones), WT/DS26/R/USA (18 August 1997); Panel Report, *United States – Measures Concerning the Importation, Marketing and Sale of Tuna and Tuna Products* (US – Tuna II (Mexico)), WT/DS381/R (15 September 2011). On the EU-US Boeing dispute see originally EC-US Agreement on Trade in Large Civil Aircraft, OJ L 301 of 17 October 1992; Appellate Body Report United States – *Measures affecting Trade in Large Civil Aircraft*, 892 WT/DS353/AB/R (12 March 2012); Library of the European Parliament, 'Principal EU-US disputes' (22 April 2013), www.europarl.europa.eu/RegData/bibliotheque/briefing/2013/130518/LDM_BRI(2013)130518_REV1_EN.pdf accessed 25 February 2022; MA Pollack and GC Shaffer, *When Cooperation Fails: The International Law and Politics of Genetically Modified Foods* (Oxford University Press, 2009) Chs 1 and 7; Pollack and Shaffer, *Transatlantic Governance in the Global Economy* (n 11); Petersmann, 'Transformative Transatlantic Free Trade Agreements without Rights and Remedies of Citizens?' (n 4); N Krisch, 'Pluralism in Postnational Risk Regulation: The Dispute over GMOs and Trade' (2010) 1 *Transnational Legal Theory* 1.

[25] See the resolution of the EU-US Boeing-Airbus Trade Dispute from 15 June 2021, agreeing to extend a tariff truce for five years, ending a dispute over aircraft subsidies given to Airbus and Boeing, with $11.5 billion of duties being imposed on each other's exports, originating in a dispute from 2004 where the US lodged proceedings at the WTO against the EU over Member States' support to Airbus for commercial aircraft development, with the EU opening a parallel case arguing that Boeing benefited from US subsidies as well as space and military contracts. In 2019, the WTO authorised the US to levy tariffs on $7.5 billion of EU exports annually over government support for Airbus. The EU then

disputes, eg the Airbus-Boeing Large Civil Aircraft in 2021, is highly significant but is perhaps an important side issue to the main 'act'. Some would suggest that the history of transatlantic relations shows a fine line between cooperation and conflict. The engagement of the EU and US on the future reform of WTO DSB has reached a critical juncture; the US has failed to nominate judges to the body and is increasingly opposed to the forum in its existing format, with respect to the rules-based system of multilateralism to which both the US and EU have long subscribed.[26] The Biden administration appears to place the WTO DSB reform as part of a broader reform centrally with EU cooperation but still part of a bigger picture rethink on fairer and more inclusive global trade. The EU and 15 WTO members established contingency appeal arrangement for trade disputes in March 2020, with the number trebling a year later.[27] The extent to which the US will join the EU as to shared visions of WTO reform remains to be seen, particularly where new forms of transatlantic trade councils are proposed.[28] To some degree, the judicialisation of the WTO DSB has become a long-running concern of the US, seemingly fostered by the EU and US as its main litigants. Yet its institutionalisation appears to wane despite the common utility of a rules-based institutionalisation approach to global trade. Whether the EU and US will ultimately contribute to fragmentation or centralisation in this domain is still an open question.

In addition to the informal dialogues noted above, there are formal permanent political dialogues such as Annual Summits between EU and US leaders. A Transatlantic Legislators Dialogue has been ongoing since 1972 and forms an important element of the external action of the European Parliament, perhaps less so other institutions.[29] These are supported by the Transatlantic Economic Council, the EU-US Energy Council and the High-Level Working Groups.[30]

won permission to hit back with levies on $4billion of US goods. See European Commission, 'EU and US take decisive step to end aircraft dispute (Press Release)' (15 June 2021), https://ec.europa.eu/commission/presscorner/detail/en/ip_21_3001 accessed 25 February 2022; see also 'Understanding on a cooperative framework for Large Civil Aircraft' (2021) Tradoc 159645, https://trade.ec.europa.eu/doclib/docs/2021/june/tradoc_159645.pdf accessed 25 February 2022.

[26] KJ Alter and C Lafont, 'Global Governance and the Problem of the Second Best: The Example of Reforming the World Trade Organization' (2019) SSRN Paper, https://ssrn.com/abstract=3524325 accessed 25 February 2022; 'WTO modernisation: Introduction to future EU proposals' (2018) Tradoc 157331, https://trade.ec.europa.eu/doclib/docs/2018/september/tradoc_157331.pdf accessed 25 February 2022; United States Trade Representative, 'Report on the WTO Appellate Body of the World Trade Organization' (2010), https://ustr.gov/sites/default/files/Report_on_the_Appellate_Body_of_the_World_Trade_Organization.pdf accessed 25 February 2022.

[27] European Commission, 'EU and 15 World Trade Organization members establish contingency appeal arrangement for trade disputes' (2020), https://trade.ec.europa.eu/doclib/press/index.cfm?id=2127 accessed 25 February 2022 (Multi-Party Interim Appeal Arbitration Arrangement pursuant to Art 25 of the DSU).

[28] Some already suggest that the US has subscribed to the vision of the EU in its MPIA. However, the Biden adminstration has continued the longstanding US discontent with the state of the WTO DSB.

[29] See the Transatlantic Legislators Dialogue webpage, https://www.europarl.europa.eu/tld/en/home accessed 25 February 2022; *cf* Jančić, 'Transatlantic Regulatory Interdependence, Law and Governance: The Evolving Roles of the EU and US Legislatures' (n 23).

[30] For example, the EU-US Working Group on Cybercrime and Cybersecurity or the High Level Working Group on Jobs and Growth.

Yet these entities vary greatly in terms of agenda, activities and outputs. Irrespective of the administration, EU and US representatives maintain regular contact. Today, the EU delegation to the US employs approximately 90 staff, about 30 of whom are EU diplomats.[31] The European Parliament also has a liaison office in Washington DC which increasingly attempts to develop its own autonomy and shed the 'baggage' of the critique of the Transatlantic Legislator's Dialogue as an ineffective 'talking-shop'.[32] It can be said that institutionalising even 'talking-shops' yields many benefits for the EU and the reach of its soft power. Beyond dialogues, deeper forms of governance have been attempted, although their success and objectives is contested. For instance, there are many US liaison officers in the EU, in The Hague for example, posted to the European Cybercrime Centre.[33] Anthony Gardner, former US Ambassador to the EU, reminds us in his book *Stars with Stripes* that US Big Tech industry has never sought US representation to lobby in the EU in recent times, preferring to 'go it alone'.[34] These issues as to the formalisation of engagement are notable. There is also a well-documented surge in professional US lobbyists in Brussels, often US qualified lawyers working at Brussels-based law firms, with sizeable departments dedicated to following sectoral EU law and policy developments.[35] Further work on the areas of law the subject to engagement and the representation of public and private interests here will also be of value.[36] Nonetheless, it adds another layer of context to the nature of the transatlantic dialogues that are emerging and the institutional forums in which they take place – many, varied and multi-level.

Ultimately, transatlantic relations are a story of largely cooperative and lively institutional interactions across many individual points that perhaps have outgrown traditional typologies of the multi-level nature of EU-US relations.[37] Even at the lowest point of EU-US relations in 60 years (and there were many during the Trump administration; the US refusing to diplomatically acknowledge the EU

[31] See Delegation of the European Union to the United States website: https://eeas.europa.eu/delegations/united-states-america/27290/about_en accessed 25 February 2022.

[32] See European Parliament Office in Washington DC website: www.europarl.europa.eu/unitedstates/en/ accessed 25 February 2022.

[33] Operational Agreements (*Europol*), www.europol.europa.eu/partners-collaboration/agreements/operational-agreements accessed 25 February 2022.

[34] A Gardner, *Stars with Stripes: The Essential Partnership between the European Union and the United States* (Palgrave, 2020).

[35] E Lipton and D Hakim, 'Lobbying Bonanza as Firms Try to Influence European Union' *The New York Times* (18 October 2013), www.nytimes.com/2013/10/19/world/europe/lobbying-bonanza-as-firms-try-to-influence-european-union.html accessed 25 February 2022; J Power, 'Facebook pressed Irish ambassador to lobby US Congress members' *The Irish Times* (25 February 20121) www.irishtimes.com/business/facebook-pressed-irish-ambassador-to-lobby-us-congress-members-1.4494200 accessed 25 February 2022; E Sánchez Nicolás, '"Big Five" tech giants spent €19m lobbying EU in 2020' (*EU Observer*, 1 March 2021), https://euobserver.com/science/151072?utm_source=euobs&utm_medium=email accessed 25 February 2022; J Espinoza, 'Google in last-ditch lobbying attempt to influence incoming EU tech rules' *Financial Times* (10 January 2022), www.ft.com/content/8c7527bc-7ab4-41cd-ba94-3145208da9c3 accessed 25 February 2022.

[36] See D Coen et al, *Business Lobbying in the European Union* (Oxford University Press, 2020).

[37] eg Pollock and Shaffer, *Transatlantic Governance in the Global Economy* (n 11).

probably ranks highly), US government, agencies and actors actively continue to engage with the EU.[38] For example, the US mission to the EU gave extraordinarily constructive feedback on the EU's GDPR in its two-year review in early 2020, during the Covid-19 pandemic, alongside dozens of US tech companies, notably praising and drawing attention to transatlantic data privacy cooperation and alignment.[39] As is considered below, three US government bodies wrote a lengthy report in 2020 to criticise the CJEU's decision in *Schrems II* that struck down the EU-US Privacy Shield.[40] One might say that, irrespective of the content, such an engagement shows the variety of ongoing engagements between the EU and US. These engagements take place through and by institutional actors, interested in each other's affairs and actively engaging in them.

This chapter suggests that significant convergence may conceivably be emerging between EU and US regulators on the need to weaken Big Tech. Transatlantic convergence on regulatory standards from competition law to privacy and speech law suggests a commonality of regulatory capture. The EU-US Joint Agenda for Global Change includes a EU-US TTC which has begun to take effect with significant effects already. Advocating for a loose institutionalisation of key global challenges currently not well covered or dealt with by, for example, the WTO, seems like a useful way of generating transatlantic convergence.

This chapter contains the following sections: (II) institutionalisation attempts in EU-US digital trade and data flows; (III) transatlantic data flow regimes: law and governance; (IV) from EU-US Safe Harbour to the EU-US Privacy Shield agreements; (V) the *Schrems* litigation of the EU-US Privacy Shield; (VI) the future of transatlantic data institutionalisation; and (VII) conclusions.

II. Institutionalisation Attempts in EU-US Digital Trade and Data Flows

After several decades of sophisticated legal integration, transatlantic data flows are still exceptionally well regulated, governed and relatively integrated, however imperfectly.[41] To an outsider, stronger institutionalisation of transatlantic privacy policy might appear to be the next logical step in the light of the importance of

[38] 'US Downgraded EU's Diplomatic Status (but Didn't Say Anything)' (n 6).

[39] See the summary of responses in European Commission, 'Commission report: EU data protection rules empower citizens and are fit for the digital age' (Press Release, 24 June 2020), https://ec.europa.eu/commission/presscorner/detail/en/ip_20_1163 accessed 25 February 2022.

[40] Case C-311/18 *Data Protection Commissioner v Facebook Ireland Limited, Maximillian Schrems* (*Schrems II*) EU:C:2020:559; 'White Paper: Information on US Privacy Safeguards Relevant to SCCs and Other EU Legal Bases for EU-US Data Transfers after Schrems II' (2020), www.commerce.gov/sites/default/files/2020-09/SCCsWhitePaperFORMATTEDFINAL508COMPLIANT.PDF accessed 25 February 2022.

[41] See Gardner, *Stars with Stripes* (n 34); 'US Downgraded E.U.'s Diplomatic Status (but Didn't Say Anything)' (n 6).

transatlantic data flows. Yet the meaning of institutionalisation here remains very elusive. In the past, the EU and US have set up multiple forms of transatlantic institutions but none of them have been based on a shared consensus as to the meaning of privacy, and instead have relied on a learning or changing remit to evolve the concept. Transatlantic relations in the area of data and privacy have mostly relied on domestic institutions, in recent or historical forms of agreement. TTIP, the largest-scale form of transatlantic collaboration in recent history, expressly excluded data flows from its negotiations. Its negotiation of e-commerce could have been pivotal given the growing gap between the TPP and EU agreements as to data flows but also the gap emerging as to the formulation of digital trade between the EU and US.[42] As the TTIP was paused at the end of the Obama administration, and given that the Biden administration is unlikely to restart the TTIP negotiations, it is possible that we will never know the place of highly institutionalised cooperation with data *outside* of its remit. While the quest for regulatory convergence to promote more seamless and efficient trade amongst partners and ensure competitiveness and business facilitation was a major goal of the TTIP negotiations, data issues were initially excluded from their ambit and were a major source of conflict between the US and the EU, particularly audio-visual services on cultural exception grounds. These were excluded from the negotiating mandate of the European Commission, after significant political pressure from the European Parliament. Intellectual property issues also garnered very significant civil society opposition. The available texts after 15 rounds of negotiations provide an interesting insight into the possible state of the transatlantic position.[43] TTIP texts (initially leaked) exposed significant the divergence between the US and the EU on data protection, particularly given that TTIP was being negotiated before the adoption of the GDPR. Thus, while the so-called 'Washington Consensus' or US domination in alignment with the values of Silicon Valley of the TPP text 'lives on' in the CPTPP adopting APEC-CBPR standards on privacy, the US shift towards

[42] M Burri and R Polanco, 'Digital Trade Provisions in Preferential Trade Agreements: Introducing a New Dataset' (2020) 23 *Journal of International Economic Law* 187.

[43] European Commission, 'TTIP: Initial proposal on trade in services, investment and e-commerce' (31 July 2015), http://trade.ec.europa.eu/doclib/docs/2015/july/tradoc_153669.pdf accessed 25 February 2022; European Commission, 'TTIP: Annexes to the services, investment and e-commerce initial proposal' (31 July 2015), http://trade.ec.europa.eu/doclib/docs/2015/july/tradoc_153670.pdf accessed 25 February 2022; European Commission, 'A reading guide to the EU proposal on services, investment and e-commerce for the Transatlantic Trade and Investment Partnership' (31 July 2015), http://trade.ec.europa.eu/doclib/docs/2015/july/tradoc_153668.pdf accessed 25 February 2022; European Parliament, 'TTIP Legislative Train Schedule' (2020), www.europarl.europa.eu/legislative-train/theme-international-trade-inta/file-ttip-services-investment-and-e-commerce accessed 25 February 2022. See M Burri, 'The Regulation of Data Flows Through Trade Agreements' (2017) 48 *Georgetown Journal of International Law* 407; W Berka, 'CETA, TTIP, TiSA, and Data Protection' in S Griller et al (eds), *Mega-Regional Trade Agreements: CETA, TTIP, and TiSA: New Orientations for EU External Economic Relations* (Oxford University Press, 2017); A Renda and C Yoo, 'Telecommunications and Internet Services: The Digital Side of the TTIP' (2015) CEPS, TIPP in Balance Project Paper No 8, www.ceps.eu/download/publication/?id=9012&pdf=SR112%20Renda%20and%20Yoo%20Telecoms%20TTIP.pdf accessed 25 February 2022.

the need for federal privacy laws, agencies and standards could radically shift the understanding of the outcome of the TPP agreement and TTIP negotiations.[44]

Although the scale and valorisation of data is notoriously complex and contested, transatlantic data flows are extremely salient from economic, legal and political perspectives because of their scale. It is beyond dispute that transatlantic data flows are economically valuable and critical to global economic development. Digital trade is the fastest growing segment of the global economy, representing nearly $10 trillion a year and rising. By contrast goods and services trade rose at an average rate of just 2.4 per cent in the last decade. In 2017, the US exported $204 billion digitally deliverable services to the EU while importing $124 billion of such services from the EU. However, the value of the data is an issue, where cross-border data flows are not picked up by international trade statistics.[45] In 2021, the transatlantic economy amounted to one third of global GDP.[46] The economic and legal value of the relationship is far from a continuum. Still, the institutionalisation of EU-US data flows and data privacy taking place in recent times appears to pivot away from the looser decentralisation prevailing until recently, to some extent at least moving towards convergence and an emphasis on the need for regulatory capture, oversight and accountability – and will doubtless impact upon the modelling of its economic value in the future.[47]

III. Transatlantic Data Flow Regimes: Law and Governance

The EU and US have many forms of data flow agreements, broadly speaking, in the areas of commercial and security-related transfer regimes. They mostly date to the post-9/11 era, though not exclusively. They notably have uniform modes of governance, review processes and structures and have generated important means to reflect upon institutionalisation. All EU-US data flow regimes (EU-US

[44] T Streinz, 'Digital Megaregulation Uncontested? TPP's Model for the Global Digital Economy' in B Kingsbury et al (eds), *Megaregulation Contested* (Oxford University Press, 2019).

[45] Some value products and services relating on the transatlantic transfer of data to add $1 trillion to the EU-US relationship between 2016–2026. See G Workmann, 'TTIP Underlining the Importance of Digital Trade' (*US Chamber of Commerce*, 5 May 2016), www.uschamber.com/article/ttip-underlining-the-importance-digital-trade accessed 25 February 2022; Gardner, *Stars with Stripes* (n 34) 164; D Hamilton and J Quinlan, US Chamber of Commerce, *The Transatlantic Economy 2019* (Brookings, 2019).

US Chamber of Commerce, 'The Transatlantic Economy 2020', www.uschamber.com/international/the-transatlantic-economy-2020 accessed 25 February 2022.

[46] D Hamilton and J Quinlan, US Chamber of Commerce, *The Transatlantic Economy 2021* (2021), www.amchameu.eu/sites/default/files/publications/files/transatlanticeconomy2021_fullreporthr.pdf accessed 25 February 2022.

[47] P Schwartz, 'The EU-US Privacy Collision: A Turn to Institutions and Procedure' (2013) 126 *Harvard Law Review* 1996.

Passenger Name Records (EU-US PNR) Agreement and EU-US Terrorist Financial Tracking Programme (EU-US TFTP) Agreement, Umbrella Agreement, Safe Harbour, Privacy Shield) generally adopt a reasonably standard model of transatlantic governance that entails annual joint reviews involving both the EU and US administrations, formalizing cooperation on various levels and subjecting uneven enforcement and implementation to a standardised form of review.[48] More are in the process of being negotiated (Privacy Shield replacement and EU-US e-evidence regime) and demonstrate the vibrancy of the cooperation. The European Parliament voted to suspend all EU-US data transfer agreements on the basis of its inquiry into mass surveillance by the US.[49] The suspension did not occur but, over the course of nearly two decades after 9/11, the European Parliament, in particular its LIBE Committee continues unfailingly to 'contest' transatlantic issues.[50] EU-US data privacy innovations are arguably very modest and empower local actors with joint governance much more than a transnational institutional body generally, with one main exception: the EU-US Privacy Shield. The account thus sketches the contours of the agreements and then focuses in detail on arguably the most topical and significant of these, the EU-US Privacy Shield.

Two of the most prominent agreements entered into by the EU and the US in the post 9/11 period, designed to communicate air passenger data and to target the financing of terrorism, are the EU-US PNR Agreement and EU-US TFTP Agreement.[51] The EU-US PNR was infamously struck down by the Court of Justice in 2004 in litigation by the Europan Parliament that is commonly viewed as problematic, leaving the EU forced to negotiate an even worse outcome with the US.[52] These agreements have generated much controversy on account of their limitations on redress and their uneven application of US law to EU citizens, not enabling the latter to fully realise their rights to redress and review.[53] The formulation of the character of rights, remedies and redress is distinctively

[48] E Fahey, 'Law and Governance as Checks and Balances in Transatlantic Security: Rights, Redress, and Remedies in EU-US Passenger Name Records and the Terrorist Finance Tracking Program' (2013) 32 *Yearbook of European Law* 368.

[49] European Parliament, 'Resolution of 26 May 2016 on transatlantic data flows' (2016/2727(RSP)) [2016] OJ C76/82.

[50] Joint Press Statement following EU-US Justice and Home Affairs Ministerial Meeting of 18 November 2013, Council 16418/13 (18 November 2013). See Council of the European Union, 'Report on the Findings by the EU Co-chairs of the Ad Hoc EU-US Working Group on Data Protection' Council document 16987/13 and European Commission, 'Rebuilding Trust in EU-US Data Flows' COM (2013) 846 final.

[51] See Agreement between the United States of America and the European Union on the use and transfer of Passenger Name Record Data to the United States Department of Homeland (EU-US PNR) [2012] OJ L215/5, approved by the European Parliament in April 2012; Agreement between the European Union and the United States of America on the processing and Transfer of Financial Messaging data from the European Union to the United States for the purposes of the Terrorist Finance Tracking Program (hereafter TFTP) [2010] OJ L 195/5.

[52] Joined cases C-317/04 and C-318/04 *European Parliament v Council of the European Union and Commission of the European Communities* ECLI:EU:C:2006:346.

[53] See Fahey, 'Law and Governance as Checks and Balances in Transatlantic Security: Rights, Redress, and Remedies in EU-US Passenger Name Records and the Terrorist Finance Tracking Program' (n 48).

replicated in both agreements in a broad time frame, extending well after a decade post-9/11.[54] As a result, they are perceived to form very prominent examples of the limits of mutual recognition of justice in transatlantic relations.[55] Moreover, the use of detailed governance or review mechanisms to monitor the operation of these agreements has generated little in the way of substantive change, though some forms of institutionalisation have evolved, including EU officials in the US.[56] While on one level the governance of EU-PNR has deepened and widened considerably over the years and across agreements,[57] the oversight and accountability thereof appears spare and difficult to judge. PNR litigation as to other third countries has generated CJEU decisions highlighting its problematic forms, most acutely with the US, eg Canada.[58] Ongoing negotiations with Canada on PNR draw attention to how difficult it is to reimagine these regimes and how complex the case law of the Court is to implement with other sovereign entities and highly developed constitutional orders.

A. EU-US PNR

After 9/11 the US infamously introduced legislation which required all airlines flying into the country to supply Passenger Name Records (PNR) data to the US Customs and Border Control.[59] It was a development which would change the face of data transfer law and governance globally, but in particular EU law. This legislation was problematic from the outset from an EU law perspective as Article 25 of the then in force Data Protection Directive provided that personal information originating from within EU Member States may be transferred to a third country only if that country 'ensures an adequate level of protection',[60] a level of protection which had not formally been established between the EU and US. In

[54] On reciprocity and its limits see G Shaffer, 'Reconciling Trade and Regulatory Roles: The Prospects and Limits of New Approaches to Transatlantic Governance Through Mutual Recognition and Safe Harbor Agreements' (2002) 9 *Columbia Journal of European Law* 29; V Mitsilegas, 'Constitutional Implications of Mutual Recognition in Criminal Matters in the EU' (2006) 43 *Common Market Law Review* 1277, 1283.

[55] Fahey, 'Law and Governance as Checks and Balances in Transatlantic Security: Rights, Redress, and Remedies in EU-US Passenger Name Records and the Terrorist Finance Tracking Program' (n 48).

[56] eg M de Goede and M Wesseling, 'Secrecy and Security in Transatlantic Terrorism Finance Tracking' (2017) 39 *Journal of European Integration* 253; Case T-529/09 *In 't Veld v Council* EU:T:2012:215.

[57] De Goede and Wesseling, 'Secrecy and Security in Transatlantic Terrorism Finance Tracking' (n 56).

[58] Agreement between the European Community and the Government of Canada on the processing of Advance Passenger Information and Passenger Name Record data [2006] OJ L 82/15; Opinion 1/15 of the Court (Grand Chamber) of 26 July 2017, pursuant to Article 218(11) TFEU – Draft agreement between Canada and the European Union – Transfer of Passenger Name Record data from the European Union to Canada EU:C:2017:592.

[59] Aviation and Transportation Security Act of 2001, s 1447.

[60] Directive 95/46 of the European Parliament and of the Council of 24 October 1995 on the protection of individuals with regard to the processing of personal data and on the free movement of such data [1995] OJ L281/31.

2003, the EU launched negotiations with the US on an Agreement which would govern the transfer of PNR data and a draft Agreement was reached in 2004.[61] The Commission then adopted an Adequacy Decision, asserting that undertakings offered by the Customs and Border Protection Agency provided adequate protection for the data of EU citizens travelling to the US. Under threat of litigation to the CJEU by the European Parliament, who had become increasingly vocalised in its opposition to such data transfer, principally on civil liberties grounds, an agreement between the EU and US came into force in 2004. The European Parliament quickly sought annulment both of the Commission Adequacy Decision and of the Council Decision authorising the signature of the Agreement. The litigation would result in one of the worst outcomes for EU international relations and the also the European Parliament for some time.[62]

After a high-profile, rushed and difficult hearing, the CJEU handed down a decision on 30 May 2006 which concluded that ex Article 95 EC (now Article 114 TFEU), the legal basis for internal market harmonisation or approximation of laws, as the legal basis of the Council Decision read in conjunction with the Data Protection Directive, did not provide an adequate legal basis for the transfer of the data, entailing that the agreement had to be annulled.[63] The consequences were significant; notably, the Court preserved the effect of the Adequacy Decision until 30 September 2006 to allow time for a new agreement to be negotiated – an action that would not necessarily follow in future similar CJEU decisions. A provisional seven-year agreement was then concluded in 2007 to replace the earlier agreement. The end result was a significantly worse legal agreement, with the US taking advantage of the renegotiation to considerably extend data-retention periods and the EU institutions, in particular the European Parliament, becoming internally more concerned about the need for a global strategy on PNR.[64] A new agreement was reached in 2011, enhancing data protection mechanisms and limiting the use of data.[65] It became apparent to all that the negative judicialisation of the EU-US PNR would have significant consequences. The controversy has not abated and the EU has since introduced its own PNR system internally, itself the subject of strategic litigation against its existence by NGOs and civil liberties organisations.[66] The CJEU also handed down a significant opinion in Opinion 1/15 on the EU-Canada

[61] Undertakings of US CBP issued on 11 May 2004, OJ [2004] L 1235/11.

[62] E Fahey, 'Of "One Shotters" and "Repeat Hitters": A Retrospective on the Role of the European Parliament in the EU-US PNR Litigation' in F Nicola and B Davies (eds), *EU Law Stories: Contextual and Critical Histories of European Jurisprudence* (Cambridge University Press, 2017).

[63] Joined Cases C-317/04 and C-318/04 *European Parliament v Council and Commission* EU:C:2006:346.

[64] European Commission, 'Communication from the Commission on the Global Approach to Transfers of Passenger Name Record (PNR) Data to Third Countries' COM (2010) 492 final.

[65] European Commission, 'New EU-US Agreements on PNR improves data protection and fights crime and terrorism' (2011) IP/11/1368, https://ec.europa.eu/commission/presscorner/detail/en/IP_11_1368 accessed 25 February 2022. See Fahey, 'Of "One Shotters" and "Repeat Hitters": A Retrospective on the Role of the European Parliament in the EU-US PNR Litigation' (n 62).

[66] See C-817/19 *Ligue des droits humains v Conseil des ministers*, pending.

PNR Agreement, considered above, requiring independence in oversight of processing and use of PNR. It is widely understood to be a complex opinion to implement and to constitute a troublesome precedent for the character of EU-US PNR agreements.[67] Additionally, in the wake of *Schrems II*, the fate of other PNR agreements, eg with the UK embedded with the TCA or under negotiation with Japan, remains to be seen. Certain US scholars suggest that administrative oversight and prior independent authorisation on the use of PNR may not prove so complex for the US, possibly able to adapt existing domestic mechanisms.[68] However, the complicated position of certain Member States, increasingly rebelling against the CJEU's imposition of data restrictions on national security activities, may inure to the benefit of third countries.[69] Indeed, as the discussion above suggests, the equilibrium in EU law between security and privacy as to bulk data collection and retention for security purposes appears all the more in flux after a series of CJEU decisions. Irrespective of the substantive outcome, in all instances EU law increasingly pushes for further and deeper degrees of institutionalisation through design and the autonomy of actors. Whether international partnership can meet CJEU requirements as to oversight remains to be seen, but most likely not.

B. TFTP Law and Governance

The EU-US 'SWIFT' or TFTP Agreement came to public knowledge when *The New York Times* newspaper published details disclosing secret access obtained by the US to the Belgian Society for Worldwide Interbank Financial Telecommunications (SWIFT), by over 2000 organisations and revealed that the US Central Intelligence Agency (CIA) was running a secret programme, overseen by the US Treasury, obtaining financial messaging data in order to track terrorist financing. The EU-US TFTP Agreement was entered into so as to legitimise the US program and meet data privacy concerns concerning the US extraction, use and transfer of financial messaging data without a warrant. Soft law 'representations' were undertaken by the US. They were subsequently described when published in the Official Journal in 2006 (in the form of a highly unusual letter from the US Department of Treasury), providing that the: '… TFTP contains multiple, overlapping layers of

[67] See Opinion 1/15 of the Court (Grand Chamber) of 26 July 2017, EU:C:2017:592. See also E Guild and E Mendos Kuşkonmaz, 'EU Exclusive Jurisdiction on Surveillance Related to Terrorism and Serious Transnational Crime: Case Review on Opinion 1/15' (2018) 43 *European Law Review* 583; E Guild and E Mendos Kuşkonmaz, 'A critical take on Opinion 1/15: is the glass half full or half empty?' [2019] *European Yearbook on Human Rights* 111; C Kuner, 'International agreements, data protection, and EU fundamental rights on the international stage: Opinion 1/15, EU-Canada PNR' (2018) 55 *Common Market Law Review* 857, 858.

[68] Eg, K Propp, 'Avoiding the next transatlantic security crisis: The looming clash over passenger name record data' (*Atlantic Council*, 1 July 2021), www.atlanticcouncil.org/in-depth-research-reports/issue-brief/the-looming-clash-over-passenger-name-record-data/ accessed 25 February 2022.

[69] *cf* Case C-817/19 *Ligue des droit humains*, pending.

governmental and independent controls to ensure that the data … are used strictly for counterterrorism purposes …'.

These representations were followed by the agreement of the US to the appointment of an 'Eminent European Person' to review the data, subsequently producing reports classified as secret and rendering its remarks as to its efficacy difficult to assess. An EU-US TFTP Agreement – finally reached for technical reasons when SWIFT made changes to its systems in 2009 – was vetoed by the European Parliament in 2010 pursuant to Article 218 TFEU because of the lack of information provided.[70] A second SWIFT agreement was reached and entered into force also in 2010 pursuant to Articles 87(2)(a) and 88(2) TFEU; Article 16 TFEU. The EU-US TFTP Agreement provides in Article 1 that its purpose is to prevent, investigate, detect and prosecute terrorist financing, by providing to the US Treasury exclusively data stored in the territory of the EU. It is thus a highly unusual form of agreement. Europol is a Designated Provider pursuant to Article 4 of the Agreement.[71] Much controversy has ensued as to its legal base, governance, its engagement with territory and sovereignty, oversight and accountability. Yet again, joint governance here proves highly problematic but is also couched in weak institutional design.

C. The EU-US Umbrella Agreement

An EU-US so-called Umbrella Agreement for the transfer of data for law enforcement purposes was finally adopted in 2016.[72] The agreement was intended to improve protection for personal data relating to the prevention, investigation, detection, and prosecution of criminal offences although its operation has largely been shrouded in secrecy since its entry into force. There is no statement of competence or legal basis for the agreement in its published form. It is stated in Article 1 that:

> The purpose of this Agreement is to ensure a high level of protection of personal information and enhance cooperation between the United States and the European Union and its Member States, in relation to the prevention, investigation, detection or prosecution of criminal offences, including terrorism.

[70] See A Ripoll Servent and A MacKenzie, 'The European Parliament as norm-taker? EU-US relations after the SWIFT Agreement' (2012) 17(5) *European Foreign Affairs Review* 71; De Goede and Wesseling, 'Secrecy and Security in Transatlantic Terrorism Finance Tracking' (n 56).

[71] It is served with requests from the US Treasury for data which it must consider pursuant to Art 4(2) as to whether it is identified as clearly as possible, that its necessity is substantiated and that the request is tailored as narrowly as possible to minimise the amount of data sought. See Fahey, 'Law and Governance as Checks and Balances in Transatlantic Security: Rights, Redress, and Remedies in EU-US Passenger Name Records and the Terrorist Finance Tracking Program' (n 48).

[72] EU-US Agreement on the Protection of Personal Information Relating to the Prevention, Investigation, Detection and Prosecution of Criminal Offenses (EU-US Umbrella Agreement) [2016] OJ L 336/3.

It thus represented a very significant form of collaboration on privacy. In 2016, President Obama signed the Judicial Redress Act into law. This granted non-US citizens privacy rights, including a private right of action for breaches of privacy violations that occurred in the US.[73] At first sight, this seemed like a significant development. The Act was signed after Congress approved an amendment that limits the right to sue to only those citizens of countries which permit the 'transfer of personal data for commercial purposes' to the US, and did not impose personal data transfer policies that 'materially impeded' US national security interests. It was a significant step to enable the advancement of the EU-US Privacy Shield and was important also in the evolution of the EU-US Umbrella Agreement. As Severson stated:

> At this stage, the US government has chosen a policy that maintains the status quo, while tinkering at the edges. Ultimately, perhaps the greatest change to come from PPD-28 is a public acknowledgement that foreigners have a legitimate privacy interest. The directive states that when conducting US signals intelligence activities, the US government 'must take into account that all persons should be treated with dignity and respect, regardless of their nationality or wherever they might reside, and that all persons have legitimate privacy interests in the handling of their personal information.' While even this pronouncement is limited – since it applies only to the handling of information, not its collection – still, the statement opens the door for further oversight and reform.[74]

Such developments were vulnerable to change under the new and more EU-hostile US Trump administration and were swiftly reversed.[75]

The agreement is broad in its scope, which is defined in Article 3 as relating to:

> personal information transferred between the Competent Authorities of one Party and the Competent Authorities of the other Party, or otherwise transferred in accordance with an agreement concluded between the United States and the European Union or its Member States, for the prevention, detection, investigation, and prosecution of criminal offences, including terrorism.

Article 5 delineates its effects and perhaps underlines the broad range of data transfer agreements existing, by stating that:

> This Agreement supplements, as appropriate, but does not replace, provisions regarding the protection of personal information in international agreements between the Parties, or the United States and Member States that address matters within the scope of this Agreement.

[73] See US Department of Justice, 'Judicial Redress Act of 2015 & US-Eu Data Protection And Privacy Agreement' (*USDJ*, 9 October 2020), www.justice.gov/opcl/judicial-redress-act-2015 accessed 25 February 2022.

[74] D Severson, 'American Surveillance of Non-US Persons: Why New Privacy Protections Offer Only Cosmetic Change' (2015) 56 *Harvard International Law Journal* 465, 513.

[75] 'Meijers Committee Note on the EU-US Umbrella Agreement' (2016) CM 1613. The Meijers Committee has raised concerns as to the relationship between this superstructure and the existing EU-US Agreements (Europol, Eurojust, MLA, Bilateral MLA treaties, TFTP and PNR) with regard to the sustainability of an adequacy requirement.

Its use and limitations are outlined in Article 6 to the effect that the 'transfer of personal information shall be for specific purposes authorised by the legal basis for the transfer as set forth in Article 1'. The Umbrella Agreement includes various protections: eg data use limitations, onward transfer requirements, publicly available retention periods, access and rectification rights, data breach notification and judicial redress and enforceability.

On 1 February 2017, the EU-US data protection umbrella agreement entered into force. Article 14 explicitly provides for accountability, stating that the parties shall have in place measures to promote accountability for processing personal information within the scope of the agreement by their Competent Authorities, and any other of their authorities to which personal information has been transferred. Article 23 of the agreement requires the Commission and the US Government to conduct an initial joint review no later than three years after it enters into force. The implications of the invalidation of the EU-US Privacy Shield and the increased pressure on cloud providers falling under the US Foreign Intelligence Surveillance Act (FISA), section 702 and transferring data using standard contractual clauses for the right of judicial redress also appear to be complex contextual issues and are discussed further below. In this regard, a premium is placed on joint reviews on account of the loose institutional set-up, similar to all EU-US data flow regimes.[76] It is thus quite loose in terms of its institutionalised components yet is still a significant metric of closeness between the two legal orders. There is very limited information as to its operation, which appears entirely non-transparent and solely through the Commission at its executive discretion. It is arguably one of the least transparent of the EU-US regimes but still very much in the style of emerging law and governance of EU-US relations, predicated on weak and loose institutionalisation of data transfer regimes and highly esoteric and incomplete structures.

D. The EU-US E-Evidence Agreement Negotiations

The most recent of the transatlantic data regimes under negotiation relates to e-evidence and is perhaps the one most imbued with global consequences.[77] Highly

[76] EU-US Umbrella Agreement, Art 23.

[77] Council of the European Union, 'Information note from the European Commission services following the stock-taking meeting with the US on an EU-US Agreement on cross-border access to electronic evidence, 26 March 2021' (2021) 7295/21. The EU side was represented by representatives from *inter alia* European Commission DGs in Justice and Home Affairs as well as the European External Action Service. The US side was represented by the Department of Justice and the Department of State. The US mission in Brussels and the EU Delegation in Washington also attended. The US updated the EU side on the state of play on the US CLOUD Act, including implementation of the US-UK agreement and on negotiations with third states under the CLOUD Act. The US stated that the US-UK agreement had not entered into force yet, as there were a number of pending issues still to be addressed. As for Australia, the US said work was ongoing and the US was optimistic things would move forward. The US also said they were looking at opening negotiations with other third countries, without giving further detail.

significant legislative developments have been taking place globally to provide for formal recognition of public-private cooperative mechanisms with respect to e-evidence across borders. Here, the EU's efforts to institutionalise emerging regimes are notable but are replicating other global systems. Developments began in the US, and in an extraordinary setting and place. In 2018, US Congress enacted the Clarifying Lawful Overseas Use of Data Act, or 'CLOUD Act', in the midst of the Microsoft litigation on appeal to the US Supreme Court.[78] It allowed US federal law enforcement authorities to compel US-based data companies to provide data regardless of whether the data was stored in the US or on foreign soil. In this long-running litigation, US law enforcement sought data on a user of Microsoft services in relation to a drug trafficking case; Microsoft said that the data in question was located exclusively in a data centre in Ireland, and access would have to be worked out with Irish authorities. In 2018, the Supreme Court heard arguments in the case, with privacy NGOs urging the Supreme Court to respect international privacy standards, citing key cases from the European Court of Human Rights and the CJEU.[79] The Act authorises US law enforcement to unilaterally demand access to data stored outside the US, drawing widespread criticism from the international community. It thus adopts long-established US principles on extra-territoriality to the effect that a company subject to US jurisdiction could be required to produce data the company controls, regardless of where it is stored at any point in time. Some state that law enforcement agencies around the world were encouraged that the innovative international agreements envisioned by the legislation would offer a solution to burgeoning difficulties in obtaining access to electronic evidence located in the US.[80] Most significantly, however, it had no in-built specific guarantees for data relating to non-US citizens.

[78] *Microsoft v United States*, 829 F3d 197 (2d Cir 2016). In that case, the US government served upon Microsoft a warrant that had been approved by the FBI to turn over emails of a target account stored in Ireland, who had found probable cause to believe the electronic data sought by the government related to the commission of a narcotics crime. The appellate court held, for the first time since the Stored Communications Act (SCA) was enacted in 1986, that the SCA did not require Microsoft to disclose information in its custody and control that it had stored on a server in Ireland. The decision was on appeal to the US Supreme Court when the CLOUD Act was enacted, making the decision moot.

[79] eg *EPIC Amicus US v Miscrosoft* [2018] No 17-2 SCUS, www.supremecourt.gov/DocketPDF/17/17-2/28360/20180118172113162_17-2%20bsac%20Electronic%20Privacy%20Information%20Center.pdf accessed 25 February 2022.

[80] Only the UK has emerged with an agreement so far and this has drawn much criticism, from the EU and also from human rights bodies: see Agreement between the Government of the United States of America and the Government of the United Kingdom of Great Britain and Northern Ireland on Access to Electronic Data for the Purpose of Countering Serious Crime' (3 October 3, 2019). See eg J Daskal and P Swire, 'The U.K.-US CLOUD Act Agreement Is Finally Here, Containing New Safeguards' (*Lawfare Blog*, 8 October 2019), www.lawfareblog.com/uk-us-cloud-act-agreement-finally-here-containing-new-safeguards accessed 25 February 2022; T Christakis, '21 Thoughts and Questions about the UK-US CLOUD Act Agreement: (and an Explanation of How it Works – with Charts)' (*European Law Blog*, 17 October 2019), https://europeanlawblog.eu/2019/10/17/21-thoughts-and-questions-about-the-uk-us-cloud-act-agreement-and-an-explanation-of-how-it-works-with-charts/ accessed 25 February 2022; E Kyriakides, 'The CLOUD Act, E-Evidence, and Individual Rights' (2019) *European Data Protection Law Review* 99; M Rojszczak, 'CLOUD Act Agreements from an EU Perspective' (2020) *Computer Law & Security Review* 105445.

Simultaneously, in the same time period, the EU also proposed similarly 'sweeping' changes allowing EU enforcement agencies to preserve and collect cloud-based evidence outside of the mutual legal assistance treaty system, the so-called e-evidence package.[81] In 2018, the Commission introduced e-evidence legislation to facilitate the sharing of electronic evidence amongst EU Member States, including a regulation for European Production and Preservation Orders as well as a proposed directive supplementary thereto to mandate the establishment of legal representatives of service provides within the EU that could be served with orders.[82] Then, in early 2019, the European Commission began negotiations with the US on a comprehensive EU-US agreement on access to electronic evidence, ie an international agreement dealing precisely with cross-border access requests to electronic evidence with negotiating directives adopted by the Council in 2019.[83] EU bodies such as the European Data Protection Board (EDPB) and the European Parliament have stressed that an international agreement *must* contain sufficient adequate data protection safeguards, ie have 'strong procedural and substantive fundamental rights'. Whether they will complement existing complex EU-US Mutual Legal Assistance agreements remains to be seen.[84] An e-evidence

[81] A Aguinaldo and P De Hert, 'European Law Enforcement and US Data Companies: A Decade of Cooperation Free from Law' (2020) 6(26) *Brussels Privacy Hub Working Paper*.

[82] European Commission, 'Proposal for a Regulation of the European Parliament and of the Council on European Production and Preservation Orders for electronic evidence in criminal matters' COM (2018) 225 final; European Commission, 'Proposal for a Directive of the European Parliament and of the Council laying down harmonised rules on the appointment of legal representatives for the purpose of gathering evidence in criminal proceedings' COM (2018) 226 final; European Commission Staff Working Document, 'Impact Assessment Accompanying the document Proposal for a Regulation of the European Parliament and of the Council on European Production and Preservation Orders for electronic evidence in criminal matters and Proposal for a Directive of the European Parliament and of the Council laying down harmonised rules on the appointment of legal representatives for the purpose of gathering evidence in criminal proceedings' SWD (2018) 118 final.

[83] European Commission, 'Recommendation for a Council Decision authorising the opening of negotiations in view of an agreement between the European Union and the United States of America on cross-border access to electronic evidence for judicial cooperation in criminal matters' COM (2019) 70 final; European Commission, 'Annex to the Recommendation for a Council Decision authorising the opening of negotiations in view of an agreement between the European Union and the United States of America on cross-border access to electronic evidence for judicial cooperation in criminal matters' COM (2019) 70 final; European Commission, 'Questions and Answers: Mandate for the EU-US cooperation on electronic evidence' (Press Release, 5 February 2019), https://ec.europa.eu/commission/presscorner/detail/en/MEMO_19_863 accessed 25 February 2022; European Commission, 'Report of the Commission services on the second round of negotiations in view of an agreement between the European Union and the United States of America on cross-border access to electronic evidence for judicial cooperation in criminal matters' (6 November 2019) 13713/19; EDPB–EDPS, 'Joint Response to the LIBE Committee on the impact of the US Cloud Act on the European legal framework for personal data protection' (10 July 2019), https://edpb.europa.eu/our-work-tools/our-documents/letters/edpb-edps-joint-response-libe-committee-impact-us-cloud-act_en accessed 25 February 2022.

[84] In 2003, the EU and US signed two treaties on extradition and mutual legal assistance so as to simplify the extradition process and promote better prosecutorial cooperation, as part of efforts to improve transatlantic security cooperation post 9/11. The Agreements were historic as they were the first law enforcement agreements conducted between the EU and US and the first cooperation agreements to be negotiated by the Council in criminal matters pursuant to ex Arts 24 and 38 Treaty of the European Union (TEU). The negotiation of bilateral instruments with 15 EU Member States followed

agreement would incorporate and potentially expand upon existing data protection safeguards contained in the EU-US Agreement on the Protection of Personal Information Relating to the Prevention, Investigation, Detection and Prosecution of Criminal Offenses (also referred to as the Umbrella Agreement). Were the institutional characteristics robust enough, these additional safeguards would help mitigate the concerns expressed in the privacy and civil liberties community about the lesser degree of judicial involvement in responding to e-evidence requests.[85] The question increasingly arises as to whether an EU-level approach is essential here in order to avoid the potential negative consequences of a fragmented patchwork of non-harmonised bilateral executive agreements between the US and EU Member States that would be concluded under the US CLOUD Act.[86] Identifying what the legal base of such an agreement would be has constituted a complex task, particularly as to the institutional design and governance that would be 'court proof' and also likely to pass muster with the European Parliament; matters on the US side look similarly complex.[87] The EU also has significant difficulties in the Council of Europe as to the Budapest Convention and its amendment, as discussed above.[88] It remains to be seen how this new era of international law will impact on EU law-making and whether the Biden administration will evolve transatlantic law-making efforts in an era of the autonomy of the EU legal order.

thereafter as well as the negotiation with 10 new accession States in 2004. After the 2007, two full extradition treaties and two bilateral mutual assistance instruments were concluded with Bulgaria and Romania in 2007. An exchange of instruments between the EU and US took place in 2009 and all instruments and the Agreements entered into force on 1 February 2010. See E Fahey, 'Transatlantic Cooperation in Criminal Law' in V Mitsilegas et al (eds), *Research Handbook on EU Criminal Law* (Edward Elgar, 2018).

[85] See J Daskal, 'Privacy and Security across Borders' (2019) *Yale Law Journal Forum* 1029, www.yalelawjournal.org/pdf/Daskal_v3q35qwf.pdf accessed 25 February 2022. Daskal and Wire envision two options as a matter of EU law: either the EU and US negotiate an agreement outside of the CLOUD Act; or the EU and US opt for a CLOUD Act executive agreement.

[86] T Christakis and F Terpan, 'EU-US Negotiations on Law Enforcement Access to Data: Divergences, Challenges and EU Law Procedures and Options' (2021) *International Data Privacy Law* 1; T Christakis, 'Data, Extraterritoriality and International Solutions to Transatlantic Problems of Access to Digital Evidence. Legal Opinion on the Microsoft Ireland Case (Supreme Court of the United States) (November 29, 2017)' (2017) The White Book: Lawful Access to Data: The US v. Microsoft Case, Sovereignty in the Cyber-Space and European Data Protection, CEIS & The Chertoff Group White Paper, https://ssrn.com/abstract=3086820 accessed 25 February 2022; T Christakis, 'E-Evidence in the EU Parliament: Basic Features of Birgit Sippel's Draft Report' (*EU Law Blog*, 21 January 2020), https://europeanlawblog.eu/2020/01/21/e-evidence-in-the-eu-parliament-basic-features-of-birgit-sippels-draft-report/ accessed 25 February 2022.

[87] See Christakis and Terpan, 'EU-US Negotiations on Law Enforcement Access to Data: Divergences, Challenges and EU Law Procedures and Options' (n 86) 20–21.

[88] The Commission held a stock-taking meeting with the US on 26 March 2021 ahead of the EU-US Justice and Home Affairs Senior Officials Meeting on 14–15 April 2021. The discussions appear to be highly sensitive (leaked via civil liberties NGO Statewatch) and appear to consist more of US discussions of third country agreements as to Australia and the UK rather than EU-US relations. See Council of the European Union, 'Information note from the European Commission services following the stock-taking meeting with the US on an EU-US Agreement on cross-border access to electronic evidence, 26 March 2021' (2021) 7295/21; 'EU-USA: Action against encrypted communications to be discussed at senior officials' meeting in April' (*Statewatch*, 24 March 2021), www.statewatch.org/news/2021/march/eu-usa-action-against-encrypted-communications-to-be-discussed-at-senior-officials-meeting-in-april/

IV. From EU-US Safe Harbour to the EU-US Privacy Shield Agreements: The Ever Weaker Institutionalisation of Hybrid Governance

The Safe Harbour Agreement is a significant form of transatlantic relations, in its typical style of scattered hybrid governance, dispersed amongst decisions, annexes and letters. Yet its scale and breadth with commercial and security implications entailed that it was an important departure for transatlantic relations with a so-called 'hybrid' style governance.[89] In July 2000, the US Department of Commerce and the European Commission formalised an agreement creating a set of so-called 'Safe Harbour Principles' (the Principles) on data privacy protection, principles that became known as the Safe Harbour Agreement. Under the Safe Harbour 'understanding', US based firms could self-certify that they would abide by the Safe Harbour Principles and thus avoid the restrictions on data transfers to the US imposed by European law. The Safe Harbour program set forth seven core data privacy principles for industry to follow. It thus operated under the premise that the EU formally acknowledged the Principles as 'adequate' and so the Principles provide US businesses with a 'safe harbour'. Despite its unusual formula, the Principles are understood to constitute an agreement.

As Shaffer stated (many years ago now), for some the principles constitute a unique development in the governance of EU-US economic relations, adding a coercive extraterritorial reach to EU privacy standards. Yet for others, they constituted a capitulation by trade bureaucrats to US trading concerns through a weak agreement filled with loopholes, or perhaps simply a compromise through new institutional developments balancing EU concerns.[90] What was principally innovative about this form of governance was that it constituted a loose form of de facto harmonisation of social standards going beyond previous EU-US mutual recognition agreements yet also somehow going beyond regulatory requirements in the US. It led to the assertion that the EU was 'ratecheting up' US privacy standards, through a form of intuitional development thereof, through 'spillover' and 'convergence' built into the system for cross-border transfers of data.[91] The degree of institutional form here was always open to question, bringing out a classic

accessed 25 February 2022; 'EU-USA: "Sensitive" European Commission information note on cross-border access to electronic evidence' (*Statewatch*, 11 May 2021), www.statewatch.org/news/2021/may/eu-usa-sensitive-european-commission-information-note-on-cross-border-access-to-electronic-evidence/ accessed 25 February 2022.

[89] Where the principles went beyond the regulatory requirements prevailing in the US. Still, the lack of a uniform body of privacy law or regulation and no specialised enforcement authorities meant that it was widely assumed that US law would not be regarded as 'adequate'; *cf* G Shaffer, 'Reconciling Trade and Regulatory Goals: The Prospects and Limits of New Approaches to Transatlantic Governance through Mutual Recognition and Safe Harbour Agreements' (2002) 9 *Columbia Journal of European Law* 29, 77.

[90] Shaffer, 'Reconciling Trade and Regulatory Goals: The Prospects and Limits of New Approaches to Transatlantic Governance through Mutual Recognition and Safe Harbour Agreements' (n 89).

[91] ibid.

critique of the EU as institution-based unlike the US market-based approach, although it is hard to see this as anything other than a form of fusion of the two.[92] It was symptomatic of an era where the EU increasingly negotiated with the US as a state-like entity and its market-based power and clout on regulatory standards was becoming apparent, driven through institutional frameworks. The Safe Harbour Principles were importantly 'endorsed' by the European Commission in a Decision,[93] the key binding legal element thereof.

As is developed below in further detail, in 2015, in *Schrems v Data Protection Commission*[94] (*Schrems I*) the CJEU invalidated the EU-US Safe Harbour Agreement. Prior to this, however, the Snowdon affair broke out, igniting massive European scepticism about US surveillance practices.[95] The initial outcome of *Schrems I* was to subvert the claim that the Internet could be free from regulation. Whether it promoted a general decentralisation of authority to national authorities as a form of institutionalisation is debatable. It appeared to theoretically empower the emerging enforcement agenda with regard to data rights and EU law.[96] A new replacement for Safe Harbour was quickly adopted in 2016, nominally renamed and rebranded with marketing-style logos as the EU-US Privacy Shield.[97] It was developed so swiftly thereafter, as Anthony Gardner reminds us in his book accounting for his time as Ambassador to the EU from the US, as a greatly rushed diplomatic intervention to 'mop up' the aftermath of *Schrems I*.[98] *Schrems I* thus bore striking parallels to the PNR CJEU decision of the Court several years earlier and the Privacy Shield was by all accounts only likely in these circumstances to bear similarities to the Safe Harbour Agreement. The Privacy Shield had high ambitions: it purported to evolve the oversight and accountability

[92] J R Reidenberg, 'E-Commerce and Trans-Atlantic Privacy' (2001) 38 *Houston Law Review* 717, 743–46; A Lukas, 'Safe Harbor or Stormy Waters? Living with the EU Data Protection Directive' (2001) 16 Trade Briefing Papers, CATO Institute Center for Trade Policy Studies; M Cutler, 'Information Technology: Lawyers Say US, EU on Collision Course over E-commerce as Competitiveness Issues' (2002) 18 *International Trade Review (BNA)* 1868 (arguing that EU laws 'inhibit the ability of US companies to compete within the EU'). See generally G Shaffer, 'Globalization and Social Protection: The Impact of EU and International Rules in the Ratcheting Up of US Privacy Standards' (2000) 25 *Yale Journal of International Law* 70.

[93] Commission Decision of 26 July 2000 pursuant to Directive 95/46/EC of the European Parliament and of the Council on the adequacy of the protection provided by the safe harbour privacy principles and related frequently asked questions issued by the US Department of Commerce, 2000/520/EC [2000] OJ L 215/7. Article 25 of the Directive provided that Member States would prohibit all data transfers to a third country if the Commission did not find that they ensured an adequate level of protection.

[94] Case C-362/14 *Schrems v Data Commissioner (Schrems I)* EU:C:2015:650.

[95] European Commission, 'Rebuilding Trust in EU-US Data Flows' COM (2013) 846 final.

[96] JP Barlow, 'A Declaration of the Independence of Cyberspace' (1996), www.eff.org/cyberspace-independence accessed 25 February 2022.

[97] Commission Implementing Decision (EU) 2016/1250 of 12 July 2016 pursuant to Directive 95/46/EC of the European Parliament and of the Council on the adequacy of the protection provided by the EU-US Privacy Shield (notified under document C (2016) 4176).

[98] Gardner, *Stars with Stripes* (n 34).

dimensions of Safe Harbour.[99] The Privacy Shield established a set of mutually agreed principles, subject to the 'investigatory and enforcement powers' of the US Federal Trade Commission, the Department of Transportation and other statutory bodies that could ensure compliance.[100] The EU-US Privacy Shield decision was adopted in mid-2016 and the Privacy Shield framework became operational shortly thereafter in 1 August 2016. Its express function was to protect the fundamental rights of anyone in the EU whose personal data was transferred to certified companies in the US for commercial purposes. It was thus developed with the objective of bringing legal clarity to businesses relying on transatlantic data transfers. The Privacy Shield was a thus key overarching framework approved by the EU and the US government to ensure compliance with EU data protection requirements when data is transferred between the US and the EU and EEA. It was not explicitly mentioned by the GDPR. Organisations are deemed to provide 'adequate' protection of personal information as required by the GDPR if they abided by the seven key principles: (1) notice; (2) choice; (3) accountability for onward transfer; (4) security; (5) data integrity and purpose limitation; (6) access; and (7) recourse, enforcement, and liability. They were thus *the same* principles as applicable to the Safe Harbour Agreement. EU enforcement rested with national DPAs (Data Protection Authorities), whereas US enforcement rested with the Federal Trade Commission (FTC). However, as Brkan states in the Commission's adequacy decision on Privacy Shield, adopted in the aftermath of the *Schrems* case, the Commission implicitly stated that US legislation no longer interfered with the essence of the fundamental right to privacy under EU law, because it did not allow storage of personal data on a generalised basis.[101] Rather, US intelligence activities were excluded.[102] It was also argued that section 702 of the US FISA is described in the Privacy Shield as allowing access to content 'targeting certain non-US persons outside the United States …' despite there being numerous challenges before US courts against this section of FISA and it being contestable whether it was generalised or not.[103]

One key difference with respect to the Privacy Shield was to be the breadth of governance and the actors of the governance regime. As to the actors, the Privacy

[99] V Jourová and E O'Reilly, 'Follow-up reply from the European Ombudsman to Commissioner Jourová on the use of the title "Ombudsperson" in the EU-US Privacy Shield agreement' (*European Ombudsman*, 2 May 2016), www.ombudsman.europa.eu/en/correspondence/en/66926 accessed 25 February 2022.

[100] See 'EU-US Privacy Shield Framework Principles Issued by The US Department Of Commerce', www.privacyshield.gov/servlet/servlet.FileDownload?file=015t00000004qAg accessed 25 February 2022.

[101] Commission Implementing Decision (EU) 2016/1250 of 12 July 2016 pursuant to Directive 95/46/EC of the European Parliament and of the Council on the adequacy of the protection provided by the EU-US Privacy Shield (notified under document C(2016) 4176) OJ L207/1; M Brkan, 'The Essence of the Fundamental Rights to Privacy and Data Protection: Finding the Way Through the Maze of the CJEU's Constitutional Reasoning' (2019) 20 *German Law Journal* 864, 865.

[102] Commission Implementing Decision (EU) 2016/1250 (n 101) para 90.

[103] ibid.

Shield Annex Part III provides that the Ombudsperson was to be a senior official within the US Department of State who was independent from US intelligence agencies. As outlined below, the EU executive had begun to lose patience with the US's alleged lack of compliance on this issue. The Privacy Shield Ombudsperson was a new mechanism set up under the Privacy Shield to facilitate the processing of and response to requests relating to possible access for national security purposes by US intelligence authorities to personal data transmitted from the EU to the US.[104] The Ombudsperson was to deal with requests relating to data transferred not just pursuant to the Privacy Shield, but also on the basis of other frameworks such as the Standard Contractual Causes (SCCs), binding corporate rules (BCRs) or derogations. The US had an interim ombudsman, Manisha Singh, in place despite continued EU pressure to make a permanent appointment. On 20 June 2019, Keith Krach was confirmed by the US Senate to become the Trump administration's first permanent Privacy Shield Ombudsperson at the State Department. The role of the Privacy Shield Ombudsperson was to act as an additional avenue of redress for all EU data subjects whose data is transferred from the EU or Switzerland to the US under either the EU-US or the Swiss-US Privacy Shield Framework, the Swiss version being a replica parallel agreement to the EU-US Agreement. Assisted by a number of staff, the Ombudsperson was obliged to ensure that requests are properly investigated and addressed in a timely manner, and that confirmation was received that the relevant US laws were complied with or – crucially – to provide adequate remedies.

The Commission then further committed to reviewing the arrangement on an annual basis, to assess whether it continued to ensure an adequate level of protection for personal data. Over the course of 2017, 2018 and 2019, the EU and US engaged in joint annual reviews of the operation of the EU-US Privacy Shield, involving a not inconsiderable number of EU and US public, private sector, government and agencies actors.[105] The first review made a variety of recommendations as to the commercial aspects of the Privacy Shield as well as the national security

[104] See European Commission, 'Privacy Shield request form under Ombudsperson mechanism'. https://ec.europa.eu/newsroom/article29/items/610144 accessed 25 February 2022.

[105] The annual review was conducted for the EU by representatives of the European Commission's Directorate General for Justice and Consumers. The EU delegation also included eight representatives designated by the Article 29 Working Party, the advisory body bringing together the national data protection authorities (DPAs) of the Member States as well as the European Data Protection Supervisor. On the US side, representatives of the Department of Commerce (DoC), the Federal Trade Commission (FTC), the Department of Transportation, the Department of State, the Office of the Director of National Intelligence and the Department of Justice participated in the review, as well as the acting Ombudsperson, a Member of the Privacy and Civil Liberties Oversight Board (PCLOB) and the Office of the Inspector General of the Intelligence Community. Moreover, representatives of organisations that offer independent dispute resolution under the Privacy Shield, the American Arbitration Association as administrator of the Privacy Shield Arbitration Panel and some Privacy Shield-certified companies provided input during the annual review. For the third annual review, the Commission gathered information from Privacy Shield-certified companies through their respective trade associations and non-governmental organisations active in the field of fundamental rights.

matters. The US Department of State was said to have taken measures to ensure that the Ombudsperson mechanism was fully functional and ready to receive and address complaints. The EU asked that US Congress would consider favourably enshrining in the Foreign Intelligence Surveillance Act the protections for non-Americans offered by Presidential Policy Directive 28 (PPD-28) and asked the US administration to swiftly appoint a permanent Privacy Shield Ombudsperson, as well as the missing members of the Privacy and Civil Liberties Oversight Board (PCLOB). Overall, the report was broadly positive. In the second annual review it was noted that significant progress has been made in the commercial aspects of the Privacy Shield. More US oversight and enforcement actions were suggested, with regard to the compliance of Privacy Shield certified organisations. One of the main concerns expressed remained a lack of oversight in the US of three new members of the PCLOB, including its Chair. The Federal Trade Commission also confirmed that its investigation into the Facebook/Cambridge Analytica case was ongoing and positive sentiments were expressed by the Commission as to the development of Federal Privacy law.[106] Also lauded was the US Amendments Reauthorization Act of 2017, which amended the Foreign Intelligence Surveillance Act of 1978, introduced some limited additional privacy safeguards, for instance in the area of transparency.[107] In the third annual review in 2019, the Commission welcomed the fact that the Department of Commerce was carrying out proactive compliance 'spot-checks' on a regular basis and in a systematic manner.[108] However, it noted that these 'spot-checks' tended to be limited to formal requirements and the Commission would have expected a more vigorous approach regarding enforcement action on substantive violations of the Privacy Shield Principles.

The reviews involved a diverse range of public and private sector officials, lawyers, business, users and others involved in the implementation of the Privact Shield. The findings are thus of much significance for the very mixed picture they present as to the operative nature of the Privacy Shield and its uneven enforcement, foundations and functionality. The delays in the Trump administration appointing an Ombudsman led to arguably the only point of real political conflict, with the European Parliament applying pressure within the EU institutions for the appointment to be made. Limited US enforcement of transgressions of the Privacy Shield received largely mild critique, with the overall result that the three reviews largely generated positive reports from a vast range of sources and produced mostly short reports encouraging rollout implementation and enforcement.[109] The

[106] eg see Federal Trade Commission, 'In the Matter of Cambridge Analytica LLC' (2019), www.ftc.gov/enforcement/cases-proceedings/182-3107/cambridge-analytica-llc-matter accessed 25 February 2022.

[107] See Foreign Intelligence Surveillance Act Amendments Reauthorization Act of 2017, s 139.

[108] European Commission, 'Report from the Commission to the European Parliament and the Council on the third annual review of the functioning of the EU-US Privacy Shield' COM (2019) 495 final.

[109] See European Commission, 'First Annual Review of the EU-US Privacy Shield' (2017), https://ec.europa.eu/commission/presscorner/detail/en/MEMO_17_3967 accessed 25 February 2022;

Privacy Shield met its fate in July 2020, when the CJEU struck it down because of its 'weak' institutionalisation and the place of US national security laws. This arguably showed the 'damp squid' nature of the reviews conducted.[110] Such a narrative is not per se conventional and most commentators suggest that US surveillance law, rather than the institutionalisation problem, was the primary issue. Still, it is argued that the framing of the Ombudsman and institutionalisation issues together are more closely linked than some suggest, and indeed more pivotal to understanding the dynamic of the surveillance issues.

Prior to examining its future, the chapter next considers other significant litigation taking place with respect to the Privacy Shield from the moment of its adoption to its annulment in July 2020.

V. The *Schrems* Litigation on the EU-US Privacy Shield

The Privacy Shield was the subject of several sets of judicial review proceedings, as was its predecessor Safe Harbour. As has already been outlined, in *Schrems I* in 2015, the CJEU struck down the Safe Harbour Agreement in a landmark decision, annulling the data transfer agreement.[111] As former US Ambassador to the EU Anthony Gardner has detailed in his account of Obama-era transatlantic diplomacy, *Stars with Stripes*, there was an unimaginably short period of time in which to negotiate a new regime.[112] The economic repercussions of a legal lacuna were appreciable. The EU-US Privacy Shield came into force shortly thereafter to replace the US Safe Harbour Agreement, and specifically to address the concerns about data collection and privacy that had arisen in the *Schrems* case; but the NSA, Snowdon and PRISM revelations were also relevant.[113] It has spurred the development of other instruments and enforcement regimes. Yet, as explained below, the Privacy Shield itself was struck down in 2020, just five years after its introduction. This raises significant questions surrounding the meaning of innovations

European Data Protection Board, 'EU-US Privacy Shield – Second Annual Joint Review report – 22/01/2019', https://edpb.europa.eu/our-work-tools/our-documents/other-guidance/eu-us-privacy-shield-second-annual-joint-review-report_en accessed 25 February 2022 and European Data Protection Board, 'EU-US Privacy Shield – Third Annual Joint Review report – 12/11/2019' (2019), https://edpb.europa.eu/our-work-tools/our-documents/eu-us-privacy-shield-third-annual-joint-review-report-12112019_en accessed 25 February 2022.

[110] E Fahey and F Terpan, 'Torn between Institutionalisation and Judicialisation: the Demise of the EU-US Privacy Shield' (2021) 28 *Indiana Journal of Global Legal Studies* 205.

[111] See Statement of the Article 29 Working Party on the implementation of the Judgment of the ECJ of 6 October 2015 in *Schrems I* (n 94); L Azoulai and M Van der Sluis, 'Institutionalizing Personal Data Protection in Times of Global Institutional Distrust: Schrems' (2016) 53 *Common Market Law Review* 1343.

[112] See Gardner, *Stars with Stripes* (n 34).

[113] Commission Implementing Decision (EU) 2016/1250 of 12 July 2016 pursuant to Directive 95/46/EC of the European Parliament and of the Council on the adequacy of the protection provided by the EU-US Privacy Shield (notified under document C (2016) 4176) [2016] OJ L207/1; *Schrems I* (n 94); Azoulai and Van der Sluis (n 111).

with regard to actors and institutionalisation and non-institutionalisation in this context. Whether the Privacy Shield became substantially *more* institutionalised and a *more* effective mode of governance seems debateable. It ultimately appears as study of modest institutional innovations taking place at transnational level despite grander ambitions: a difficult mismatch. It thus forms a ripe case study for consideration here.

The *Schrems* litigation began with one Austrian law student acting alone, and would eventually become synonymous with the most key transatlantic data transfer litigation in EU law. This status of Schrems would be further litigated in *Maximilian Schrems v Facebook Ireland Limited (Schrems I)*.[114] There are few litigants who can claim to have contributed as much to the development of secondary EU law as Maximilian Schrems.[115] Schrems brought a first series of complaints in 2011 and 2013 against Facebook and the way in which the company used the personal data of its users, which ultimately led to the annulment of the Safe Harbour framework between the EU and the US.[116] Meanwhile, Schrems also rallied support for a class action against Facebook, in which he invited other users to assign him their claims with regard to the company's alleged violations of privacy and data-protection law. Over 20,000 users assigned their claims to Schrems; he brought proceedings against Facebook in the courts of his country of domicile, Austria, based on his rights and those of seven other users. The CJEU in *Schrems v Facebook* considered a preliminary ruling concerning the interpretation of Articles 15 and 16 of Council Regulation (EC) No 44/2001 of 22 December 2000 on jurisdiction and the recognition and enforcement of judgments in civil and commercial matters. The request was made in proceedings between Schrems and Facebook Ireland Limited, concerning applications seeking declarations and an injunction, disclosure, production of accounts and payment in the amount of €4,000 in respect of private Facebook accounts of both Mr Schrems and the seven other persons who had assigned to him their claims relating to those accounts. Schrems was a privacy activist, whose publications, talks, lectures and non-profit organisation used 'targeted and strategic litigation' to enforce privacy and data protection laws across Europe. The CJEU had to consider whether Schrems could still rely on the special rules for consumers provided in (what are now) Articles 17–19 of Regulation No 1215/2012 on jurisdiction and the recognition and enforcement of judgments in civil and commercial matters (Brussels Ia) and seize the courts of his own domicile. In a small chamber, the CJEU held that although

[114] Case C-498/16 *Schrems v Facebook Ireland* ECLI:EU:C:2018:37; Council Regulation (EC) No 44/2001 of 22 December 2000 on jurisdiction and the recognition and enforcement of judgments in civil and commercial matters (Brussels I) [2001] OJ L12/1.

[115] T Lutzi, 'What's a consumer?' (Some) clarification on consumer jurisdiction, social-media accounts, and collective redress under the Brussels Ia Regulation: Case C-498/16 Maximilian Schrems v. Facebook Ireland Limited, EU:C:2018:37' (2018) 25 *Maastricht Journal of European and Comparative Law* 374.

[116] ibid.

Schrems could still be considered a consumer, his resulting capacity to seize the courts of his domicile would be limited to his own claims. It found that Article 15 of Regulation No 44/2001 had to be interpreted as meaning that the activities of publishing books, lecturing, operating websites, fundraising and being assigned the claims of numerous consumers for the purpose of their enforcement did not entail the loss of a private Facebook account user's status as a '*consumer*' within the meaning of that article.[117] This enlargement of Schrems' status is significant. A less than successful attempt to enlarge the cohort of actors capable of litigating the Privacy Shield occurred in the *Digital Rights Ireland* case. The General Court ruled as inadmissible a challenge brought by Digital Rights Ireland, an Irish digital rights NGO advocacy group that had already successfully won litigation against the Data Retention Directive in 2014, where it sought the annulment of the 'Privacy Shield', arguing that it did not ensure an adequate level of data protection.[118] On one level, this stricter view of standing is notable given the broad interpretation of a 'consumer' by the Court because it limits the range of actors, entities and subjects who can litigate the Privacy Shield.[119]

In Summer 2020, the CJEU invalidated the EU-US Privacy Shield in its decision in *Facebook Ireland v Schrems* (*Schrems II*).[120] Thus, this was the second time that the CJEU invalidated a data transfer mechanism: the Safe Harbour Principles had also been declared invalid by the CJEU in Case C-362/14 (*Schrems I*), in relatively similar circumstances, terms and form. After the invalidation of Safe Harbour, Facebook used SCCs,[121] along with the EU-US Privacy Shield, to transfer data outside of the EU. Thereafter, pursuant to an amended complaint in 2015, Schrems challenged the validity of Facebook's use of SCCs to transfer EU citizens' data to the US, arguing that the access to such data for mass surveillance by US intelligence agencies violated Articles 7, 8 and 47 of the EU Charter of Fundamental Rights (CFR). In a draft decision in 2016, the Irish Data Protection Commissioner held that the SCCs could not overcome the challenges of US surveillance laws and they instigated proceedings in the Irish High Court, seeking a preliminary reference on the validity of the SCCs to the CJEU and their compliance with the CFR.

[117] *Schrems v Facebook Ireland* (n 114) para 41; P de Miguel Asensio, *Conflict of Laws and the Internet* (Edward Elgar, 2020) Ch 6.

[118] In Case T-670/16 *Digital Rights Ireland v European Commission* ECLI:EU:T:2017:838.

[119] Ibid. Case T-738/16 *La Quadrature du Net v Commission* ECLI:EU:T:2020:638; C-623/17 *Privacy International* EU:C:2020:790 and Case C-511/18 *La Quadrature du Net and Others* ECLI:EU:C:2020:791; Case C-512/18 *French Data Network and Others* and Case C-520/18 *Ordre des barreaux francophones et germanophone*. The case of *La Quadrature du Net v Commission* substantively begun the process of challenging *the Privacy Shield*. The CJEU does not analyse the EU-US Privacy Shield.

[120] Case C-311/18 *Data Protection Commissioner v Facebook Ireland Ltd, Maximillian Schrems* (*Schrems II*) EU:C:2020:559.

[121] The standard contractual clauses (SCCs) were pre-approved by the European Commission to act as terms and conditions for extraterritorial data transfers offering safeguards on data protection for the data transferred internationally, under the Commission Decision 2010/87. See Commission Decision of 5 February 2010 on standard contractual clauses for the transfer of personal data to processors established in third countries under Directive 95/46/EC of the European Parliament and of the Council (notified under document C(2010) 593) [2010] OJ L39/5.

In 2017, the Irish Court held that US surveillance laws permitted 'mass processing' of personal data and that a reference to the CJEU was necessary in order to determine the validity of SCCs.[122] Accordingly, by a preliminary ruling in 2018, the Irish Court referred 11 questions[123] to the CJEU which generally questioned the legality of SCCs and the EU-US Privacy Shield as adequate means of ensuring compliant data transfers to the third countries. Advocate General Saugmandsgaard Øe in an Opinion in late 2019 stated that the Ombudsperson was designated by the Secretary of State and was an integral part of the US State Department. There was nothing in that designation to indicate that the revocation of the Ombudsperson or the cancellation of his appointment would be accompanied by any particular guarantees. Although the Ombudsperson was presented as being independent of the 'intelligence community', he reported to the Secretary of State and was therefore not independent of the executive. As a result, Advocate General Øe stated:

> Consequently, the establishment of the Ombudsperson does not to my mind provide a remedy before an independent body offering the persons whose data are transferred a possibility of relying on their right of access to the data or of contesting any infringements of the applicable rules by the intelligence services.[124]

A short few months later, in Summer 2020 and towards the end of the Trump administration, the CJEU held that the European Commission's adequacy determination for Privacy Shield was invalid, on the basis that the US surveillance programs that the Commission assessed in its Privacy Shield decision, were not limited to what was strictly necessary and proportional as required by EU law, and hence they did not meet the requirements of Article 52 of the EU CFR. Second, it held that, with regard to US surveillance, EU data subjects lacked actionable judicial redress and lacked the right to an effective remedy in the US, as required by Article 47 of the EU Charter. The CJEU held that the institutional dimension to the redress provided for was deficient, stating that:

> […] [T]here is nothing in that decision to indicate that that ombudsperson has the power to adopt decisions that are binding on those intelligence services and does not mention any legal safeguards that would accompany that political commitment on which data subjects could rely […] Therefore, the ombudsperson mechanism to which the Privacy Shield Decision refers does not provide any cause of action before a body which offers the persons whose data is transferred to the United States guarantees essentially equivalent to those required by Article 47 of the Charter […]. Therefore, in finding, in

[122] *Data Protection Commissioner v Facebook Ireland Limited* [2017] IEHC 545. Further litigation ensued in Ireland instigated by Facebook to inhibit the unrestricted entitlement of national courts under Irish law to refer questions to the CJEU: see *Data Protection Commissioner v Facebook Ireland Ltd & Another* [2019] IESC 46.

[123] Ie what obligations are incumbent upon the DPC? Is the Privacy Shield an adequacy decision? Whose laws must satisfy whom? How should US law be understood and interpreted in Europe precisely? It may consider: where there is a violation of rights through transfer, what precisely is the comparator? The adequacy of the Ombudsman under the Privacy Shield was also the subject of the reference.

[124] *Schrems II* (n 120), Opinion of AG Øe, EU:C:2019:1145, para 339.

> Article 1(1) of the Privacy Shield Decision, that the United States ensures an adequate level of protection for personal data transferred from the Union to organisations in that third country under the EU-US Privacy Shield, the Commission disregarded the requirements of Article 45(1) of the GDPR, read in the light of Articles 7, 8 and 47 of the Charter.[125]

Much analysis of the decision has focused on the place of remedies rather than the structural challenges of weak and limited institutionalisation, as if the former were disconnected from the latter.[126] Ultimately, it is argued here that the non-autonomous actor – the key 'innovation' of the Privacy Shield – clearly amounted to weak institutionalisation (eg as to the Ombudsman) which could not provide adequate oversight in the face of such surveillance. In other words, the decision was not exclusively about US surveillance but also the fragile construct of institutionalisation on which the entire architecture ultimately hinged.[127]

VI. The Future of Transatlantic Data Institutionalisation: Towards Convergence?

The development of an architecture of class actions has been argued to be a key remedy for the successful exchange of data post-*Schrems II*.[128] Much of the aftermath of *Schrems II*, as discussed below, has focused on the specifics of the transfer regime, perhaps in place of examining the broader operation of many transatlantic regimes that are equally prone to allegations of deficiency. For instance, the European Parliament passed a wide-ranging resolution on *Schrems II*, to encourage the Commission to proactively monitor the use of mass surveillance technologies in the US as well as in other third countries, which could be the subject of an adequacy finding. It remarked that, while the recent entry into force in the US of the California Consumer Privacy Act (CCPA) was significant and steps were ongoing at federal level for legislative shifts, neither the CCPA nor any of the federal

[125] *Schrems II* (n 120) paras 196–98.

[126] eg A Joel and F Oliveira, 'Redress: What is the problem?' (*European Law Blog*, 28 September 2021). https://europeanlawblog.eu/2021/09/28/redress-what-is-the-problem/ accessed 25 February 2022; C Kuner, 'The Schrems II judgment of the Court of Justice and the future of data transfer regulation' (*European Law Blog*, 17 July 2020), https://europeanlawblog.eu/2020/07/17/the-schrems-ii-judgment-of-the-court-of-justice-and-the-future-of-data-transfer-regulation/ accessed 25 February 2022; K Propp and P Swire, 'After Schrems II: A Proposal to Meet the Individual Redress Challenge' (*Lawfare Blog*, 13 August 2020), www.lawfareblog.com/after-schrems-ii-proposal-meet-individual-redress-challenge accessed 25 February 2022; D Korff, 'Transfers of personal data from the EU to non-EU countries under the EU General Data Protection Regulation after "Schrems II": not a "Mission Impossible"' (*Ian Brown*, April 2021), www.ianbrown.tech/wp-content/uploads/2021/04/KORFF-The-EU-regime-on-data-transfers-after-Schrems-II-210422.pdf accessed 25 February 2022.

[127] Fahey and Terpan, 'Torn between Institutionalisation and Judicialisation: the demise of the EU-US Privacy Shield' (n 110).

[128] Korff, 'Transfers of personal data from the EU to non-EU countries under the EU General Data Protection Regulation after "Schrems II": not a "Mission Impossible"' (n 126).

proposals so far met the requirements of the GDPR for an adequacy finding. The European Parliament further encouraged the US legislator to enact legislation that met those requirements, though even such a move would not remedy the fundamental issues on mass surveillance by US intelligence services and the insufficient access to remedies that the Court had found. These would require an amendment to section 702 of the FISA, and the US President to amend EO 12333 and PPD-28. This, along with a legally enshrined mechanism to ensure that non-US citizens have enforceable rights beyond the Judicial Redress Act, was still required. Also, the extent to which the CJEU again backed EU negotiators into a corner, particularly after the EU-Canada PNR opinion, rendered the force of the judgment very difficult to carry forward. Indeed, it could be argued that as a result of *Schrems II* and in the EU-Canada PNR Opinion, all EU-US data transfer agreements were clearly imperilled.

More acutely, the *Schrems II* decision drew unfavourable attention to the EU's regular exchange of personal data with the US under the EU-US TFTP and the EU-US PNR as well as several other exchange programs, mechanisms and procedures.[129] The European Parliament formally requested the Commission to analyse the impact of the *Schrems I* and *II* judgments on these data exchanges. The question then arises as to the future of the EU-US Privacy Shield in the wake of a new US administration.[130] Immediately after *Schrems II*, litigation began in Ireland on the part of the Irish Data Protection Authority to halt the transfer of Facebook data to the US. Under the Trump administration then prevailing, the US announced initially that the Department of Commerce 'would continue to administer the Privacy Shield program', as the *Schrems II* ruling 'does not relieve participating organizations of their Privacy Shield obligations'.[131] In late September 2020, three significant US entities, namely the US Department of Commerce, US Department of Justice and US Office of the Director of National Intelligence, published a 22-page 'White Paper' on the *Schrems II* decision of the CJEU. This extraordinary paper accused the CJEU of being misinformed in its decision and omitting key information on US privacy law. The paper is labelled as an 'information' document, perhaps caustically so, entitled 'Information on US Privacy Safeguards Relevant to SCCs and other EU Legal Bases for EU-US Data Transfers after

[129] The European Parliament referenced: '… The automatic exchange of tax information via the intergovernmental agreements implementing the US Foreign Tax Compliance Act (FATCA), which adversely affects "accidental Americans", as …. adverse effects of the US Foreign Account Tax Compliance Act (FATCA) on EU citizens and in particular "accidental Americans"; recalls that the US continues to have access to Member States' law enforcement databases containing EU citizens' fingerprints and DNA data …' See European Parliament, 'Resolution of 20 May 2021 on the ruling of the CJEU of 16 July 2020 – Data Protection Commissioner v Facebook Ireland Limited and Maximillian Schrems ("Schrems II"), Case C-311/18' (2020) 2020/2789 (RSP).

[130] A Chander, 'Is Data Localization a Solution for Schrems II?' (2020) 23 *Journal of International Economic Law* 771.

[131] US Department of Commerce, 'US Secretary of Commerce Wilbur Ross Statement on Schrems II Ruling and the Importance of EU-US Data Flows' (2020).

Schrems II'.[132] On one level, it is unusual and controversial to see a foreign government oppose and critique an international court in this way, and in such detail. It is all the more remarkable given the general convergence of the EU and US towards higher shared standards of data privacy and protection. A Senate hearing on the *Schrems II* decision took place in late 2020 and the new US administration quickly appointed negotiators.[133] In the meantime, the European Commission, together with the Department of Commerce, issued a statement outlining their efforts to find a solution to preserve transatlantic data flows. The EDPB welcomed the CJEU ruling in *Schrems II*, stating that it was 'ready to provide the European Commission with assistance and guidance to help it build, together with the US, a new framework that fully complies with EU data protection law' but without a grace period.[134] Many sought the rapid re-adoption of the Privacy Shield and to involve *more* actors rather than framing it as an institutionalisation issue.[135] In January 2021, the EDPB and the European Data Protection Supervisor (EDPS) adopted joint opinions on two sets of SCCs,[136] with one opinion on the SCCs for contracts between controllers and processors and one on the SCCs for the transfer of personal data to third countries. Their complexity and workability cannot be understated. The EDPB has provided a roadmap to support the application of the principle of accountability in data transfers,[137] where multiparty accountability

[132] US Department of Commerce, US Department of Justice and US Office of the Director of National Intelligence, 'Information on US Privacy Safeguards Relevant to SCCs and Other EU Legal Bases for EU-US Data Transfers after *Schrems II*', www.commerce.gov/sites/default/files/2020-09/SCCsWhitePaperFORMATTEDFINAL508COMPLIANT.PDF accessed 25 February 2022.

[133] US Senate Committee on Commerce, Science and Technology, 'The Invalidation of the EU-US Privacy Shield and the Future of Transatlantic Data Flows' (2020), www.commerce.senate.gov/2020/12/the-invalidation-of-the-eu-us-privacy-shield-and-the-future-of-transatlantic-data-flows accessed 25 February 2022.

[134] European Data Protection Board, 'Statement on the Court of Justice of the European Union Judgment in Case C-311/18 – *Data Protection Commissioner v Facebook Ireland and Maximillian Schrems*' (2020), https://edpb.europa.eu/news/news/2020/statement-court-justice-european-union-judgment-case-c-31118-data-protection_en accessed 25 February 2022; European Data Protection Board publishes FAQ document on CJEU judgment C-311/18 (Schrems II)' (2020), https://edpb.europa.eu/news/news/2020/european-data-protection-board-publishes-faq-document-cjeu-judgment-c-31118-schrems_en accessed 25 February 2022; J Daskal, 'What Comes Next: The Aftermath of European Court's Blow to Transatlantic Data Transfers' (*Just Security*, 17 July 2020) www.justsecurity.org/71485/what-comes-next-the-aftermath-of-european-courts-blow-to-transatlantic-data-transfers/ accessed 25 February 2022.

[135] See also P Gewirtz et al, 'A Roadmap for US-Europe Cooperation on China' (2021) Yale Law School Paul Tsai China Center Paper, https://law.yale.edu/sites/default/files/area/center/china/document/roadmap_for_us-eu_cooperation_on_china.pdf accessed 25 February 2022.

[136] 'EDPB & EDPS adopt joint opinions on new sets of SCCs' (2021), https://edpb.europa.eu/news/news/2021/edpb-edps-adopt-joint-opinions-new-sets-sccs_en accessed 25 February 2022. See EDPB-EDPS, 'Joint Opinion 1/2021 on standard contractual clauses between controllers and processors' (2021) https://edpb.europa.eu/our-work-tools/our-documents/edpbedps-joint-opinion/edpb-edps-joint-opinion-12021-standard_en accessed 25 February 2022.

[137] European Data Protection Board, Recommendations 01/2020 on measures that supplement transfer tools to ensure compliance with the EU level of protection of personal data 11 November 2020, https://edpb.europa.eu/our-work-tools/documents/public-consultations/2020/recommendations-012020-measures-supplement_en accessed 25 February 2022.

has been reflected upon for some time. Still, the Irish DPA appeared engaged in a war of words with the European Parliament as to enforcement of the Privacy Shield. The role of this DPA is still pivotal to transatlantic data flows. The aftermath of *Schrems* saw the Data Protection Commission (DPC) drafting orders to halve data flows but a short few months after *Schrems II*, in the DPC's view, Facebook could simply choose to include the agreement on data processing in a 'contract', which would make the GDPR requirements for 'consent' no longer apply; this caused international furore.[138] Ultimately, however, individuals' rights of action and reform of US surveillance laws are needed as well as a new and robust EU-US self-certification regime, perhaps along with class actions.

It is critical to note that in *Digital Rights Ireland*, the CJEU struck down the general retention of metadata under the Data Retention Directive, annulling its provisions. The CJEU has subsequently delivered many decisions on metadata retention and national security practices eg *Privacy International* and *La Quadrature du Net*, where the complex position of the EU vis-à-vis its Member States is increasingly set out, taking data protection more seriously but still permitting much surveillance regionally. This looks odd internationally, and certainly from a US perspective.[139] This complex EU position wears thin in the broader context of the position taken in *Schrems* in relation to international data transfers. Indeed, it is a significant complaint against the EU. As Cameron argues, the CJEU can hardly lecture the US on how it should do better in reconciling national security with privacy and data protection concerns if it is not also willing to say the same to EU Member States. Indeed, some commentators suggest that the *Schrems I* and *II* case law reflects the Commission's 'missionary' zeal to convert the world to the EU's global standards.[140]

As discussed in Chapter 1, the EU thus increasingly wrestles with its label as a 'soft data localisation' actor as a result of the *Schrems II* decision. Arguably, this label does little justice to the conflicted wrestling the EU actually does to develop a 'third way' on data in the digital trade and data flow context. How heavy-handed the EU will be as a 'sparring partner' for further standard setting remains to be seen. Some suggest that *Schrems II* presents a more robust internal and external approach to extraterritoriality, though it is improbable that these claims would be upheld, given the breadth of EU-US agreements on data transfer and the range of hybrid governance that they span.[141] This is perhaps reinforced by European Commission's earlier explicit promotion of the convergence of data protection

[138] V Manancourt, 'Ireland's Facebook decision triggers argument over limits of GDPR' (*Politico*, 18 October 2021) www.politico.eu/article/ireland-facebook-decision-triggers-argument-over-limits-gdpr/ accessed 25 February 2022.

[139] *Privacy International* (n 119); *cf Big Brother Watch and Others v UK* App nos 58170/13, 62322/14 and 24960/15 (ECtHR, 25 May 2021).

[140] I Cameron, 'A. Court of Justice Metadata retention and national security: Privacy International and La Quadrature du Net' (2021) 58 *Common Market Law Review* 1433.

[141] F Fabbrini et al (eds), *Data Protection Beyond Borders: Transatlantic Perspectives on Extraterritoriality and Sovereignty* (Hart Publishing, 2021).

standards at international levels.[142] Yet despite appearances, the direction of EU regulatory travel increasingly *aligns* with an international consensus on privacy, which is arguably more rather than less disposed to these concerns than ever.

More convincingly perhaps, others argue that the EU struggles with its double standards on security and surveillance, and that the US does not appreciate the complexity of the role of national security, at least not within the scope of EU law.[143] The EU is also internally greatly institutionalised in the face of a significant private sector regime prevailing in the US.[144] On whatever view, the global challenges faced by the EU are daunting, where it has to export these complex standards to third countries. A good case in point is the Brexit trade agreement reached with the UK. The European Commission has substantially shifted away from its model clauses on horizontal data flows in the EU-UK TCA.[145] It remains to be seen whether *Schrems II* has been circumvented here or whether horizontal data flow provisions are increasingly to be embedded more carefully within trade agreements. Whether the Privacy Shield can be renegotiated in a manner that is politically and legally effective is still uncertain.[146] In the formulation of the CJEU decision, the outcome is an impossible Bermuda Triangle of EU-US data blanket surveillance: to many, the preservation of EU rights and data transfer is impossible to square with US surveillance and uninhibited data flows.[147] Arguably, perceived transatlantic divergences are out of step with the direction of policy development, with the CJEU and the US agencies awkwardly speaking across one another. The US actors outlined above, in their report on the CJEU *Schrems II* decision, sought to emphasise the benefit of information sharing under the US FISA, section 702,

[142] M Tzanou, 'Schrems I and Schrems II: Assessing the Case for the Extraterritoriality of EU Fundamental Rights' in Fabbrini et al, *Data Protection Beyond Borders: Transatlantic Perspectives on Extraterritoriality and Sovereignty* (n 141); European Commission, 'Communication from the European Commission to the European Parliament and the Council: Data protection as a pillar of citizen's empowerment and the EU's approach to the digital transition – two years of application of the General Data Protection Regulation' COM (2020) 264 final, 13.

[143] Propp and Swire, 'After Schrems II: A Proposal to Meet the Individual Redress Challenge' (n 126); K Irion, 'Schrems II and Surveillance: Third Countries' National Security Powers in the Purview of EU Law' (*European Law Blog*, 24 July 2020), https://europeanlawblog.eu/2020/07/24/schrems-ii-and-surveillance-third-countries-national-security-powers-in-the-purview-of-eu-law/ accessed 25 February 2022; T Christakis, 'After Schrems II: Uncertainties on the Legal Basis for Data Transfers and Constitutional Implications for Europe' (*European Law Blog*, 21 July 2020), https://europeanlawblog.eu/2020/07/21/after-schrems-ii-uncertainties-on-the-legal-basis-for-data-transfers-and-constitutional-implications-for-europe/ accessed 25 February 2022.

[144] I am grateful to Maria Tzanou for suggestions on this issue.

[145] See Title III: Digital Trade, Chapter 2: 'Data flows and personal data protection' of Trade and Cooperation Agreement between the European Union and the European Atomic Energy Community, of the one part, and the United Kingdom of Great Britain and Northern Ireland, of the other part ST/5198/2021/INIT (EU-UK TCA) [2021] OJ L149/10.

[146] Much attention had subsequently focused on the UK-EU adequacy decision being agreed and the place of surveillance therein, causing US diplomats to assert that the US was entitled to similar treatment given their similar laws. Irrespective of the merits of this, it that is clear is that a new period of uncertainties has started. See Christakis, 'After Schrems II: Uncertainties on the Legal Basis for Data Transfers and Constitutional Implications for Europe' (n 143).

[147] eg 'EU-US data flow deal possible? Third time won't be the charm without US surveillance reform' (*Access Now*, 15 June 2021), www.accessnow.org/biden-us-eu-data-flow-deal/ accessed 25 February 2022.

stating that although it was impossible to disclose the instances in which the FISA section 702 programme has protected the safety of EU citizens and residents, nonetheless, it has done so.[148] Still, this will make uncomfortable reading for those concerned to understand the aftermath of the Snowdon/NSA affair and the extent to which the US remains wedded to its post-9/11 legacy of total surveillance. Whether further technical and policy convergence and truly institutionalised joint cooperation is probable when viewed in this light, and under a less hostile US administration, is a question still to be answered.

The place of a US-inspired GDPR is under discussion in the US now in a manner not previously thought possible.[149] Both Democratic and Republican Senators during the Trump administration advanced legislation to this effect.[150] Similarly, a US Privacy Regulator or Agency is the subject of discussion in a manner not previously anticipated.[151] Senate hearings in 2020 on the *Schrems II* decision indicate a vibrant national debate going more in the direction of European values than ever before.[152] Recent FTC fines for Facebook of $5billion show that EU-style enforcement of Big Tech is emerging in the US, and possibly indicates a dramatic shift in values.[153] The financially swingeing reach of the enforcement obligations shows a transatlantic gap for now. The EU's right to be forgotten as developed by the CJEU in *Google v Spain*, initially derided by many in the US, is now a core part of many US companies' corporate social principles and operational rules.[154] Instead of forcing many US companies to abandon the EU, evidence suggests that many companies and boards have significantly upped their privacy compliance to take into account the GDPR and privacy policy.[155] EU regulators are more closely following the leads of US regulators in thinking about more aggressive responses and more pre-emptive means of regulating Big Tech, with the US pursuing Google for illegal monopoly, and the EU pursuing

[148] It provides a limited number of declassified examples: see US Department of Commerce, US Department of Justice and US Office of the Director of National Intelligence, 'Information on US Privacy Safeguards Relevant to SCCs and Other EU Legal Bases for EU-US Data Transfers after *Schrems II*' (n 132) 4–5.

[149] eg C Kerry et al, 'Bridging the Gaps a Path forward to Federal Privacy Legislation' (2020), www.brookings.edu/wp-content/uploads/2020/06/Bridging-the-gaps_a-path-forward-to-federal-privacy-legislation.pdf accessed 25 February 2022.

[150] eg Consumer Online Privacy Rights Act, s 2968; Consumer Data Privacy and Security Act of 2020, s 3456. California legislature passed into law the California Consumer Privacy Act of 2018 (CCPA), effective 1 January 2020. Although the scope of the CCPA is not as broad as that of the GDPR, its protections are similar, differing mainly in the way by which individuals can opt-out of sales of their personal data to third parties.

[151] See Electronic Privacy Information Center: Campaigns (2021).

[152] See US Senate Committee on Commerce, Science and Technology, 'The Invalidation of the EU-US Privacy Shield and the Future of Transatlantic Data Flows' (n 133).

[153] See T Wu, *The Curse of Bigness: Antitrust in the New Gilded Age* (Columbia Global Reports, 2018). See also the appointment of Professor Lina Khan to the Biden Administration: D McCabe and C Kang, 'Biden Names Lina Khan, a Big-Tech Critic, as F.T.C. Chair' (*New York Times* 15 June 2021), www.nytimes.com/2021/06/15/technology/lina-khan-ftc.html accessed 25 February 2022.

[154] Case C-131/12 *Google Spain* ECLI:EU:C:2014:317; S Zuboff, *The Age of Surveillance Capitalism: The Fight for a Human Future at the New Frontier of Power* (Profile Books, 2019).

[155] eg KE Davis and F Marotta-Wurgler, 'Contracting for Personal Data' (2019) 94 *New York University Law* Review 662.

Amazon for competition law breaches.[156] The DSA and DMA proposals arguably witness a transatlantic alliance on the need to capture the Big Tech 'gatekeepers'. The future of Big Tech needs to take into account transatlantic standards that frequently become or constitute global standards. As noted above, Facebook has already 'quietly' moved 1.5 billion user files from Ireland to the US in April 2018 so that they would be governed by US privacy law rather than the GDPR, and Google swiftly moved millions of UK Google users to US 'control' post-Brexit in 2020, to reduce the impact of the GDPR and eliminate the possibility of any of those users filing claims in the Irish courts.[157] However, Facebook has until recently been a 'strong' advocate of EU law, of increasingly advocating for the GDPR to be the global standard, in the absence of any truly global equivalent.[158] While historically Google's Global Policy Counsel called for international privacy standards to be based on those of the Asia-Pacific Economic Cooperation (APEC), Microsoft's CEO has pointed to the EU GDPR as the global framework to be relied upon.[159] Facebook and Google may have initially 'opposed' the GDPR but ultimately they have subscribed to it and sought to advocate a US-style GDPR. They have helped a transatlantic settlement emerge. Instead of pointing out the possible reasons for divergence with EU law and acceptance thereof under essential equivalence principles, it might be said that the US and EU are converging more than ever on data privacy and data regulation. What is laudable is how much US entities engage with EU law, and how engagement is constructive and regular, as the two-year GDPR amply demonstrates. The depth of US companies' engagement with EU law shows how constructive it is to continue to engage across the Atlantic, as forms of transatlantic convergence are already happening on the ground. Beyond this, significant agreemeent may conceivably be emerging between EU and US regulators on the need to weaken Big Tech. Transatlantic convergence on regulatory standards from competition law to privacy and speech law suggests a commonality of regulatory capture.[160] Nonetheless, the EU emerges as a heavily institutionalised regulator in all such contexts, with a plethora of subjects and objects. In the wake of the EU-US

[156] US Department of Justice, 'Justice Department Sues Monopolist Google For Violating Antitrust Laws' (Justice News, 20 October 2020), www.justice.gov/opa/pr/justice-department-sues-monopolist-google-violating-antitrust-laws accessed 25 February 2022; Case AT.40462 Amazon Marketplace of the European Commission; European Commission, 'Antitrust: Commission sends Statement of Objections to Amazon for the use of non-public independent seller data and opens second investigation into its e-commerce business practices' (Press Release, 10 November 2020), https://ec.europa.eu/commission/presscorner/detail/en/ip_20_2077 accessed 25 February 2022.

[157] D Ingram, 'Exclusive: Facebook to Put 1.5 Billion Users out of Reach of New EU Privacy Law' *Reuters* (19 April 2018), www.reuters.com/article/us-facebook-privacy-eu-exclusive-idUSKBN1HQ00P accessed 24 February 2022; 'Google Moves UK User Data to US to Avert Brexit Risks' *Financial Times* (20 February 2020), www.ft.com/content/135e5b66-53fb-11ea-90ad-25e377c0ee1f accessed 24 February 2022.

[158] B Petkova, 'Privacy as Europe's first Amendment' (2019) 25 *European Law Journal* 140.

[159] Satya Nadella Microsoft CEO in D Hurst, 'Japan Calls for Global Consensus on Data Governance' *The Diplomat* (2 February 2019), https://thediplomat.com/2019/02/japan-calls-for-global-consensus-on-data-governance/ accessed 25 February 2022.

[160] J Espinoza, 'EU vs Big Tech: Brussels' bid to weaken the digital gatekeepers' (*Financial Times*, 8 December 2020), www.ft.com/content/4e08efbb-dd96-4bea-8260-01502aaf1bd7 accessed 25 February 2022.

TTC, proposing a loose institutionalisation of key global challenges currently not well covered or dealt with by, for example, the WTO, seems like a useful way of generating transatlantic convergence.[161] It is also worth stating that other important transatlantic developments may be seen increasingly in the shadow of the court-like bodies emerging from the private sector, eg Facebook's new Oversight Board, with scale and scope to institutionalise data governance like never before and with the capacity to apply international standards.[162] Much remains to be seen as to the future of soft institutionalisation and its sustainability in the face of many other challenges, not least global ones, generated internally and beyond the EU.

VII. Conclusions

Transatlantic data governance has had many iterations. Its values and institutions appear remarkably porous and fluid. Paradoxically, as outlined in Chapter 6 below, developments in EU-China relations arguably eclipse these EU-US structures and developments. It is frequently stated that the EU is closer to the US than it is to China. However, from the perspective of institutionalisation, this is not necessary the case. Irrespective of the administration, the transatlantic relationship forms a key longer-term case study of limited institutionalisation and patchy aspirations. The place of a US-inspired GDPR or a US Privacy Regulator or Agency appears central to future transatlantic convergence on privacy. Surveillance and security law issues, however, tend to eclipse such convergence. Most trade disputes between the EU and US have taken place before the WTO DSB in recent times. However, following its demise its future holds an uncertain place in the story of EU-US relations. Data disputes have largely centred on the Luxembourg court. Transatlantic convergence on regulatory standards from competition law to privacy and speech law may change this forum dynamic in a small number of respects. The EU-US Joint Agenda for Global Change includes a transatlantic TTC, which proposes a form of convergence on so many key global challenges relating to data currently not well covered or dealt with. Still, the esoteric institutionalisation of EU-US data flows and data privacy taking place in recent times appears to pivot away from the looser decentralisation that had prevailed until recently. The development of a Trans-atlantic Privacy to include a two-tier redress system, including a Data Protection Review Court could herald a significant era of change. Still, the place of self-certification envisaged suggests a road ahead of much hybrid governance and a complex pathway to deeper and wider institutionalisation.

[161] European Commission, 'Joint communication to the European Parliament, the European council and the Council: A new EU-US agenda for global change' JOIN (2021)22 final. Some suggest that the US seems to have explicitly accepted an EU policy on the Multiparty Interim Appeal Arbitration Arrangement (MPIA), spearheaded by the EU in response to the US's refusal to appoint members to the WTO Appelate Body: M Konstadinidis, 'EU-US Summit: Between Transatlantic Cooperation and Strategic Autonomy' (2021) 63 *EU Law Live! Weekend Edition*.

[162] K Klonick, 'The Facebook Oversight Board: Creating an Independent Institution to Adjudicate Online Free Expression' (2020) 129 *Yale Law Journal* 2418.

5

East Asian Convergence: EU-Japan Relations and Data

I. Overview of EU-Japan Relations in Context: The Slow-burn of Convergence

The EU's engagement with Japan is longstanding, with institutional ties which date back to the 1970s.[1] While the period until the late 1980s was marked by trade friction, in the 1990s and in particular after the evolution of the Single Market and the fall of the Berlin Wall, the EU and Japan were poised to play an increasing role in international affairs as economic success stories.[2] The EU-Japan relationship was historically characterised as the 'weak link' in a US-EU-Japan triangle.[3] While today, this triangle has become geopolitically significant to the EU – even under the more hostile Trump presidency, historically EU-Japan relations were not so close. An EU-Japan partnership was established by way of a Joint Declaration in 1991, one of the many soft law instruments that would dominate the relationship until 2018 and an incipient form of institutionalisation.[4] The subsequent EU-Japan Action Plan (2001) was considerably more detailed about EU-Japan economic cooperation, though it fell short of being an actual trade agreement.[5] Its Comprehensive Action Plan

[1] F Bindi, 'European Union Foreign Policy: A Historical Overview' in F Bindi and I Angelescu (eds), *The Foreign Policy of the European Union: Assessing Europe's Role in the World*, 2nd edn (Brookings Institution Press, 2012); T Tanaka, 'EU-Japan Relations' in T Christiansen et al (eds), *The Palgrave Handbook of EU-Asia Relations* (Palgrave Macmillan, 2013); T Ueta and É Remacle (eds), *Japan and Enlarged Europe: Partners in Global Governance* (Peter Lang, 2005); C Hosoya, 'Relations between the European Communities and Japan' (1979) 18 *Journal of Common Market Studies* 159.

[2] PJ Cardwell, 'The EU-Japan Relationship: from Mutual Ignorance to Meaningful Partnership?' (2004) 2(2) *Journal of European Affairs* 11; PJ Cardwell, 'Brexit, the EU and Japan' (*UK in a Changing EU*, 2017), https://ukandeu.ac.uk/brexit-the-eu-and-japan/ accessed 25 February 2022; S Strange, 'European Business in Japan: A Policy Crossroads?' (1995) 33 *Journal of Common Market Studies* 1.

[3] Cardwell, 'The EU-Japan Relationship: from Mutual Ignorance to Meaningful Partnership?' (n 2); Cardwell, 'Brexit, the EU and Japan' (n 2). See also B Heitger and J Stehn (1990) 'Japanese Direct Investments in the EC – Response to the Internal Market 1993?' (1990) 29 *Journal of Common Market Studies* 1.

[4] EU Japan Partnership and Cooperation Agreements, https://eu-japan.com/eu-japan-agreements/eu-japan-partnership-agreements/ accessed 25 February 2022. I am grateful to Isabella Mancini for her reflections on this point.

[5] EU-Japan Summit, Joint Press Statement (8 December 2001), https://eeas.europa.eu/archives/docs/japan/docs/2001_jpr_en.pdf accessed 25 February 2022.

gave a new impetus to bilateral relations by providing the foundations for both sides to build a 'decade of Japan-Europe cooperation'. Both parties undertook to implement the Action Plan, pursuing its four main objectives: promoting peace and security; strengthening the economic and trade partnership; coping with global and societal challenges; and bringing together people and cultures.

The broader context of the limited legal engagement in this new era between the EU and Japan is worth noting. A major task for Japanese trade policy in the first decade after World War II was to promote exports for foreign currency reserves in order to import foods and industrial raw materials, both of which were necessary to support the Japanese economy, which had been severely damaged by the war.[6] Another prime aim was to participate in the world trading system as soon as possible, to secure vitally important trade relations with foreign countries. Overcoming significant opposition from European countries, Japan finally joined the General Agreement on Tariffs and Trade (GATT) in 1955, but was still treated in a somewhat discriminatory manner.[7] This seemed to be the main reason for Japan's longstanding wariness toward preferential/discriminatory regional trade arrangements (RTAs). Japan was largely a passive participant in the world trading system after World War II, concentrating on its own economic restoration under the US security umbrella, and having difficulties in liberalising its trade in agricultural products, especially rice. Until the early 2000s Japan avoided playing a role in regional framework formation in Asia due to the negative legacy of the war.[8]

On 22 October 2000, Japanese Prime Minister Yoshiro Mori and Singapore Prime Minister Goh Chok Tong agreed to formal negotiations for the Japan-Singapore Economic Agreement for a New Age Partnership (JSEPA) in 2001. For Japan the JSEPA marked a major turning point in promoting regional economic integration, in view of the above context.[9] Still, Japan's attempts to project greater influence on international institutions in the twentieth century are understood to have been hampered by three factors: the dominance of the US, and Japan's unwillingness to risk a rupture with the world's sole superpower; the historical legacy

[6] T Ogita, 'An Approach towards Japan's FTA Policy' (2002) IDE APEC Study Center Working Paper Series 01/02 – No 4, 2.

[7] 'Japan and the GATT' (1954) 9(3) *International Journal* 216; A Forsberg, 'The Politics of GATT Expansion: Japanese Accession and the Domestic Political Context in Japan and the United States, 1948–1955' (1998) 27 *Business and Economic History* 185.

[8] Ogita, 'An Approach towards Japan's FTA Policy' (n 6) 10, citing N Munakata, 'Nihon no Chiiki Keizai Togo Seisaku no Keisei' (The Formation of Japan's Regional Economic Integration Policy) in N Munakata (ed), *Nicchu Kankei no Tenki* (Turning Point of Japan-China Relations) (Toyo Keizai Shimpo Sha, 2001).

[9] Ogita, 'An Approach towards Japan's FTA Policy' (n 6) 10; MS Manger, 'Competition and Bilateralism in Trade Policy: The Case of Japan's Free Trade Agreements' (2005) 12 *Review of International Political Economy* 804, 805.

in Asia of suspicion and distrust of Japan; and Japan's own parochial politics.[10] Featuring in all of this is a limited engagement with international institutions generally. It is said that the key outcome of the EU-Japan 2001 action plan was the start of a deregulation dialogue between the EU and Japan, which mirrored another dialogue with the US.[11] Each side submitted issues of regulatory and related difficulties that were experienced by its firms and citizens, and this gave the European Commission an opportunity to call for sweeping reforms in Japan to make its economy more open to European firms. Meanwhile, Japan's points of concern as to the EU were often related to issues of unevenness in the Single Market, but sometimes covered matters under national, rather than EU competence, which the Commission transmitted to the Member States to deal with.[12] It is said that the long-running deregulation dialogue was thus a necessary precursor to building up respective knowledge, awareness and trust. Further, by placing the EU on an equal footing with the US, it signalled how significant the EU had become for Japan.[13] The informality of the deregulation dialogue was said to tackle effectively some of the major regulatory, institutional and even cultural barriers to trade, and enabled this mutual learning process to propel the parties towards successful trade negotiations.[14] The relationship has dramatically evolved in recent times to become one of the largest free trade areas in the world and one of the largest areas for the free flow of data, along with a significant strategic partnership, ie the EU-Japan Economic Partnership Agreement (EPA), EU-Japan Adequacy Decision and EU-Japan Strategic Partnership Agreement (SPA), considered next in greater detail. The former constitute binding 'hard-law' agreements and are, as this chapter explores, grounded in significant efforts to institutionalise relations, particularly as to data. They are thus important landmarks in efforts to evolve the partnership beyond a law-light, institution-light regime. Ultimately, however, cultural and legal differences between the systems of the respective parties indicate a 'lighter' form of institutionalisation imposed on the partner. Regulatory cooperation is mired by the depth of norm convergence sought. Instead, a more general convergence with EU values appears mostly as a key outcome to date.

Chapter 5 contains the following sections: (II) the EU-Japan EPA and SPA; (III) the EU-Japan EPA negotiations; (IV) criticism of the EU-Japan Adequacy Decision; (V) EU-Japan EPA: digital trade and data flow as best practice; (VI) EU-Japan digital regulatory cooperation; and (VII) Conclusions.

[10] M Nolan, 'Japan and International Economic Institutions' (*PIIE*, 6 July 2000), https://www.piie.com/commentary/speeches-papers/japan-and-international-economic-institutions accessed 25 February 2022.

[11] Cardwell, 'The EU-Japan Relationship: from Mutual Ignorance to Meaningful Partnership?' (n 2).

[12] EU-Japan Industrialists Roundtables provide useful detail of this deregulation dialogue taking effect, eg in labour and the environment. See 'The 5th EU-Japan Industrialists Round Table' (Press Release, 10 October 1998).

[13] R Oshiba, 'A Japanese View of the EU' (2012) 20(2) *Perspectives* 103.

[14] Cardwell, 'The EU-Japan Relationship: from Mutual Ignorance to Meaningful Partnership?' (n 2).

II. The EU-Japan EPA and SPA: Going Beyond a Law-Light Institution-Light Partnership

On 1 February 2019, after nine years of preparations and negotiations, the EU-Japan EPA came into force. It was the biggest free trade agreement (FTA) either side had ever concluded, covering nearly 640 million citizens, a third of global Gross Domestic Product, and around 40 per cent of global trade.

Japan emerged as one of the major developed economies to be targeted by the EU in its post-Lisbon 'pivot to Asia', mimicking or rivalling the US Obama administration pivot to Asia, but with the overall goal being to develop counter-weights to China.[15] There was much scepticism about the need for and nature of what could be a successful partnership, given the demographics thereof and competitiveness challenges of such an economy with its automotives sector.[16] The EU-Japan FTA negotiations marked an important moment for the development of a gold-standard agreement in trade, setting out the parameters of a deeper trade agenda with another highly developed economy. The agreement was significant to complete the pivot to Asia, going beyond the earlier Korea and Singapore agreements for the EU, with the most ambitious and powerful nation of the ASEAN region, Japan, after many years of EU-ASEAN engagements, which had proved to be unrewarding and tedious as an inter-organisational learning experience.[17]

[15] D Twining, 'Europe's Incomplete Pivot to Asia' (*The German Marshall Fund of the United States*, 9 April 2015); J Gilson, *EU-Japan Relations and the Crisis of Multilateralism* (Routledge 2019); P Nelson, 'Taking the Lead in Current and Future Trade Relationships' in A Berkofsky et al (eds), *The EU-Japan Partnership in the Shadow of China* (Routledge, 2019); B Gaens, 'The EU-Japan Partnership: Stepping Stone For A Stronger Presence In Asia?' (2017) FIIA Briefing Paper 218, https://css.ethz.ch/content/dam/ethz/special-interest/gess/cis/center-for-securities-studies/resources/docs/FIIA-The%20EU%20Japan%20Partnership.pdf accessed 25 February 2022; D Hallinan, 'Partnership in a Competitive Order: Understanding the EU-Japan FTA' (2016) European Trade Study Group Paper, www.etsg.org/ETSG2016/Papers/425.pdf accessed 25 February 2022; J-P Bassino, 'Global Context and European Motivations for the EU-Japan Partnership Agreement (EPA)' (2019) 55(1–2) *The Review of Economics and Commerce* 43; European Parliamentary Research Service, 'Bilateral trade deal with Japan – largest to date for EU' (February 2019) PE 633.164; European Parliamentary Research Service, 'Japan and prospects for closer EU ties' (October 2017) PE 608.739. See K Ang, 'Europe Pivots to Indo-Pacific with "Multipolar" Ambitions' (*Nikkei Asia*, 2 February 2021), https://asia.nikkei.com/Spotlight/Asia-Insight/Europe-pivots-to-Indo-Pacific-with-multipolar-ambitions accessed 25 February 2022.

[16] eg D Hallinan, 'Partnership in a Competitive Order: Understanding the EU-Japan FTA' (2016) University College Dublin Paper No 425, 1: 'The EU's decision to enter into a PTA with Japan is arguably puzzling, given a long history of economic competition, Japan's relatively modest growth potential, and the massive scale of increased import-competition in sensitive sectors of European industry that a PTA with Japan will entail. Major European industrial interest groups and particular EU MSs have expressed concern that an FTA with Japan will present limited benefits for European exporters in key sectors where Japan is highly competitive such as automotives, machinery and electronics, due to Japan's low rates of growth and concerns regarding long-term demographic trends which are likely to continue to weigh on growth going forward …'

[17] G Butler, 'The Future of EU International Agreements as Legal Instruments in the ASEAN Region' (2020) 7(2) *Journal of International and Comparative Law* 287, 288; J-U Wunderlich, 'The EU an Actor *Sui Generis*? A Comparison of EU and ASEAN Actorness' (2012) 50 *Journal of Common Market Studies* 653.

From a Japanese perspective, the EU-Korea FTA, which entered into force in 2011, presented Japanese firms with a severe disadvantage in the EU market vis-à-vis their Korean competitors.

The EU and Japan agreed an EPA and an SPA in 2018. On 1 February 2019, the Economic Partnership Agreement (EPA) between the European Union (EU) and Japan entered into force.[18] The SPA (together with the EPA) was signed at the Tokyo summit on 17 July 2018.[19] The SPA represents a framework strengthening the overall partnership, by promoting political and sectoral cooperation and joint actions in more than 40 areas of common interest. The EU-Japan SPA and EPA are legally independent and separate and this is intentionally so, as the EPA has no essential elements clause, unlike CETA for example. This is deliberate, to protect the Japanese use of the death penalty from triggering such clauses.[20] There are no legal 'linkage provisions', as Article 43(8) of the SPA underscores, and this is a highly salient issue here. The SPA represents institutionalised political/policy dialogue and secures long-term mutual commitments, to be handled through diplomatic negotiations. Japan is an interesting case where the death penalty still exists, and where women's rights and labour rights vary greatly from those in the EU in very significant fundamental rights areas of EU law, unlike other more recent developed partner countries, eg Canada. Yet the lack of a linkage clause here between the EPA and SPA and lack of an essential elements clause does not reflect these realities. There is minimal place for institutions in the SPA where political dialogue is instead prioritised. The reason for this state of affairs appears to be because Japan was particularly concerned about a binding link between the EPA and SPA and its use as to the death penalty in an essential elements clause, hence its exclusion.[21] More importantly, it highlights the weaker institutional set-up of the broader relationship, although grounded in a progressive widening of the relationship, and a range of key areas, not least relating to contemporary security challenges such as cybersecurity.

[18] eg M Frennhoff Larsén, 'Parliamentary Influence Ten Years after Lisbon: EU Trade Negotiations with Japan' (2020) 58 *Journal of Common Market Studies* 1540.

[19] Agreement between the European Union and Japan for an Economic Partnership (EU-Japan EPA) [2018] OJ L 330/3; Council Decision (EU) 2018/1197 on the Signing, on Behalf of the European Union, and Provisional Application of the Strategic Partnership Agreement between the European Union and its Member States, of the one Part, and Japan, of the other Part [2018] OJ L216/1; Strategic Partnership Agreement between the European Union and its Member States, of the one Part, and Japan, of the other Part (EU-Japan SPA) [2018] OJ L 216/4.

[20] P Bacon and H Nakamura, 'Diffusing the Abolitionist Norm in Japan: EU "Death Penalty Diplomacy" and the Gap between Rhetoric and Reality in EU-Japan Relations' (2021) 59 *Journal of Common Market Studies* 1230.

[21] K Meissner and L McKenzie, 'The Paradox of Human Rights Conditionality in EU Trade Policy: When Strategic Interests Drive Policy Outcomes' [2018] *Journal of European Public Policy* 1; Bacon and Nakamura, 'Diffusing the Abolitionist Norm in Japan: EU "Death Penalty Diplomacy" and the Gap between Rhetoric and Reality in EU-Japan Relations' (n 20); E Fahey and I Wieczorek, 'The European Parliament as a Defender of EU Values in EU-Japan Agreements: What Role for Soft Law and Hard Law Powers?' (2022) *European Law Review*, forthcoming.

The trade agreement itself is built around an atypical EU trade agreement structure, at least atypical of post-Lisbon so-called 'deeper' trade agreements. It comprises a Joint Committee and a myriad of other forms of committees and working groups. All of these entities have evolved since its inception, meet regularly and operate in accordance with procedural forms that are atypical of EU procedures.[22] Of these, one of the most interesting for present purposes is that on regulatory cooperation. The other relates to electronic commence, which is part of the Committee on Trade in Services, Investment Liberalisation and Electronic Commerce and follows the same form, meeting operationalisation (of at least two meetings being held to date) as the rest of the EPA, which are outlined further below.

However, digital trade cooperation and the protection of privacy form interesting and key (binding) parts of the EPA and are discussed in detail, given the developments taking place in Japanese law that are outlined below.

III. The EU-Japan EPA Negotiations: The Moving Place of Data Towards the Adequacy Decision

During the negotiations of the EU-Japan EPA, data emerged as a controversial issue, where EU and Japan's interests did not align.[23] During the trade negotiations with the EU, Japan repeatedly stated its interest in free data flows and expressed concern at EU-specific data rights formulations.[24]

Not only had the relationship between data and trade been dismissed by the EU. it had also been overlooked in the economic analyses behind the trade agreement.[25] The adequacy decision was thus significant in ensuring that the EU's data protection rules under the GDPR would not disrupt the EU's services trade with Japan, kept intentionally separate from the trade agreement. As noted above, the EU currently has adequacy decisions with 14 countries, mostly highly developed economies, one of which was the negotiations with the UK after Brexit

[22] See European Commission, 'EU-Japan Economic Partnership Agreement (EPA) – Meetings and documents', https://trade.ec.europa.eu/doclib/press/index.cfm?id=2042 accessed 25 February 2022.

[23] See I Mancini, 'A deep trade agenda for fundamental rights: framing fundamental rights for the new generation EU trade agreements with other developed countries' (DPhil Thesis, City, University of London 2021). See the European Commission, 'Report of the 15th EU-Japan FTA/EPA Negotiating Round' (2016), https://trade.ec.europa.eu/doclib/docs/2016/march/tradoc_154368.pdf accessed 25 February 2022; and European Commission, 'Report of the 18th EU-Japan FTA/EPA Negotiating Round' (2017), https://trade.ec.europa.eu/doclib/docs/2017/april/tradoc_155506.pdf accessed 25 February 2022.

[24] E Fahey and I Mancini, 'The EU as an Intentional or Accidental Convergence Actor? Learning From the EU-Japan Data Adequacy Negotiations' (2020) 26 *International Trade Law and Regulation* 99.

[25] A Sapir et al, 'The EU-Japan Economic Partnership Agreement' (*Bruegel*, 3 October 2018), https://bruegel.org/2018/10/the-eu-japan-economic-partnership-agreement/ accessed 25 February 2022.

as part of the UK-EU Trade and Cooperation Agreement (TCA).[26] The criteria setting out how adequacy decisions are made are outlined in the GDPR and corresponding CJEU case law.[27] It is a matter of controversy as to how much the CJEU has become involved in the adequacy process after *Schrems* I and II, rendering many past and future adequacy decisions uncertain. Considerable disquiet was expressed by the European Parliament in a resolution on the prospective UK adequacy decision and to declaring US law to be adequate in the wake of the US adoption of the GDPR in California.[28] Concerns expressed as to Japan were much more muted overall and not communicated until later in the process.[29]

Following the conclusion of the EU-Japan talks on personal data protection in July 2018, in September 2018 the European Data Protection Board, adopted an Opinion on the EU-Japan adequacy decision on the basis of an assessment pursuant to documentation of the European Commission.[30] It assessed whether the Commission had ensured sufficient guarantees for the adequacy of data protection of individuals within Japanese law – not to replicate EU data protection law, but rather to assess equivalence.[31] The decision thus raises interesting questions as to institutionalisation and Europeanisation and its relationship to convergence. Convergence arguably emerges as an essential principle of adequacy because, pursuant to Article 45 of the GDPR, a third country's legislation needs to be aligned to the essence of the GDPR driven by convergence of values and objectives.[32] EU information materials published on the EU-Japan Adequacy Decision also convey the 'closeness' of Japanese standards to EU law.[33] In the Japan decision, the Commission wrote that the requirements set forth in Supplementary Rule 4 exclude the use of transfer instruments that do not create a binding relationship

[26] These countries are Andorra, Argentina, Canada (as to commercial organisations), Faroe Islands, Guernsey, Israel, Isle of Man, Japan, Jersey, New Zealand, Republic of Korea, Switzerland, the UK and Uruguay. See European Commission, 'Adequacy Decisions', https://ec.europa.eu/info/law/law-topic/data-protection/international-dimension-data-protection/adequacy-decisions_en accessed 25 February 2022.

[27] See O Patel and N Lea, 'EU-UK Data Flows, Brexit and No-Deal: Adequacy or Disarray?' (August 2019) UCL European Institute, https://www.ucl.ac.uk/european-institute/sites/european-institute/files/eu-uk_data_flows_brexit_and_no_deal_updated.pdf accessed 25 February 2022.

[28] European Parliament resolution of 12 February 2020 on the proposed mandate for negotiations for a new partnership with the United Kingdom of Great Britain and Northern Ireland (2020/2557(RSP)); Fahey and Wieczorek (n 21).

[29] See in more detail Fahey and Wieczorek (n 21).

[30] European Data Protection Board, 'Opinion 28/2018 regarding the European Commission Draft Implementing Decision on the Adequate Protection of Personal Data in Japan' (5 December 2018), https://edpb.europa.eu/sites/edpb/files/files/file1/2018-12-05-opinion_2018-28_art.70_japan_adequacy_en.pdf accessed on 25 February 2022.

[31] Fahey and Mancini, 'The EU as an Intentional or Accidental Convergence Actor? Learning From the EU-Japan Data Adequacy Negotiations' (n 24).

[32] ibid.

[33] Fahey and Mancini, 'The EU as an Intentional or Accidental Convergence Actor? Learning From the EU-Japan Data Adequacy Negotiations' (n 24); B Zeller et al, 'The Right to be Forgotten – the EU and Asia Pacific Experience (Australia, Indonesia, Japan and Singapore)' (2019) 1 *European Human Rights Law Review* 23, 25.

between the Japanese data exporter and the country data importer and that do not guarantee the required level of protection.[34] Japan could thus no longer rely on the Asia-Pacific Economic Cooperation Cross-Border Privacy Rules (APEC CBPR) system for onwards transfer.[35]

It is thus significant that Japan has negotiated specific, structured rules which are binding and enforceable and applicable only to personal data transferred from the EU.[36] The EU-Japan Adequacy Decision was the first adequacy decision concluded since the entry into force of the GDPR[37] and set a significant precedent. The decision has as its goal a degree convergence of legal frameworks rather than replication. It has been designed with some intention of convergence that is indirect, more latent and constructed. Many decisions receive harsh critique as to whether the legal order in fact is 'essentially equivalent' to EU law and the politicisation of the process has become significant.[38]

IV. Criticism of the EU-Japan Adequacy Decision: Forced Convergence?

Despite it being clear that enforcement and redress must be demonstrated in practice, and not only exist on paper, the draft Adequacy Decision appeared to overlook this.[39] It listed many examples of where Japan's Personal Information Protection Commission (PPC) or the courts can, in theory under legislative provision, take enforcement actions, but it did not give any examples of specific penalties issued or compensation granted, either administrative or judicial. A related issue was whether, even if it was enforced, a law which has maximum penalties for breaches of US$10,000 in the Act (or US$3,000 in the Supplementary Rules) is capable of being 'essentially equivalent' to the GDPR, where penalties are some orders of magnitude higher? Other key arguments related to the

[34] Commission Implementing Decision (EU) 2019/419 of 23 January 2019 pursuant to Regulation (EU) 2016/679 of the European Parliament and of the Council on the adequate protection of personal data by Japan under the Act on the Protection of Personal Information (EU-Japan Adequacy Decision) [2019] OJ L 76/1, para 79.

[35] ibid.

[36] Japan's Personal Information Protection Commission, Supplementary rules on the Act on the Protection of Personal Information (Act No 57 of 2003 as amended), released 24 August 2018, https://www.ppc.go.jp/files/pdf/Supplementary_Rules.pdf (in Japanese) accessed 25 February 2022.

[37] See Regulation (EU) 2016/679 of the European Parliament and of the Council of 27 April 2016 on the protection of natural persons with regard to the processing of personal data and on the free movement of such data, and repealing Directive 95/46/EC (GDPR) [2016] OJ L119/1, Art 99(2) according to which the Regulation shall apply from 25 May 2018.

[38] G Greenleaf, 'Questioning "Adequacy" (Pt I) – Japan' (2017) 150 *Privacy Laws & Business International Report* 6; G Greenleaf, 'Japan: EU Adequacy Discounted' (2018) 155 *Privacy Laws & Business International Report* 8.

[39] See G Greenleaf, 'Japan's Proposed EU Adequacy Assessment: Substantive Issues and Procedural Hurdles' (2018) 154 *Privacy Laws & Business International Report* 1, 3–8; Greenleaf, 'Questioning "Adequacy" (Pt I) – Japan' (n 38).

exclusion of Japanese citizens under the decision, sectoral exclusions and gaps between EU law and Japanese law, eg requirements for data protection by design and by default; data portability; and de-linking (ie the 'right to be forgotten'). In 2018, the European Parliament issued a strongly worded critique of Japanese law and the adequacy process,[40] referring to indiscriminate mass surveillance.

Article 13 of the Constitution of Japan 1947 protects the right to life, liberty and the pursuit of happiness. The Japanese Supreme Court has said that this includes a right to privacy but only to the extent that it does not interfere with welfare. It is important to note that the process of constitutional revision in Japan is burdensome and Japan's 1947 Constitution has never been revised. The Supreme Court has rarely found violations of privacy to exist. A high-profile example of the court refusing to find a constitutional violation of privacy as to the fingerprinting of foreign residents is *Ikuta v Moriguchi City*.[41] Otherwise, the protections are extremely weak and contrast with other Asian regional partners. It is important to note that GDPR Article 45 explicitly requires 'effective and enforceable data subject rights' and 'effective judicial and administrative redress'. Some commentators suggest that Japan increasingly signs up to so many competing regimes that its approach to international data transfers and regimes is becoming highly inconsistent, perhaps understandably for a middle-power caught between many regimes.[42] There is concern that Japan has become a signatory to so many key global data transfer instruments and digital trade regimes (eg APEC CBPR and EU-Japan Adequacy Decision, the Regional Comprehensive Economic Partnership and the Comprehensive and Progressive Agreement for Trans-Pacific Partnership) that it has lost the credibility of its focus.[43] The case law of the Japanese Supreme Court appeared to indicate that Japanese law was closer to EU standards of rights rather than other legal orders or traditions, or indeed communitarian values.[44]

[40] European Parliament, 'Report containing a motion for a non-legislative resolution on the draft Council decision on the conclusion of the Agreement between the European Union and Japan for an Economic Partnership' (9 September 2018) (07964/2018 – C8-0382/2018 – 2018/0091M(NLE))). The Parliament overall stated that there was a high concern in terms of principles, safeguards and individual rights as well as oversight and enforcement after the adoption of the amended APPI but also relevant differences even after the PPC adopted the Supplementary rules. The Parliament called for further binding supplementary rules, made specific calls for further fines and welcomed the development of legally binding powers.

[41] G Greenleaf, 'The Right to Privacy in Asian Constitutions' (2020) University of New South Wales Law Research Series No 53, referencing the Juki-net decision of 2008 on Art 13 – *Ikuta v Moriguchi City*, 62 *Minshu* 665 (6 March 2008); H Miyashita, 'The Evolving Concept of Data Privacy in Japanese Law' (2011) 1(4) *International Data Privacy Law* 229.

[42] M Bartl and K Irion, 'The Japan EU Economic Partnership Agreement: Flows of Personal Data to the Land of the Rising Sun' (2017) Amsterdam Centre for Information Law Institute Working Paper, 9, https://www.ivir.nl/publicaties/download/Transfer-of-personal-data-to-the-land-of-the-rising-sun-FINAL.pdf accessed 25 February 2022.

[43] ibid.

[44] Fahey and Mancini, 'The EU as an Intentional or Accidental Convergence Actor? Learning From the EU-Japan Data Adequacy Negotiations' (n 24); F Zufall, 'Challenging the EU's Right to Be Forgotten: Society's Right to Know in Japan' (2019) 5 *European Data Protection Law Review* 17; IFLA, 'The Right to be Forgotten in National and Regional Contexts', https://www.ifla.org/files/assets/clm/statements/rtbf_background.pdf accessed 25 February 2022.

There are many who have suggested that the EU's adequacy decision with Japan lacks sufficient justification that Japan meets the EU's criteria for adequacy, described as guaranteeing levels of protection that are essentially equivalent to those ensured within the EU.[45] The Japanese legal order is not a federalised system and the balance of power between central and local government has been decidedly towards centralisation and away from autonomy in regions, agencies and prefectural governments, the direct opposite to the EU's data transfer regime.[46] It is perhaps no surprise that the EU has accorded adequacy decisions to its major new trading partners, the beneficiaries of new broader framework agreements. However, the Japan adequacy decision was the first to be awarded post-GDPR and thus received even more international scrutiny than ever. For instance, some suggested, prior to the adoption of the decision, that Japanese data privacy laws had received negligible enforcement.[47] In respect of the draft Decision concerning the private sector, it was argued to lack sufficient justification that Japan meets the EU's criteria for adequacy, described in the Decision as requiring that Japan 'guarantees a level of protection "essentially equivalent" to that ensured' within the EU. Accordingly, it was said to be difficult to assert that Japan's enforcement regime was essentially equivalent to that of the EU, with consent as an insufficient basis for onwards transfer.[48] Greenleaf takes issue with the extent of the gaps between Japanese and EU laws, including requirements for data protection by design and default and also whether by preventing APEC CBPR compliance as a basis for onwards transfers, its replacement with an almost entirely consent-based mechanism is protective enough.[49] Nonetheless, European Commission and EU data protection authorities met in 2021 to conduct the first review of the EU-Japan mutual adequacy arrangement, with extensive references being made to 'convergence' of standards and values throughout the contacts, arguably highly indicative of the direction of the adequacy process.[50] Such triumphalism may be short-lived, however, given the current state of the EU-Japan Passenger Name Records (PNR) agreement negotiations. These are currently causing considerable headaches in Japan, as

[45] Bartl and Irion, 'The Japan EU Economic Partnership Agreement: Flows of Personal Data to the Land of the Rising Sun' (n 42); Greenleaf, 'Japan: EU Adequacy Discounted' (n 37).

[46] D Rosen, 'Regionalism Rses in Japan to Confront Covid-19' (*University of Melbourne*), https://law.unimelb.edu.au/centres/alc/engagement/asian-legal-conversations-covid-19/alc-original-articles/regionalism-rises-in-japan-to-confront-covid-19 accessed 25 February 2022.

[47] Greenleaf, 'Japan: EU Adequacy Discounted' (n 37).

[48] ibid.

[49] G Greenleaf, 'Questioning "Adequacy" (Pt II) – South Korea' (2018) 151 *Privacy Laws & Business International Report* 14–16 (February 2018). The EU adequacy decision with Korea was similarly impugned, including also its self-assessment regime, similarly the adequacy decision with the UK post-Brexit.

[50] European Commission, 'Joint Statement on the First Review of the EU-Japan Mutual Adequacy Arrangement' (News, 26 October 2021), https://ec.europa.eu/newsroom/just/items/724795/en accessed 25 February 2022.

in many other third countries, as to how to implement the increasingly strict criteria of the CJEU as to independent oversight, enforcement and accountability in relation to international data transfers.[51]

V. EU-Japan EPA: Digital Trade and Data Flows as Best Practice?

The EU-Japan EPA is similar in structure and substance to the EU-Singapore agreement as part of the EU's post-Lisbon FTAs, but in terms of e-commerce it is somewhat apart.[52] As noted above, it is significantly more comprehensive and broad-ranging than any previous EU agreement and was thus significant at the point of its adoption, however fast-moving the overall field may generally be considered.[53] Some go as far as to suggest that it was a watershed in trade agreements for digital trade at the time, despite the complex placement of e-commerce which, unlike in CETA, is not in a separate chapter.[54] The EU-Japan EPA includes e-commence as one of six sections in the chapter on services, investment and commerce. It does not form a standalone chapter, unlike the US-Mexico-Canada Agreement (USMCA), for example, which has a chapter on digital trade. As a result, there is somewhat less detail in the EU-Japan EPA. Digital products are not defined. The EU-Japan EPA has a mortarium on customs duties for electronic transmission and requires non-discriminatory treatment for electronic transmissions. The EPA underlines the importance of maintaining and adopting consumer protection measures pursuant to Article 8.78, tackled in greater detail and in a standalone clause. While the USCMA makes explicit reference to the UNICITRAL Model law on e-commerce,[55] the EU-Japan EPA only states

[51] See Fahey and Wieczorek (n 21).

[52] P Sauvé and M Soprana, 'The Evolution of the EU Digital Trade Policy' in M Hahn and G Van der Loo (eds), *Law and Practice of the Common Commercial Policy* (Brill Nijhoff, 2020); JA Micallef, 'Digital Trade in EU FTAs: Are EU FTAs Allowing Cross Border Digital Trade to Reach Its Full Potential?' (2019) 53 *Journal of World Trade* 855; G Pasadilla, 'E-commerce Provisions in RTAs: Implications for Negotiations and Capacity Building' (2020) ASIA-Pacific Research and Training Network on Trade Working Paper No 192, https://www.unescap.org/sites/default/files/AWP192%20Pasadilla%20Gloria_0.pdf accessed 25 February 2022; M Kanetake and S de Vries, 'EU-Japan Economic Partnership Agreement: Data Protection in the Era of Digital Trade and Economy' (*Renforce Blog*, 18 December 2018), http://blog.renforce.eu/index.php/en/2018/12/18/eu-japan-economic-partnership-agreement-data-protection-in-the-era-of-digital-trade-and-economy/ accessed 25 February 2022; European Parliament, 'Study: The EU – Japan Economic Partnership Agreement' (2018) Policy Department Study PE 603.880.

[53] Sauvé and Soprana, 'The Evolution of the EU Digital Trade Policy' (n 52).

[54] EU-Japan EPA, Ch 8, s F; Comprehensive Economic and Trade Agreement (CETA) between Canada, of the one part, and the European Union and its Member States, of the other part [2017] OJ L11/23, ch 16. See Micallef, 'Digital Trade in EU FTAs: Are EU FTAs Allowing Cross Border Digital Trade to Reach Its Full Potential?' (n 52) 860.

[55] See UNCITRAL Model Law on Electronic Commerce (1996) with additional Art 5 as adopted in 1998.

that measures must be administrated in a reasonable, objective and impartial way, thereby downplaying internationalisation measures. On many key issues, e-commerce provisions are addressed in very similar ways in the EU-Japan EPA and USMCA: eg electronic signature, consumer protection, unsolicited e-communication, e-authentication, cybersecurity and source codes. The EU-Japan EPA has no provisions on the location of computing facilities or third-party liability for interactive computer services.

The major difference between the EU-Japan EPA and major US agreements such as USCMA is on cross-border data flows. The EU-Japan EPA and USMCA are both clear that measures must take account of international guidelines such as APEC's Privacy Framework or the OECD Council Recommendations. The significant difference as to the EU-Japan EPA is that on the cross-border transfer of international data, the parties must investigate the free flow of data after three years of the date of the entry into force of the agreement.[56] There is an article on regulatory dialogues in EU-Japan e-commerce cooperation outlined, including in multilateral fora on a range of issues, discussed below, but notably it does not include cooperation on personal data. As was considered in Chapter 2, this is in contrast to the USMCA, which allows for cooperation on personal information along with cybersecurity for example, which highlights the APEC CBPR as a mechanism for interoperability of data privacy rules. The EU-Japan EPA is a useful study of best contemporary modern practice in next generation EU trade agreements with a developed economy. The e-commerce chapter of the EU-Japan EPA is arguably more substantial than those in the EU-Korea and EU-Canada FTAs,[57] except that the former does not have provisions on computing facilities, and its requirements on consumer and data protection are soft.[58]

A landmark clause on free flows of data for the EU is set out in Article 8.81 – discussed further above – which postpones the key issues therein, providing for a review clause three years from the entry into force of the agreement. This clause is also to be found in the modernised EU-Mexico Agreement. The aftermath of these cautious approaches was the development of the EU's Horizontal Approach to data by the Commission, as outlined above, also after calls from various EU Member States.[59]

The e-commerce provisions of the EU-Japan EPA are commonly understood to be much more substantial than those in EU-Korea and EU-Canada FTAs.[60]

[56] Pasadilla, 'E-Commerce Provisions in RTAs: Implications for Negotiations and Capacity Building' (n 52).

[57] S Hamanaka, 'The Future Impact of Trans-Pacific Partnership's Rule-Making Achievements: The Case Study of E-commerce' (2019) 42 *World Economy* 561.

[58] ibid.

[59] See Letter on data flows to the Vice President of the European Commission Frans Timmermans, dated 16 May 2015, www.government.nl/binaries/government/documents/letters/2017/05/19/like-minded-letter-on-data-flows-in-trade-agreements/Like+Minded+Letter+on+Data+Flows+in+Trade+Agreements.pdf accessed 25 February 2022.

[60] Eg S Hamanaka, 'The Future Impact of Trans-Pacific Partnership's Rule-Making Achievements: The Case Study of E-commerce' (n 57) 552, 561.

Significantly, the digital trade provisions of the EPA were also alleged to be capable of being seen as bypassed by the UK-Japan CEPA, agreed in late 2020.[61] It is notably not a digital trade chapter standalone and is instead merged with services and investment in the nomenclature of e-commerce. Later EU trade agreements have included digital trade as a separate and standalone chapter, reflecting an evolution in thinking and also of nomenclature. The EU-Japan EPA merges e-commerce with services. It is possible to see this as forward-thinking, similar to the synergies between services and digital trade in the UK-EU TCA.[62]

The EU-Japan EPA includes specific commitments on domestic regulation, meaning that each party must ensure that all its measures of general application that affect e-commerce are administered in a reasonable, objective, and impartial manner. This is accompanied by a best effort commitment not to impose prior authorisation – or any other requirement having equivalent effect – on the provision of services by electronic means.[63] The EPA includes provisions stating that the parties shall not adopt or maintain measures regulating electronic transactions that deny the legal effect, validity or enforceability of a contract, solely on the grounds that it is concluded by electronic means, or otherwise create obstacles to the use of contracts concluded by electronic promotion.[64] While some agreements aim to 'facilitate trade in digital products' or through 'electronic means or technologies', and to improve the effectiveness and efficiency of electronic commerce, or consider e-commerce facilitation as part of general common cooperation activities, other agreements have more concrete obligations – such as the EU-Japan EPA.[65]

There are some important and new examples of 'best practice' in digital trade that are worthy of closer study. An immediate question arises as to what is understood by best practice in such a complex and emerging field, which appears still more institution-light. One example might be the Digital Economy Partnership Agreement (DEPA) between New Zealand, Chile and Singapore, and its provisions on cooperation in areas key to ensure market access and consumer welfare and its provisions on paperless trade using data exchange mechanisms. However, the DEPA is merely a cooperation agreement rather than a regulatory regime and is a significantly different form of modular regime. Notably, DEPA does not use the term 'digital trade' but rather strengthens the obligations of conventional

[61] 'Cutting-edge digital & data provisions that go far beyond the EU-Japan deal. These will enable free flow of data whilst maintaining high standards of protection for personal data. We have also committed to uphold the principles of net neutrality, as well as introducing a ban on data localisation, which will prevent British businesses from having the extra cost of setting up servers in Japan': see UK Government, 'UK and Japan Agree Historic Free Trade Agreement' (Press release, 11 September 2020), https://www.gov.uk/government/news/uk-and-japan-agree-historic-free-trade-agreement accessed 25 February 2022.

[62] EU-Japan EPA; Council Decision (EU) 2018/1197 (n 19); Strategic Partnership Agreement (n 19).

[63] EU-Japan EPA, Arts 8.74 and 8.75.

[64] EU-Japan EPA, Art 8.76.

[65] Hamanaka, 'The Future Impact of Trans-Pacific Partnership's Rule-Making Achievements: The Case Study of E-commerce' (n 57) 561.

digital trade provisions, eg customs duties on electronic transmissions, non-discriminatory treatment, promotion and facilitation of e-commerce, rules on data flows, paperless trading, authentication and data localisation as well as rules for algorithms, digital inclusion, fin tech and AI.[66] Here, such a regime provides a platform for the evolution of rule-making, perhaps more akin to the EU-USTTC than anything else.

The framing of digital trade chapters is also significant for our understanding of best practice. Whether they unduly focus on preventing barriers from being put in place as technological changes emerge rather than removing them remains to be seen and is open to debate. Their quantification is also highly problematic. Given that their economic benefits are extremely difficult to quantify, it is also difficult to put a value on 'good practice' or 'best practice' here, other than the number of barriers that could be removed. Many other barriers outside of digital trade provisions are increasingly seen to be significant in understanding good or best practice, eg as to mutual recognition of professional qualifications or intellectual property issues. More broadly, views on informational sovereignty and digital protectionism constitute overarching issues that colour the singular content of digital trade chapters. As stated above, while many new-generation trade agreements have provisions on digital trade, they are not consistent, coherent, or cohesive. New datasets on digital trade provisions of all new preferential trade agreements are revealing; several trade agreements with e-commerce chapters (47 treaties) include provisions to promote and facilitate e-commerce.[67] However, these provisions are largely non-binding and vary across agreements. Still, the EU's efforts to evolve its own practice with another significant developed economy are important for their breadth. The nature of the ongoing renegotiation of the key clauses as to the institutionalisation of regulatory cooperation is arguably also of much importance.

VI. EU-Japan Digital Trade Regulatory Cooperation: Incipient Institutionalisation

Just as there is no shared idea of digital trade in regional trade agreements, similarly there is no shared international understanding of regulatory cooperation in trade agreements. Regulatory cooperation is of much importance because it prevents

[66] S Peng et al (eds), *Artificial Intelligence and International Economic Law* (Cambridge University Press, 2021) 19. As noted above, the digital trade provisions of the EPA were also alleged to be significantly capable of being seen as bypassed by the UK-Japan CEPA agreed in late 2020, although it appears heavily dependent upon data standard protections adopted as stated above, where the UK seems to diverge from the GDPR and accede to CPTPP. CEPA adopts CPTPP standards on privacy and a generally more economic view of data flows, which the UK attempts to pursue: see UK Government, 'UK and Japan Agree Historic Free Trade Agreement (Press release)' (n 61).

[67] M Burri and R Polanco, 'Digital Trade Provisions in Preferential Trade Agreements: Introducing a New Dataset' (2020) 23 *Journal of International Economic Law* 187, 203.

regulatory divergences and removes some of the most significant barriers to trade. The EU has sought to include regulatory cooperation in the area of digital trade or e-commerce in all of its post-Lisbon trade agreements with all major developed global economies. Article 8.80 of the EU-Japan EPA provides that:

> 1. The Parties shall, where appropriate, cooperate and participate actively in multilateral fora to promote the development of electronic commerce.
> 2. The Parties agree to maintain a dialogue on regulatory matters relating to electronic commerce with a view to sharing information and experience … including on related laws, regulations and their implementation, and best practices with respective to electronic commerce. (…)

These commitments to multilateralism are laudable of course but also – as explored in Chapter 2 – sit against a backdrop of a significant lack of activity at multilateral level, in particular at the WTO.

The EU-Japan EPA has important voluntary cooperation commitments that are understood to be best practice, eg to 'maintain a dialogue' on regulatory issues, which thus seek to institutionalise cooperation between the parties.[68] While some agreements merely recognise the protection of personal information in different ways as to processing and dissemination of data, records and accounts and so on or that it should be protected, in several treaties parties specifically commit to adopting or maintaining legislation or regulations that protect personal data.[69] The EU-Japan EPA provides for a reassessment within three years of its entry into force of the need to include provisions on the free flow of data into the Agreement, ongoing at the time of writing, as a form of *rendezvous* clause.[70] This *rendezvous* took effect in 2020 and negotiations appear to have been complex, slow and tedious – hurdles which are not unexpected in the face of the complexity of the EU's positions.[71] How the EU engages with the spirit of the design of these clauses is also highly controversial; after all, precisely what is it that the EU strives for. As Burri states, the regulatory environment for digital trade has historically been substantially influenced by US FTAs and so the EU's capacity to set international standards remains quite significant, especially where substantial differences lie as to cross border data flows, human rights and security.[72]

[68] EU-Japan EPA, Art 8.80.2(f).

[69] See Agreement establishing an association between the European Community and its Member States, of the one part, and the Republic of Chile, of the other part [2002] OJ 359, Art 30; Free Trade Agreement between the European Union and its Member States, of the one part, and the Republic of Korea, of the other part [2011] OJ L127/6, Art 7.43; EU-Canada CETA, Art 16.4 and 5; Free Trade Agreement between the European Union and the Socialist Republic of Viet Nam [2019] OJ L186/2, Art 8.45.

[70] EU-Japan EPA, Art 8.81.

[71] Micallef, 'Digital Trade in EU FTAs: Are EU FTAs Allowing Cross Border Digital Trade to Reach Its Full Potential?' (n 52) 864.

[72] M Burri, 'The Governance of Data and Data Flows in Trade Agreements: The Pitfalls of Legal Adaptation' (2017) 51(56) *University of California Davis Law Review* 65, 99. See also S Aaronson, 'Why Trade Agreements Are Not Setting Information Free: The Lost History and Reinvigorated Debate over Cross-Border Data Flows, Human Rights, and National Security' (2015) 14 *World Trade Review* 671, 675; European Parliament, 'Study: The EU – Japan Economic Partnership Agreement'.

However, some suggest that the textual content of the EU-Japan EPA on regulatory cooperation and data amounts to a lot less than best practice. For example, Bartl and Irion contended on an earlier draft of the EPA that while the regulatory cooperation chapter explicitly states that it does not to interfere with parties' autonomy to regulate in pursuit or furtherance of its public policy objectives, among others, in personal data, the provision does not exclude data flows from the scope of activities, and therefore data privacy issues could be tabled as part of the regulatory cooperation mechanisms.[73] However, it is important to note that the EU-Japan EPA provisions were in a final draft and in existence along with texts on the EU-Mexico modernisation provisions when the EU published its model horizontal texts for the place of trade and privacy in trade agreements.[74] In other words, important developments in EU practice took place at this key point in the development of the GDPR and the EU's practices – and perhaps *earlier* critique is overshadowed as a result. It also should arguably be seen in context of the substantive development of convergence of standards in recent case law. In fact, the EU's convergence practices cannot be underestimated, given their success and their grounding in internationalisation.[75]

VII. Conclusions

EU-Japan relations ultimately constitute a significant study of the convergence of legal norms and standards, with lighter institutionalisation. It is a more remarkable study given the strong push to EU standards in this narrative, via courts adopting EU law principles, far beyond their previous legal parameters. The context of the EU-Japan relationship has stronger economic ties at its heart, yet ultimately shows the evolution of a broad partnership. The EU-Japan EPA is a very interesting study of framing, as data that was initially left outside of the negotiations has paradoxically ultimately become very central to all of the parties and has become a best practice element of the EPA, for a while at least, until its renegotiation arose as to its rendezvous clause. While it may not be the broadest of trade agreements in the end, its span is still worthy of study and highly indicative of EU best practice post-Lisbon. The Adequacy Decision appears to have generated convergence with EU legal standards in data privacy – not necessarily directly through institutionalisation but rather more indirectly through a form of convergence. While

[73] Bartl and Irion, 'The Japan EU Economic Partnership Agreement: Flows of Personal Data to the Land of the Rising Sun' (n 42).

[74] European Commission, 'Horizontal Provisions for Cross-Border Data Flows and for Personal Data Protection (in EU Trade and Investment Agreements)' (May 2018) Tradoc No 156884, template Art B.1, https://trade.ec.europa.eu/doclib/docs/2018/may/tradoc_156884.pdf accessed 25 February 2022.

[75] See E Fahey (ed), *Framing Convergence with the Global Legal Order: The EU and the World* (Hart Publishing, 2020) Ch 1.

the level of institutionalisation resulting from EU-Japan data adequacy and digital trade negotiations overall appears limited, it is difficult to underestimate the extent of the convergence which is generated or the push towards multilateralism and regulatory cooperation through institutionalisation in the EPA. As a long-standing trading partner of Europe, but also a representative Asian legal order not predisposed towards institutions, enforcement and regulatory cultures in the same way as Europe, it is a striking example of the nature of the cooperation and its significant outcomes for all. Given that the EU-Japan EPA appears now to have model or best practice chapters as to digital trade/electronic commerce, it becomes more significant than ever to probe the nature of the relationship.

6

East Asian Reverse Convergence with the EU? Closing Down the Gap in Emerging EU-China Relations

I. Overview: EU-China Relations: No Overarching Legal Framework

China has evolved a heavily state-directed approach to international economic ordering which has made it a complex partner for many, not least the EU. China is the EU's second largest trading partner, accounting for 15.4 per cent of the EU's total trade.[1] There are many longstanding links between the EU and China but they have not been embedded legally in any meaningful way – beyond dialogues at least – until more recent times, particularly since 2014.[2] In this regard, EU-China relations share some similarities with law-making in EU-US relations.[3] For some, China presents both a challenge and opportunity for the EU in relation to its conceptualisation of global justice.[4] There is now an official EU-China legal affairs dialogue.[5] It is one of the 14 strategic partnerships that the EU has, in contrast to the over 70 that China has, which are institutionalised and planned socialisation projects as to international economic law embedded in careful diplomatic language. Relations with China have encountered unprecedented strain during the Covid-19 crisis, where disputes as to disinformation, propaganda and the information provided about Covid-19 and its entry

[1] Data available at https://webgate.ec.europa.eu/isdb_results/factsheets/country/details_china_en.pdf accessed 26 February 2022.

[2] A Michalski and Z Pan, 'Role Dynamics in a Structured Relationship: The EU-China Strategic Partnership' (2017) 55 *Journal of Common Market Studies* 611; Z Chen, 'China, the European Union and the Fragile World Order' (2016) 54 *Journal of Common Market Studies* 775.

[3] There are a number of EU funded projects initiating developments in the field, focusing on its innovations with respect to EU law, eg Jean Monnet Network 'EU-China Legal and Judicial Cooperation' (EUPLANT), www.qmul.ac.uk/euplant/ accessed 26 February 2022.

[4] M Burnay and W Muller (eds), Special Issue on 'China and Global Governance: Between the International Rule of Law and the International Rule of Power?' (2018) 31 *The Hague Yearbook of International Law* 2020; M Burnay et al (eds), Special Issue on 'The Rule of Law as a Strategic Priority in EU External Action' (2016) 14 *Asia-Europe Journal*.

[5] With three having taken place by 2019, launched 'by consensus' in 2015: ibid.

into Europe.[6] Still, China has long had a complex history in relation to EU procurement, EU foreign direct investment and EU international fisheries policies, where its exclusion appears as a central goal of EU actions, policies and practices or where double-standards routinely operate.[7] The EU and China jointly adopted the EU-China 2020 Strategic Agenda for Cooperation.[8] The two sides agreed to implement the Strategic Agenda for Cooperation through their annual Summit, which provides strategic guidance to their relationship: (i) through the three pillars directly underpinning the Summit (the annual High Level Strategic Dialogue, the annual High Level Economic and Trade Dialogue, and the bi-annual People-to-People Dialogue); (ii) through their regular meetings of counterparts; and (iii) through their broad range of sectoral dialogues. This has included: strengthening coordination and cooperation, working for just, reasonable and effective rules in key fields, such as international trade and investment, finance, environment and climate change, the Internet and a new generation of wireless communication technology. Institutions are thus firmly embedded within these soft-law mechanisms: for example, institutions are mentioned four times in the Strategic Agenda and the relationship itself is carefully outlined in typical EU modes of engagements with third countries through dialogues, groups, meetings etc, ie China co-opts into the classical modes of EU international relations law. These developments have also come about because of multiple annual EU-China strategic documents and visions couched in relatively similar terms. Yet its broader context is still far more complex.

In 1978, China accounted for less than 1 per cent of global trade; by 2000 this had grown to 3 per cent, and a decade later its share had more than tripled, with and China becoming the world's top exporter, surpassing the US to become the world's largest trading nation in 2013. In 2020, it was the world's largest exporter and trading nation.[9] Many questions arise as to how to count the Chinese economy as the largest or second largest in the world, how to understand its hybrid market economy or how to reframe the problem of Chinese state capitalism more broadly.[10] The EU increasingly openly questions the actual 'largesse' of China – given the complex formula of the state there, the notion of 'China, Inc' permits

[6] M Peel, 'China hits back at EU disinformation claims' (*Financial Times*, 25 April 2020), www.ft.com/content/6cbb9b22-8735-46ba-88a7-cb3e04cad6db accessed 26 February 2022.

[7] *cf* J Odom, 'Europe's Double Standard for China's Overfishing' (*EJIL Talk!*, 16 April 2020), www.ejiltalk.org/europes-double-standard-for-chinas-overfishing/ accessed 26 February 2022.

[8] See Delegation of the European Union to China, 'EU-China 2020 Strategic Agenda for Cooperation' (2020), https://eeas.europa.eu/archives/docs/china/docs/eu-china_2020_strategic_agenda_en.pdf accessed 26 February 2022.

[9] WTO, 'World Trade Statistical Review 2020', www.wto.org/english/res_e/statis_e/wts2020_e/wts20_toc_e.htm accessed 26 February 2022.

[10] M Wu, 'The "China, Inc." Challenge to Global Trade Governance' (2016) 57 *Harvard International Law Journal* 261, 262; A Lang, 'Heterodox Markets and "Market Distortions" in the Global Trading System' (2019) 22 *Journal of International Economic Law* 677; US Trade Representative, 'Report on the Appellate Body of the World Trade Organisation' (2020) https://ustr.gov/sites/default/files/Report_on_the_Appellate_Body_of_the_World_Trade_Organization.pdf accessed 26 February 2022.

increasing EU scepticism on this.[11] China has liberalised its markets in significant ways since joining the WTO, through a process of marketisation that has taken place experimentally and incrementally. Its rise in the world economy has been matched by the number of WTO disputes concerning China. It was involved in nearly a quarter of all WTO cases between 2006 and 2015, joining the EU and US as the main litigators before the WTO.[12] This rise in economic and institutional power is by no means a straightforward development. The EU is not a neutral bystander in US-China disputes, which are heavily rooted in the awkward place of China in the development of the WTO. The EU mostly agrees with US on distortions of state capitalism. However, the EU has sought to address these issues *within* the WTO, involving rules-based procedures and institutionalised understanding of trade, and has emphasised to the US its need to contribute in like mind and form. It is a remarkable state of affairs to see the erosion of the dispute settlement system at a time where China was increasingly formalising its involvement in the institutionalised procedures. The EU increasingly enhances diversification of its international relations while at the same time seeking to address the distortive effect of foreign subsidies, arguably with China at the top of its regulatory agenda.[13] It is a complex balancing act for the EU to continue to juggle with an 'entity' that has become difficult to engage with. EU-China relations increasingly appear as an emerging story of possible institutionalisation, perhaps more accurately framing 'creeping' institutionalisation, against, as explored below, a backdrop of reverse convergence.

The EU has been developing a subsidies Regulation – arguably with China as its key subject and object – to be used against state-supported foreign companies operating in the EU. Foreign handouts are said to distort the European market when applied to market competition, mergers and acquisitions, and public procurement.[14] The Foreign Direct Investments (FDI) Screening Regulation[15] establishes a framework for the screening of FDI into the EU and is an important tool with which to address risks to security or public order brought about by foreign investments that target the EU's or Member States' critical assets. However, in terms of the scope of application, the FDI Screening Regulation is to

[11] Wu, 'The "China, Inc." Challenge to Global Trade Governance' (n 10).

[12] ibid 262; J Pauwelyn, 'The WTO 20 Years On: "Global Governance by Judiciary" or, Rather, Member-driven Settlement of (Some) Trade Disputes between (Some) WTO Members?' (2016) 27 *European Journal of International Law* 1119, 1123; G Shaffer and H Gao, 'China's Rise: How It Took on the US at the WTO' (2018) *University of Illinois Law Review* 115, 132. See also the masterly P Mavroidis and A Sapir, *China and the WTO: Why Multilateralism Still Matters* (Princeton University Press, 2021).

[13] See European Commission, 'Proposal for a Regulation of the European Parliament and of the Council on foreign subsidies distorting the internal market {SWD(2021) 99 final} – {SWD(2021) 100 final} – {SEC(2021) 182 final}' COM(2021) 223 final.

[14] European Commission, 'Commission proposes new Regulation to address distortions caused by foreign subsidies in the Single Market' (5 May 2021), https://ec.europa.eu/commission/presscorner/detail/en/ip_21_1982 accessed 26 February 2022.

[15] Regulation (EU) 2019/452 of the European Parliament and of the Council of 19 March 2019 establishing a framework for the screening of foreign direct investments into the Union [2019] OJ L79I/1.

determine the likely impact of foreign direct investment on security and public order by considering its effects, amongst others, on critical infrastructure, critical technologies and critical inputs; it does not specifically tackle the issue of distortions caused by foreign subsidies. Some suggest that the EU's lengthy list of legal tools against China continues to grow: eg evolving trade defence instruments (anti-dumping and anti-subsidy duties); allowing those duties to be used against companies subsidised by the Chinese government but exporting from another country; tightening up screening of inward FDI for national security reasons; developing an anti-coercion tool to use against foreign governments acting illegally; producing a toolbox for Member States to manage risky entities (such as Huawei) in 5G networks; banning imports made with forced labour; and requiring European companies to exercise 'due diligence' in eliminating labour and environmental abuses from their supply chains.[16] Arguably, however, many of these legal tools are 'hangovers' from the EU's engagement with China in the midst of the Trump administration, and much may change in how they evolve. Nonetheless, they represent an emerging deepening institutional design of EU regulatory surveillance architecture, with China as a clear subject and object, in a broad range of trade-related fields. Importantly for present purposes, many of these capture or relate to data law through a mixture of subject, design, schema or bureaucratisation.

Chapter 6 contains the following sections: (II) EU-China CAI and GI Agreements; (III) EU Member States' engagement with the law-light, institution-light Belt and Road Initiative; (IV) cyber law, the State and China; (V) the Chinese approach to cyber security; (VI) privacy and Chinese law; (VII) global alternatives to the 'gold standard' of EU data laws for China; and (VIII) conclusions.

II. The EU-China CAI and GI Agreements: Beyond a Limited Institutionalisation Agenda

The EU and China launched negotiations on the Comprehensive Agreement on Investment (CAI) in 2014. The negotiations aimed to replace the 25 outdated bilateral investment treaties (BITs) that China and EU Member States had concluded prior to the Treaty of Lisbon. While Asia is the home of some of the world's fastest growing economies, such as China and the Southeast Asian countries and it goes without saying that China is its most significant. China repeatedly emphasised its developing economy status in investment negotiations with the EU.[17] The CAI

[16] A Beattie, 'The EU is trailing China's trade distortions all round the world' (*Financial Times*, 10 May 2021), www.ft.com/content/0e94cd4e-16f9-4bfc-8bba-333027fb95ed accessed 26 February 2022.

[17] G Grieger, 'EU-China Comprehensive Agreement on Investment: Levelling the playing field with China' (2020) European Parliamentary Research Service PE 652.066; C Brandi and W Cheng, 'The Disputed Status of Developing Countries in the WTO' (*DIE Blog*, 14 March 2019) https://blogs.

is a noteworthy agreement on many levels but principally because it aims to go beyond traditional investment protection to also cover market access, investment-related sustainable development, and level-playing-field issues, such as transparency of subsidies, and rules on state-owned enterprises (SOEs) and forced technology transfer.[18] A significant issue for negotiations was level-playing-field issues and the ownership of companies in China, particularly in terms of state ownership, control and enterprise with respect to its complex developing economy status. Although the EU and China agreed in 2016 on the scope of the future agreement – that it would go beyond a traditional investment protection agreement to cover market access for investment and a number of important disciplines – after 33 rounds of negotiations in 2020, the first significant bilateral trade agreement was signed between the EU and China, albeit not in those areas.[19] In late December 2020, at the end of the German presidency of the European Council and when Germany was eager to preside over its conclusion, agreement in principle was finally reached on an investment agreement.[20] This provoked a wide range of reactions and controversies on Chinese human rights standards, conflicts between EU institutional actors, and also an initial transatlantic divide.[21] Above all, the CAI is a very limited form of agreement on investment only and is not a trade agreement. Its 'comprehensiveness' has thus drawn much derision. The emerging role of institutions and law here is of much interest. It is an innovative form of investment agreement which aims to liberalise investment alone but it is also one that proposes an institutionalised *and* embedded regulatory cooperation framework 12 years after the introduction of its new investment competences in the Treaty of Lisbon. Thus Section VI of the published texts of January 2021, subject to legal scrubbing changes and subject to agreement (which is highly irregular), outline 'institutional and final provisions' which provide for a series of Investment Committees referencing EU-China Economic and Trade Dialogues involving the European Commission and State

die-gdi.de/2019/03/14/the-disputed-status-of-developing-countries-in-the-wto/ accessed 26 February 2022; The World Bank, 'GDP (current US$) – China, European Union, United States, Japan', https://data.worldbank.org/indicator/NY.GDP.MKTP.CD?locations=CN-EU-US-JP&most_recent_value_desc=true accessed 26 February 2022.

[18] See European Parliament Research Service, 'EU-China Comprehensive Agreement on Investment Levelling the playing field with China' (September 2020), www.europarl.europa.eu/RegData/etudes/BRIE/2020/652066/EPRS_BRI(2020)652066_EN.pdf accessed 26 February 2022.

[19] European Commission, 'EU and China reach agreement in principle on investment' (30 December 2020), https://ec.europa.eu/commission/presscorner/detail/en/ip_20_2541?mc_cid=51ec175ba0&mc_eid=d59f683373 accessed 26 February 2022.

[20] ibid. See draft text: https://trade.ec.europa.eu/doclib/docs/2021/january/tradoc_159341.pdf accessed 26 February 2022; European Commission, 'Commission publishes market access offers of the EU-China investment agreement' (12 March 2021), https://trade.ec.europa.eu/doclib/press/index.cfm?id=2253 accessed 26 February 2022. See also J Ewing and SL Myers, 'China and EU Leaders Strike Investment Deal, but Political Hurdles Await' (*New York Times*, 30 December 2020), www.nytimes.com/2020/12/30/business/china-eu-investment-deal.html accessed 26 February 2022.

[21] N Barkin, 'Watching China in Europe – January 2021' (2021), https://sites-gmf.vuturevx.com/61/6509/january-2021/january-2021(1).asp?sid=504eaec4-a13f-4a0b-bd39-56dbbc033363 accessed 26 February 2022.

Council of China. It also refers to working groups on investment (Article 3), sustainable development (Article 4), and final provisions predicated on dialogue involving non-state stakeholders (Article 1 of sub-section 2 final provisions). These provisions are also accompanied by regulatory frameworks. It remains to be seen whether the agreement can be evolved to a conclusion and whether in particular it would be a mixed agreement or simply an EU-only agreement. In total, it adopts a uniform framework for investment relations by replacing 25 existing bilateral investment treaties between China and the EU Member States, modernising the patchwork of previous agreements. This itself suggests that the CAI has the potential to engage in infrastructure innovations as to investment. However, it is significantly different from CETA-style or OECD BIT-style investment, eg making no provision for fair and equitable treatment and not providing for investor-state dispute settlement.

The CAI was largely innovative as an agreement because it goes beyond protection provisions on investment. It covers market access, investment-related sustainable development, levelling-the-playing-field issues, transparency of subsidies, forced transfer of technology. It is also first agreement to take on board binding investment in many sectors and is thus wide ranging. It is said to improve market access conditions for EU companies in China and to level the playing field for them, addressing perceived asymmetries between the EU and China, for example prohibitions, equity caps, authorisation regimes, forced technology transfers etc. However, its innovations can be criticised, despite its efforts to procure binding protections in a legal agreement, to prevent possible back-sliding on the part of China and its efforts to nudge a broader set of developments at multilateral level.[22] There has been much criticism of the place of human rights in the CAI from the moment of the agreement, particularly in the European Parliament, a significant veto holder in the trade agreement process since the introduction of its powers in the Treaty of Lisbon.[23] The CAI is about the liberalisation of investment between the parties through a structured framework. It establishes this proposed liberalisation through a series of institutional mechanisms to monitor implementation, engaging with a complex partner facing large socio-economic challenges. China's 'liberalisation' in the domain of trade has otherwise mainly been conducted via the WTO and autonomously, and not through bilateralism until the CAI. Labour rights in particular are addressed in

[22] Criticism of CAI: J Carafano et al, 'The Pitfalls of the China-EU Comprehensive Agreement on Investment' (*The Diplomat*, 22 January 2021), https://thediplomat.com/2021/01/the-pitfalls-of-the-china-eu-comprehensive-agreement-on-investment/ accessed 26 February 2022.

[23] See European Parliament, 'MEPs refuse any agreement with China whilst sanctions are in place' (Press Release, 20 May 2021), https://www.europarl.europa.eu/news/en/press-room/20210517IPR04123/meps-refuse-any-agreement-with-china-whilst-sanctions-are-in-place accessed 26 February 2022; European Parliament, 'Resolution on Chinese countersanctions on EU entities and MEPs and MPs 2021/2644(RSP)' (2021), https://oeil.secure.europarl.europa.eu/oeil/popups/ficheprocedure.do?lang=en&reference=2021/2644(RSP) accessed 26 February 2022; European Parliament; 'Resolution of 16 September 2021 on a new EU-China strategy (2021/2037(INI))' (16 September 2021).

the sustainable development chapter but also in the Preamble, referencing the non-binding comprehensive strategy partnership but not international law.[24] There are thus many reasons to be positive about the CAI. However, one may say that overall the 'comprehensive' nature of the CAI is perhaps something of an overstatement. The state of the CAI negotiations appears highly complex in terms of their likely successful conclusion.[25] The CAI provides for institutional structures to maintain the agreement which are of much note because they break the mould of law-light, institution-light structures. However, in May 2021, the CAI negotiations were frozen after sanctions were imposed on EU law-makers, including five Members of the European Parliament and the Subcommittee on Human Rights, as a retaliatory response to the EU's decision to enact restrictive measures against four Chinese officials over human rights abuses against the Muslim Uyghur minority in the Xinjiang region.[26]

Prior to and apart from the agreement in principle of the CAI, the European Council has adopted decisions on the signature of the agreement between the EU and the government of China on geographical indications (GIs). This agreement also includes a mechanism to add more GIs in 2024.[27]

These developments between the two legal orders are highly significant with regard to legalisation. This form of convergence of values matters because it deepens institutionalisation. These developments, particularly the agreement in principle, signify a very significant legalisation of the EU-China relations, which is considered below.

III. EU Member States' Engagement with the Law-Light, Institution-Light Belt and Road Initiative

China has embarked on an ambitious Belt and Road Initiative (BRI) with the aim of extending and straightening its regional, megaregional and global influence.[28]

[24] Including references to forced labour. The word 'law' remarkably appears 60 times in the CAI Negotiation Schedules.

[25] Some suggest that the German Presidency Council's undue efforts to accelerate the agreement resulted in a rushed CAI: H von der Burchard, 'Merkel pushes EU-China investment deal over the finish line despite criticism' (*Politico*, 29 December 2020), www.politico.eu/article/eu-china-investment-deal-angela-merkel-pushes-finish-line-despite-criticism/ accessed 26 February 2022.

[26] European Parliament, 'MEPs refuse any agreement with China whilst sanctions are in place' (n 23); M Telo, 'Controversial Developments of EU-China Relations: Main Drivers and Geopolitical Inplications of the Comprehensive Agremeent on Investments' (2021) *Journal of Common Market Studies* 1.

[27] Agreement between the European Union and the Government of the People's Republic of China on cooperation on, and protection of, geographical indications, Council doc No 8361/20 (9 July 2020).

[28] eg M Brunnermeier et al, 'Beijing's Bismarckian Ghosts: How Great Powers Compete Economically' (2018) 41 *Washington Quarterly* 161, 171; J Chaisse and M Matsushita, 'China's "Belt And Road" Initiative: Mapping the World Trade Normative and Strategic Implications' (2018) 52 *Journal of World Trade* 163; H Wang, 'China's Approach to the Belt and Road Initiative: Scope, Character and Sustainability' (2019) 22 *Journal of International Economic Law* 29.

It is a most remarkable project, fluid and constantly increasing. It generally forms a largely law-light, institution-light, treaty-light, top-down regulatory effort spanning a significant part of Asia and Europe, in a massive carving-up of the geopolitical order. It is dependent upon the disregard for law, for example local environmental or labour, and is centred rather around investment (and not law).[29] It is comprised predominantly of two great global circuits of transport infrastructure – trade and finance – in the form of the Silk Road Economic Belt and the Maritime Silk Road, and perhaps – as outlined below – also a Digital Silk Road, mostly in the form of soft law 'projects'.[30] This 'alegal' approach to international law and global governance perhaps is not necessarily truly representative of Chinese practice. For example, subsequent to this, China has adopted a civil legal code in early 2021 after decades of development. It also then joined the Regional Comprehensive Economic Partnership (RCEP) and even applied to join the Comprehensive and Progressive Agreement for Trans-Pacific Partnership (CPTPP) – as well as reaching agreement with the EU on an EU-China CAI.[31] Indeed as Gao states, what is most significant, other than the already notable step of actually joining, is that China is agreeing in such forums to rules on cross-border data transfer and the localisation of data, positions that were previous unthinkable for China or which had been widely regarded as impossible for China to accept.[32] These comments are also applicable in the context of the CAI, where China has signed up to a structured dispute settlement mechanism on sustainable development, including labour and the environment.[33] This considerable legalisation of Chinese engagement with the global legal order, and the breadth of it, perhaps helps put the BRI into perspective and context, particularly where the EU seeks to oppose it with its own form of oppositional framework.

That this is a turning point is important. ASEAN, Japan, and South Korea accounted for significant parts of the EU's global trade. The dynamic economic development of Asian countries has led to a period of reaction and adjustment in the EU's trade policy towards the area. As a result, this region has become central to the EU's economic growth. Beyond economic interests, the EU has significant geopolitical interests in the Asian region, where risks of political conflict remain, eg the South China Sea disputes and the China-Taiwan conflict.[34]

[29] S Rolland and D Trubek, *Emerging Powers in the International Economic Order* (Cambridge University Press, 2019) 196.

[30] MS Erie, 'Chinese Law and Development' (2021) 62 *Harvard International Law Journal* 51; *cf* H Wang, 'China's Approach to the Belt and Road Initiative' (2019) 22 *Journal of International Economic Law* 59.

[31] H Jiang, 'The Making of a Civil Code: Promises and Perils of a New Civil Law' (2021) 95 *Tulane Law Review* 777, also noting the major problem of applying contract law to SOEs, with the lack of competitiveness of market conditions in which SOEs operate.

[32] H Gao, 'WTO Reform and China: defining or defiling the multilateral trading system?' (2021) 62 *Harvard International Law Journal* 1, 36.

[33] ibid 36.

[34] European Commission, 'Joint Communication to the European Parliament, the Council, the European Economic and Social Committee, the Committee of the Regions and the European Investment Bank: Connecting Europe and Asia – Building blocks for an EU Strategy' JOIN(2018) 31 final.

At the first BRI forum in May 2017, Chinese President Xi Jinping announced that Big Data would be integrated into the BRI to create the Digital Silk Road of the twenty-first century. The Digital Silk Road, also called the 'Information Silk Road,' brings advanced IT infrastructure to BRI countries, such as broadband networks, e-commerce hubs and smart cities, apparently driven by Chinese tech giants such as Huawei, who are in a position to deliver high-quality fibre optic cables at lower costs than European and US competitions. Such Chinese firms, for example, have opened cloud data centres in Africa and have been active in participating in national digitalisation strategies there.[35]

The relationship between the BRI and Europe is an important one in the broader scheme of reflecting on regulatory reach and markets outside of institutions. China has, as a result, sought to expand its influence through instruments other than formal international law, principally the BRI.[36] The BRI has gained a strong foothold in Europe and has arguably managed to divide the EU bilaterally and carve up the Member States in ways that no other global power has managed. The BRI is ultimately a set of highly domestic policies and economic instruments, supported by Chinese domestic institutions and law, but devoid of multilateral or bilateral agreements. Hungary was the first European country to sign a BRI-related memorandum of understanding with China in 2015. By 2019, at least two dozen European countries had signed BRI co-operation instruments, largely untraceable through their soft law origins.[37] In this period, the Commission opened an investigation into China's successful bid to build a high-speed railway connection between Belgrade and Budapest, albeit that nothing further was investigated.[38] A detailed BRI agreement between China and Italy – rare for the BRI – appears to have been signed in April 2019, ironically concluded *before* the EU Council met on 22 March 2019 to discuss a common EU strategy toward China,[39] unaware of developments taking place *outside* of binding law

[35] T Hinane El Kadi, 'The Promise and Peril of the Digital Silk Road' (*Chatham House*, 6 June 2019), https://www.chathamhouse.org/2019/06/promise-and-peril-digital-silk-road accessed 26 February 2022; M Erie and T Streinz, 'The Beijing Effect: China's "Digital Silk Road" as Transnational Data Governance' (2021) 54(1) *New York University Journal of International Law and Politics* 1.

[36] S Rolland and D Trubek, *Emerging Powers in the International Economic Order* (Cambridge University Press, 2019) 192; E Fahey and J Brsakoska Bazerkoska, 'Critical Perspectives on Social and Legal Relevance of Sincere Cooperation in EU External Relations Law in the Era of Expanding Trade: The Belt & Road Initiative in Context' (Hart Publishing, 2022).

[37] Eg T Matura, 'The Belt and Road Initiative Depicted in Hungary and Slovakia' (2018) 7 *Journal of Contemporary East Asia Studies* 174; J Macri, 'How Hungary's Path Leads to China's Belt and Road' (*The Diplomat*, 11 April 2019), https://thediplomat.com/2019/04/how-hungarys-path-leads-to-chinas-belt-and-road/ accessed 26 February 2022.

[38] F Bindi, 'Why Did Italy Embrace the Belt and Road Initiative?' (*Carnegie Endowment for International Peace*, 20 May 2019) https://carnegieendowment.org/2019/05/20/why-did-italy-embrace-belt-and-road-initiative-pub-79149 accessed 26 February 2022; F van der Eijk and A Pandita Gunavardana, 'The Road that Divided the EU: Italy Joins China's Belt and Road Initiative' (*European Law Blog*, 25 June 2019), https://europeanlawblog.eu/2019/06/25/the-road-that-divided-the-eu-italy-joins-chinas-belt-and-road-initiative/ accessed 26 February 2022.

[39] European Council, 'Conclusions March 21–22 2019 EUCO 1/19', 4. See G Martinico, 'Comparative Law Reflections on the Use of Soft Law in the Belt and Road Initiative' in G Martinico and X Wu (eds),

and *outside* of institutions. Unilateral membership of the BRI has appeared at times to undermine the EU's international agenda, complicating EU-China and EU-UN efforts.[40]

Given the vast number of EU Member States involved in the BRI in various ways and the EU's intensifying relations with China, the place of the EU in the BRI – or at least how to deal with it – appears more critical than ever. There are many who contend that the EU itself should join the BRI. It has long been asserted that the EU needs to create its own BRI rival and this finally appears to have been initated in 2021, as part of an EU strategic autonomy initiative. Ultimately, the EU has generally pursued an ambiguous set of ambitions in Asia. This has hinged on bilateralism with developed economies above all else (Korea, Japan), until recently at the exclusion of China where indirectly possible. Global governance literature focuses mostly on the sheer size of China and its emerging role in the global legal order as it seeks to establish its place through globalising its own legal order.[41] China stands, however, as a highly complex place; despite its size and rapid growth since embarking on economic reforms and opening up, it remains a developing country and its market reforms are considered to be incomplete.[42] The large size of its economy and population, its substantial economic and political influence and its long bureaucratic tradition differentiate it from many other developing countries. The effects of the gradual legalisation and institutionalisation of Chinese legal engagements in the broadest sense, eg with the WTO, remain to be seen in its dealings with the EU, particularly as to the CAI and not least because of the complexity of the issues emerging in relation to human rights and labour issues.[43]

A Legal Analysis of the Belt and Road Initiative: Towards a New Silk Road? (Palgrave Macmillan, 2020). See also H Wang, 'The Belt and Road Initiative Agreements: Characteristics, Rationale, and Challenges' (2021) 20 *World Trade Review* 282.

[40] Such as the Greek blockade of the EU statement at the UN in June 2017, criticising China's human rights record shortly after significant investment in Greece by China: see 'Greece Blocks EU Statement on China Human Rights at UN' (*Euroactiv*, 19 June 2017), www.euractiv.com/section/china/news/greece-blocks-eu-statement-on-china-human-rights-at-un/ accessed 26 February 2022.

[41] PK Lee et al, 'China in Darfur: Humanitarian Rule-maker or Rule-taker?' (2012) 38 *Review of International Studies* 423; S Kennedy (ed), *From Rule Takers to Rule Makers: The Growing Role of Chinese in Global Governance* (Indiana University Research, 2012); L Choukroune, 'China and the WTO Dispute Settlement System' (2012) 1 *China Perspectives* 49.

[42] Lang, 'Heterodox Markets and "Market Distortions" in The Global Trading System' (n 10) 679.

[43] Nonetheless, China does face some of the challenges that other developing and transition countries encounter in adopting and enforcing its laws, eg in cutting-edge market reform areas such as competition law and limited institutional capabilities. See W Ng, *The Political Economy of Competition Law in China* (Cambridge University Press, 2018) Ch 1, p 19, citing The World Bank, 'China Overview' (*World Bank*, 6 April 2016), www.worldbank.org/en/country/china/overview accessed 26 February 2022. As Brunnermeier, Doshi and James state, China today uses many of the techniques used by Germany a century ago – state-led industrial policy, generous state contracts, civil-military integration, bans on rival product, forced mergers, pursuit of third world markets and even international treaties to set its standards: M Brunnermeier et al, 'Beijing's Bismarckian Ghosts: How Great Powers Compete Economically' (2018) 41 *Washington Quarterly* 161, 165–66.

The EU has launched – to much fanfare – an 'EU Global Gateway' as a response to the BRI. The Global Gateway is lauded to:

> bring together the EU, Member States with their financial and development institutions, including the European Investment Bank (EIB), and the European Bank for Reconstruction and Development (EBRD) and seek to mobilise the private sector in order to leverage investments for a transformational impact.[44]

However, it is largely understood to be less about developing infrastructure itself and more about engaging with the private sector. It has been met by widespread scepticism and concern.[45]

IV. Cyber Law, the State and China: Behind the Great Firewall of China

State-owned enterprises prove problematic for many aspects of legal issues relating to China.[46] China is now at the forefront in developing world-leading technology in several areas such as 5G telecoms and AI. It exports this technology to more than 100 countries, who are participating in the BRI. It is also said to be seeking to boost its influence in the UN and other standard-setting bodies, to enhance the interests of its own companies.[47] China's use of subsidies and investment restrictions is well-documented: tentacles of 'China, Inc' extend wide and deep.[48] In international economic law terms, China continues to converge around Western models and institutionalise their bureaucracy within its own legal order and within international organisations.[49] To this end, some argue that the BRI is better seen as a globalisation study.[50] While this appears true to a degree, the place

[44] European Commission, '€300 billion for the European Union's strategy to boost sustainable links around the world' (Press Release, 1 December 2021), https://ec.europa.eu/commission/presscorner/detail/en/ip_21_6433? accessed 26 February 2022.

[45] 'Clear ambition is required if Europe is to rival China's Belt and Road' *Financial Times* (5 December 2021), https://www.ft.com/content/2d8ba39f-565f-4917-af3b-b993f6d9d826 accessed 26 February 2022.

[46] Wu, 'The "China, Inc." Challenge to Global Trade Governance' (n 10).

[47] J Kynge and N Liu, 'From AI to Facial Recognition: How China is Setting the Rules in New Tech' (*Financial Times*, 7 October 2020), https://www.ft.com/content/188d86df-6e82-47eb-a134-2e1e45c777b6 accessed 26 February 2022.

[48] M Wu, 'Testimony before US-China Economic and Security Revision Commission Hearing on US Companies in China' (28 February 2019) 9; H Shen, *Alibaba: Infrastructuring Global China* (Routledge, 2022).

[49] eg it has significantly bureacratised its legal order to be able to engage with the WTO. See Shaffer and Gao, 'China's Rise: How It Took on the US at the WTO' (n 12); Lang, 'Heterodox Markets and "Market Distortions" in The Global Trading System' (n 10); *cf* E Economy, 'The China Model: Unexceptional Exceptionalism' Essay Series of the Hoover Institution: Human Prosperity Project' (*Hoover*, 4 December 2020), https://www.hoover.org/research/china-model-unexceptional-exceptionalism accessed 26 February 2022; Erie, 'Chinese Law and Development' (n 30).

[50] ibid.

of legalisation within this is easily overlooked and it seems clear that the place of soft law has been key in the fast-paced and broad development of the BRI. China's increasing legalisation, internally through a civil law code and externally through internationalisation, participating more in international organisations and signing more regional trade agreements, has also been overlooked.

Unsurprisingly, EU country reports on China, issued in accordance with its new trade defence rules, identify a huge array of sources of state disruption in the Chinese economy.[51] In a staggeringly long list, these range from state and party involvement in corporate management, the basic legal structure of socialist market economy, the risk assessment practices of financial firms, preferential government procurement practices, mechanisms for allocating land, investment screening systems, divergence of Chinese labour laws and practices from fundamental international labour standards, as well as a wide range of sector-specific policies, from research and development subsidies, preferential loads to favoured enterprises, export restrictions and incentives, tax incentives, land use cost relief, employment stabilisation plans and much more.[52] This evaluation of state disruption in the Chinese economy has encountered significant critique from some quarters, for its over-zealousness and also its alignment with US ideals and philosophies on the nature of the Chinese state system.[53] There was a danger for Europe of repeating Chinese state capitalism in the EU with its Covid-19 approach to state aid. Critique of the concept of the state and its reach becomes all the more complex in the post- Covid era. Nonetheless, it is important to bear in mind that China is universally agreed to be extremely restrictive on digital trade, scoring one of the highest levels of digital trade restrictiveness in the world in recent surveys.[54] Covid-19 arguably had a dramatically negative impact on China with respect to information flows and international leadership, initially at least. Paradoxically, China is also very digitally-oriented compared to many other countries. Its digital economy is fast-moving, and its advanced e-commerce market is already one of the biggest in the world – and looks likely to remain so.[55]

China's 'Great Firewall' remains an enigma and is well known for its restrictions.[56] It is a term of art or colloquial expression of the 'splintering' of

[51] European Commission, 'Staff Working Document on Significant Distortions in the Economy of the People's Republic of China for the Purposes of Trade Defence Investigations' SWD (2017) 483 final/2.

[52] ibid.

[53] Lang, 'Heterodox Markets and "Market Distortions" in The Global Trading System' (n 10); US Trade Representative (n 10).

[54] MF Ferracane et al, 'ECIPE Digital Trade Restrictiveness Survey Index' (2018) ECIPE, https://ecipe.org/wp-content/uploads/2018/05/DTRI_FINAL.pdf accessed 26 February 2022.

[55] See R Mitter, *China's Good War How World War II Is Shaping a New Nationalism* (Harvard University Press, 2020).

[56] Wu, 'The "China, Inc." Challenge to Global Trade Governance' (n 10); D Mac Síthigh and M Siems, 'The Chinese Social Credit System: A Model for Other Countries?' (2019) 82 *Modern Law Review* 1071 (as to many related policies flowing from this restrictiveness).

the global internet that is most dramatically evident in China. Although countries other than China impose regulations on cyber flows, and have done so for many decades in fact, the scale of these regulations and enforcement tools in China are in a league of their own.[57] Many attempts have been made to raise the issue of data flows in the WTO Work Programme on e-commerce by the US and Japan but so far unsuccessfully. In data matters, the 'state' is similarly an immensely challenging idea when it comes to China. In the realm of trade, China has vigorously sought to institutionalise itself within the WTO legal order by training officials and thus embedding its bureaucracy. It also has sought to litigate and defend vigorously before the WTO Dispute Settlement Body.[58] In the areas of cross-border data flows, law enforcement and electronic communications, extraordinary divergences exist between China and much of the rest of the world. However, beyond China, the future of global technology appears also to be predicated on the complex model of surveillance capitalism that has developed.[59] This complexity appears innately comfortable or institutionally aligned with the China in many respects as to data flows, and shows that the Great Firewall metaphor has some significant nuances.[60]

Data and security appear to have a highly complex relationship. In 2015, the EU and China signed an agreement in the global race to develop 5G networks, during an EU-China High Level Economic and Trade Dialogue in Beijing. In 2018, with a global market share of 29 per cent, the nominally private Huawei Technologies ranked first among the top seven global telecoms equipment vendors, ahead of American Cisco and Ciena, Swedish Ericsson, Finnish Nokia, South Korean Samsung and Chinese state-owned ZTE Corpo. China uses advanced technologies for the systematic digital surveillance of its population, notably in its restive Xinjiang province, while the EU pursues a human-centric approach to advanced technologies, with the protection of the digital rights of the individual being key.[61] By 2021, however, Huawei issues had developed an entirely different meaning and outlook and 5G had then become politically toxic. The pace of change, as much as politics, law, technology and culture, is thus highly significant in EU-China relations.

[57] Wu, 'The "China, Inc." Challenge to Global Trade Governance' (n 10) 318, fnn 307–309; C Kuner, 'Data Nationalism and Its Discontents' (2015) *Emory Law Journal Online*, https://scholarlycommons.law.emory.edu/cgi/viewcontent.cgi?article=1024&context=elj-online accessed 26 February 2022.

[58] *cf* W Ng, 'Changing Global Dynamics and International Competition Law: Considering China's Potential Impact' (2019) 30 *European Journal of International Law* 1409.

[59] S Zuboff, *The Age of Surveillance Capitalism: The Fight for a Human Future at the New Frontier of Power* (Profile Books, 2019).

[60] X Chu and X Gao, 'Comparing the EU's and China's approaches in digital governance: on power and regulatory capture' in E Fahey and I Mancini (eds), *Understanding The EU As A Good Global Actor: Whose Metrics?* (Edward Elgar 2022, forthcoming).

[61] European Parliament, '5G in the EU and Chinese telecoms suppliers' (April 2019), https://www.europarl.europa.eu/RegData/etudes/ATAG/2019/637912/EPRS_ATA(2019)637912_EN.pdf accessed 26 February 2022.

Linked to the 'Great Wall' phenomenon, China has one of the highest digital trade restrictiveness metrics in the world.[62] It imposes a wide range of measures that directly impact cross-border data flows. China has a general data localisation rule which requires companies to store the data they collect only on servers inside China.[63] The recent Cybersecurity Law has a 'wide' data localisation requirement and applies to network operators, managers and network service providers (Article 76 of the Cybersecurity Law). The new law includes requirements for the personal information of Chinese citizens and 'important data' collected by 'key information infrastructure operators' (KIIOs) to be kept within the borders of China. If there are business reasons for the KIIOs to transfer this data outside of China, security assessments must be conducted. China also requires ISPs to retain users' data for a minimum period of 60 days whilst the Administrative Provisions on Information Services of Mobile Internet Application Programs also require that app providers keep records of users' activities for 60 days. China additionally has strict and detailed consent requirements for the collection of data. The State Security Law permits the state security organ, when necessary, to access any information or data held by anyone in China.[64] As explored above, significant developments in the 'Personal Information Protection Law' (PIPL) 2021 appear to move Chinese law further towards the European GDPR status quo, albeit to a degree.

V. The Chinese Approach to Cybersecurity: Deeper Institutionalisation but Away From the EU?

As a country that treats sovereignty as a defining issue of international law, China is an extremely interesting and challenging case study of the intersection of security and trade. China, as noted above, scores very highly in world surveys of digital trade restrictiveness.[65] The relationship between the BRI and China's regional security issues is a thorny one, particularly as to longer term ambitions.[66] It appears that BRI has fuelled Chinese interest in revamping the

[62] Ferracane et al, 'ECIPE Digital Trade Restrictiveness Survey Index' (n 54).

[63] There are notably also a series of ad hoc data localisation rules in the financial sectors, healthcare sector, taxi sector, electronic media, as well as on mapping services and trade secrets.

[64] In addition, the Law of the People's Republic of China on Protection of Consumer Rights and Interests gives the regulator the right to shut down and de-register the business in case of a data breach. The English version of the Act is available at http://english.mofcom.gov.cn/aarticle/lawsdata/chineselaw/200211/20021100053545.html accessed 26 February 2022.

[65] Ferracane et al, 'ECIPE Digital Trade Restrictiveness Survey Index' (n 54). They measure: (1) fiscal restrictions and market access; (b) establishment restrictions; (c) restrictions on data, and finally (d) trading restrictions. China is followed by Russia, India, Indonesia and Vietnam. They all have very restrictive regimes for digital trade.

[66] M Li, 'The Belt and Road Initiative: Geo-Economics and Indo-Pacific Security Competition' (2020) 96 *International Affairs* 169, at 179, citing Z Minghao, 'Yidai yilu jianshe de anquan baozhang wenti chuyi' [Analysing the Security Measures for the BRI] (2016) 18(2) *Guoji luntan [International Forum]* 1.

regional security order in the Asia Pacific. BRI connects Eurasia to continental and maritime infrastructures, raising the possibility that standards for smart infrastructure – which is connected to the Internet through sensors and software – may eventually be set by China and may deny US companies interoperability. China's decision to ban Western companies like Facebook have allowed its indigenous alternatives to become the domestic standard. China has been active in advancing its own agenda internationally on cybersecurity and information issues, defining the issue as one of information security, similar to Russia.[67] The US, UK and other Western states seek to frame the problem as one of cybersecurity and seek a multi-stakeholder model of governance including state and non-state actors.[68] For instance, security interests have dominated the EU's trade agreements with Eastern and Southern European countries motivated by the EU's desire to provide the economic stability necessary for political stability.[69] Against this complex tableau, the Huawei 5G affair has brought to centre-stage the salience of the trade/security nexus at the heart of the contemporary global legal order and, to a lesser extent, also cybersecurity. However a significant divide remains between legal literature on security and trade as to EU-China relations and China and much of the global legal order. The EU has had a long and complex preliminary engagement with China, predominantly formally in trade but also structurally in a variety of areas, and it is as yet just an embryonic partnership. How the security nexus evolves and how it contrasts with the US-Sino tech war remain to be seen.

As stated above, political developments rapidly evolve when it comes to China, from a Hong Kong security law, Huawei 5G to Tiktok. Prior to significant developments in EU-China trade taking place, the Standing Committee of China's National People's Congress adopted the National Security Law in Hong Kong on 30 June 2020.[70] The High Representative, Josep Borrell, responded to the effect that the EU reiterated its grave concerns about this law, adopted without any meaningful prior consultation of Hong Kong's Legislative Council and civil society. It was reiterated that the EU has a strong stake in the continued stability and prosperity of Hong Kong under the 'One Country, Two Systems' principle, attaching importance to the preservation of Hong Kong's high degree

[67] See A Roberts, 'Disruptions Leading to a Competitive World Order' in A Roberts, *Is International Law International?* (Oxford University Press, 2017) 16.

[68] See F Delarue, *Cyber Operations and International Law* (Cambridge University Press, 2020).

[69] P Manoli, 'Political Economy Aspects of Deep and Comprehensive Free Trade Agreements' (2013) 4(2) *Eastern Journal of European Studies* 51.

[70] 'The Law of the People's Republic of China on Safeguarding National Security in the Hong Kong Special Administrative Region' (2020), www.gld.gov.hk/egazette/pdf/20202448e/egn2020244872.pdf accessed 26 February 2022; C Chan, 'Thirty Years from Tiananmen: China, Hong Kong, and the Ongoing Experiment to Preserve Liberal Values in an Authoritarian State' (2019) 17(2) *International Journal of Constitutional Law* 439, 441; H Fu, 'China's Imperatives for National Security Legislation' in C Chan and F de Londras (eds), *China's National Security: Endangering Hong Kong's Rule of Law?* (Hart Publishing, 2020) 41.

of autonomy, in line with the Basic Law and with international commitments.[71] For many, the Hong Kong law is a reminder of the uncertain and complex place of China as to security and the breadth of its powers; it is a useful touchstone of the complexity of China.

In a country such as China, where the party-state controls the media and alternative sources of information, the Internet has raised significant issues as to the contours of privacy and data protection and how – if at all – they are enforced.[72] At the start of the twenty-first century, the NGO Privacy International ranked China almost last in a ranking of countries, denoting an endemic surveillance society (with a score of 1.3).[73] On account of the absence of an EU-China adequacy decision to date, and a limited program on trade-related issues, there is very little scholarship on the interaction between Europe and China in the area of data flows. China is one of the important jurisdictions that have emulated the EU's data protection law, at least superficially.[74] This may change in due course, with the adoption of the PIPL in 2021. For instance, as discussed below, it has recently enacted data protection laws, in 2017, 2019, and most comprehensively in 2021.[75] The Cybersecurity Law of 2019 builds on early non-binding measures of the government, for example Guidelines on the protection of personal information in public and commercial service information systems GB Z2881202012, which came into effect on 1 February 2013. The Cybersecurity Law incorporates several GDPR concepts into Chinese law, eg data must be adequate, relevant and not excessive to the purses for which it

[71] Council of the European Union, 'Declaration of the High Representative on behalf of the European Union on the adoption by China's National People's Congress of a National Security Legislation on Hong Kong' (1 July 2020).

[72] 'China Media Bulletin: 2019 internet freedom trends, Shutterstock censorship, Huawei "safe cities"' (*Freedom House*, November 2019) 140 *China Media Bulletin*, https://freedomhouse.org/report/china-media-bulletin/2020/china-media-bulletin-2019-internet-freedom-trends-shutterstock accessed 26 February 2022; 'China's Internet Freedom Hit a New Low in 2019, and the World Could Follow' (*The Diplomat*, 19 November 2019), https://thediplomat.com/2019/11/chinas-internet-freedom-hit-a-new-low-in-2019-and-the-world-could-follow/ accessed 26 February 2022; 'Human Rights Watch World Report: China Events of 2018' (*Human Rights Watch*, 2019), https://www.hrw.org/world-report/2019/country-chapters/china-and-tibet accessed 26 February 2022. See 'China: Freedom on the Net 2021 Country Report' (*Freedom House*, 2021), https://freedomhouse.org/country/china/freedom-net/2021 accessed 26 February 2022; 'China: Freedom on the Net 2020 Country Report' (*Freedom House*, 2020), https://freedomhouse.org/country/china/freedom-net/2020 accessed 26 February 2022; *cf* Mac Síthigh and Siems, 'The Chinese Social Credit System: A Model for Other Countries?' (n 56), who outline its similarities with respect to platform economy credit systems (eg Uber, Paypal) or financial system credits, although without any regard to privacy decisions.

[73] 'Privacy International National Ranking 2007 – Leading Surveillance Societies Around the World'. The UK and US also joined in this category ranking at levels of 1.4 and 1.5 respectively. This document, previously accessible on the Internet, became unavailable in January 2022.

[74] A Bradford, *The Brussels Effect: How the European Union Rules the World* (Oxford University Press, 2020).

[75] R Creemers et al, 'Translation: Cybersecurity Law of the People's Republic of China (Effective June 1, 2017)' (*New America*, 29 June 2018), https://www.newamerica.org/cybersecurity-initiative/digichina/blog/translation-cybersecurity-law-peoples-republic-china/ accessed 26 February 2022.

is processed.[76] The data subject must give his explicit consent, which mirrors purpose limitation and consent requirements in the GDPR. However, in terms of institutional design and enforcement, any EU content is merely superficial.[77]

Chinese scholars also support EU-style regulation in China, noting that its reliance on EU-style government as opposed to US-style self-government by the industry provided a better fit. Yet in reality it is unclear how much influence the EU has really had on China's data protection regime: China is universally known for its restrictions on criticism and internet freedom.[78] In fact, its digital authoritarianism, from social points to facial recognition, represents 'a stark departure' from the Internet governance and privacy principles of the EU. China continues to block and filter online content on a large scale and several companies have been prohibited from operating in the country. Companies such as Google have also withdrawn from China because of its censorship rules and attempts at hacking.[79] China's commitment to EU-style data privacy is understood to be questionable, after reports surfaced of China's large-scale deployment of facial recognition techniques for law enforcement purposes. Its social credit system, where citizens are rated for their trustworthiness by paying taxes or in committing crimes, has also been widely noted and studied, garnering international concern,.[80] These social credit ratings have significant negative consequences, in that citizens with poor 'social credit' may be banned from travelling by train or aeroplane. China's data privacy practices for social control purposes are a stark reminder that any de jure 'Brussels Effect' on paper does not translate into the use of EU law in a meaningful way.[81]

As adverted to above, a vast amount of scholarship engages in 'discovery mode' as to the nuances of understanding Chinese legal regulation.[82] This arguably emphasises differences between the regimes. In order words, such literature focuses more on the *separate* analysis of both regimes. However, it is likely that this form of interaction will continue and perhaps even increase due, for example, to the expansion of 5G networks and the fundamental role, as one of the world's technological leaders, that China plays in new legal and technical challenges.

[76] See eg S Wang Han and A Bakar Munir, 'Information Security Technology – Personal Information Security Specification: China's Version of the GDPR' (2018) 4 *European Data Protection Review* 535; E Pernot-Leplay, 'China's Approach on Data Privacy Law: A Third Way Between the U.S. and the EU?' (2020) 8 *Penn State Journal of Law & International Affairs* 51, 63; G Greenleaf, 'China Issues a Comprehensive Draft Data Privacy Law' (2020) 168 *Privacy Laws & Business International Report* 6.

[77] EU influence may also be seen in the China-EU Information Society Project, a cooperation initiative between China and the EU from 2005–2009. The EU provided funding and technical advice to the Ministry of Commerce in China as part of the cooperation with the specific objective to design a regulatory framework by introducing best practices from the EU.

[78] Bradford, *The Brussels Effect: How the European Union Rules the World* (n 74).

[79] Obviously, China has not had controversial cases against Google in China because Google is banned in China.

[80] Mac Sithigh and Siems, 'The Chinese Social Credit System: A Model for Other Countries?' (n 56).

[81] Bradford, *The Brussels Effect: How the European Union Rules the World* (n 74) 154.

[82] eg Erie, 'Chinese Law and Development' (n 30).

Chinese law requires data localisation in fields ranging from financial information, population health information, online publication and online lending to online taxi reservation and online map services. The recent Cybersecurity Law provides that personal information and data collected and produced by critical information infrastructure operators arising from their operations in China must be stored within China.[83] Chinese personal jurisdiction and applicable law for online data protection are thus mostly territorially based, not because Chinese legislators adopt the exceptionalist view, but rather because a territorially-based private international law fits into China's broader economic data localisation policy and strict censorship systems.[84] Also, it is consistent with Chinese private international law, which generally refrains from the extra-territorial application of law.[85]

Concerns exist about Chinese influence on security, with respect to its reach into the Digital Silk Road. China has, for example, hosted sessions on its system of censorship and surveillance for media officials from Morocco, Egypt and Libya, and it is said that these sessions have been followed by the adoption in those countries of repressive cybersecurity laws resembling those of China.[86] Egypt signed a Memorandum of Agreement with Chinese IT companies in 2019 to deepen cooperation in AI, cloud computing and surveillance systems, raising concerns about the installation of Chinese digital surveillance tools without adequate legal safeguards being in place for privacy.[87] It is difficult to suggest that most of these events could happen in Europe, given that the respective starting points are different. However, it underscores how limited the institutionalisation of data privacy has been in China and how the convergence of rules, norms and standards is far more chequered and multifarious than may have been realised.

As Bersick, Christou and Yi state, unlike the EU approach to cybersecurity, which is defensive, centred on law and resilience and focused on multi-stakeholder approaches, China's perspective on cybersecurity is driven by the central objective of establishing cyber sovereignty within China.[88] This ensures that respect for national sovereignty becomes one of the guiding principles governing global cyberspace. This comes directly from China's national security culture, with an emphasis on securing China's so-called cyber sovereign borders. The EU-China

[83] J Huang, 'Chinese Private International Law and Online Data Protection' (2019) 15 *Journal of Private International Law* 186, 194.

[84] Y Hong, 'The Cross-Border Data Flows Security Assessment: An Important Part of Protecting China's Basic Strategic Resources' (2017) Yale Law School, Paul Tsai China Center Working Paper.

[85] Huang, 'Chinese Private International Law and Online Data Protection' (n 83) 208.

[86] El Kadi, 'The Promise and Peril of the Digital Silk Road' (n 35).

[87] El Kadi, 'The Promise and Peril of the Digital Silk Road' (n 35).

[88] S Bersick et al, 'Cybersecurity and EU-China Relations' in E Kirchner et al (eds), *Security Relations between China and the European Union: From Convergence to Cooperation?* (Cambridge University Press, 2016) 169.

Strategic 2020 Agenda for Cooperation agreed enhanced cooperation, mutual trust and understanding as its core pillars.[89] However, the diverse approaches of the EU and China in cyberspace are said to be too diametrically opposed for any concrete outcome.[90] The EU has also largely focused on soft cyber power and this is understood to be too far apart from the Chinese approach to amount to a credible engagement. In 'EU-China – A Strategic Outlook', the EU views China as 'an economic competitor in the pursuit of technological leadership'.[91] China and the EU apply different approaches towards global cyber governance, with China adopting a state-centric view, perhaps promoting the 'balkanisation' of the Internet.[92] However, whether this view holds good after the CJEU *Schrems II* decision, which promotes significant data localisation and ostensibly impedes data flows, remains to be seen.

There are still a great number of bilateral agreements between EU Member States and China. These agreements cover a wide range of topics within the area of international judicial cooperation and in some instances data transfers. For instance, in 2014 China and Italy pledged to increase their cooperation in strategic areas such as law enforcement and the fight against transnational crime and terrorism.[93] It is thought that China prefers to 'deal' with Member States rather than the EU as a whole, using a divide-and-rule strategy. Many ongoing 5G network issues are largely unrelated to exclusive external competences and cyber competences not falling under trade competences per se. This renders this area a complex one for law enforcement generally. However, returning to the separateness or differences between the EU and China, the next section looks at privacy and Chinese law and its convergence towards the EU.

VI. Privacy and Chinese Law: Moving Gradually Towards the EU?

The Chinese Constitution lists the fundamental rights and duties of citizens but is generally non-justiciable.[94] It is a coincidence that the most significant case about the justiciability of constitutional rights, *Qi Yuling v Chen Xiaoqi*, was a

[89] European Commission, 'European Commission and HR/VP contribution to the European Council, EU-China – A Strategic Outlook (2019).

[90] Ibid; *cf* Chinese Ministry of Foreign Affairs, 'China's Policy Paper on the EU: Deepen the China-EU Comprehensive Strategic Partnership for Mutual Benefit and Win-Win Cooperation' (2014).

[91] European Commission, 'EU-China – A Strategic Outlook' (n 89).

[92] F Russo, 'Assessing the EU-China Relationship in Cyberspace' (*EIAS*, 2020), www.eias.org/op-ed/assessing-the-eu-china-relationship-in-cyberspace/ accessed 26 February 2022.

[93] See Martinico, 'Comparative Law Reflections on the Use of Soft Law in the Belt and Road Initiative' (n 39).

[94] See G Greenleaf, 'The Right to Privacy in Asian Constitutions' (2020) University of New South Wales Law Research Series No 53.

case concerning privacy and identity theft.[95] A positive reply to the complaint by the Shandong Appeal Court, referred to the Supreme People's Court, is understood to confirm that it was no longer possible for individuals to raise constitutional rights in China in civil disputes. There are significant developments in Chinese privacy law in recent times which suggest that officially there is an increasing orientation towards aspects of the EU's GDPR regime that could conceivably pave the way for adequacy issues to be satisfied. Shortly before the China Cybersecurity Law came into effect, China's State Internet Information Office published draft measures to assess whether personal information and important data could be moved out of China.[96] As noted above, China's National Standardisation Committee introduced 'Information Security Techniques – Personal Information Security Specification' (the National Standard) in 2017, to become effective May 2018. The National Standard applies to all private sector organisations involved in 'personal information', the definition of which could potentially be interpreted more broadly than under some European laws. The definition of personal sensitive information is open-ended and is understood to be broader than comparable laws.[97]

After 1 May 2018, the National Standard was applauded for providing clarity on what is expected from data protection compliance programmes in China. It had been functioning as China's de facto soft law for some time, and it was important for companies to evaluate personal data protection programmes against the National Standard. Bundled consent has not been discouraged and there is a specific requirement for consent to process the activities or core and extended function. There is no choice of lawful basis other than consent in China and the predominant consent-based regime has faced various challenges. The proposed revision to the National Standard also includes the same requirements that the controller provides opt-out mechanisms for personalised display or listing and advertisement. The revised National Standard introduces a documentation requirement similar to Article 30 of the GDPR with respect to accountability. As to due diligence and control over third party APR, the revised draft requires the controller to document certain due diligence on the data protection compliance, though not to the same extent as required in controller to processor data sharing under the GDPR. There is also an important obligation in Article 42 of the Cybersecurity Law for reporting data breaches to both Chinese authorities

[95] *Qi Yuling v Chen Xiaoqi* [2001] 5 SPC Gazette, http://en.pkulaw.cn/display.aspx?cgid=1970324837041542&lib=case accessed 26 February 2022; Greenleaf, 'The Right to Privacy in Asian Constitutions' (n 94).

[96] Huang, 'Chinese Private International Law and Online Data Protection' (n 83) 195; 'Measures to Assess Whether Personal information and Important Data Can be Moved outside of China' (draft), published for public opinions by State Internet Information Office (11 April 2017).

[97] G Greenleaf and S Livingston, 'China's Personal Information Standard: the Long March to a Privacy Law' (2017) 150 *Privacy Laws and Business international Report* 25, 53.

and the affected data subject. A certificate centre set up in 2018 had yet to report any company. In 2019, China's National Standardisation Technical Committee proposed certain revisions to the National Standard personal Information Security Specification, for public consultation (35273-2017). In February 2019, the China Cyber Security Review Technology and Certification Centre announced that the personal data protection compliance programme of some companies, for example Alipay, Tencent Cloud and others, had passed certification based on the National Standard. There was also a joint announcement in 2019 by four ministers to curb certain privacy practices such as bundled consent throughout 2019. The revisions to Chinese law in 2019 are thus notable, given that the previous draft thereof was understood to closely track EU law.[98]

As noted above, China has in the past decade been strengthening its data protection framework and has granted foreigners equal legal protection with Chinese nationals.[99] China has also adopted protection for consumers pursuant to its e-commerce Law in 2019 with respect to platform operators. This does not mean, however, that it satisfies adequacy requirements under EU law, in particular in view of China's law enforcement problem, popular law breaches and the likely window-dressing of the Binding Corporate Rules.[100] With Huawei's increasing share of products on European markets, including smartphones, tablets and network infrastructures facilities, from WLAN routes to fibre optic cables, there is little doubt that the personal data of EU customers and consumers has been transferred to China.[101] Such data may be highly valuable to the Chinese intelligence agencies, as well as to Chinese businesses seeking EU markets. Yet there are few legally binding international agreements or treaties dealing with the Internet, and geographically-bound adequacy approaches may not be the optimal way of dealing with data transfers.[102] Theoretically, there are legal remedies available to EU citizens when their data is processed in China, whether they may sue directly in China or from their EU domiciles, but there is not a single reported case of data privacy breach.[103] It is possible that excessive amounts of attention are focused on transatlantic transfers, rather than EU-Asian transfers. Instead, much may depend on whether an EU data subject's Member State of domicile has a mutual judicial assistance agreement with China to enforce EU court judgments and arbitral awards. This indicates that the EU's Charter of Fundamental Rights is evidently

[98] On the revisions to the China data protection framework see D Luo, 'China – Data Protection Overview' (*One Trust Data Guidance*, November 2021), https://www.dataguidance.com/notes/china-data-protection-overview accessed 26 February 2022.

[99] B Zhao and GP Mifsud Bonnici, 'Protecting EU Citizens Personal Data in China: a Reality or a Fantasy?' (2019) 24(2) *International Journal of Law and Information Technology* 128, 148.

[100] ibid 149.

[101] See Zhao and Bonnici, 'Protecting EU Citizens Personal Data in China: a Reality or a Fantasy?' (n 99).

[102] C Kuner, 'The Internet and the Global Reach of EU Law' in M Cremona and J Scott (eds), *EU Law Beyond EU Borders: The Extraterritorial Reach of EU Law* (Oxford University Press, 2019).

[103] Zhao and Bonnici, 'Protecting EU Citizens Personal Data in China: a Reality or a Fantasy?' (n 99).

not evenly applied as it stands. Ultimately, an EU-China form of Privacy Shield is urgently required, though politically and legally, post-*Schrems II*, this seems far out of reach. Significant differences exist between the EU and China's respective regimes on data protection; these seem likely to render impossible data transfers between them for law enforcement purposes.[104] Whether this remains the case in the light of the widening agenda of EU-China relations remains to be seen.

As noted above China's National People's Congress Standing Committee recently passed China's first comprehensive data privacy law, the PIPL, which took effect on 1 November 2021.[105] Its framing is notable, as merely a framework law rather than a comprehensive attempt at law-making; it does not directly address privacy. There are many notable changes in the text. One that is framed most concretely, in binding and hard law terms rather than as a framing principle, is the explicit outlawing of automated decision-making for price discrimination, to protect consumers from differentiated treatment. This perhaps veers towards EU law on the matter in terms of convergence. Another highly notable element of the framework law is its openness to international cross-border transfers. The PIPL is said to encourage Chinese participation in international protection law-making and also, in Article 12, to promote mutual recognition of personal information protection rules. Some suggest that it is unclear whether Chinese regulators are seeking to facilitate interoperability between Chinese laws, or to bring international rules closer to Chinese law, or both. In this regard, there are many unknowns in the future of Chinese internationalisation of the digital sphere. However, the increasing legalisation of Chinese national practice appears highly distinctive, however framed, and is allied with significant internationalisation developments, for example joining international agreements or applying to join major regional agreements; it is a story of increasing convergence.[106]

VII. Global Alternatives to the 'Gold Standard' of EU Data Laws for China?

While China has adopted many EU standards, it is difficult to see this as the end point of the Chinese data narrative. The EU's data privacy regime is widely

[104] P de Hert and V Papakonstantinou, 'The Data Protection Regime in China' (2015) European Parliament, Committee on Civil Liberties, https://www.europarl.europa.eu/RegData/etudes/IDAN/2015/536472/IPOL_IDA(2015)536472_EN.pdf accessed 26 February 2022.

[105] It is said to have a history stretching back more than 15 years to an earlier, aborted legislative effort, and it continued to evolve through the first and second published drafts, straight through to the final text. See 'Seven Major Changes in China's Finalized Personal Information Protection Law' (*DigiChina*, August 23, 2021) https://digichina.stanford.edu/news/seven-major-changes-chinas-finalized-personal-information-protection-law accessed 26 February 2022.

[106] *cf* H Gao, 'Data Regulation with Chinese Characteristics' in M Burri (ed), *Big Data and Global Trade Law* (Cambridge University Press, 2021).

considered one of the most ambitious, stringent and gold-standard protections of the individual's data rights globally.[107] Whether other entities internally will adopt European standards, or indeed emulate them as global standards, is a very different matter. There are some suggestions in the US that EU-styled GDPR or regulatory bodies could be viably proposed but no suggestions that the Asia-Pacific Economic Cooperation (APEC) Cross-Border Privacy Rules (CBPR) will rival it.[108] The precise impact of the GDPR on international agreements and instruments remains to be seen. When it comes to alternatives to the EU regime, the first one which is consistently mooted is Convention 108 of the Council of Europe. Convention 108 is said to be increasingly of relevance to Asian data privacy laws, with four Asian states as observers and likely to accede, which is briefly considered in Chapter 2 above.[109] Whilst accession to Convention 108 will have a positive effect on applications for adequacy under the GDPR, the extent of compliance is not yet known. Most arguments as to the force of Convention 108+ assume some significance for Council of Europe and European Court of Human Rights jurisprudence, for example, which is hardly applicable in much of Asia.[110] Treaty-based harmonisation seems unlikely to emerge any time soon. There is little appetite currently in major Western economies outside of the EU to accede. Convention 108+ is also said to lack any 'killer' features that might induce 'fear' since it lacks a sanctions regime and also lacks extraterritoriality. Also, most importantly, China is not a signatory to the Convention and its additional protocol; it is asserted that China is likely to be barred from accession, as a non-democratic society.[111] Ultimately, it seems difficult to see it as a parallel institutionalisation of data. If its core attraction is that it is distinctly not institutionalised – in the EU sense of design, enforcement, compliance, multilevel actors – it currently also lacks competing factors that

[107] See J Polakiewicz, 'Convention 108 as a Global Privacy Standard' (International Data Protection Conference, Budapest, 2011), https://rm.coe.int/16806b294e accessed 26 February 2022; LA Bygrave, 'The "Strasbourg Effect" on Data Protection in Light of the "Brussels Effect": Logic, Mechanics and Prospects' (2021) 40 *Computer Law & Security Review* 1.

[108] See G Greenleaf, 'Will Asia-Pacific Trade Agreements Collide with EU Adequacy and Asian Laws?' (2020) 167 *Privacy Laws & Business International Report* 18.

[109] C Sullivan, 'EU GDPR or APEC CBPR? A Comparative Analysis of the Approach of the EU and APEC to Cross Border Data Transfers and Protection of Personal Data in the IoT Era' (2019) 35(4) *Computer Law & Security Review* 380; Bygrave, 'The "Strasbourg Effect" on Data Protection in Light of the "Brussels Effect": Logic, Mechanics and Prospects' (n 107); G Greenleaf, 'A World Data Privacy Treaty? "Globalisation" and "Modernisation" of Council of Europe Convention 108' in N Witzleb et al (eds), *Emerging Challenges in Privacy Law: Comparative Perspectives* (Cambridge University Press, 2014) 92.

[110] Eg Bygrave, 'The "Strasbourg Effect" on Data Protection in Light of the "Brussels Effect": Logic, Mechanics and Prospects' (n 107) 3: '… the Strasbourg Effect on data protection did not begin with the adoption of C108 +. Ever since the 1970s, the CoE has been enormously influential in shaping regulatory discourse in the field, primarily within Europe but also beyond': see ibid 10.

[111] Nor is China a signatory of the OECD Guidelines on the Protection of Privacy and Transborder flows of personal data and so many gaps easily appear in this argumentation.

might make it a gold standard, whether these factors relate to the Convention itself specifically or in a broader context.

As noted briefly in Chapter 1 above, the other major global standard to be considered is the CBPR system, which was first established in 2011 by the APEC as a 'regional economic forum' of 21 Asia-Pacific member economies.[112] The APEC Privacy Framework is a set of principles and implementation guidelines that were created in order to establish effective privacy protections that avoid barriers to information flows, and ensure continued trade and economic growth in all 27 countries of the APEC region. The APEC Privacy Framework set in motion the process of creating the APEC CBPR system. However, unlike the GRPR – which is a binding regulation that applies to all EU countries – the CBPR is a voluntary, principles-based framework that only extends to APEC members that have formally joined. Notably, China, an APEC member economy that endorsed the CBPR system in 2011, has never expressed any interest in joining.[113] China also has not ratified the International Convention on Civil and Political Rights (ICCPR), which also protects privacy.

CPTPP, in its Chapter 14 (e-commerce), includes commitments to privacy but *without* specifying APEC-CBR and China is not yet a party to the CPTPP.[114] As to the electronic commerce chapter, the CPTPP text is the same as that found in the earlier versions of TPP, particularly as to the key provision, noticeably including references to broader international frameworks, ie the APEC CBPR systems.[115]

Overall, the question of a rival 'gold standard' appears moot absent China joining CPTPP. However, in 2021, China officially applied to joint CPTPP; whether this is likely to realistically result in accession is an open question at the time of writing.[116] China's application to CPTPP followed closely after China joined the RCEP in late 2020, making it the world's largest trading bloc, involving

[112] Like the EU GDPR, the CBPR also governs the transfer of personal information across the borders of participating nations. To date, eight nations have joined the CBPR system: the US, Canada, Mexico, Japan, Singapore, Taiwan, Australia and the Republic of Korea; G Greenleaf, *Asian Data Privacy Laws: Trade and Human Rights Perspectives* (Oxford University Press, 2014); G Greenleaf, 'The Right to Privacy in Asian Constitutions' (2020) University of New South Wales Law Research Series No 53.

[113] A Gribakov, 'Cross-Border Privacy Rules in Asia: An Overview' (*Law Fare Blog*, 3 January 2019), www.lawfareblog.com/cross-border-privacy-rules-asia-overview accessed 26 February 2022. Unlike the GDPR, which is a directly applicable regulation, the CBPR system does not displace or change a country's domestic laws and regulations. Where there are no applicable domestic privacy protection requirements in a country, the CBPR system is intended to provide a minimum level of protection.

[114] Trans-Pacific Partnership Agreement (TPP), Art 148 (personal information protection), Art 14.11 (cross border transfer of information by electronic means), Art 14(13) location of computing facilities. Article 14.8 CPTPP (Personal information protection), imposes positive obligation on each party to provide that they shall maintain or adopt a legal framework that provides for the protection of the personal information of the users of electronic commerce: T Streinz, 'Digital Megaregulation Uncontested? TPP's Model for the Global Digital Economy' in B Kingsbury et al (eds), *Megaregulation Contested* (Oxford University Press, 2019) 313.

[115] Notably the UK intends to pursue accession to the CPTPP as part of its trade negotiations programme.

[116] 'China officially applies to join CPTPP, as the US increasingly isolated in trade' (*The Global Times*, 17 September 2021), www.globaltimes.cn/page/202109/1234550.shtml accessed 26 February 2022.

ASEAN nations (eg Brunei, Cambodia, Indonesia, Laos, Malaysia, Myanmar, Philippines, Singapore, Thailand, and Vietnam) and ASEAN FTA partners (Australia, China, India, Japan, New Zealand and Republic of Korea).[117] RCEP includes digital trade provisions, specifically enabling the free flow of 'business information', some exceptions, a ban on data localisation and a personal data protection floor. It is widely understood as a significant 'retreat' from TPP, where its e-commerce chapter is not enforcement by state-state dispute settlement (Article 17); there is no provision on source code; the right of covered business to transfer of data offshore and localisation bans are subject to self-judging public policy tests (Articles 15 and 16); bans on data localisation are subject to self-judging and non-disputable national security exceptions and a moratorium on customs duties on electronic transmission is not made permanent (Article 12). Most significantly, the privacy provisions (Article 9) are weak and differ greatly from TPP, in that only a law providing for protection of personal information is required and there is no minimum standard.[118] RCEP thus has provisions on data transfer, data localisation and cross-border transfers of data by electronic means. However, RCEP has weaker rules and market access commitments than CPTPP, for example, though is does have a chapter on e-commerce (Chapter 12). This appears an important development for China. Gao and Shaffer have argued that e-commerce in the RCEP provides ample evidence of the fact that the RCEP is not led and dominated by China, particularly when it comes to the provisions on data localisation (eg Article 12.14, which provides that businesses are not required to locate computing facilities in its territory or to restrict cross-border transfer of information by electronic means for business purposes).[119] Exceptionally, such measures may be deployed under certain conditions. It is in this regard that RCEP deviates from TPP. Under TPP, parties need to show that their measures pursue a legitimate public policy objective and are not arbitrary, unjustifiably discriminatory, or a disguised restriction on trade, and that the restrictions are no greater than necessary. If need be, these questions could get adjudicated in state-state dispute settlement proceedings. In contrast, under RCEP, it is for each country itself to decide what 'it considers necessary' to achieve a legitimate public

[117] H-W Liu, 'Data Localization and Digital Trade Barriers: ASEAN in Megaregionalism' in PL Hsieh and B Mercurio (eds), *ASEAN Law in the New Regional Economic Order: Global Trends and Shifting Paradigms* (Cambridge University Press, 2019); MF Ferracane and L Mosi, 'What Kinds of Rules are Needed to Support Digital Trade?' in B Hoekman et al (eds), *Rebooting Multilateral Trade Cooperation: Perspectives from China and Europe* (CEPR, 2021); P Leblond, 'Governing Cross-Border Data Flows Beyond Trade Agreements to Support Digital Trade: Inspiration from International Financial Standards-Setting Bodies' in I Borchert and LA Winters (eds), *Addressing Impediments to Digital Trade* (CERP, 2021); H Gao and G Shaffer, 'The RCEP: Great Power Competition and Cooperation over Trade' (2021) UC Irvine School of Law Research Paper No 2021-09; J Chaisse and Richard Pomfret, 'The RCEP and the Changing Landscape of World Trade: Assessing Asia-Pacific Investment Regionalism Next Stage' (2019) 12 *Law and Development Review* 159.

[118] J Kelsey, 'Important Differences between the Ffinal RCEP Electronic Commerce Chapter and the TPPA and Lessons for E-commerce in the WTO' (*Bilaterals*, 10 February 2020), https://www.bilaterals.org/?important-differences-between-the accessed 26 February 2022.

[119] Gao and Shaffer, 'The RCEP: Great Power Competition and Cooperation over Trade' (n 117).

policy objective. As a footnote makes clear, 'the Parties affirm that the necessity behind the implementation of such legitimate public policy shall be decided by the implementing Party'. Other parties may only allege that a measure is arbitrary, unjustifiably discriminatory, or a disguised restriction on trade but they cannot claim that it does not pursue a legitimate public policy objective or that it is not necessary. Parties retain even greater leeway with regard to measures they consider necessary for the protection of 'essential security interests'. Such measures are protected from other parties' scrutiny altogether. In contrast to TPP, RCEP does not foresee the use of state-state dispute settlement for data governance commitments (but it does contemplate that this could be revisited when the agreement is reviewed, in which case parties may opt in to state-state dispute settlement). Instead, RCEP encourages good faith consultations between the parties and within RCEP's Joint Committee. Some have argued that on data governance issues, the parallels between TPP and RCEP are more pronounced, as it mimics the TPP in letting the mere existence of any kind of data protection and privacy framework suffice (noting that Cambodia, Laos, and Myanmar have five years in which to create such frameworks).[120] As in TPP, protection of personal information is seen as desirable for economic reasons, commitment to data protection and privacy as human rights. The requirement to publish the relevant data protection laws is a welcome contribution to comparative data protection law scholarship and practice. RCEP even includes an entirely new provision, which continues the trend towards business conduct regulation in international economic law, requiring parties to encourage companies to publish their privacy policies. The RCEP countries commit to take evolving global data protection standards into account, but do not explicitly reference any, including the APEC Privacy Framework. Commentators suggest that the RCEP's e-commerce chapter is built on the CPTPP's framework, which is not surprising, given that many CPTPP member states are also members of the RCEP. However, the RCEP adds and removes language in order to give its member states all the leeway they need to adopt restrictive measures to digital trade and data flows, should they wish to do so. This may imply that that China, which tightly protects its digital realm from the outside world, is behind the weaker language.[121] China has thus ensured that the RCEP will allow it to keep its Great Firewall intact.

[120] Streinz argues that RCEP echoes TPP's and other agreements' commitment to data mobility as a new objective of international economic law and uses TPP as its blueprint but modifies it in a way that retains countries' ability to craft restrictive data policies when they deem it necessary: T Streinz, 'RCEP's Contribution to Global Data Governance' (*Afronomics Law*, 19 February 2021), https://www.afronomicslaw.org/category/analysis/rceps-contribution-global-data-governance-0 accessed 26 February 2022.

[121] P Leblond, 'Digital Trade: Is RCEP the WTO's Future?' (*CIGI*, 23 November 2020), https://www.cigionline.org/articles/digital-trade-rcep-wtos-future/ accessed 26 February 2022; J Kelsey, 'Important Differences between the Final RCEP Electronic Commerce Chapter and the TPPA and Lessons for E-commerce in the WTO' (*Bilaterals*, 10 February 2020), https://www.bilaterals.org/?important-differences-between-the accessed 26 February 2022.

Should the WTO's Joint Statement Initiative negotiations ever lead to an agreement, it would most likely resemble the RCEP's Chapter 12: ie, an agreement that is aspirational in nature but does little to effectively promote cross-border digital and data flows. Those countries that wish to maintain tight controls on such flows would remain legally free to do so. Overall, the likelihood of Chinese leadership on this issue currently remains slim, irrespective of the forum.[122] While it is said that the world is 'voting with its feet' for data privacy laws with moderated or modified versions of 'European' standards, arguably Brexit will be another test beyond China as a measure of how much of a gold standard the GDPR constitutes.[123] It also remains to be seen how China will engage with emerging transatlantic institutionalisation initiatives, eg a Trade and Technology Council standalone or developments at the WTO to reform this area, with China as a key protagonist. Will China gradually legalise and converge even more? The notion of a gold standard thus is open to certain interpretation and of much interest in the Asian context.

VIII. Conclusions

Ostensibly, China is a key example of the 'reverse Brussels Effect', incapable of being institutionalised in a 'European' sense yet still converging with EU data privacy law, even if in reverse. The Chinese legal order appears theoretically open to much European-style institutionalisation, yet its depth and actual convergence is much less clear. To view China as a surveillance state is a nuanced idea in an era shifting towards global 'surveillance capitalism' worldwide. China adopts many EU data privacy laws and norms but arguably only on paper and evidently lacks institutionalisation of data law in a European sense. China has limited engagement with international law norms in the area of data privacy, and this appears significant against the backdrop of its engagement with EU law. But it is not fully accurate to say that it has entirely limited engagement. The relationship between trade and security becomes all the more pivotal, eg as to BRI, and initially showed a developing engagement with Europe but in a manner which is distinctly law-light and institution-light. China has preferred bilateral engagement with EU Member States, at least prior to the CAI. However, the esoteric nature of this much appears clear, particularly in the light of ongoing shifts, such as the development of

[122] Streinz, 'RCEP's Contribution to Global Data Governance' (n 120).

[123] This is possibly because of the fact that the UK plans to join CPTPP and has made considerable 'triumphalist' communications concerning its FTA with Japan, in particular as to its digital trade chapter. There, the UK has stated that its provisions go considerably further than the EU-Japan EPA as to data standards. It remains to be seen what this means and how this aligns with its joining of CPTPP. China and perhaps even the EU joining CPTPP going forward could substantially alter this dynamic.

a civil code within Chinese law that will probably lead to the juridification of legal culture. The BRI and Global Gateway developments aside, increasing legalisation of all forms of international relations is likely to have a profound effect on China and its legal culture in the future. Deepening legalisation and the emerging institutionalisation frameworks, eg through the CAI, indicate that highly significant change could still be likely.

Conclusions

This book has argued that the EU is globally unique in its commitment to internal and external institutionalisation practices. It has shown how institutionalisation forms a spectrum for analysis which is 'process-based' and possibly incomplete or is dynamic and under development. In the above text, institutionalisation has been shown to incorporate a sliding scale of minimalist enforcement, bottom-up processes of development, accountability processes, stabilisation and actorness all merging together as part of a 'process' narrative. A legal view of institutionalisation has been argued to be, by its nature, 'bottom up', piecing together a range of instruments, regimes, practices, norms and enforcement issues. It may involve a consideration of rights and effectiveness of good governance and how existing institutions shape norms. It has been shown here to be a valuable metric of the evolution of EU policies.

Institutionalisation has a complex relationship with global governance and non-state actors. Nonetheless, more and more areas and countries are subject to heavy institutionalisation – often viewed through the lens of neoliberal institutionalism – and this has operated as a positive force for change in the world. This book has argued that institutionalisation is understood to be of significance in trade and data regulation to secure positive outcomes, to enforcement mutual agreement, to reduce redistributive problems and provide solutions and ensure equal distribution of benefits of an agreement. In an age of the critique of international institutions and institutionalisation generally, it is still important to understand their usefulness and purpose in the grander scheme of things. Arguably, institutionalisation is embryonically understood in legal circles. It may have 'thin' or 'thick' connotations and is highly dependent on executive understandings of norms and their capacity for development and interpretation. There is no self-evident form for the institutionalisation of regional trade integration. Nor even is there a taxonomy or a menu of options or best practices. Thickness in institutional design does not necessarily translate into dynamic transnational or supranational governance. It is also worth stating that there is no hard and fast rule as to regulatory coherence and institutionalisation. It is self-evident that the transformation of Europe was substantially shaped by the European Court of Justice, national courts and significant institutional enforcement. Newer forms of economic integration appear predicated on looser forms of intergovernmentalism and a turn away from 'thicker' forms of institutionalisation, shifting away from the EU model. Yet the EU has mitigated this by its own consistent advocacy of institutionalisation in international relations. In fact, seen through this lens, many of the case studies are revealing more of the EU's international relations strategies perhaps than legal culture, system and architectural nuances of enforcement and remedies.

This book has focused on how legal scholarship has historically been programmed to be concerned with enforcement and compliance aspects of regulatory design, as opposed to the design process itself and its rollout, which is often much more embryonic, bitty, piecemeal and 'unclean'. As to data, it is arguably one of the most vibrant research agendas, ever.

BIBLIOGRAPHY

'10 Point-Manifesto Towards European Digital Strategic Autonomy' (*Eurosmart*, 2019) https://www.eurosmart.com/towards-european-digital-strategic-autonomy-digital-sovereignty/ accessed 8 March 2022.

Aaronson, S, 'Why Trade Agreements Are Not Setting Information Free: The Lost History and Reinvigorated Debate over Cross-Border Data Flows, Human Rights, and National Security' (2015) 14 *World Trade Review* 671.

—— 'What Are We Talking about When We Talk about Digital Protectionism?' (2019) 18(4) *World Trade Review* 541.

—— 'Could Trade Agreements Help Address the Wicked Problem of Cross Border Disinformation' (2021) SSRN Paper, p 19, https://papers.ssrn.com/sol3/papers.cfm?abstract_id=3820213 accessed 8 March 2022.

Acemoglu, D et al, 'Too Much Data: Prices and Inefficiencies in Data Markets' (2019) National Bureau of Economic Research, Working Paper No 26296.

Aggarwal, V, 'The Dynamics of Trade Liberalisation' (Princeton, 2005) https://www.princeton.edu/~hmilner/Conference_files/KEOHANE/aggarwal.pdf accessed 8 March 2022.

Aguinaldo, A and De Hert, P, 'European Law Enforcement and US Data Companies: A Decade of Cooperation Free from Law' (2020) 6(26) Brussels Privacy Hub Working Paper.

Ahmed, U, 'The Importance of Cross-Border Regulatory Cooperation in an Era of Digital Trade' (2019) 18 *World Trade Law Review* 99.

Aitken, H, 'The Pandemic, UN cyber negotiations and international law and norms' (*EJIL Talk!*, 13 September 2021) https://www.ejiltalk.org/the-pandemic-un-cyber-negotiations-and-international-law-and-norms/ accessed 8 March 2022.

Alschner, W, *The New Terrain of International Law: Courts, Politics, Rights* (Princeton University Press 2014).

Alschner, W, Pauwelyn, J and Puig, S, 'The Data-Driven Future of International Economic Law' (2017) 20 *Journal of International Economic Law* 217.

Alter, KJ, 'The European Court's Political Power' (1996) 19 *West Europe Politics* 45.

Alter, KJ, Helfer, LR and Madsen, MR, *International Court Authority* (Oxford University Press, 2018).

Alter, KJ and Lafont, C, 'Global Governance and the Problem of the Second Best: The Example of Reforming the World Trade Organization' (2019) SSRN Paper https://ssrn.com/abstract=3524325 accessed 8 March 2022.

Alvarez, JE, *The Impact of International Organizations on International Law* (Brill Nijhoff 2016).

Ang, K, 'Europe pivots to Indo-Pacific with 'multipolar' ambitions' (*Nikkei Asia*, 2 February 2021) https://asia.nikkei.com/Spotlight/Asia-Insight/Europe-pivots-to-Indo-Pacific-with-multipolar-ambitions accessed 8 March 2022.

Anghel, S et al, 'On the Path to "Strategic Autonomy": The EU in an Evolving Geopolitical Environment' (2020) European Parliamentary Research Service, PE 652.096.

'Apple and Facebook trade accusations over data privacy' (*Financial Times*, November 20 2020) https://www.ft.com/content/54c54efb-7c80-4468-bf8f-c646e2bbe07f accessed 8 March 2022.

Babinet, G, Jadot, T and Lenoir, T, 'Digital Services Act: Moderating Content and Protecting Minors' (*Institut Montaigne*, 18 September 2020) https://www.institutmontaigne.org/en/blog/digital-services-act-moderating-content-and-protecting-minors accessed 8 March 2022.

Bacon, P and Nakamura, H, 'Diffusing the Abolitionist Norm in Japan: EU 'Death Penalty Diplomacy' and the Gap between Rhetoric and Reality in EU-Japan Relations' (2021) 59 *Journal of Common Market Studies* 1230.

Barker, T, 'Europe Can't Win the Tech War It Just Started' (*Foreign Policy*, 16 January 2020) https://foreignpolicy.com/2020/01/16/europe-technology-sovereignty-von-der-leyen/ accessed 8 March 2022.

Barkin, N, 'Watching China in Europe- January 2021' (2021) https://sites-gmf.vuturevx.com/61/6509/january-2021/january-2021(1).asp?sid=504eaec4-a13f-4a0b-bd39-56dbbc033363 accessed 8 March 2022.

Barlow, JP, 'A Declaration of the Independence of Cyberspace' (1996) https://www.eff.org/cyberspace-independence accessed 8 March 2022.

Barshefsky, C 'EU digital protectionism risks damaging ties with the US' (*Financial Times*, 2 August 2020) https://www.ft.com/content/9edea4f5-5f34-4e17-89cd-f9b9ba698103 accessed 8 March 2022.

Bartl, M and Fahey, E, 'A Postnational Marketplace: Negotiating the Transatlantic Trade and Investment Partnership (TTIP) in E Fahey and D Curtin (eds), *A Transatlantic Community of Law: Legal Perspectives on the Relationship between the EU and US legal orders* (Cambridge University Press, 2014).

Bartl, M and Irion, K, 'The Japan EU Economic Partnership Agreement: Flows of Personal Data to the Land of the Rising Sun' (2017) Amsterdam Centre for Information Law Institute Working Paper, https://www.ivir.nl/publicaties/download/Transfer-of-personal-data-to-the-land-of-the-rising-sun-FINAL.pdf accessed 8 March 2022.

Bassino, J-P, 'Global context and European motivations for the EU-Japan Partnership Agreement (EPA)' (2019) 55(1–2) *The Review of Economics and Commerce* 43.

Beattie, A, 'The EU is trailing China's trade distortions all round the world' (*Financial Times*, 10 May 2021) https://www.ft.com/content/0e94cd4e-16f9-4bfc-8bba-333027fb95ed accessed 8 March 2022.

Bellamy, R, Lacey, J and Nicolaïdis, K (eds), *European Boundaries in Question?* (Routledge 2018).

Bendiek, A, 'The EU as a Force for Peace in International Cyber Diplomacy' (2018) SWP Comment No 19/2018, https://www.ssoar.info/ssoar/handle/document/57428 accessed 8 March 2022.

Benvenisti, E, 'Upholding Democracy Amid the Challenges of New Technology: What Role for the Law of Global Governance?' (2018) 29 *European Journal of International Law* 9.

Berka, W, 'CETA, TTIP, TiSA, and Data Protection' in S Griller, W Obwexer and E Vranes (eds), *Mega-Regional Trade Agreements: CETA, TTIP, and TiSA: New Orientations for EU External Economic Relations* (Oxford University Press, 2017).

Bernik, I, *Cybercrime and Cyber Warfare* (John Wiley and Sons 2014).

Bersick, S, Christou, G and Yi, S, 'Cybersecurity and EU-China Relations' in EJ Kirchner, T Christiansen and H Dorussen (eds), *Security Relations between China and the European Union: From Convergence to Cooperation?* (Cambridge University Press, 2016).

Bignami, F and Charnovitz, S, 'Transnational Civil Society Dialogues' in M Pollack and G Shaffer (eds), *Transatlantic Governance in the Global Economy* (Rowman & Littlefield, 2001).

Binder, C and Hofbauer, J, 'The Perception of the EU Legal Order in International Law: An In- and Outside View' (2017) 8 *European Yearbook of International Economic Law* 139.

Bindi, F, 'European Union Foreign Policy: A Historical Overview' in F Bindi and I Angelescu (eds), *The Foreign Policy of the European Union: Assessing Europe's Role in the World*, 2nd edn (Brookings Institution Press, 2012).

—— 'Why Did Italy Embrace the Belt and Road Initiative?' (*Carnegie Endowment for International Peace*, 20 May 2019) https://carnegieendowment.org/2019/05/20/why-did-italy-embrace-belt-and-road-initiative-pub-79149 accessed 8 March 2022.

Black, J and Murray, A, 'Regulating AI and Machine Learning: Setting the Regulatory Agenda' (2019) 10 *European Journal of Law and Technology*.

Bordin, FL, 'Is the EU Engaging in Impermissible indirect regulation of UN action? Controversies over the GDPR' (*EJIL: Talk!*, 11 December 2020) ejiltalk.org/is-the-eu-engaging-in-impermissible-indirect-regulation-of-un-action-controversies-over-the-general-data-protection-regulation/ accessed 8 March 2022.

Borrell, J, 'Cyber sanctions: time to act' (*European External Action Service*, 30 July 2020) https://eeas.europa.eu/headquarters/headquarters-homepage/83627/cyber-sanctions-time-act_en accessed 8 March 2022.

—— 'Europe Must Learn Quickly To Speak The Language Of Power' (*EJIL:Talk!*, 25 October 2020) https://www.ejiltalk.org/europe-must-learn-quickly-to-speak-the-language-of-power-part-i/ accessed 8 March 2022.

Bradford, A, 'The Brussels Effect' (2012) 107 *Northwestern University Law Review* 1.

—— *Brussels Effect: How the European Union Rules the World* (Oxford University Press, 2020).

Brandi, C and Cheng, W, 'The disputed status of developing countries in the WTO' (*DIE Blog*, 14 March 2019) https://blogs.die-gdi.de/2019/03/14/the-disputed-status-of-developing-countries-in-the-wto/ accessed 8 March 2022.

Brkan, M, 'The Essence of the Fundamental Rights to Privacy and Data Protection: Finding the Way Through the Maze of the CJEU's Constitutional Reasoning' (2019) 20 *German Law Journal* 864.

Brunnermeier, M, Doshi, R and James, H, 'Beijing's Bismarckian ghosts: how Great Powers compete economically' (2018) 41 *Washington Quarterly* 161.

Buchan, R, *Cyber-Espionage and International Law* (Hart Publishing, 2018).

Bull, R et al, 'New Approaches to International Regulatory Cooperation: The Challenge of TTIP, TPP, and Mega-Regional Trade Agreements' (2015) 78 *Law and Contemporary Problems* 1.

Burley, A-M and Mattli, W, 'Europe Before the Court: a Political Theory of Legal Integration' (1993) 47 *International Organization* 41.

Burley, A-M and Muller, W (eds), Special Issue on 'China and Global Governance: Between the International Rule of Law and the International Rule of Power?' (2018) 31 *The Hague Yearbook of International Law* 2020.

Burley, A-M, Raube, K and Wouters, J (eds), Special Issue on 'The Rule of Law as a Strategic Priority in EU External Action' (2016) 14 *Asia-Europe Journal.*

Burri, M, 'Should There Be New Multilateral Rules for Digital Trade?' (2013) E15 Expert Group on Trade and Innovation.

—— 'The International Economic Law Framework for Digital Trade' (2015) 135 *Zeitschrift für Schwezerisches Recht* 10.

—— 'Designing Future-Oriented Multilateral Rules for Digital Trade' in P Sauve and M Roy (eds), *Research Handbook on Trade in Services* (Edward Elgar, 2016).

—— 'The Governance of Data and Data Flows in Trade Agreements: The Pitfalls of Legal Adaptation' (2017) 51(56) *University of California Davis Law Review* 65.

—— 'The Regulation of Data Flows Through Trade Agreements' (2017) 48 *Georgetown Journal of International Law* 407.

—— 'How Should the WTO Respond to the Data-driven Economy' (*CIGI*, 4 May 2020) https://www.cigionline.org/articles/how-should-wto-respond-data-driven-economy accessed 8 March 2022.

—— 'Data Flows and Global Trade Law' in M Burri (ed), *Big Data and Global Trade Law* (Cambridge University Press, 2021).

Burri, M and Polanco, R, 'Digital Trade Provisions in Preferential Trade Agreements: Introducing a New Dataset' (2020) 23 *Journal of International Economic Law* 187.

Burwell, FG and Propp, K, 'The European Union and the Search for Digital Sovereignty: Building "Fortress Europe" or Preparing for a New World?' (*Atlantic Council*, June 2020) https://www.atlanticcouncil.org/wp-content/uploads/2020/06/The-European-Union-and-the-Search-for-Digital-Sovereignty-Building-Fortress-Europe-or-Preparing-for-a-New-World.pdf accessed 8 March 2022.

Butler, G, 'The Future of EU International Agreements as Legal Instruments in the ASEAN Region' (2020) 7(2) *Journal of International and Comparative Law* 287.

Bygrave, LA, 'The "Strasbourg Effect" on Data Protection in Light of the 'Brussels Effect': Logic, Mechanics and Prospects' (2021) 40 *Computer Law & Security Review* 1.

Cambridge Econometrics for UK Department of International Trade and Department of Digital, Culture, Media & Sport, 'Understanding and measuring cross-border digital trade' (14 May 2020) https://assets.publishing.service.gov.uk/government/uploads/system/uploads/attachment_data/file/885174/Understanding-and-measuring-cross-border-digital-trade.pdf accessed 8 March 2022.

Cameron, I, 'A. Court of Justice Metadata retention and national security: Privacy International and La Quadrature du Net' (2021) 58 *Common Market Law Review* 1433.

Caporaso, J, 'Europe's Triple Crisis and the Uneven Role of Institutions: the Euro, Refugees and Brexit' (2018) 56 *Journal of Common Market Studies* 1345.

Cappelletti, M, Seccombe, M and Weile, JH, *Integration through law: Europe and the American federal experience*, vol 1 (De Gruyter 1986).

Carafano, J, Gupta, A and Smith, J, 'The Pitfalls of the China-EU Comprehensive Agreement on Investment' *The Diplomat* (22 January 2021) https://thediplomat.com/2021/01/the-pitfalls-of-the-china-eu-comprehensive-agreement-on-investment/ accessed 8 March 2022.

Cardwell, PJ, 'The EU-Japan Relationship: from Mutual Ignorance to Meaningful Partnership?' (2004) 2(2) *Journal of European Affairs* 11.

—— 'Brexit, the EU and Japan' (*UK in a Changing EU*, 2017), https://ukandeu.ac.uk/brexit-the-eu-and-japan/ accessed 8 March 2022.

Carrapico, H and Barrinha, A, 'The EU as a Coherent (Cyber)Security Actor?' (2017) 55 *Journal of Common Market Studies* 1254.

Carrapico, H and Farrand, B, 'Blurring Public and Private: Cybersecurity in the Age of Regulatory Capitalism' in O Bures and H Carrapico (eds), *Security Privatization: How Non-Security-Related Businesses Shape Security Governance* (Springer, 2018).

—— 'Discursive Continuity and Change in the Time of Covid-19: the Case of EU Cybersecurity Policy' (2020) 42 *Journal of European Integration* 1111.

—— 'When Trust Fades, Facebook Is No Longer a Friend: Shifting Privatisation Dynamics in the Context of Cybersecurity as a Result of Disinformation, Populism and Political Uncertainty' (2021) 59 *Journal of Common Market Studies* 1160.

Catá Backer, L, 'Global Panopticism: States, Corporations and the Governance Effects of Monitoring Regimes' (2008) 15(1) *Indiana Journal of Global Legal Studies* 101.

Chaisse, J and Matsushita, M, 'China's 'Belt And Road' Initiative: Mapping the World Trade Normative and Strategic Implications' (2018) 52 *Journal of World Trade* 163.

Chaisse, J and Kirkwood, J, 'Chinese Puzzle: Anatomy of the (Invisible) Belt and Road Investment Treaty' (2020) 23 *Journal of International Economic Law* 245.

Chaisse, J and Pomfret, R, 'The RCEP and the Changing Landscape of World Trade: Assessing Asia-Pacific Investment Regionalism Next Stage' (2019) 12 *Law and Development Review* 159.

Chan, C, 'Thirty years from Tiananmen: China, Hong Kong, and the ongoing experiment to preserve liberal values in an authoritarian state' (2019) 17(2) *International Journal of Constitutional Law* 439.

Chander, A, 'Googling Freedom' (2011) 99 *California Law Review* 1.

—— *The Electronic Silk Road: how the Web binds the World Together in Commerce* (Yale University Press 2013).

—— 'Is Data Localization a Solution for Schrems II?' (2020) 23 *Journal of International Economic Law* 771.

Chander, A and Lê, UP, 'Breaking the Web: Data Localization vs. the Global Internet' (2014) UC Davis Legal Studies Research Paper No 378, https://ssrn.com/abstract=2407858 accessed 8 March 2022.

—— 'Data Nationalism' (2015) 64 *Emory Law Journal* 677.

Chen, Z, 'China, the European Union and the Fragile World Order' (2016) 54 *Journal of Common Market Studies* 775.

'China Media Bulletin: 2019 internet freedom trends, Shutterstock censorship, Huawei "safe cities"' (*Freedom House*, November 2019) 140 *China Media Bulletin*, https://freedomhouse.org/report/china-media-bulletin/2020/china-media-bulletin-2019-internet-freedom-trends-shutterstock accessed 8 March 2022.

'China officially applies to join CPTPP, as the US increasingly isolated in trade' (*The Global Times*, 17 September 2021) https://www.globaltimes.cn/page/202109/1234550.shtml accessed 8 March 2022.

'China: Freedom on the Net 2020 Country Report' (*Freedom House*, 2020) https://freedomhouse.org/country/china/freedom-net/2020 accessed 8 March 2022.

'China's Internet Freedom Hit a New Low in 2019, and the World Could Follow' (*The Diplomat*, 19 November 2019) https://thediplomat.com/2019/11/chinas-internet-freedom-hit-a-new-low-in-2019-and-the-world-could-follow/ accessed 8 March 2022.

Choukroune, L, 'China and the WTO Dispute Settlement System' (2012) 1 *China Perspectives* 49.

Christakis, T, 'Data, Extraterritoriality and International Solutions to Transatlantic Problems of Access to Digital Evidence. Legal Opinion on the Microsoft Ireland Case (Supreme Court of the United States) (November 29, 2017)' (2017) The White Book: Lawful Access to Data: The US v. Microsoft Case, Sovereignty in the Cyber-Space and European Data Protection, CEIS & The Chertoff Group White Paper, https://ssrn.com/abstract=3086820 accessed 8 March 2022.

—— '21 Thoughts and Questions about the UK-US CLOUD Act Agreement: (and an Explanation of How it Works – with Charts)' (*European Law Blog*, 17 October 2019) https://europeanlawblog.eu/2019/10/17/21-thoughts-and-questions-about-the-uk-us-cloud-act-agreement-and-an-explanation-of-how-it-works-with-charts/ accessed 8 March 2022.

—— 'E-Evidence in the EU Parliament: Basic Features of Birgit Sippel's Draft Report' (*EU Law Blog*, 21 January 2020) https://europeanlawblog.eu/2020/01/21/e-evidence-in-the-eu-parliament-basic-features-of-birgit-sippels-draft-report/ accessed 8 March 2022.

—— 'After Schrems II: Uncertainties on the Legal Basis for Data Transfers and Constitutional Implications for Europe' (*European Law Blog*, 21 July 2020) https://europeanlawblog.eu/2020/07/21/after-schrems-ii-uncertainties-on-the-legal-basis-for-data-transfers-and-constitutional-implications-for-europe/ accessed 8 March 2022.

—— '"European Digital Sovereignty": Successfully Navigating Between the "Brussels Effect" and Europe's Quest for Strategic Autonomy' (2020) Multidisciplinary Institute on Artificial Intelligence/Grenoble Alpes Data Institute, https://ssrn.com/abstract=3748098 accessed 8 March 2022.

Christakis, T and Terpan, F, 'EU-US Negotiations on Law Enforcement Access to Data: Divergences, Challenges and EU Law Procedures and Options' (2021) 11(2) *International Data Privacy Law* 81.

Christou, G, 'Transatlantic Cooperation in Cybersecurity: Converging on Security as Resilience?' in G Christou, *Cybersecurity in the European Union* (Palgrave Macmillan, 2016).

—— 'The EU's Approach to Cybersecurity' (2017) University of Essex Discussion Paper: EU-Japan Security Cooperation: Challenges and Opportunities project.

Chrysoloras, N, 'EU Set to Allow US Participation in Joint Defence Projects' (*Bloomberg*, 4 November 2019) https://www.bloomberg.com/news/articles/2019-11-04/eu-set-to-allow-u-s-participation-in-joint-defense-projects accessed 8 March 2022.

Chu, X and Gao, X, 'Comparing the EU's and China's approaches in digital governance: on power and regulatory capture' in E Fahey and I Mancini (eds), *Understanding The EU As A Good Global Actor: Whose Metrics?* (Edward Elgar, forthcoming).

Cichowski, R, *The European Court and Civil Society: Litigation, Mobilization and Governance* (Cambridge University Press, 2009).

Ciuriak, D and Ptashkina, M, 'Toward a Robust Architecture for the Regulation of Data and Digital Trade' (2020) CIGI Paper No 240.

—— 'Cybersecurity, National Security and Trade in the Digital Era' (2021) SSRN Paper, https://ssrn.com/abstract=3374886 accessed 8 March 2022.

'Civil Liberties MEPs want EU-US Privacy Shield suspended by September' *Euractiv* (June 2018) https://www.euractiv.com/section/data-protection/news/civil-liberties-meps-want-eu-us-privacy-shield-suspended-by-september/ accessed 8 March 2022.

'Clear ambition is required if Europe is to rival China's Belt and Road' (*Financial Times*, 5 December 2021) https://www.ft.com/content/2d8ba39f-565f-4917-af3b-b993f6d9d826 accessed 8 March 2022.

Coen, D, 'Lobbying in the European Union' (2007) Directorate General Internal Policies of the Union Briefing Paper PE 393.266.

Coen, D, Katsaitis, A and Vannon, M, *Business Lobbying in the European Union* (Oxford University Press, 2020).

Cohen, J, *Globalization and Sovereignty Rethinking Legality, Legitimacy, and Constitutionalism* (Cambridge University Press, 2012).

Cole, D, and Fabbrini, F, 'Bridging the Transatlantic Divide? The United States, the European Union, and the Protection of Privacy across Borders' (2016) 14 *International Journal of Constitutional Law* 220.

Conant, L, *Justice Contained: Law and Politics in the European Union* (Cornell University Press 2002).

Cory, N 'How the EU-U.S. Trade and Technology Council Can Navigate Conflict and Find Meaningful Cooperation on Data Governance and Technology Platforms' *(ITIF*, 2 December 2021) https://itif.org/publications/2021/12/02/how-eu-us-trade-and-technology-council-can-navigate-conflict-and-find accessed 8 March 2022.

Creemers, R, Triolo, P and Webster, G, 'Translation: Cybersecurity Law of the People's Republic of China (Effective June 1, 2017)' (*New America*, 29 June 2018) https://www.newamerica.org/cybersecurity-initiative/digichina/blog/translation-cybersecurity-law-peoples-republic-china/ accessed 8 March 2022.

Cremona, M, 'The Opinion procedure under Article 218(11) TFEU: Reflections in the light of Opinion 1/17' (2020) *Europe and the World: A Law Review*, https://www.scienceopen.com/hosted-document?doi=10.14324/111.444.ewlj.2020.22 accessed 8 March 2022.

Cutler, M, 'Information Technology: Lawyers Say U.S., EU on Collision Course over E-commerce as Competitiveness Issues' (2002) 18 *International Trade* Review (BNA) 1868.

Daskal, J, 'Microsoft Ireland, the CLOUD Act, and International Law making 2.0' (2018) 17 *Stanford Law Review Online.*

—— 'Privacy and Security across Borders' (2019) *Yale Law Journal Forum* 1029, https://www.yalelawjournal.org/pdf/Daskal_v3q35qwf.pdf accessed 8 March 2022.

—— 'A European Court Decision May Usher in Global Censorship' (*State*, 3 October 2019) https://slate.com/technology/2019/10/european-court-justice-glawischnig-piesczek-facebook-censorship.html accessed 8 March 2022.

—— 'What Comes Next: The Aftermath of European Court's Blow to Transatlantic Data Transfers' (*Just Security*, 17 July 2020) https://www.justsecurity.org/71485/what-comes-next-the-aftermath-of-european-courts-blow-to-transatlantic-data-transfers/ accessed 8 March 2022.

Daskal, J and Kennedy-Mayo, D, 'Budapest Convention: What Is It and How Is It Being Updated?' (*Cross Border Data Forum*, 2 July 2020) https://www.crossborderdataforum.org/budapest-convention-what-is-it-and-how-is-it-being-updated/ accessed 8 March 2022.

Daskal, J and Klonick, K, 'When a Politician Is Called a 'Lousy Traitor, Should Facebook Censor It?' (*New York Times*, 27 June 2019) https://www.nytimes.com/2019/06/27/opinion/facebook-censorship-speech-law.html accessed 8 March 2022.

Daskal, J and Swire, P, 'The U.K.-U.S. CLOUD Act Agreement Is Finally Here, Containing New Safeguards' (*Lawfare Blog*, 8 October 2019) https://www.lawfareblog.com/uk-us-cloud-act-agreement-finally-here-containing-new-safeguards accessed 8 March 2022.

De Froment, C, 'Digital Services Act: New Forms of Work' (*Institut Montaigne*, 15 September 2020) https://www.institutmontaigne.org/en/blog/digital-services-act-new-forms-work accessed 8 March 2022.

De Goede, M and Wesseling, M, 'Secrecy and Security in Transatlantic Terrorism Finance Tracking' (2017) 39 *Journal of European Integration* 253.

De Hert, P and Czerniawski, M, 'Expanding the European Data Protection Scope Beyond Territory: Article 3 of the General Data Protection Regulation in its Wider Scope' (2016) 6 *International Data Privacy Law* 3.

De Hert, P and Papakonstantinou, V, 'The data protection regime in China' (2015) European Parliament, Committee on Civil Liberties, https://www.europarl.europa.eu/RegData/etudes/IDAN/2015/536472/IPOL_IDA(2015)536472_EN.pdf accessed 8 March 2022.

De Miguel Asensio, P, *Conflict of Laws and the Internet* (Edward Elgar 2020).

De Streel, A et al, 'Digital Markets Act: Making economic regulation of platforms fit for the digital age' (2020) CERRE Report, https://cerre.eu/wp-content/uploads/2020/11/CERRE_DMA_Making-economic-regulation-of-platforms-fit-for-the-digital-age_Full-report_December2020.pdf accessed 8 March 2022.

De Terwangne, C, 'Is a Global Data Protection Regulatory Model Possible?' in S Gutwirth et al (eds), *Reinventing Data Protection?* (Springer, 2009).

Dehousse, R, *The European Court of Justice: the Politics of Judicial Integration* (Springer 1998).

Deibert, R, 'Toward a Human-Centric Approach to Cybersecurity' (2018) 32 *Ethics & International Affairs* 411.

Delarue, F, *Cyber Operations and International Law* (Cambridge University Press, 2020).

Desierto, D, 'Human Rights Regulation in the Tech Sector? The European Court of Justice's Facebook Decision and California's AB5 Gig Economy Bill' (*EJIL:Talk!*, 8 October 2019) https://www.ejiltalk.org/human-rights-regulation-in-the-tech-sector-the-european-court-of-justices-facebook-decision-and-californias-ab5-gig-economy-bill/ accessed 8 March 2022.

Docksey, C, 'The Coronavirus Crisis and EU Adequacy Decisions for Data Transfers' (*European Law Blog*, 3 April 2020) https://europeanlawblog.eu/2020/04/03/the-coronavirus-crisis-and-eu-adequacy-decisions-for-data-transfers/ accessed 8 March 2022.

Doctorow, C and Schmon, C, 'The EU's Digital Markets Act: There Is a Lot to Like, but Room for Improvement' (*Electronic Frontier Foundation*, 15 December 2020) https://www.eff.org/deeplinks/2020/12/eus-digital-markets-act-there-lot-room-improvement accessed 8 March 2022.

Dressel, B (ed), *The Judicialization of Politics in Asia* (Routledge 2012).

Dri, C, 'Limits of the Institutional Mimesis of the European Union: The Case of the Mercosur Parliament' (2010) 1(1) *Latin American Policy* 52.

Dumortier, F, Papakonstantinou, V and De Hert, P, 'EU sanctions against cyber-attacks and defense rights: Wanna Cry?' (*European Law Blog*, 28 September 2020) https://europeanlawblog.eu/2020/09/28/eu-sanctions-against-cyber-attacks-imposed-and-defense-rights-wanna-cry/ accessed 8 March 2022.

Dyevre, A and Ovádek, M, 'Experimental Legal Methods in the Classroom' (2020) 16 *Utrecht Law Review* 1.

Dyevre, A, Wijtvliet, W, and Lampach, N, 'The Future of European Legal Scholarship: Empirical Jurisprudence' (2019) 26 *Maastricht Journal of European and Comparative Law* 348.

Eckes, C, 'The Law and Practice of EU Sanctions' in S Blockmans and P Koutrakos (eds), *Research Handbook on EU Common Foreign and Security Policy* (Edward Elgar, 2019).

—— 'Common Foreign and Security Policy: The Consequences of the Court's Extended Jurisdiction' (2016) 22 *European Law Journal* 492.

Economy, E, 'The China Model: Unexceptional Exceptionalism' Essay Series of the Hoover Institution: Human Prosperity Project (*Hoover*, 4 December 2020) https://www.hoover.org/research/china-model-unexceptional-exceptionalism accessed 8 March 2022.

Eeckhout, P, 'Opinion 2/13 on EU Accession to the ECHR and Judicial Dialogue: Autonomy or Autarky' (2015) 38(4) *Fordham International Law Journal* 955.

Egan, M, 'Toward a New History in European Law: New Wine in Old Bottles?' (2013) 28 *American University International Law Review* 1223.

Eifert, M et al, 'Taming the giants: The DMA/DSA package' (2021) 58 *Common Market Law Review* 987.

Elsig, M and Klotz, S, 'Initiator conditions and the diffusion of digital trade-related provisions in PTAs (2021) *International Interactions*.

Erie, SM, 'Chinese Law and Development' (2021) 62 *Harvard International Law Journal* 51.

Erie, SM and Streinz, T, 'The Beijing Effect: China's "Digital Silk Road" as Transnational Data Governance' (2021) *New York University Journal of International Law and Politics*, forthcoming.

Espinoza, J, 'EU vs Big Tech: Brussels' bid to weaken the digital gatekeepers' (*Financial Times*, 8 December 2020) https://www.ft.com/content/4e08efbb-dd96-4bea-8260-01502aaf1bd7 accessed 8 March 2022.

—— 'Google in last-ditch lobbying attempt to influence incoming EU tech rules' (*Financial Times*, 10 January 2022) https://www.ft.com/content/8c7527bc-7ab4-41cd-ba94-3145208da9c3 accessed 8 March 2022.

Espinoza, J and Politi, J, 'US warns EU against anti-American tech policy' (*Financial Times*, 15 June 2021) https://www.ft.com/content/2036d7e9-daa2-445d-8f88-6fcee745a259 accessed 8 March 2022.

'European readers still blocked from some US news sites' (*BBC*, 26 June 2018) https://www.bbc.co.uk/news/technology-44614885 accessed 8 March 2022.
'EU-US Privacy Shield Framework Principles Issued by the US Department of Commerce' https://www.privacyshield.gov/servlet/servlet.FileDownload?file=015t00000004qAg accessed 8 March 2022.
'EU-US data flow deal possible? Third time won't be the charm without US surveillance reform' (*Access Now*, 15 June 2021) https://www.accessnow.org/biden-us-eu-data-flow-deal/accessed 8 March 2022.
'EU-USA: "Sensitive" European Commission information note on cross-border access to electronic evidence' (*Statewatch*, 11 May 2021) https://www.statewatch.org/news/2021/may/eu-usa-sensitive-european-commission-information-note-on-cross-border-access-to-electronic-evidence/ accessed 8 March 2022.
'EU-USA: Action against encrypted communications to be discussed at senior officials' meeting in April' (*Statewatch*, 24 March 2021) https://www.statewatch.org/news/2021/march/eu-usa-action-against-encrypted-communications-to-be-discussed-at-senior-officials-meeting-in-april/ accessed 8 March 2022.
Ewing, J and Myers, SL, 'China and EU Leaders Strike Investment Deal, but Political Hurdles Await' (*New York Times*, 30 December 2020) https://www.nytimes.com/2020/12/30/business/china-eu-investment-deal.html accessed 8 March 2022.
Fabbrini, F, Celeste, E, Quinn, J (eds), *Data Protection Beyond Borders: Transatlantic Perspectives on Extraterritoriality and Sovereignty* (Hart Publishing, 2021).
Fahey, E 'Law and Governance as Checks and Balances in Transatlantic Security: Rights, Redress, and Remedies in EU-US Passenger Name Records and the Terrorist Finance Tracking Program' (2013) 32 *Yearbook of European Law* 368.
—— 'On The Use of Law in Transatlantic Relations: Legal Dialogues Between the EU and US' (2014) 20(3) *European Law Journal* 368.
—— 'The EU's Cybercrime and Cybersecurity Rule-Making: Mapping the Internal and External Dimensions of EU Security' (2014) 5 *European Journal of Risk Regulation* 46.
—— 'The Global Dimension of the EU's AFSJ: On Internal Transparency and External Practice' (2014) Jean Monnet Working Paper Series 2014/4.
—— 'Of "One Shotters" and "Repeat Hitters": A Retrospective on the Role of the European Parliament in the EU-US PNR Litigation' in F Nicola and B Davies (eds), *EU Law Stories: Contextual and Critical Histories of European Jurisprudence* (Cambridge University Press, 2017).
—— (ed), *Institutionalisation beyond the Nation State* (Springer 2018).
—— 'Introduction: Institutionalisation beyond the Nation State: New Paradigms? Transatlantic Relations: Data, Privacy and Trade Law' in E Fahey (ed), *Institutionalisation beyond the Nation State* (Springer, 2018).
—— *Introduction to Law and Global Governance* (Edward Elgar, 2018).
—— 'Transatlantic Cooperation in Criminal Law' in V Mitsilegas, M Bergström and T Konstadinides (eds), *Research Handbook on EU Criminal Law* (Edward Elgar 2018).
—— 'Hyper-legalisation and Delegalisation in the AFSJ: on Contradictions in the External Management of EU Migration' in S Carrera, J Santos Vara and T Strik (eds), *Constitutionalising the External Dimensions of EU Migration Policies in Times of Crisis: Legality, Rule of Law and Fundamental Rights Reconsidered* (Edward Elgar, 2019).
—— 'Digital trade and data equivalency: Research briefing for the Welsh parliament' (2020) Wales, UK: Welsh Parliament.
—— *Framing Convergence with the Global Legal Order: The EU and the World* (Hart Publishing, 2020).
—— 'Future-Mapping the Directions of European Union (EU) Law: How Do We Predict the Future of EU Law?' (2020) 7(S2) *Journal of International and Comparative Law* 265.
—— 'Institutionalising EU Cyber Law: Can the EU institutionalise its many subjects and objects?' (2020) EIF Working Paper Series 01/2020.
—— (ed), 'The Future of Transatlantic Trade' (2021) 52 *EU Law Live Special Issue*.
—— 'The Rise and Fall of International Law in the Post-Lisbon AFSJ Legislation Cycles' (2021) 1 *Groningen Journal of European Law* 1.

—— 'Developing EU Cybercrime and Cybersecurity: On legal challenges of EU institutionalisation of cyber law-making' in T Hoerber, G Weber and I Cabras (eds), *The Routledge Handbook of European Integrations* (Routledge, 2022).

Fahey, E and Brsakoska Bazerkoska, J, 'Critical Perspectives on Social and Legal Relevance of Sincere Cooperation in EU External Relations Law in the Era of Expanding Trade: The Belt & Road Initiative in Context' (forthcoming).

Fahey, E and Mancini, I, 'The EU as an Intentional or Accidental Convergence Actor? Learning From the EU-Japan Data Adequacy Negotiations' (2020) 26 *International Trade Law and Regulation* 99.

Fahey, E and Terpan, F, 'Torn between Institutionalisation and Judicialisation: the demise of the EU-US Privacy Shield' (2021) 28 *Indiana Journal of Global Legal Studies* 205.

Fahey, E and Wieczorek, I, 'The European Parliament as a Defender of EU Values in EU-Japan Agreements: What Role for Soft Law and Hard Law Powers?' (2022) *European Law Review*, forthcoming.

Fanou, M, 'The CETA ICS and the Autonomy of the EU Legal Order in Opinion 1/17 – A Compass for the Future' (2020) 22 *Cambridge Yearbook of European Legal Studies* 106.

Farrell, H and Newman, A, *Of Privacy and Power: The Transatlantic Struggle over Freedom and Security* (Princeton University Press, 2019).

Federal Trade Commission Staff Report, 'Internet of Things: Privacy and Security in a Connected World' (2015) https://www.ftc.gov/system/files/documents/reports/federal-trade-commission-staff-report-november-2013-workshop-entitled-internet-things-privacy/150127iotrpt.pdf accessed 8 March 2022.

Ferracane, MF, Lee-Makiyama, H, and Van der Marel, E, 'ECIPE Digital Trade Restrictiveness Survey Index' (ECIPE, 2018) https://ecipe.org/wp-content/uploads/2018/05/DTRI_FINAL.pdf accessed 8 March 2022.

Ferracane, MF and Mosi, L, 'What kinds of rules are needed to support digital trade?' in B Hoekman, T Xinquan and W Dong (eds), *Rebooting Multilateral Trade Cooperation: Perspectives from China and Europe* (CEPR, 2021).

Fisher, A and Streinz, T, 'Confronting Data Inequality' (2021) IILJ Working Paper 2021/1.

Fleischer, P Global Privacy Counsel, 'Call for global privacy standards' (*Public Policy*, 14 September 2007) https://publicpolicy.googleblog.com/2007/09/call-for-global-privacy-standards.html accessed 8 March 2022.

Floridi, L, 'The Fight for Digital Sovereignty: What It Is, and Why It Matters, Especially for the EU' (2020) 33 *Philosophy and Technology* 369.

Forsberg, A, 'The Politics of GATT Expansion: Japanese Accession and the Domestic Political Content in Japan and the United States, 1948–1955' (1998) 27 *Business and Economic History* 185.

Frennhoff Larsén, M, 'Parliamentary Influence Ten Years after Lisbon: EU Trade Negotiations with Japan' (2020) 58 *Journal of Common Market Studies* 1540.

Fu, H, 'China's imperatives for national security legislation' in C Chan and F De Londras (eds), *China's National Security: Endangering Hong Kong's Rule of Law?* (Hart Publishing, 2020) 41.

Gaens, B, 'The EU-Japan Partnership: Stepping Stone For A Stronger Presence In Asia?' (2017) FIIA Briefing Paper 218, https://css.ethz.ch/content/dam/ethz/special-interest/gess/cis/center-for-securities-studies/resources/docs/FIIA-The%20EU%20Japan%20Partnership.pdf accessed 8 March 2022.

Gao, H, 'Digital or Trade? The Contrasting Approaches of China and US to Digital Trade' (2017) 21 *Journal of International Economic Law* 297.

—— 'The Regulation of Digital Trade in the TPP: Trade Rules for the Digital Age' in J Chaisse, H Gao and C Lo (eds), *Paradigm Shift in International Economic Law Rule-Making* (Springer, 2017).

—— 'Data Regulation with Chinese Characteristics' in M Burri (ed), *Big Data and Global Trade Law* (Cambridge University Press, 2021).

—— 'WTO Reform and China: defining or defiling the multilateral trading system?' (2021) 62 *Harvard International Law Journal* 1.

Gao, H, and Shaffer, G, 'The RCEP: Great Power Competition and Cooperation over Trade' (2021) UC Irvine School of Law Research Paper No 2021-09.

Gardner, A, *Stars with Stripes: The Essential Partnership between the European Union and the United States* (Palgrave 2020).

General Assembly of the United Nations, 'Guidelines for the Regulation of Computerized Personal Data Files' UN DOC.E/CN.4/1990/72 of 14 December 1990.

Gewirtz, P et al, 'A Roadmap for US-Europe Cooperation on China' (2021) Yale Law School Paul Tsai China Center Paper, https://law.yale.edu/sites/default/files/area/center/china/document/roadmap_for_us-eu_cooperation_on_china.pdf accessed 8 March 2022.

Gilson, J, *EU–Japan Relations and the Crisis of Multilateralism* (Routledge 2019).

Golberg, E, 'Regulatory Cooperation – A Reality Check' (2019) M-RCBG Associate Working Paper Series No 115, https://www.hks.harvard.edu/sites/default/files/centers/mrcbg/img/115_final.pdf accessed 8 March 2022.

Goldsmith, JL, 'Against Cyberanarchy' (1996) 65 *University of Chicago Law Review* 1199.

'Google moves UK user data to US to avert Brexit risks' (*Financial Times*, 20 February 2020) https://www.ft.com/content/135e5b66-53fb-11ea-90ad-25e377c0ee1faccessed 8 March 2022.

'Greece Blocks EU Statement on China Human Rights at UN' (*Euroactiv*, 19 June 2017) https://www.euractiv.com/section/china/news/greece-blocks-eu-statement-on-china-human-rights-at-un/ accessed 8 March 2022.

Green Cowles, M, 'The Transatlantic Business Dialogue: Transforming the New Transatlantic Dialogue' in M Pollack and G Shaffer (eds), *Transatlantic Governance in the Global Economy* (Rowman & Littlefield, 2001).

Green, M and Purser, L, 'The Faculty of the Future: A Transatlantic Dialogue' (2000) https://www.acenet.edu/Documents/transatlantic-dialogue.pdf accessed 8 March 2022.

Greenleaf, G, *Asian Data Privacy Laws: Trade and Human Rights Perspectives* (Oxford University Press, 2014).

—— 'A World Data Privacy Treaty? "Globalisation" and "Modernisation" of Council of Europe Convention 108' in N Witzleb et al (eds), *Emerging Challenges in Privacy Law: Comparative Perspectives* (Cambridge University Press, 2014).

—— 'Renewing Convention 108: The CoE's 'GDPR Lite' Initiatives' (2016) 142 *Privacy Laws & Business International Report* 14.

—— 'Questioning 'adequacy' (Pt I) – Japan' (2017) 150 *Privacy Laws & Business International Report* 6.

—— 'Japan: EU Adequacy Discounted' (2018) 155 *Privacy Laws & Business International Report* 8.

—— 'Japan's Proposed EU Adequacy Assessment: Substantive Issues and Procedural Hurdles' (2018) 154 *Privacy Laws & Business International Report* 1.

—— 'Looming Free Trade Agreements Pose Threats to Privacy' (2018) 152 *Privacy Laws & Business International Report* 23.

—— '"Modernised" Data Protection Convention 108 and the GDPR' (2018) 154 *Privacy Laws and business international Report* 22.

—— 'China Issues a Comprehensive Draft Data Privacy Law' (2020) 168 *Privacy Laws & Business International Report* 6.

—— 'The Right to Privacy in Asian Constitutions' (2020) University of New South Wales Law Research Series No 53.

—— 'Will Asia-Pacific trade agreements collide with EU adequacy and Asian laws?' (2020) 167 *Privacy Laws & Business International Report* 18.

Greenleaf, G and Livingston, S, 'China's Personal Information Standard: the Long March to a privacy Law' (2017) 150 *Privacy Laws and Business international Report* 25.

Grevi, G, 'Strategic autonomy for European choices: The key to Europe's shaping power' (2019) European Policy Centre Discussion Paper.

Gribakov, A, 'Cross-Border Privacy Rules in Asia: An Overview' (*Law Fare Blog*, 3 January 2019) https://www.lawfareblog.com/cross-border-privacy-rules-asia-overview accessed 8 March 2022.

Grieger, G, 'EU-China Comprehensive Agreement on Investment: Levelling the playing field with China' (2020) European Parliamentary Research Service PE 652.066.

Groussot, X and Öberg, ML, 'The Web of Autonomy of the EU Legal Order: Achmea' in G Butler and R Wessel (eds), *EU External Relations Law: The Cases in Context* (Oxford University Press, 2021).

Grüll, P, '"Geopolitical" Europe aims to extend its digital sovereignty from China' (*Euractive*, 9 September 2020) https://www.euractiv.com/section/digital/news/geopolitical-europe-aims-to-extend-its-digital-sovereignty-versus-china/ accessed 8 March 2022.

Guild, E and Mendos Kuşkonmaz, E, 'EU Exclusive Jurisdiction on Surveillance Related to Terrorism and Serious Transnational Crime: Case Review on Opinion 1/15' (2018) 43 *European Law Review* 583

—— 'A critical take on Opinion 1/15: is the glass half full or half empty?' [2019] *European Yearbook on Human Rights* 111.

Guilfoyle, D, 'The International Criminal Court Independent Expert Review: questions of accountability and culture' (*EJIL: Talk!*, 7 October 2020).

Hallinan, D, 'Partnership in a Competitive Order: Understanding the EU-Japan FTA' (2016) European Trade Study Group Paper, https://www.etsg.org/ETSG2016/Papers/425.pdf accessed 8 March 2022.

Hamanaka, S, 'The Future Impact of Trans-Pacific Partnership's Rule-Making Achievements: The Case Study of E-commerce' (2019) 42 *World Economy* 552.

Hamilton, D and Quinlan, J, US Chamber of Commerce, *The Transatlantic Economy 2019* (Brookings 2019).

—— US Chamber of Commerce, *The Transatlantic Economy 2021* (2021) http://www.amchameu.eu/sites/default/files/publications/files/transatlanticeconomy2021_fullreporthr.pdf accessed 8 March 2022.

Hathaway, O et al, 'The Law of Cyber-Attack' (2012) 100 *California Law Review* 817.

Heclo, H, 'Thinking Institutionally' in SA Binder, RAW Rhodes and BA Rockman, *The Oxford Handbook of Political Institutions* (Oxford University Press, 2008).

Heitger, B and Stehn, J, 'Japanese Direct Investments in the EC – Response to the Internal Market 1993?' (1990) 29 *Journal of Common Market Studies* 1.

Hernández, GI, 'The Judicialization of International Law: Reflections on the Empirical Turn' (2014) 25 *European Journal of International Law* 919.

Herpig, S and Schuetze, J, 'Transatlantic Cyber Forum – Cooperating on Borderless Cyber Security Challenges' in D Feldner (ed), *Redesigning Organizations* (Springer, 2020).

Herzog, D, *RIP Sovereignty* (Yale University Press, 2020).

Hillman, J and Grundhoefer, S, 'Can the US-EU Trade and Technology Council Succeed?' (*Council on Foreign Affairs*, 29 October 2021) https://www.cfr.org/blog/can-us-eu-trade-and-technology-council-succeed accessed 8 March 2022.

Hinane El Kadi, T, 'The Promise and Peril of the Digital Silk Road' (*Chatham House*, 6 June 2019) https://www.chathamhouse.org/2019/06/promise-and-peril-digital-silk-road accessed 8 March 2022.

Hirschl, R, *Towards Juristocracy* (Harvard University Press 2004 & 2007).

—— 'The Judicialization of Politics' in GA Caldeira et al (eds), *The Oxford Handbook of Law and Politics* (Oxford University Press, 2018).

Hobbs, C (ed), *Europe's Digital Sovereignty: From Rulemaker to Superpower in the Age of US-China Rivalry* (Essay Collection, European Council of Foreign Affairs 2020) https://ecfr.eu/wp-content/uploads/europe_digital_sovereignty_rulemaker_superpower_age_us_china_rivalry.pdf accessed 8 March 2022.

Hoekman, B, 'Fostering Transatlantic Regulatory Cooperation and Gradual Multilateralization' (2015) 18 *Journal of International Economic Law* 609.

—— 'International Regulatory Cooperation and Trade Agreements' in E Brousseau, J-M Glachant and J Sgard (eds), *The Oxford Handbook of Institutions of International Economic Governance and Market Regulation* (Oxford University Press, 2019).

Hofmann, S, 'Elastic Relations: Looking to both Sides of the Atlantic in the 2020 US Presidential Election Year' (2021) 59(S1) *Journal of Common Market Studies* 150.

Hong, Y, 'The cross-border data flows security assessment: an important part of protecting China's basic strategic resources' (2017) Yale Law School, Paul Tsai China Center Working Paper.

Horn, H, Mavroidis, P and Sapir, A, 'Beyond the WTO? An Anatomy of EU and US Preferential Trade Agreements' (2010) 33 *The World Economy* 1565.

Hosoya, C, 'Relations between the European Communities and Japan' (1979) 18 *Journal of Common Market Studies* 159.

Howse, R, 'The Institutions of TPP11: Back to the Future?' in B Kingsbury et al, *Megaregulation Contested: Global Economic Ordering after TPP* (Oxford University Press, 2019).

Huang, J, 'Chinese private international law and online data protection' (2019) 15 *Journal of Private International Law* 186.

Huang, K, Madnick, S and Johnson, S, 'Framework for Understanding Cybersecurity Impacts on International Trade' (2019) CISL Working Paper No 2019-23, https://ssrn.com/abstract=3555341 accessed 8 March 2022.

Hübner, K, Deman, A-S and Balik, T, 'EU and Trade Policymaking: the Contentious Case of CETA' (2017) 39 *Journal of European Integration* 843.

'Human Rights Watch World Report: China Events of 2018' (*Human Rights Watch*, 2019) https://www.hrw.org/world-report/2019/country-chapters/china-and-tibet accessed 8 March 2022.

Hurst, D 'Japan Calls for Global Consensus on Data Governance' (*The Diplomat*, 2 February 2019) https://thediplomat.com/2019/02/japan-calls-for-global-consensus-on-data-governance/ accessed 8 March 2022.

Ibáñez Colomo, P, 'The Draft Digital Markets Act: A Legal and Institutional Analysis' (2021) SSRN Paper, https://papers.ssrn.com/sol3/papers.cfm?abstract_id=3790276 accessed 8 March 2022.

IFLA, 'The Right to be Forgotten in National and Regional Contexts', https://www.ifla.org/files/assets/clm/statements/rtbf_background.pdf accessed 8 March 2022.

Information Security Policy Council Japan, 'International Strategy on Cybersecurity Cooperation: J-Initiative for Cybersecurity' (2013) https://www.nisc.go.jp/eng/pdf/InternationalStrategyonCybersecurityCooperation_e.pdf accessed 8 March 2022.

Ingram, D, 'Exclusive: Facebook to put 1.5 billion users out of reach of new EU privacy law' (*Reuters*, 19 April 2018) https://www.reuters.com/article/us-facebook-privacy-eu-exclusive-idUSKBN1HQ00P accessed 8 March 2022.

Internet Corporation for Assigned Names and Numbers, 'ICANN Org Comments on the Two-Year Review Exercise of the GDPR' (April 2020) https://ec.europa.eu/info/law/better-regulation/have-your-say/initiatives/12322-Report-on-the-application-of-the-General-Data-Protection-Regulation/F514217 accessed 8 March 2022.

Irion, K, 'Schrems II and Surveillance: Third Countries' National Security Powers in the Purview of EU Law' (*European Law Blog*, 24 July 2020) https://europeanlawblog.eu/2020/07/24/schrems-ii-and-surveillance-third-countries-national-security-powers-in-the-purview-of-eu-law/ accessed 8 March 2022.

Jacobides, MG and Lianos, I, 'Regulating platforms and ecosystems: an introduction' (2021) 30(5) *Industrial and Corporate Change* 1131.

Jančić, D, 'Transatlantic Regulatory Interdependence, Law and Governance: The Evolving Roles of the EU and US Legislatures' (2015) 17 *Cambridge Yearbook of European Legal Studies* 334.

Janow, M and Mavroidis, P, 'Digital Trade, E-Commerce, the WTO and Regional Frameworks' (2019) 18(S1) *World Trade Review* 1.

'Japan and the GATT' (1954) 9(3) *International Journal* 216.

Jiang, H, 'The Making of a Civil Code: Promises and Perils of a New Civil Law' (2021) 95 *Tulane Law Review* 777.

Joel, A and Oliveira, F, 'Redress: What is the probelm?' (*European Law Blog*, 28 September 2021) https://europeanlawblog.eu/2021/09/28/redress-what-is-the-problem/ accessed 8 March 2022.

Joh, E, 'The Undue Influence of Surveillance Technology Companies on Policing' (2017) 92 *New York University Law Review* 19.

Johnson, DR and Post, D, 'Law and Borders: The Rise of Law in Cyberspace' (1996) 48 *Stanford Law Review* 1367.

Jourová, V and O'Reilly, E, 'Follow-up reply from the European Ombudsman to Commissioner Jourová on the use of the title "Ombudsperson" in the EU-US Privacy Shield agreement' (*European Ombudsman*, 2 May 2016) https://www.ombudsman.europa.eu/en/doc/correspondence/en/66926 accessed 8 March 2022.

Kagan, RA 'Globalization and Legal Change: the "Americanization" of European Law?' (2007) 1 *Regulation and Governance* 99.

Kaminski, M, 'Why Trade Is Not the Place for the EU to Negotiate Privacy' (*Internet Policy Review*, 23 January 2015) https://policyreview.info/articles/news/why-trade-not-place-eu-negotiate-privacy/354 accessed 8 March 2022.

Kanetake, M and De Vries, S, 'EU-Japan Economic Partnership Agreement: Data Protection in the Era of Digital Trade and Economy' (*Renforce Blog*, 18 December 2018) http://blog.renforce.eu/index.php/en/2018/12/18/eu-japan-economic-partnership-agreement-data-protection-in-the-era-of-digital-trade-and-economy/ accessed 8 March 2022.

Kasper, A, 'EU Cybersecurity Governance – Stakeholders and Normative Intentions Towards Integration' in M Harwood, S Moncada and R Pace (eds), *The future of the European Union: Demisting the Debate* (Msida, 2020).

Kasper, A and Antonov, A, 'Towards Conceptualizing EU Cybersecurity Law' (2019) ZEI Discussion Paper C253, https://www.researchgate.net/profile/Center-For-European-Integration-Studies/publication/338038206_ZEI_Discussion_Paper_C_253_Towards_Conceptualizing_EU_Cybersecurity_Law/links/5dfb5630a6fdcc28372c19eb/ZEI-Discussion-Paper-C-253-Towards-Conceptualizing-EU-Cybersecurity-Law.pdf accessed 8 March 2022.

Kayali, L, 'Inside Facebook's fight against European regulation' (*Politico*, 23 January 2019) https://www.politico.eu/article/inside-story-facebook-fight-against-european-regulation/ accessed 8 March 2022.

Keane Woods, A, 'Litigating Data Sovereignty' (2018) 128 *Yale Law Journal* 328.

Keeleng, D, 'In Praise of Judicial Activism, but What Does it Mean? And Has the European Court of Justice Ever Practiced It?' in F Mancini, *Scritti In Onore* (Giuffrè Editori, 1998).

Kelemen, DK, 'The European Union's Authoritarian Equilibrium' (2020) 27 *Journal of European Public Policy* 481.

Kelemen, RD, *Eurolegalism: the transformation of law and regulation in the European Union* (Harvard University Press 2011).

Kelsey, J, 'Important differences between the final RCEP electronic commerce chapter and the TPPA and lessons for e-commerce in the WTO' (*Bilaterals*, 10 February 2020) https://www.bilaterals.org/?important-differences-between-the accessed 8 March 2022.

Kennedy, S (ed), *From Rule Takers to Rule Makers: The Growing Role of Chinese in Global Governance* (Indiana University Research 2012).

Keohane, R 'Ironies of Sovereignty: The European Union and the United States' (2002) 42 *Journal of Common Market Studies* 743.

Kerry, C et al, 'Bridging the Gaps: a Path forward to Federal Privacy Legislation' (2020) https://www.brookings.edu/wp-content/uploads/2020/06/Bridging-the-gaps_a-path-forward-to-federal-privacy-legislation.pdf accessed 8 March 2022.

Kingsbury, B, 'Infrastructure and InfraReg: on Rousing the International Law 'Wizards of Is' (2019) 8(2) *Cambridge International Law Journal* 171.

Kingsbury, B et al, 'Introduction: The Essence, Significance, and Problems of the Trans-Pacific Partnership' in B Kingsbury et al, *Megaregulation Contested: Global Economic Ordering after TPP* (Oxford University Press, 2019).

Kleimann, D and Kübek, G, 'The Signing, Provisional Application, and Conclusion of Trade and Investment Agreements in the EU: The Case of CETA and Opinion 2/15' (2018) 45 *Legal Issues of Economic Integration* 13.

Klimburg, A, *National Cyber Security Framework Manual. NATO CCD COE Publication* (NATO, 2013).

Klonick, K, 'The Facebook Oversight Board', in City Law School Working Paper 2020/2 'The Law of Facebook'.

—— 'The Facebook Oversight Board: Creating an Independent Institution to Adjudicate Online Free Expression' (2020) 129 *Yale Law Journal* 2418.

Knauss, J and Trubek, D, 'The Transatlantic Labor Dialogue: Minimal Action in a Weak Structure' in M Pollack and G Shaffer (eds), *Transatlantic Governance in the Global Economy* (Rowman & Littlefield, 2001).

Komaitis, K, 'Europe's pursuit of digital sovereignty could affect the future of the Internet' (*TechEU*) https://tech.eu/features/32780/europe-digital-sovereignty/ accessed 8 March 2022.

Konstadinidis, M, 'EU-US Summit: Between Transatlantic Cooperation and Strategic Autonomy' (2021) 63 *EU Law Live! Weekend Edition.*

Korff, D, 'Transfers of personal data from the EU to non-EU countries under the EU General Data Protection Regulation after "Schrems II": not a "Mission Impossible"' (*Ian Brown*, April 2021) https://www.ianbrown.tech/wp-content/uploads/2021/04/KORFF-The-EU-regime-on-data-transfers-after-Schrems-II-210422.pdf accessed 8 March 2022.

Korkea-Aho, E, 'EU Soft Law in Domestic Legal Systems: Flexibility and Diversity Guaranteed?' (2009) 16(3) *Maastricht Journal of European and Comparative Law* 27.

Krasner, SD, *Sovereignty. Organised Hypocrisy* (Princeton: Princeton University Press, 1999).

Kriebernegg, U, *The Transatlantic Dialogue on Higher Education: An Analysis of Cultural Narratives* (Logos Verlag Berlin GmbH, 2011).

Krisch, N, 'Pluralism in Postnational Risk Regulation: The Dispute over GMOs and Trade' (2010) 1 *Transnational Legal Theory* 1.

Krishnamurthy, V, 'A Tale of Two Privacy Laws: The GDPR and the International Right to Privacy' (2020) 114 *American Journal of International Law Unbound* 26.

Krotz, U, Patel, KK and Romero, F, *Europe's Cold War Relations: The EC Towards a Global Role* (Bloomsbury 2019).

Kukuvec, D, 'The Court of Justice of the European Union for Hedgehogs' Jean Monnet Working Paper 1/21, https://jeanmonnetprogram.org/wp-content/uploads/JMWP-01_Damjan-Kukovec.pdf accessed 8 March 2022.

Kuner, C, 'Requiring Local Storage of Internet Data Will Not Protect Privacy' (*Oxford University Press Blog*, 2013) http://blog.oup.com/2013/12/data-security-privacy-storage-law/ accessed 8 March 2022.

—— 'Data Nationalism and Its Discontents' (*Emory Law Journal Online*, 2015) https://scholarlycommons.law.emory.edu/cgi/viewcontent.cgi?article=1024&context=elj-online accessed 8 March 2022.

—— 'Extra Territoriality and Regulation of International Data Transfers in EU Data Protection Law' (2015) 5 *International Data Privacy Law* 242.

—— 'International agreements, data protection, and EU fundamental rights on the international stage: Opinion 1/15, EU-Canada PNR' (2018) 55 *Common Market Law Review* 857.

—— 'The Internet and the Global Reach of EU Law' in M Cremona and J Scott (eds), *EU Law Beyond EU Borders: The Extraterritorial Reach of EU Law* (Oxford University Press, 2019).

—— 'The Schrems II judgment of the Court of Justice and the future of data transfer regulation' (*European Law Blog*, 17 July 2020) https://europeanlawblog.eu/2020/07/17/the-schrems-ii-judgment-of-the-court-of-justice-and-the-future-of-data-transfer-regulation/ accessed 8 March 2022.

Kynge, J and Liu, N, 'From AI to Facial Recognition: How China is Setting the Rules in New Tech' (*Financial Times*, 7 October 2020) https://www.ft.com/content/188d86df-6e82-47eb-a134-2e1e45c777b6 accessed 8 March 2022.

Kyriakides, E, 'The CLOUD Act, E-Evidence, and Individual Rights' (2019) *European Data Protection Law Review* 99.

Laidlaw, E, 'Privacy and Cybersecurity in Digital Trade: The Challenge of Cross Border Data Flows' (2021) *Global Affairs Canada Paper*, https://ssrn.com/abstract=3790936 accessed 8 March 2022.

Lamadrid de Pablo, A and Bayón Fernández, N, 'Why the Proposed DMA Might be Illegal Under Article 114 TFEU, and How To Fix It' (2021) https://antitrustlair.files.wordpress.com/2021/04/why-the-proposed-dma-might-be-illegal-under-article-114-tfeu-and-how-to-fix-it-3.pdf accessed 8 March 2022.

Landfried, C, 'The Judicialization of Politics in Germany' (1994) 15 *International Politics Law Review* 113.

Lang, A, 'Heterodox Markets and "Market Distortions" in the Global Trading System' (2019) 22 *Journal of International Economic Law* 677.

Lazarou, E, 'The future of multilateralism: crisis or opportunity?' (2017) European Parliamentary Research Service Paper PE 603.922, https://www.europarl.europa.eu/RegData/etudes/BRIE/2017/603922/EPRS_BRI(2017)603922_EN.pdf accessed 8 March 2022.

Leblond, P, 'Digital Trade at the WTO – The CPTPP and CUSMA Pose Challenges to Canadian Data Regulation' (2019) CIGI Papers No 227, https://www.cigionline.org/sites/default/files/documents/no.227.pdf accessed 8 March 2022.

—— 'Digital Trade: Is RCEP the WTO's Future?' (*CIGI*, 23 November 2020) https://www.cigionline.org/articles/digital-trade-rcep-wtos-future/ accessed 8 March 2022.

—— 'Governing cross-border data flows beyond trade agreements to support digital trade: Inspiration from international financial standards-setting bodies' in I Borchert and LA Winters (eds), *Addressing Impediments to Digital Trade* (CERP, 2021).

Lee, PK, Chan, G and Chan, LH, 'China in Darfur: Humanitarian Rule-maker or Rule-taker?' (2012) 38 *Review of International Studies* 423.

Lee, Y-S, 'The Eagle Meets the Dragon – Two Superpowers, Two Mega RTAs, and So Many in between: Reflections on TPP and RCEP' (2016) 50(3) *Journal of World Trade* 475.

Lee-Makiyama, H, 'On New Regulation of Europe's Digital Markets' (*Wilson Center*, 5 April 2021) https://www.wilsoncenter.org/article/new-regulation-europes-digital-markets accessed 8 March 2022.

'Legal Opinion on Budapest Cybercrime Convention: use of disconnection clause in Second Additional Protocol to the Council of Europe Convention on Cybercrime' (29 April 2019) https://www.coe.int/en/web/dlapil/-/use-of-a-disconnection-clause-in-the-second-additional-protocol-to-the-budapest-convention-on-cybercri-1 accessed 8 March 2022.

Lenaerts, K, Lecture, Brussels, 2013.

Lenz, T, *Interorganizational Diffusion in International Relations: Regional Institutions and the Role of the European Union* (Oxford University Press, 2021).

Lewis, M, 'Criminalizing China' (2020) 111 *Journal of Criminal law and Criminology* 145.

Li, M, 'The Belt and Road Initiative: Geo-economics and Indo-Pacific security competition' (2020) 96 *International Affairs* 169.

Library of the European Parliament, 'Principal EU-US disputes' (22 April 2013) https://www.europarl.europa.eu/RegData/bibliotheque/briefing/2013/130518/LDM_BRI(2013)130518_REV1_EN.pdf accessed 8 March 2022.

Lippert, B, Von Ondarza, N and Perthes, V (eds), 'European Strategic Autonomy: Actors, Issues, Conflicts of Interests' (2019) SWP Research Paper 2019/RP 04.

Lipton, E and Hakim, D, 'Lobbying Bonanza as Firms Try to Influence European Union' *The* (*New York Times*, 18 October 2013) https://www.nytimes.com/2013/10/19/world/europe/lobbying-bonanza-as-firms-try-to-influence-european-union.html accessed 8 March 2022.

Liu, H-W, 'Data Localization and Digital Trade Barriers: ASEAN in Megaregionalism' in PL Hsieh and B Mercurio (eds), *ASEAN Law in the New Regional Economic Order: Global Trends and Shifting Paradigms* (Cambridge University Press, 2019).

Lock, T 'Walking on a Tightrope: The Draft ECHR Accession Agreement and the Autonomy of the EU Legal Order' (2011) 48 *Common Market Law Review* 1025.

Lockett, J, 'What cybersecurity means for global trade' (*World Economic Forum*, 15 September 2015) https://www.weforum.org/agenda/2015/09/what-cybersecurity-means-for-global-trade/accessed 8 March 2022.

Lopez-Gonzalez, J and Jouanjean, MA, 'Digital Trade: Developing a Framework for Analysis' (2017) OECD Trade Policy Papers No 205.

Luciano, BT, 'A Clash between Creature and Creator? Contemporary Relations between the Pan-African Parliament and the European Parliament' (2020) 58 *Journal of Common Market Studies* 1182.

Lukas, A, 'Safe Harbor or Stormy Waters? Living with the EU Data Protection Directive' (2001) 16 Trade Briefing Papers, CATO Institute Center for Trade Policy Studies.

Luo, D, 'China – Data Protection Overview' (*One Trust Data Guidance*, November 2021) https://www.dataguidance.com/notes/china-data-protection-overview accessed 8 March 2022.

Lustig, D and Weiler, JHH, 'Judicial Review in the Contemporary World – Retrospective and Prospective' (2018) 16 *I-CON* 1.

Lutzi, T, 'What's a consumer?' (Some) clarification on consumer jurisdiction, social-media accounts, and collective redress under the Brussels Ia Regulation: Case C-498/16 Maximilian Schrems v. Facebook Ireland Limited, EU:C:2018:37' (2018) 25 *Maastricht Journal of European and Comparative Law* 374.

Lynn, W, 'Defending a New Domain the Pentagon's Cyber Strategy' (2010) 89(5) *Foreign Affairs* 98.
Lynskey, O, 'Deconstructing Data Protection: The Added Value of a Right to Data Protection in the EU Legal Order' (2014) 63 *International and Comparative Law Quarterly* 3.
—— 'The Europeanisation of Data Protection Law' [2016] *Cambridge Yearbook of European Legal Studies* 1.
—— 'Delivering Data Protection: The Next Chapter' (2020) 21(S1) *German Law Journal* 80.
'Marietje Schaake: EU needs to think bigger than Big Tech' (*Tech Monitor*, 27 November 2020) https://techmonitor.ai/interviews/marietje-schaake-eu-think-bigger-than-big-tech accessed 8 March 2022.
Mac Síthigh, D and Siems, M, 'The Chinese Social Credit System: A Model for Other Countries?' (2019) 82 *Modern Law Review* 1071.
Macri, J, 'How Hungary's Path Leads to China's Belt and Road' (*The Diplomat*, 11 April 2019) https://thediplomat.com/2019/04/how-hungarys-path-leads-to-chinas-belt-and-road/ accessed 8 March 2022.
Manancourt, V, 'Ireland's Facebook decision triggers argument over limits of GDPR' (*Politico*, 18 October 2021) https://www.politico.eu/article/ireland-facebook-decision-triggers-argument-over-limits-gdpr/ accessed 8 March 2022.
Manancourt, V and Heikkilä, M, 'EU eyes tighter grip on data in "tech sovereignty" push' (*Politico*, 29 October 2020) https://www.politico.eu/article/in-small-steps-europe-looks-to-tighten-grip-on-data/ accessed 8 March 2022.
Mancini, I, 'Fundamental Rights in the EU's External Trade Relations: From Promotion "Through" Trade Agreements to Protection "In" Trade Agreements' in E Kassoti and R Wessel (eds), *EU Trade Agreements and the Duty to Respect Human Rights Abroad* (CLEER, 2020).
—— 'A deep trade agenda for fundamental rights: framing fundamental rights for the new generation EU trade agreements with other developed countries' (DPhil Thesis, City, University of London 2021).
Manger, MS, 'Competition and Bilateralism in Trade Policy: The Case of Japan's Free Trade Agreements' (2005) 12 *Review of International Political Economy* 804.
Manoli, P, 'Political Economy Aspects of Deep and Comprehensive Free Trade Agreements' (2013) 4(2) *Eastern Journal of European Studies* 51.
Markopoulou, D, Papakonstantinou, V and De Hert, P, 'The new EU cybersecurity framework: The NIS Directive, ENISA's role and the General Data Protection Regulation' (2019) 35(6) *Computer Law & Security Review* 105336.
Martinico, G, 'Comparative Law Reflections on the Use of Soft Law in the Belt and Road Initiative' in G Martinico and X Wu (eds), *A Legal Analysis of the Belt and Road Initiative: Towards a New Silk Road?* (Palgrave Macmillan, 2020).
Martins dos Santos, B and Morar, D, 'Four lessons for US legislators from the EU Digital Services Act' (*Brookings*, 6 January 2021) https://www.brookings.edu/blog/techtank/2021/01/06/four-lessons-for-u-s-legislators-from-the-eu-digital-services-act/ accessed 8 March 2022.
Matsubara, M, 'How Japan's New Cybersecurity Strategy Will Bring the Country up to Par With the Rest of the World' (*Council on Foreign Relations*, 4 June 2018) https://www.cfr.org/blog/how-japans-new-cybersecurity-strategy-will-bring-country-par-rest-world accessed 8 March 2022.
Matsudaira, T, 'Judicialization of Politics and the Japanese Supreme Court' (2010) 88 *Washington University Law Review* 1559.
Mattli, W and Woods, N, 'In Whose Benefit? Explaining Regulatory Change in Global Politics' in W Mattli and N Woods (eds), *The Politics of Global Regulation* (Princeton University Press, 2009).
Matura, T, 'The Belt and Road Initiative depicted in Hungary and Slovakia' (2018) 7 *Journal of Contemporary East Asia Studies* 174.
Mavroidis, P, 'Trade Regulation, and Digital Trade' (2017) Columbia School of International and Public Affairs Working Paper.
Mavroidis, P and Sapir, A, *China and the WTO: Why Multilateralism Still Matters* (Princeton University Press, 2021).
Mayr, S, 'CETA, TTIP, TiSA, and Their Relationship with EU Law' in S Griller, W Obwexer and E Vranes (eds), *Mega-Regional Trade Agreements: CETA, TTIP, and TiSA: New Orientations for EU External Economic Relations* (Oxford University Press, 2017).

McCabe, D and Kang, C, 'Biden Names Lina Khan, a Big-Tech Critic, as FTC Chair' (*New York Times*, 15 June 2021) https://www.nytimes.com/2021/06/15/technology/lina-khan-ftc.html accessed 8 March 2022.

McKinsey Global Institute, 'By 2025, Internet of Things Applications Could Have US$11 Trillion Impact' (2015) https://www.mckinsey.com/mgi/overview/in-the-news/by-2025-internet-of-things-applications-could-have-11-trillion-impact 31 December 2021

—— 'DigitalGlobalization: The New Era of Global Flows' (2016) https://www.mckinsey.com/business-functions/mckinsey-digital/our-insights/digital-globalization-the-new-era-of-global-flows accessed 8 March 2022.

'Meijers Committee Note on the EU-US Umbrella Agreement' (2016) CM 1613.

Meissner, K and McKenzie, L, 'The Paradox of Human Rights Conditionality in EU Trade Policy: When Strategic Interests Drive Policy Outcomes' (2018) *Journal of European Public Policy* 1.

Meltzer, J and Kerry, C, 'Cybersecurity and digital trade: Getting it right' (*Brookings*, 18 September 2019) https://www.brookings.edu/research/cybersecurity-and-digital-trade-getting-it-right/ accessed 8 March 2022.

Meltzer, J, 'The Internet, Cross-Border Data Flows and International Trade' (2013) Center for Technology Innovation at Brookings, Issues in Technology Innovation No 22, https://www.brookings.edu/wp-content/uploads/2016/06/internet-data-and-trade-meltzer.pdf accessed 8 March 2022.

—— 'Governing Digital Trade' (2019) 18 *World Trade Review* 23.

—— 'Cybersecurity, Digital Trade, and Data Flows: Re-thinking a Role for International Trade Rules' (2020) Global Economy & Development WP No 132.

Micallef, JA, 'Digital Trade in EU FTAs: Are EU FTAs Allowing Cross Border Digital Trade to Reach Its Full Potential?' (2019) 53 *Journal of World Trade* 855.

Michalski, A and Pan, Z, 'Role Dynamics in a Structured Relationship: The EU–China Strategic Partnership' (2017) 55 *Journal of Common Market Studies* 611.

Milner, H and Moravscik, A (eds), *Power, Interdependence, and Nonstate Actors in World Politics* (Princeton University Press, 2009).

Minghao, Z, 'Yidai yilu jianshe de anquan baozhang wenti chuyi' [Analysing the security measures for the BRI] (2016) 18(2) *Guoji luntan [International Forum]* 1.

Mishra, N, 'The Trade: (Cyber)Security Dilemma and Its Impact on Global Cybersecurity Governance' (2020) 54 *Journal of World Trade* 567.

Mitchell, AD, 'Towards Compatibility: The Future of Electronic Commerce within the Global Trading System' (2001) 4 *Journal of International Economic Law* 685.

Mitchell, AD and Hepburn, J, 'Don't Fence Me In: Reforming Trade and Investment Law to Better Facilitate Cross-Border Data Transfer' (2016) *The Yale Journal of Law and Technology* 1.

Mitsilegas, V, 'Constitutional Implications of Mutual Recognition in Criminal Matters in the EU' (2006) 43 *Common Market Law Review* 1277.

—— 'Autonomous Concepts Diversity Management and Mutual Trust in Europe's Area of Criminal Justice' (2020) 57 *Common Market Law Review* 45;.

Mitter, R, *China's Good War How World War II Is Shaping a New Nationalism* (Harvard University Press 2020).

Miyashita, H, 'The evolving concept of data privacy in Japanese law' (2011) 1(4) *International Data Privacy Law* 229.

Mondré, A et al, 'Uneven Judicialization: Comparing International Dispute Settlement in Security, Trade, and the Environment' (2010) 4 *New Global Studies.*

Monteiro, J-A and Teh, R, 'Provisions on Electronic Commerce in Regional Trade Agreements' (2017) WTO Working Paper ERSD-2017-11.

Moravcsik, A and Emmons, C, 'A Liberal Intergovernmentalist Approach to EU External Action' in S Gstohl and S Schunz (eds), *The External Action of the European Union – Concepts, Approaches, Theories* (Macmillan, 2021).

Moret, E and Pawlak, P, 'The EU Cyber Diplomacy Toolbox: towards a cyber sanctions regime?' (2017) European Union Institute for Security Studies, 24 Brief Issue, https://www.iss.europa.eu/sites/default/files/EUISSFiles/Brief%2024%20Cyber%20sanctions.pdf accessed 8 March 2022.

Munakata, N, 'Nihon no Chiiki Keizai Togo Seisaku no Keisei' (The Formation of Japan's Regional Economic Integration Policy) in N Munakata (ed), *Nicchu Kankei no Tenki* (Turning Point of Japan-China Relations) (Toyo Keizai Shimpo Sha, 2001).

Mussche, N, and Lens, D, 'The ECJ's Construction of an EU Mobility Regime-Judicialization and the Posting of Third-country Nationals' (2019) 57 *Journal of Common Market Studies* 1247.

Nakagawa, J, 'Regulatory Co-operation and Regulatory Coherence through Mega-FTAs: Possibilities and Challenges' in J Chaisse and T Lin (eds), *International Economic Law and Governance: Essays in Honour of Mitsuo Matsushita* (Oxford University Press, 2016).

Navarro, J, 'The Creation and Transformation of Regional Parliamentary Assemblies: Lessons from the Pan-African Parliament' (2010) 16(2) *Journal of Legislative Studies* 195.

Nelson, P, 'Taking the lead in current and future trade relationships' in A Berkofsky et al (eds), *The EU-Japan Partnership in the Shadow of China* (Routledge, 2019).

Ng, W, *The Political Economy of Competition Law in China* (Cambridge University Press, 2018).

—— 'Changing Global Dynamics and International Competition Law: Considering China's Potential Impact' (2019) 30 *European Journal of International Law* 1409.

Nitta, Y, 'Japan's Approach towards International Strategy on Cyber Security Cooperation' (2013) 2013 World Cyberspace Cooperation Summit IV (WCC4) https://cybersummit.info/sites/cybersummit.info/files/Japan_edited%20v2.pdf-FINAL.pdf accessed 8 March 2022.

Nolan, M, 'Japan and International Economic Institutions' (*PIIE*, 6 July 2000) https://www.piie.com/commentary/speeches-papers/japan-and-international-economic-institutions accessed 8 March 2022.

North, DC, *Institutions, Institutional Change, and Economic Performance* (Cambridge University Press, 1990).

Odermatt, J, 'When a Fence Becomes a Cage: The Principle of Autonomy in EU External Relations Law' (2016) EUI Working Paper MWP 2016/07.

—— 'The European Union as a cybersecurity actor' in S Blockmans and P Koutrakos (eds), *Research Handbook on the EU's Common Foreign and Security Policy* (Edward Elgar, 2018).

Odom, J, 'Europe's Double Standard for China's Overfishing' (*EJIL Talk!*, 16 April 2020) https://www.ejiltalk.org/europes-double-standard-for-chinas-overfishing/ accessed 8 March 2022.

OECD Digital Economy Papers, 'Measuring the economic value of data and cross-border data flows' (*OECD*, 26 August 2020) https://www.oecd-ilibrary.org/docserver/6345995e-en.pdf?expires=1605107203&id=id&accname=guest&checksum=7631AE9F2929B79DAB35E25BC1124DEE accessed 8 March 2022.

OECD, Council Recommendation, 'Guidelines on the Protection of Privacy and Transborder Flows of Personal Data' (OECD 1980).

—— 'International Regulatory Co-operation – Adapting Rules to an Interconnected World' (2020) https://www.oecd.org/gov/regulatory-policy/irc.htm accessed 8 March 2022.

Ogita, T, 'An Approach towards Japan's FTA Policy' (2002) IDE APEC Study Center Working Paper Series 01/02 – No 4, 2.

Oh, E, 'Digital Trade Regulation in the Asia-Pacific: Where Does It Stand? Comparing the RCEP E-commerce Chapter with the CPTPP and the JSI' (2021) 48 *Legal Issues of Economic Integration* 403.

Opinion of the Economic, Social and Environmental Council (France), 'Towards a European Digital Sovereignty Policy' (*ESEC*, 13 March 2019) https://www.lecese.fr/sites/default/files/travaux_multilingue/2019_07_souverainete_europeenne_numerique_GB_reduit.pdf accessed 8 March 2022.

Oshiba, R, 'A Japanese View of the EU' (2012) 20(2) *Perspectives* 103.

Oxford English Dictionary, 3rd edn (Oxford University Press, 2016).

Pasadilla, G, 'E-commerce provisions in RTAs: Implications for negotiations and capacity building' (2020) ASIA-Pacific Research and Training Network on Trade Working Paper No 192, https://www.unescap.org/sites/default/files/AWP192%20Pasadilla%20Gloria_0.pdf accessed 8 March 2022.

Pauwelyn, J, 'The WTO 20 Years On: "Global Governance by Judiciary" or, Rather, Member-driven Settlement of (Some) Trade Disputes between (Some) WTO Members?' (2016) 27 *European Journal of International Law* 1119.

Pawlak, P and Biersteke, T (eds), 'Guardian of the galaxy: EU cyber sanctions and norms in cyberspace' (2019) European Union Institute for Security Studies, Chaillot Paper 155, https://www.iss.europa.eu/sites/default/files/EUISSFiles/cp155.pdf accessed 8 March 2022.

Peel, M, 'China hits back at EU disinformation claims' (*Financial Times*, 25 April 2020) https://www.ft.com/content/6cbb9b22-8735-46ba-88a7-cb3e04cad6db accessed 8 March 2022.

Penfrat, J, 'DSA should promote open and fair digital environment, not undermine the rule of law' (*EDRi*, 2020) https://edri.org/our-work/dsa-must-promote-open-and-fair-digital-environment-not-undermine-the-rule-of-law/ accessed 8 March 2022.

Peng, S, Lin, C-F and Streinz, T (eds) *Artificial Intelligence and International Economic Law* (Cambridge University Press, 2021).

Pernot-Leplay, E, 'China's Approach on Data Privacy Law: A Third Way between the US and the EU?' (2020) 8 *Penn State Journal of Law & International Affairs* 51.

Perzanowski, A and Schultz, J, *The End of Ownership: Personal Property in the Digital Economy* (MIT Press, 2016).

Petersmann, E-U, 'Transformative Transatlantic Free Trade Agreements without Rights and Remedies of Citizens?' (2015) 18 *Journal of International Economic Law* 579.

Petkova, B, 'Privacy as Europe's first Amendment' (2019) 25 *European Law Journal* 140.

Plantin, JC et al, 'Infrastructure studies meet platform studies in the age of Google and Facebook' (2018) 20(1) *New Media & Society* 293.

Polakiewicz, J, 'Convention 108 as a Global Privacy Standard' (International Data Protection Conference, Budapest, 2011) https://rm.coe.int/16806b294e accessed 8 March 2022.

—— 'A Council of Europe perspective on the European Union: Crucial and complex cooperation' Europe and the world: a law review (April 2021) https://www.scienceopen.com/hosted-document?doi=10.14324/111.444.ewlj.2021.30 accessed 8 March 2022.

—— 'The Emperor's New Clothes – Data Privacy and Cybersecurity from a European Perspective' in E Fahey and I Mancini (eds), *Understanding The EU As A Good Global Actor: Whose Metrics?* (Edward Elgar, forthcoming).

Pollack, M, 'The New Transatlantic Agenda at Ten: Reflections in an experiment in International Governance' (2005) 43 *Journal of Common Market Studies* 899.

Pollack, M and Shaffer, G (eds), *Transatlantic Governance in the Global Economy* (Rowman & Littlefield, 2001).

—— *When Cooperation Fails: The International Law and Politics of Genetically Modified Foods* (Oxford University Press, 2009).

Porcedda, MG, 'Patching the patchwork: appraising the EU regulatory framework on cyber security breaches' (2018) 34 *Computer Law & Security Review* 1077.

Portela, C, 'The Spread of Horizontal Sanctions' (*CEPS*, 7 March 2019) https://www.ceps.eu/the-spread-of-horizontal-sanctions/ accessed 8 March 2022.

Post, D, 'Against "Against Cyberanarchy" (2002) 17 *Berkeley Technology Law Review* 1365, 2092.

Power, J, 'Facebook pressed Irish ambassador to lobby US Congress members' (*The Irish Times*, 25 February 2021) https://www.irishtimes.com/business/facebook-pressed-irish-ambassador-to-lobby-us-congress-members-1.4494200 accessed 8 March 2022.

Propp, K, 'Data flows across the Channel: The emerging UK-EU digital trade relationship' (*Atlantic Council*, 3 June 2020) https://www.atlanticcouncil.org/blogs/new-atlanticist/data-flows-across-the-channel-the-emerging-uk-eu-digital-trade-relationship/ accessed 8 March 2022.

—— 'Avoiding the next transatlantic security crisis: The looming clash over passenger name record data' (*Atlantic Council*, 1 July 2021) https://www.atlanticcouncil.org/in-depth-research-reports/issue-brief/the-looming-clash-over-passenger-name-record-data/ accessed 8 March 2022.

Propp, K and Swire, P, 'After *Schrems II*: A Proposal to Meet the Individual Redress Challenge' (*Lawfare Blog*, 13 August 2020) https://www.lawfareblog.com/after-schrems-ii-proposal-meet-individual-redress-challenge accessed 8 March 2022.

Purtova, N, 'The Law of Everything. Broad Concept of Personal Data and Future of EU Data Protection Law' (2018) 10 *Law, Innovation and Technology* 40.

Quick, R, 'Regulatory Cooperation – A Subject of Bilateral Trade Negotiations or Even for the WTO' (2008) 42 *Journal of World Trade* 391.

Reding, V, 'Digital Sovereignty: Europe at a Crossroads' (*EIB Institute*, 2016) https://institute.eib.org/wp-content/uploads/2016/01/Digital-Sovereignty-Europe-at-a-Crossroads.pdf accessed 8 March 2022.

Regalado, A, 'Who Coined "Cloud" Computing' (*MIT Technology Review*, 31 October 2011) https://www.technologyreview.com/2011/10/31/257406/who-coined-cloud-computing/ accessed 8 March 2022.

Reidenberg, JR, 'E-Commerce and Trans-Atlantic Privacy' (2001) 38 *Houston Law Review* 717.

Renard, T, 'EU Cyber Partnerships: Assessing the EU Strategic Partnerships with Third Countries in the Cyber Domain' (2018) 19(3) *European Politics and Society* 321.

Renda, A and Yoo, C, 'Telecommunications and Internet Services: The Digital Side of the TTIP' (2015) CEPS, TIPP in Balance Project Paper No 8, https://www.ceps.eu//download/publication/?id=9012&pdf=SR112%20Renda%20and%20Yoo%20Telecoms%20TTIP.pdf accessed 8 March 2022.

Resnik, J, 'Globalization(s), privatization(s), constitutionalization, and statization: Icons and experiences of sovereignty in the 21st century' (2013) 11 *I-CON*.

Riffel, C, 'The CETA Opinion of the European Court of Justice and its Implications – Not that Selfish After All' (2019) 22 *Journal of International Economic Law* 503.

Ripoll Servent, A and MacKenzie, A, 'The European Parliament as norm-taker? EU-US relations after the SWIFT Agreement' (2012) 17(5) *European Foreign Affairs Review* 71.

Ripoll Servent, A and Trauner, F (eds), *Routledge Handbook of Justice and Home Affairs* (Routledge, 2017).

Roberts, A, 'Disruptions Leading to a Competitive World Order' in A Roberts, *Is International Law International?* (Oxford University Press, 2017).

Roger, C, *The Origins of Informality: Why the Legal Foundations of Global Governance are Shifting, and Why It Matters* (Oxford University Press, 2020).

Rojszczak, M, 'CLOUD act agreements from an EU perspective' (2020) *Computer Law & Security Review* 105445.

Rolland, S and Trubek, D, *Emerging Powers in the International Economic Order* (Cambridge University Press, 2019).

Rosen, D, 'Regionalism rises in Japan to confront COVID-19' (*University of Melbourne*) https://law.unimelb.edu.au/centres/alc/engagement/asian-legal-conversations-covid-19/alc-original-articles/regionalism-rises-in-japan-to-confront-covid-19 accessed 8 March 2022.

Rotenberg, M, '*Schrems II*, from Snowden to China: Toward a new alignment on transatlantic data protection' (2020) 26 *European Law Journal* 141.

Russo, F, 'Assessing the EU-China relationship in Cyberspace' (*EIAS*, 2020) https://eias.org/op-ed/assessing-the-eu-china-relationship-in-cyberspace/ accessed 8 March 2022.

Ryngaert, C, 'Symposium Issue on Extraterritoriality and EU Data Protection' (2015) 5 *International Data Privacy Law* 4.

Sadl, U and Madsen, M, 'A "Selfie" from Luxembourg: The Court of Justice and the Fabrication of the Pre-Accession Case-Law Dossiers' (2016) 22 *Columbia Journal of European Law* 327.

Sadl, U and Palmer Olsen, H, 'Can Quantitative Methods Complement Doctrinal Legal Studies? Using Citation Network and Corpus Linguistic Analysis to Understand International Courts' (2017) 30 *Leiden Journal of International Law* 327.

Sadl, U and Panagis, I, 'The Force of EU Case Law: An Empirical Study of Precedential Constraint' (2016) iCourts Working Paper Series No 68, https://ssrn.com/abstract=2787119 accessed 8 March 2022.

Sánchez Nicolás, E, '"Big Five" tech giants spent €19m lobbying EU in 2020' (*EU Observer*, 1 March 2021), https://euobserver.com/science/151072?utm_source=euobs&utm_medium=email accessed 8 March 2022.

Sapir, A, Chowdhry, S and Terzi, A, 'The EU-Japan Economic Partnership Agreement' (*Bruegel*, 3 October 2018) https://bruegel.org/2018/10/the-eu-japan-economic-partnership-agreement/ accessed 8 March 2022.

Sassen, S, *Losing Control? Sovereignty in the Age of Globalization* (Columbia University Press, 1996).

Saurugger, S, and Terpan, F, *The Court of Justice of the European Union and the Politics of Law* (Red Globe Press, 2016).

Sauvé, P and Soprana, M 'The Evolution of the EU Digital Trade Policy' in M Hahn and G Van der Loo (eds), *Law and Practice of the Common Commercial Policy* (Brill Nijhoff, 2020).

Schaake, M, 'EU needs to think bigger than Big Tech' (*Tech Monitor*, 27 November 2020) https://techmonitor.ai/interviews/marietje-schaake-eu-think-bigger-than-big-tech accessed 8 March 2022.

Schmidt, SK, *The European Court of Justice and the Policy Process* (Oxford University Press, 2018).

Schmitt, NM (ed), *Prepared by the International Group of Experts at the Invitation of the NATO Cooperative Cyber Defence Centre of Excellence: Talinn Manual on the International Law applicable to Cyber-Warfare* (Cambridge University Press, 2013).

Schmon, C, and Gullo, K, 'European Commission's Proposed Digital Services Act Got Several Things Right, But Improvements Are Necessary to Put Users in Control' (*Electronic Frontier Foundation*, 15 December 2020) https://www.eff.org/deeplinks/2020/12/european-commissions-proposed-regulations-require-platforms-let-users-appeal accessed 8 March 2022.

Schuetze, J, 'EU-US Cybersecurity Policy Coming Together: Recommendations for instruments to accomplish joint strategic goals' (2020) EU Cyber Direct Research Paper, https://eucyberdirect.eu/content_research/eu-us-cybersecurity-policy-coming-together-recommendations-for-instruments-to-accomplish-joint-strategic-goals/ accessed 8 March 2022.

—— 'The Future for EU-US Cybersecurity Cooperation' (*Directions*, 26 November 2020). https://directionsblog.eu/the-future-for-eu-us-cybersecurity-cooperation/ accessed 8 March 2022.

Schulhofer, S, 'An international right to privacy? Be careful what you wish for' (2016) 14 *International Journal of Constitutional Law* 238.

Schwartz, PM, 'The EU-US Privacy Collision: A Turn to Institutions and Procedure' (2013) 126 *Harvard Law Review* 1996.

—— 'Global Data Privacy: The EU Way' (2019) 94 *New York University Law Journal* 771.

'Seven Major Changes in China's Finalized Personal Information Protection Law' (*DigiChina*, 23 August 2021) https://digichina.stanford.edu/news/seven-major-changes-chinas-finalized-personal-information-protection-law accessed 8 March 2022.

Severson, D, 'American Surveillance of Non-US Persons: Why New Privacy Protections Offer Only Cosmetic Change' (2015) 56 *Harvard International Law Journal* 465, 513.

Shaffer, G, 'Globalization and Social Protection: The Impact of EU and International Rules in the Ratcheting up of US Privacy Standards' (2000) 25 *Yale Journal of International Law* 70.

—— 'Reconciling Trade and Regulatory Goals: The Prospects and Limits of New Approaches to Transatlantic Governance through Mutual Recognition and Safe Harbour Agreements' (2002) 9 *Columbia Journal of European Law* 29.

Shaffer, G and Gao, H, 'China's Rise: How It Took on the US at the WTO' (2018) *University of Illinois Law Review* 115.

Sharma, M, 'Approaching Data Localization' (*Medium*, 10 June 2019) https://medium.com/@madhavsharma/approaching-data-localization-cc90282cb975 accessed 8 March 2022.

Shen, H, *Alibaba: Infrastructuring Global China* (Routledge, 2022).

Sieder, R, Schjolden, L and Angell, A (eds), *The Judicialization of Politics in Latin America* (Palgrave, 2016).

Simon, F, 'Europe ready to restart transatlantic climate dialogue after Trump "parenthesis"' (*Euractive*, 9 November 2020) https://www.euractiv.com/section/energy-environment/news/europe-ready-to-restart-transatlantic-climate-dialogue-after-trump-parenthesis accessed 8 March 2022.

Singapore-Sri-Lanka Free Trade Agreement (2018).

Slaughter, A-M, 'Agencies on the Loose: Holding Government Networks Accountable' in GA Bermann, M Herdegen and P Lindseth (eds), *Transatlantic Regulatory Cooperation* (Oxford University Press, 2000).

—— 'Judicial Globalization' (2000) 40 *Virginia Journal of International Law* 1103.

Smith, M, *Europe's Foreign and Security Policy: The Institutionalisation of Cooperation* (Cambridge University Press, 2004).

Stefan, O, 'The Future of EU Soft Law: A Research and Policy Agenda for the Aftermath of Covid-19' (2020) 7(S2) *Journal of International and Comparative Law* 329.

Stefano, S, 'The EU as a Global Standard Setting Actor: The Case of Data Transfers to Third Countries' in E Carpanelli and N Lazzerini (eds), *Use and Misuse of New Technologies* (Springer, 2019).

Stein, E, 'Lawyers, Judges and the Making of a Transnational Constitution' (1981) 75 *American Journal of International Law* 1.

Stevis-Gridneff, M, 'Without Naming Huawei, EU Warns against 5G Firms From "Hostile" Powers' (*New York Times*, 9 October 2019) https://www.nytimes.com/2019/10/09/world/europe/eu-huawei-report.html accessed 8 March 2022.

Stone Sweet, A, *Governing with Judges: Constitutional Politics in Europe* (Oxford University Press, 2000).

Stone Sweet, A, Sandholtz, W and Fligstein, N, *The Institutionalization of Europe* (Oxford University Press, 2001).

Strange, S, 'European Business in Japan: A Policy Crossroads?' (1995) 33 *Journal of Common Market Studies* 1.

Streinz, T, 'Digital Megaregulation Uncontested? TPP's Model for the Global Digital Economy' in B Kingsbury et al (eds), *Megaregulation Contested* (Oxford University Press, 2019).

—— 'RCEP's Contribution to Global Data Governance' (*Afronomics Law*, 19 February 2021) https://www.afronomicslaw.org/category/analysis/rceps-contribution-global-data-governance-0 accessed 8 March 2022.

Sullivan, C, 'EU GDPR or APEC CBPR? A Comparative Analysis of the Approach of the EU and APEC to Cross Border Data Transfers and Protection of Personal Data in the IoT Era' (2019) 35(4) *Computer Law & Security Review* 380.

Suzuki, H, 'The new politics of trade: EU-Japan' (2017) 39 *Journal of European Integration* 875.

Tajima, Y, 'Japan to lead first cyber defense drill with ASEAN, US and Europe' (*Nikkei Asia*, 9 August 2020) https://asia.nikkei.com/Business/Technology/Japan-to-lead-first-cyber-defense-drill-with-ASEAN-US-and-Europe accessed 8 March 2022.

Tamma, P, 'Europe wants 'strategic autonomy' – it just has to decide what that means' (*Politico*, 15 October 2020) https://www.politico.eu/article/europe-trade-wants-strategic-autonomy-decide-what-means/ accessed 8 March 2022.

Tanaka, T, 'EU-Japan Relations' in T Christiansen, E Kirchner and P Murray (eds), *The Palgrave Handbook of EU-Asia Relations* (Palgrave Macmillan, 2013).

Telo, M, 'Controversial Developments of EU-China Relations: Main Drivers and Geopolitical Inplications of the Comprehensive Agremeent on Investments' (2021) *Journal of Common Market Studies* 1.

Terpan, F, 'Soft Law in the European Union – The Changing Nature of EU Law' (2014) 21 *European Law Journal* 68.

The World Bank, 'China Overview' (*World Bank*, 6 April 2016) https://www.worldbank.org/en/country/china/overview#1 accessed 8 March 2022.

The World Bank, 'GDP (current US$) – China, European Union, United States, Japan' https://data.worldbank.org/indicator/NY.GDP.MKTP.CD?locations=CN-EU-US-JP&most_recent_value_desc=true accessed 8 March 2022.

Trachtman, J, 'Cybersecurity versus Trade in Internet of Things Products' (2019) 16 *Manchester Journal of International Economic Law* 301.

Trans Atlantic Consumer Dialogue (TACD), 'Lack of transparency could thwart the strong consumer safeguards that must be the goal of EU-US cooperation dialogues' (*TACD*, 28 September 2021) https://tacd.org/eu-us-organisations-transparency-ttc-pr/ accessed 8 March 2022.

'Transatlantic Dialogue on sustainable development' (*Euractive*, 26 February 2002) https://www.euractiv.com/section/sustainable-dev/news/transatlantic-dialogue-on-sustainable-development/ accessed 8 March 2022.

'Transatlantic Environment Dialogue suspended' (*Euractive*, 23 November 2000), https://www.euractiv.com/section/climate-environment/news/transatlantic-environment-dialogue-suspended/ accessed 8 March 2022.

Treasury Board of Canada, 'Taking Privacy into Account before Making Contracting Decisions' (2006).

Twining, D, 'Europe's Incomplete Pivot to Asia' (*The German Marshall Fund of the United States*, 9 April 2015).

Tzanou, M 'Schrems I and Schrems II: Assessing the Case for the Extraterritoriality of EU Fundamental Rights' in F Fabbrini, E Celeste and J Quinn (eds), *Data Protection Beyond Borders: Transatlantic Perspectives on Extraterritoriality and Sovereignty* (Hart Publishing, 2021).

'U.S. Downgraded EU's Diplomatic Status (but Didn't Say Anything)' (*New York Times*, 8 January 2019) https://www.nytimes.com/2019/01/08/world/europe/eu-us-diplomatic-status.html accessed 8 March 2022.

Ueta, T and Remacle, É (eds), *Japan and Enlarged Europe: Partners in Global Governance* (Peter Lang 2005).

United Nations Conference on Trade and Development, 'Information Economy Report 2017: Digitalization, Trade and Development' (2017) https://unctad.org/system/files/official-document/ier2017_en.pdf accessed 8 March 2022.

Van der Eijk, F and Pandita Gunavardana, A, 'The Road that divided the EU: Italy joins China's Belt and Road Initiative' (*European Law Blog*, 25 June 2019) https://europeanlawblog.eu/2019/06/25/the-road-that-divided-the-eu-italy-joins-chinas-belt-and-road-initiative/ accessed 8 March 2022.

Van Der Loo, G, Vandenbussche, T and Aktoudianakis, A, 'The EU-US Trade and Technology Council: Mapping the Challenges and Opportunities for Transatlantic Cooperation on Trade, Climate, and Digital' (2021) Egmont Paper 113.

Van Gestel, R and Micklitz, H-W, 'Why Methods Matter in European Legal Scholarship' (2014) 20 *European Law Journal* 292.

Varju, M, '5G networks, (cyber)security harmonisation and the internal market: the limits of Article 114 TFEU' (2020) 45 *European Law Review* 471.

Vauchez, A, *Brokering Europe: Eurolawyers and the Making of a Transnational Polity* (Cambridge University Press, 2015).

Venzke, I and Mendes, J, 'The idea of relative authority in European and international law' (2018) 16 *International Journal of Constitutional Law* 75.

Verhelst, A and Wouters, J, 'Filling Global Governance Gaps in Cybersecurity: International and European Legal Perspectives' (2020) 15(2) *International Organisations* 141.

Viljoen, S, 'Democratic Data: A Relational Theory for Data Governance' (2020) 131 *Yale Law Journal* 370.

Von der Burchard, H, 'Merkel pushes EU-China investment deal over the finish line despite criticism' (*Politico*, 29 December 2020) https://www.politico.eu/article/eu-china-investment-deal-angela-merkel-pushes-finish-line-despite-criticism/ accessed 8 March 2022.

Voss, WG, 'Cross-Border Data Flows, the GDPR, and Data Governance' (2020) 29 *Washington International Law Journal* 485.

—— 'The Concept of Accountability in the Context of the Evolving Role of ENISA in Data Protection, ePrivacy and Cybersecurity' in A Arcuri and F Coman-Kund (eds), *Technocracy and the Law: Accountability, Governance and Expertise* (Routledge, 2021).

Vosse, W, 'Japan's Cyber Diplomacy' (2019) https://eucyberdirect.eu/research/japans-cyber-diplomacy 31 December 2021.

Walker, N, 'Late Sovereignty in the European Union' in N Walker (ed), *Sovereignty in Transition* (Hart Publishing, 2003).

Wang Han, S and Bakar Munir, A, 'Information Security Technology – Personal Information Security Specification: China's Version of the GDPR' (2018) 4 *European Data Protection Review* 535.

Wang, H, 'China's Approach to the Belt and Road Initiative: Scope, Character and Sustainability' (2019) 22 *Journal of International Economic Law* 29.
—— 'The Belt and Road Initiative Agreements: Characteristics, Rationale and Challenges' (2021) 20 *World Trade Review* 282.
Warren, S, and Brandeis, L, 'The Right to Privacy' (1980) 4 *Harvard Law Review* 193.
Weber, RH, 'Transborder Data Transfers: Concepts, Regulatory Approaches and New Legislative Initiatives' (2013) 3 *International Data Privacy Law* 117.
Weiss, T and Wilkinson, R, *Rethinking Global Governance* (Polity Press, 2018).
Weiß, W, 'Delegation to treaty bodies in EU agreements: Constitutional constraints and proposals for strengthening the European Parliament' (2018) 14(3) *European Constitutional Law Review* 532.
—— 'CETA Investment Court and EU External Autonomy: Did Opinion 1/17 Strengthen the EU's Room for Manoeuvre in External Relations?' (2020) *Hungarian Yearbook of International Law and European Law*.
Wessel, RA, 'Towards EU Cybersecurity Law: Regulating a New Policy Field' in N Tsagourias and R Buchan (eds), *Research Handbook on International Law and Cyberspace* (Edward Elgar, 2015).
Wiener, J and Alemanno, A, 'The Future of International Regulatory Cooperation: TTIP as a Learning Process Toward a Global Policy Laboratory' (2015) 78 *Law and Contemporary Problems* 103.
Wolfe, R, 'Learning about Digital Trade: Privacy and E-Commerce in CETA and TPP' (2019) 18(S1) *World Trade Review* 63.
Woods, L, 'Overview of Digital Services Act' (*EU Law Analysis*, 15 December 2020) http://eulawanalysis.blogspot.com/2020/12/overview-of-digital-services-act.html accessed 8 March 2022.
—— 'Who has jurisdiction over Facebook Ireland? The CJEU rules on the GDPR "one stop shop"' (*EU Law Analysis*, 16 June 2021), http://eulawanalysis.blogspot.com/2021/06/who-has-jurisdiction-over-facebook.html accessed 8 March 2022.
Workmann, G, 'TTIP Underlining the Importance of Digital Trade' (US Chamber of Commerce, 5 May 2016).
World Bank 'World Development Report 2021: Data for Better Lives' https://www.worldbank.org/en/publication/wdr2021 accessed 8 March 2022.
Wouters, J and Andrione-Moylan, A, 'The changing international cooperation network of the EU: The inclusion of informal (regulatory) bodies' in RA Wessel and J Odermatt (eds), *Research Handbook on the European Union and International Organizations* (Edward Elgar, 2019).
WTO, 'Joint statement on e-commerce news archives' https://www.wto.org/english/news_e/archive_e/jsec_arc_e.htm accessed 8 March 2022.
—— 'Members adopt draft decision to improve tariff and import data, discuss trade concerns' (28 May 2019) https://www.wto.org/english/news_e/news19_e/mark_28may19_e.htm accessed 8 March 2022.
—— 'Minutes of the Committee on Market Access, 9 October 2018' (2018) G/MA/M/68.
—— 'Work Programme On Electronic Commerce: General Council Decision, Adopted on 10 December 2019' (2019) WT/L/1079.
—— 'World Trade Statistical Review 2020' https://www.wto.org/english/res_e/statis_e/wts2020_e/wts20_toc_e.htm accessed 8 March 2022.
Wu, M, 'The "China, Inc." Challenge to Global Trade Governance' (2016) 57 *Harvard International Law Journal* 261.
—— 'Digital Trade-Related Provisions in Regional Trade Agreements: Existing Models and Lessons for the Multilateral Trade System' (2017) RTA Exchange International Centre for Trade and Sustainable Development and Inter-American Development Bank.
—— 'Testimony before US-China Economic and Security Revision Commission Hearing on US Companies in China' (28 February 2019).
Wu, T, *The Curse of Bigness: Antitrust in the New Gilded Age* (Columbia Global Reports, 2018).
Wunderlich, J-U, 'The EU an Actor *Sui Generis*? A Comparison of EU and ASEAN Actorness' (2012) 50 *Journal of Common Market Studies* 653.

Yadron, D, Ackerman, S and Thielman, S, 'Inside the FBI's encryption battle with Apple' (*The Guardian*, 18 February 2016) https://www.theguardian.com/technology/2016/feb/17/inside-the-fbis-encryption-battle-with-apple accessed 8 March 2022.

Yakovleva, S, 'EU's policy on cross-border data flows: navigating the thin line between liberalizing digital trade, promoting rules-based multilateralism and safeguarding fundamental rights and values' in E Fahey and I Mancini (eds), *Understanding the EU as a Good Global Actor: Whose Metrics?* (Edward Elgar, forthcoming).

Yakovleva, S and Irion, K, 'Pitching trade against privacy: reconciling EU governance of personal data flows with external trade' (2020) 10(3) *International Data Privacy Law* 201.

Young, AR, 'Liberalizing Trade, Not Exporting Rules: The Limits to Regulatory Co-Ordination in the EU's 'New Generation' Preferential Trade Agreements' (2015) 22 *Journal of European Public Policy* 1253.

—— 'The European Union as a Global Regulator? Context and Comparison' (2015) 22 *Journal of European Public Policy* 9.

Zalan, E, 'EU and US reach steel truce in effort to reset relations' (*EU Observer*, 18 May 2021) https://euobserver.com/world/151870?utm_source=euobs&utm_medium=email accessed 8 March 2022.

Zeller and B others, 'The Right to be Forgotten – the EU and Asia Pacific Experience (Australia, Indonesia, Japan and Singapore)' (2019) 1 *European Human Rights Law Review* 23.

Zhao, B and Mifsud Bonnici, GP, 'Protecting EU Citizens Personal Data in China: a Reality or a Fantasy?' (2019) 24(2) *International Journal of Law and Information Technology* 128.

Ziegler, K and Moreno-Lax, V, 'Autonomy of the EU Legal Order – A General Principle? On the Risks of Normative Functionalism and Selective Constitutionalisation' in K Ziegler, PJ Neuvonen and V Moreno-Lax (eds), *Research Handbook on General Principles in EU Law: Constructing Legal Orders in Europe* (Edward Elgar, forthcoming).

Zuboff, S, *The Age of Surveillance Capitalism: The Fight for a Human Future at the New Frontier of Power* (Profile Books, 2019).

Zufall, F, 'Challenging the EU's Right to Be Forgotten: Society's Right to Know in Japan' (2019) 5 *European Data Protection Law Review* 17.

Zürn, M, 'The Politicization of World Politics and its Effects: Eight Propositions' (2014) 6 *European Political Science Review* 47.

—— 'Opening up Europe: Next Steps in Politicisation Research' (2016) 39 *West European Politics* 16.

INDEX

www.ingramcontent.com/pod-product-compliance
Lightning Source LLC
Chambersburg PA
CBHW071351220926
51613CB00008B/74
* 9 7 8 1 5 0 9 9 5 7 0 4 0 *